HURSTPIERPOINT

– kind and charitable

Edited by

Ian Nelson

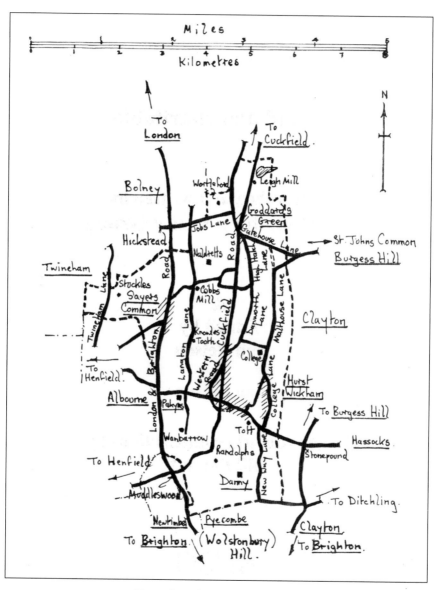

Hurstpierpoint – the framework

HURSTPIERPOINT

– kind and charitable

Researched and written by
Hurst History Study Group

&
Edited by
Ian Nelson

Cover and other illustrations by
Bill Parrott

HHSG

2001
Published by
DITCHLING PRESS LIMITED
Consort Way, Burgess Hill,
West Sussex RH15 9YS
For Hurst History Study Group
ISBN 0 9500584 6 7

British Library Cataloguing in Publication Data:

Typeset in Times New Roman, 10pt on 11 pt
Typesetting by Hurst History Study Group
Printed in UK by Ditchling Press Limited, Burgess Hill, West Sussex

The Hurst History Study Group
dedicate this book
with gratitude for all
his help and support
to

Ray Packham

CONTENTS

		Page
Acknowledgements		viii
Hurst History Study Group: Credits		ix
List of illustrations		xi
Preface		xv

1   **Man and the Land**   3
Denis Wardell &   The Inheritance
Peter Bidmead   Pre-history; Romans and Saxons;
feudal manors

2   **The Church**   25
Ian Nelson   From Ethelbert to Victoria
Domesday; St Lawrence Church;
activity and decline; dramatic change

3   **Gentry and Yeoman Farmers**   56
Denis Wardell   Changes in landownership and
farming - Elizabeth I to Victoria

4   **Craftsmen and their Trades**   74
Rose Cottis   The self-sufficient community

5   **Built to Last**   108
Audrey Rowe   Changes in styles of living and
house-building materials

6   **The Parish and its Poor**   138
Ian Nelson   A heavy parish burden

7   **In Sickness**   170
Ian Nelson   Life and death before modern
medicine and surgery

8   **Friends and Chapel-goers**   191
June Kentsley   Quakers; Methodists; Baptists and
other Dissenters

vii

9   **Law and Order**   217
    Ian Nelson   County justice; 'real' crime and
                              'social' crime

10 **A Road System Evolves**   242
    Denis Wardell   Early trackways; turnpikes; Hurst
                              joins the wider world

11 **Farming with Machines**   256
    David Blake   Agricultural developments since
                              1850

12 **Shops – a Story of Rise and Fall**   292
    Bunty & Jimmy   The shops, in the High Street and
    Parkinson

13 **Education in the 18th and 19th Centuries**   317
    Ian Nelson   National and private schools
                              elsewhere

14 **One for the Road**   343
    Rose Cottis   The Inns

15 **Hurst in the Twentieth Century**   356
    Ian Nelson   Rapid change; oral memories

    Glossary   376

    Index   384 viii

ACKNOWLEDGEMENTS

The Hurst History Study Group wish to place on record their grateful thanks to many individuals who have given freely their expertise, advice and time during the months we have been researching and writing this book. Without their help it could not have been written.

Heather Warne taught us the basic skills of document research and has continued to take a great interest in our progress. She has been readily available since for advice on many aspects, in particular deciphering early manorial evidence.

Further professional help and critical comment has been sought from, and willingly given by, a number of others: Caroline Adams, David Allam, Peter Brandon, Chris Butler, Steve Griffiths, Peter Gwynne, Annabelle Hughes and other members of the Wealden Buildings Study Group, Alison and Timothy McCann, Geoffrey Mead, Janet Pennington, Alan Readman, Peter Wilkinson.

Richard Childs and Roger Davey, the County Archivists for West and East Sussex respectively, have allowed us to publish extracts from original documents deposited in the official archives. The staff of both West and East Sussex Record Offices at Chichester and Lewes have always been unfailingly courteous and helpful when we have been struggling to trace appropriate evidence.

Local enthusiasts who have not been able to join us directly have nevertheless given freely of their time and knowledge. John Norris had previously carried out a considerable amount of research into the history of the parish church which he made available to us. Michael Clarkson helped with the transcription and translation of obscure medieval Latin. Above all, we were fortunate in having at our disposal the vast knowledge of the parish in which he was born, acquired over many years by Ray Packham, together with access to his large collection of photographs and other illustrations. We were sorry that he felt unable to join the group as an active member, but we are delighted that he has agreed to allow us to dedicate this book to him. He has been helped by his son Roger, both in gathering information for us, and in checking important sections of the text. Ray's sister Peggy Gibbs and her husband Eric live at Greenford, Middlesex, and we have made use of their proximity to the Public Record Office at Kew on several occasions, as well as Peggy's own reminiscences of her childhood village.

A number of Hurstians let us record their oral memories of the village, and thereby contributed so much to the chapter on the last century. They were: George Anscombe, Olive Beckett, Joan Black, Kathy Burdfield, Ted Crane, Margaret Georgeson, Margaret Higgs, George Lambert, Peter Nelson, Phyllis Poundsbery, Mary Shelton, Jack Spratley, Nora Talbot, Relf Waters. To all of them we are very grateful. We realise that there are many others whose reminiscences would be equally valid, and we hope they will understand that space has been the limiting factor. Some future publication will surely be able to develop this vital method of recording our more recent history. The inspection of the construction of several of the houses of the parish would not have been possible without the permission of the owners of the individual properties – we are grateful to them as well.

One other area in which we have shown our amateur status is that of computer skills. We are most grateful to Benny Coxhill, Andrew and David Parkinson, and Joanna Nelson for helping us with their expertise when 'glitches' developed in rather sudden fashion from time to time.

Publishing any book costs money. Without the generous help of the Millennium Festival Awards this project could have stalled at the typescript stage, as we would otherwise have had to look elsewhere for funding. This Award has enabled us to offer the book at a price which would be quite uneconomic in commercial terms. In addition we are most grateful for the financial support and encouragement given to us by Hurstpierpoint Parish Council. Finally, we wish to record our thanks to Lawrence Pepler and his staff at Ditchling Press Limited for suffering our amateurishness with such forbearance. We hope that the story we have put together will be an enjoyable contribution to the parish's millennium celebrations.

HURST HISTORY STUDY GROUP CREDITS

The authors of the various chapters have been credited in the table of contents, but the book is the result of collaboration between a group of individuals, and contributions to each section were made by all. In addition we have benefited from the expertise of members in other fields:

Bill Parrott designed and painted the cover illustrations, and also provided line drawings at the request of chapter authors.

Anthony Bower produced the end-paper maps; Denis Wardell and David Blake drew those in the text.

Maxine Tyler cast an eagle eye over the text to eliminate errors of spelling, punctuation and syntax as far as possible. Any remaining mistakes are the responsibility of the editor.

Anthony Bower used his considerable computer skills to carry out the typesetting, including positioning the illustrations and offering useful editorial suggestions. He also provided the group with a vast amount of data based on the parish registers, the census returns and other statistical documents.

Janet Johnson and Jimmy Parkinson have provided valuable secretarial assistance, particularly in the later stages of reviewing and revising the texts of the various chapters.

Every group needs the kind of leadership capable of directing individual efforts clearly and objectively, and shaping a mass of information and disparate ideas into a coherent whole. Ian Nelson has fulfilled this task admirably; always encouraging, sometimes cajoling, and keeping everyone positive during endless research and meetings. He has shouldered an onerous workload to ensure script was produced, deadlines met, and a book was finally published. His role as Editor has been vital, and is much appreciated by members of the Study Group.

xi

LIST OF ILLUSTRATIONS
PHOTOGRAPHS

Colour   Between pages xvi and 1
Plate
I   Bedlam Street, route of Roman road
II   Carey Hampton Borrer
III   William Borrer
IV   Nathaniel Borrer
V   Richard Davey
VI   Sarah Davey
VII   Pakyns Manor
VIII   Spotted Cow and Pigwidgeon Cottages
IX   New Inn
X   Little Park
XI   Tott Farm
XII   Danny: east elevation
XIII   Danny: south wing
XIV   Hope Baptist Chapel
XV   King's Head, Albourne
XVI   Thomas Jacket's clock
XVII   Couchman's Brewery showcard
XVIII   Ascension window from Holy Trinity Church, now in Canada

Plate		Page
1	Aerial view of Hurstpierpoint AD2000	1
2	Iron Age fort on Wolstonbury	5
3	Parish boundary bank	14
4	Parish boundary marker	15
5 & 6	East Edgeley barn	18
7	St George's Church	50
8	Peter Courthope	57
9	George, Lord Goring	57
10	Henry and Barbara Campion	57
11	Oxen plough-team	60
12	Horse plough-team	67
13	A coppiced wood	75

14	Pit Lane smithy	92
15	Hospital Carnival float	100
16	Wanbarrow Farm	115
17	Cowdrays	116
18	Home Cottage	118
19	Wickham House	121
20	Little Park: rainwater head and firemark	123
21	Little Park: Jacobean privy	124
22	Little Park: bread ovens	125
23	Little Park: salt box	126
24	Hardings cottages	128
25	Randolphs Farm	131
26	Townfield Cottages, the original workhouse building	146
27	Entrance to Pit Road	147
28	Manor Cottages	166
29	Methodist Chapel, Manor Road	205
30	Tollgate	247
31	The 'Hollow' in Brighton Road	251
32	Haymaking	262
33	Corn harvest on Randolph's Farm	265
34	Mangolds being loaded on to traditional farm cart	267
35	Sheep-shearing at Little Park	270
36	Staff of Geer & Son Ltd	272
37	Geer's nursery: inside a glasshouse	273
38	Muster of horses for the Great War	274
39	Seed harvesting at Washbrooks: leeks	286
40	Seed harvesting at Washbrooks: alyssum	287
41 & 42	Combining at Coombe Farm before the new A23 was constructed; haying at Tott Farm 1981	288
43	East end of the High Street, with George Anscombe sitting outside Jupps	303
44	William Parsons on his milk round from Latchetts Farm	304
45	Bread ovens in the High Street	305
46	Boys' entrance to the School	332
47	Stoolball in Danny Park	336
48	White Horse Inn	347
49	Hurst Brewery van	349
50	New Inn 1836	352
51	Chinese Gardens	353
52	Horse bus	366
53	George Stoner filling water cart	366

54	Crossroads	367
55	Steamroller and gang on Cuckfield Road	368
56	First motor bus	369
57	Windows of Ribbetts Cottages during World War II	373

PRINTS AND DRAWINGS

i	Mesolithic tool	3
ii	Page from Domesday Book	13
iii	Threshing with flails	20
iv	St Lawrence Church	28
v	Interior of St Lawrence Church	38
vi	Danny map	58
vii	Turn-wrest plough	60
viii	Sowing seed by hand	60
ix	Later model plough	65
x	Seed-plough and manure hopper	66
xi	Apprenticeship document	77
xii	'Jill' windmill being moved over Downs	78
xiii	Pond Lye Mill	81
xiv	Sussex wagon	95
xv	St Lawrence Fair Charter	99
xvi	Early kitchen utensils	114
xvii	Apprenticeship indenture	144
xviii	Parish officers with a pauper family	156
xix	Removal Order	157
xx	Bastardy bond	160
xxi	Bastardy Order	162
xxii	15th century herbal	183
xxiii	Collecting herbs	184
xxiv	Bleeding	185
xxv	Chapel at Trumpkins	211
xxvi	Ducking a witch	220
xxvii	Night watchman	222
xxviii	Punishment of vagrants and beggars	223
xxix	A double pillory	225
xxx	Turnpike Act	245
xxxi	Tollgate tickets	247
xxxii	Road mender	253
xxxiii	Itinerant pedlar	292

xxxiv.	Tailor's scissors	294
xxxv	Victorian shop scales	299
xxxvi	Tea-packing box and mallet	299
xxxvii	William Mitten	310
xxxviii	Flora Mitten	310
xxxix	'The written excuse'	325

FIGURES

Figure

1	Sketch map of Hurst showing some roads mentioned	ii
2	Map showing situation of Hurstpierpoint and surrounding parishes	2
3	Map showing Roman sites	7
4	Sketch map of Albourne Road and High Street	244
5–9	Sketch maps of roads and tracks	249–52

ENDNOTES AND ABBREVIATIONS

The references used relate to general matters as well as to Hurstpierpoint. They are somewhat lengthy, to suggest further reading that may be undertaken by those interested.

Abbreviations used in the endnotes are:

AMS	Additional Manuscript
ESRO	East Sussex Record Office
OS	Ordnance Survey
PRO	Public Record Office
SAC	*Sussex Archaeological Collections*
SAS	Sussex Archaeological Society
SNQ	*Sussex Notes and Queries*
SRS	*Sussex Record Society*
VCH	*Victoria County History, Sussex*
WBSG	Wealden Buildings Study Group
WSRO	West Sussex Record Office

PREFACE

To paraphrase E C Bentley, geography is about maps, while history is about chaps. The aim of this book is to tell the story of the people of Hurstpierpoint, from pre-history to the end of the last century. Inevitably the things of Hurst – the estates, the farms, the houses, the shops – will form a large part of the story, but only as evidence of the progress of human beings throughout the centuries.

The Hurst History Study Group comprises a few enthusiastic amateurs who felt that Hurst deserved such a book, one viewed from the perspective of the beginning of the third millennium AD. We have spent more than four years researching and writing. We have learnt a lot about our parish, both from the documents deposited in the record offices and from other local individuals who have amassed information themselves. There have been periods when we have been doubtful about the task ahead. At some times it has been overwhelming to discover just how much information there is, at others how much we would have liked to have known but could not find out, no matter how hard we tried. There have been the difficulties of deciphering old manuscripts, particularly when these have been written in Latin, and in a kind of shorthand. The almost infinite variations in the spelling of proper names have on many occasions presented us with the problem of precise identification of individuals. Original spelling has been retained in direct quotations, but some standardisation has been attempted in the general text. All of this has been somewhat daunting at times, but we have found the effort both very rewarding and very enjoyable, and we hope that others will find the result of interest.

We first need to understand why we are where we are. It has been said that history is built on landscape, local history even more so. For that reason a certain amount of geological and landscape background is necessary. Then archaeology will help to flesh out the early speculative history. Esther Meynell, who wrote so lovingly about Sussex said '. . . if there had been none of those boring flint implements in the [museum] glass cases it is highly probable there would have been no Brighton or Hastings . . .'[1] – or Hurstpierpoint for that matter. Man then used some of these tools to fashion huge earthworks which still provide evidence of his evolution into communities. Only when we come to preserved documents can we begin to provide much greater detail. Even then, many documents have been lost or destroyed, and so we can only tell part of the story. What remains is still a large body of evidence, leaving yet another problem – what to use and what to leave out. This is particularly so when a degree of obsession takes hold of the researchers! There has to be a limit to both the size of the book and the time spent in working on it. We know that there is enough unused material for several other books, but they must be left for another day.

We have tried to relate events in Hurst to the wider regional and national scene. Like any other parish, central government edicts were intended to provide some sort of control over activities all over the country. Even within the same county there could be wide variations in religious beliefs, in attitudes to life in general, and to secular community matters. How did Hurst conform to the norm? How did it go its own way? We hope the succeeding pages will shed some light.

A glance at the chapter titles will indicate that we have adopted a thematic approach. This inevitably results in some repetition, as the same events and individuals were involved in various aspects of village life. It would have been possible to eliminate duplication by referring the reader to the first chapter recording such an occurrence, but it is felt that this would interrupt the narrative, and so the duplications remain.

Excellent books of photographs recording aspects of the more recent history of the village have already been produced by both Ray Packham and David Robinson. Not only are we indebted to them for allowing us to use many items from their collections, but the existence of these volumes renders too much repetition unnecessary. As far as possible, illustrations have been chosen only to support the story we are telling.

A word about the sub-title. This comes from the headline of an article by Vida Herbison, who used to live where Wolstonbury Close now stands. In the June 1979 issue of *Sussex Life* she was writing about Hurstpierpoint, and referred to Henry 'Dog' Smith, a long-standing benefactor to the village, who is alleged to have made this comment. Some individuals and episodes in the history of the parish may have failed to live up to this ideal, others would seem to have tried, with varying degrees of success. It is for the reader to decide.

Ian Nelson

Hurstpierpoint
December 2000

1. Meynell E (1947): *Sussex*, 3.
2. Herbison V (1979): Hurstpierpoint – kind and charitable, *Sussex Life*, June 1979, 22- 23, 27

I. Bedlam Street, route of Roman road south of the village.

II. Carey Hampton Borrer, Rector of Hurstpierpoint 1841-98.

III. William Borrer

IV. Nathaniel Borrer of Pakyns.

V. Richard Davey, wearing a working smock, and with his hat painted to keep out the rain – outside the old St Lawrence Church.

VI. Sarah Davey 1776-1859; note the shawl drying on the clothes-line, a flat iron and a tally iron (for pressing pleats and gathers) on the table with a trivet, also the washing basket on the floor.

VII. Pakyns Manor.

VIII. Spotted Cow and Pigwidgeon
Cottages.

IX. New Inn

X. Little Park.

XI. Tott Farmhouse.

XII. Danny: east elevation.

XIII. Danny: south wing.

XIV. Hope Baptist Chapel, Western Road.

XV. Old King's Head, Albourne

XVI. Thomas Jacket's clock.

XVII. Couchman's Brewery Showcard.

XVIII. Ascension east window from Holy Trinity Church, now in Canada.

Plate 1. Aerial view of Hurstpierpoint AD2000, showing Wolstonbury Hill and the range of the South Downs in the background. (By kind permission of Hurstpierpoint and Sayers Common Parish Council).

Figure 2.
Map showing situation of Hurstpierpoint and surrounding parishes and hundreds.

1. MAN AND THE LAND

The Inheritance

THE BEGINNINGS

The first people to live and work in the Hurstpierpoint area were looking for three things: land which they would be able to cultivate, a water supply for themselves and their livestock and materials they could use to build themselves a shelter. They were subsistence farmers – they had to cultivate the land to produce food or they would starve; man was no longer primarily a hunter and gathered together in small groups for mutual help.

On the chalk downs they had found a lightly wooded land which, as time went by they were able to clear and cultivate. Evidence still remains of their labours in the strip lychetts, the narrow hillside fields and the later small, square fields of the Celtic people. Water supply was, however, always a problem.

Moving northwards from the Downs they found, at its scarp foot, bands of fertile Greensand which stretched east to west through the present Hassocks area to Albourne and beyond.[1] It was probably then also lightly wooded and easily cleared and it stretched up to, and a little beyond, a ridge of higher ground. The very name Hurst means a 'wooded hill'.

 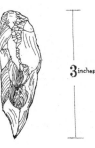

3 inches

i. Mesolithic tool 6,000–4,000BC found in Weald Close, Hurst 1980, possibly used for removing flesh from the inside of animal skins; deposited in Ditchling Museum (Catalogue No. 94.1980.1a).

It was not all good land for between the Upper and the Lower Greensand was an area of Gault Clay, hard to work and heavily wooded. It is traceable in the southern part of Danny Park and across Randolphs Copse, Foxhole Shaw and Stalkers Copse. There was a bonus as there was the narrow strip of fertile Upper Greensand [2] between the chalk and gault which formed the spring line north of the Downs and through it flowed two streams linking up to form what is now Cutlers Brook. Like all the watercourses through the Parish they are now small streams, but before the abstraction of water in the 19th century they were much larger. Together with their flood plains, which would be well watered meadowland for the livestock, they effectively covered a larger area of land.

North of the ridge of Greensand was, however, the intractable Wealden clay, stretching right up beyond our northern Parish boundary. Again heavily wooded it was useful for timber and for their animal's forage (pannage – the feeding of pigs on acorns and mast – a valuable medieval perquisite and, indeed, recorded in Domesday), but hard to clear. It was part of the Andredesweald – the great swathe of forest that stretched for many miles between Sussex and Kent. For many centuries it formed a virtual barrier to travel but, as the population grew, it was needed for agriculture and was gradually cleared for cultivation. Today there is little woodland left in this part of the parish except in field boundaries.

Within the area of clay were the watercourses with their areas of fertile flood plain. (All these flowed from south and east to the west to form tributaries of the River Adur). From Bramber well in West Town, the Langton Brook flowed north to join up with the Danworth Brook (Herrings Stream from Hassocks) which was sufficiently powerful to serve a number of later water mills from Hammonds to Ruckford and Cobbs and reinforced by the Pookbourne, flowing westwards to Herrings Mill and thence to the Adur. Further north was a watercourse serving Leigh Mill and westwards to Bolney Mill and Hookers Mill in Twineham. These watercourses were also good sources of fish until the nineteenth century and trout were, and still are, occasional visitors.

Evidence of early peoples is still being uncovered: the Mesolithic (see fig. 1) and Neolithic (Middle and New Stone Ages), with their flint tools, and most recently, that of the Bronze Age (around 1500 BC) in the area of Breachland where fragments of pottery have been found.[3]

Plate 2. Wolstonbury with its Iron Age Fort.

Overlooking the fertile land to the north was the fortress (around 500 BC) of the Iron Age Celts of Wolstonbury. This would form a place of refuge for the local people and their livestock in times of trouble, but it is unlikely that it was permanently occupied.

ROMANS AND SAXONS – 1000 YEARS

By the first century AD it is likely that the Celtic tribes had established a thriving community within the area and cleared a good percentage of the woodland for arable.

They had trading contacts with Roman Gaul and when the Romans finally invaded Britain in AD43 the inhabitants of the south, under their chief, one Cogidubnus, unlike tribes in the north, apparently seemed to have welcomed them and soon assumed a Romano-British way of life. The Romans introduced many skills, customs and building techniques previously unknown to the local people. They efficiently utilised the natural resources of the area, creating bricks and tiles from local clay, smelting iron from ironstone in the High Weald for nails, armoury and other such objects and producing corn in abundance from the Downs and lower pastures.

Although Roman occupation between AD43 – AD410 was relatively short in the span of Hurst's history, they certainly left their mark on the local landscape. They constructed a network of elaborate metalled roads for the transportation of their produce and the speedy passage of their legions. One such road, latterly named the 'Sussex Greensand Way' crossed right through the parish on its journey from Barcombe to Pulborough.[4]

Efficient use was made of the high ground formed by a natural sandstone ridge keeping traffic off the heavy Wealden clay. This road, built upon a layer of chalk, flint and any other available material, passed through Hassocks where it met the London to Portslade route at Stonepound, then continued along the southern edge of Talbot playing field and across Danny Park where its route can still be traced through Bedlam Street off the Brighton Road. (See Colour Plate 1)

Another route is thought to have branched off through Coldharbour Farm off New Way Lane and across the Downs to Pyecombe and beyond.[5] Communities sprung up alongside these routes, no doubt taking advantage of passing trade much as it does today.

Roman remains abound hereabouts, not least of all, the remarkable discovery excavated in 1925 by our own J E Couchman, one time proprietor of Hurst Brewery and local school governor. Here, in a sand quarry close to the present day Stonepound Crossroads, was found the site of a Roman burial ground.[6] The Roman custom at the time was to cremate their dead, their ashes being buried in pottery urns along with a small amount of food and drink to see them on their 'journey'. A coin was often included too in the belief that this would pay the 'ferry man' for their journey across the River Styx into the afterlife.[7]

The site yielded a large quantity of Roman pottery, mostly cremation urns, but very few domestic vessels, suggesting that the site was purely used for burial and not occupation. Coins and pottery stamps found at the cemetery indicated a period of usage between AD70 to AD250,[8] although Bronze Age and Saxon remains suggest a broad continuity of use.

Before Couchman carried out his excavations the sandpit had been in use for almost 20 years. Many of the potential artefacts would, no doubt, have been destroyed or sold by the enterprising workmen to private collectors. What was collected is now housed in the vaults of Lewes Museum.

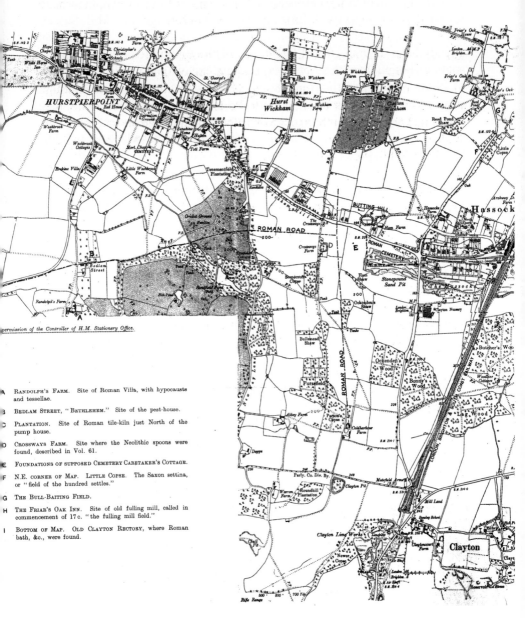

permission of the Controller of H.M. Stationery Office.

A   RANDOLPH'S FARM. Site of Roman Villa, with hypocausts and tessellae.

B   BEDLAM STREET, "BETHLEHEM." Site of the pest-house.

C   PLANTATION. Site of Roman tile-kiln just North of the pump house.

D   CROSSWAYS FARM. Site where the Neolithic spoons were found, described in Vol. 61.

E   FOUNDATIONS OF SUPPOSED CEMETERY CARETAKER'S COTTAGE.

F   N.E. CORNER OF MAP. LITTLE COPSE. The Saxon settina, or "field of the hundred settles."

G   THE BULL-BAITING FIELD.

H   THE FRIAR'S OAK INN. Site of old fulling mill, called in commencement of 17 c. "the fulling mill field."

I   BOTTOM OF MAP. OLD CLAYTON RECTORY, where Roman bath, &c., were found.

Figure 3. Map showing site of Roman activity (from *SAC* 66)

The question is where did the occupants of the cemetery come from to provide the site of at least 300 graves? The answer to that might have been revealed quite recently following the excavations of the Mid Sussex Archaeological Team at Talbot playing field off Wickham Hill. It has already been mentioned that the course of the Roman road was along the southern boundary of this field. Exploratory excavations during the autumn of 1998 revealed that flint foundations of a possible dwelling existed a few feet beneath the surface and a spoil pit yielding fragments of Roman pottery was dug nearby. Later excavations confirmed that this was indeed the site of a Roman roadside settlement and indications were that it had passed through a number of phases of occupation. Several spoil pits, both large and small, were revealed, collectively producing a large quantity of Roman pottery shards, ranging from Samian ware imported from the Continent, to East Sussex ware which may have been fired locally.

In addition some large postholes were revealed indicating the presence of two separate buildings. Excavations are planned to continue over a wider area of the site and it is hoped that this will reveal the extent of the lost community.[9]

To the north of Ham Farm, on what are now the grounds of the Friars Oak golf course, excavations were carried out prior to its development. Both Roman and Saxon remains were found here. A previously unknown Roman road was discovered, metalled with alternate layers of flint and sand. The road which could be traced south towards Ham Farm ended abruptly at a stream suggesting that it may have merely been a spur off the Greensand way, serving as access to the water way or long forgotten building located here. Quantities of tile and other Roman material found suggest the presence of a Roman building located nearby.[10]

To the south of the ancient road at Bedlam Street, the remains of a substantial Roman villa were discovered by farm labourers during 1857, close to Randolphs Farm and once part of the Danny Estate.[11] An impressive stretch of Roman pavement was uncovered beneath the field, the pavement composed almost wholly of red brick tesserae, one inch square with a few smaller ones of grey stone but without any artistic arrangement, was traced over an area of eighty feet by thirty feet. Beneath this at the southern end were found the remains of a hypocaust, providing the occupants with either under-floor heating or at least a hot bath.

Several excavations have been carried out during the last century, including an investigation by Hurstpierpoint College Antiquarian Society in 1950, although the record of their discoveries seems to have been lost. Other visits have revealed small finds of pottery and an undated bronze Roman coin providing proof of Roman or Romano-British occupation. It was often the case that building materials in the form of bricks and tiles were produced at suitable sites quite close to the property to be developed. This appears to have been the case with the villa at Randolphs Farm as, close by in the grounds of Danny, such a kiln exists measuring 6 feet by 4 feet, although now buried deep under vegetation. [12] Having found suitable clay and a convenient water source the tile maker would produce tiles, and often bricks too in what we might regard today as a primitive kiln, however, more than adequate for the purpose at the time.

Overlooking the estate halfway up the N. E. slope of Wolstonbury Hill, a slightly less elaborate settlement once existed beneath the impressive Late Bronze Age/ Early Iron Age enclosure. The occupants farming the slopes left their impressions in the soil. Here a farmstead exists with its associated field system dating to the late Romano-British period.[13] The farmstead survives as a group of at least four rectangular terraces cut into the hill slope, with traces of two circular houses constructed on two of the terraces. Subsequent excavations, including a visit from Hurstpierpoint College Antiquarian Society revealed a further six associated structures on the site. Fragments of clay roof tiles, a door key, iron nails, part of a Greensand rotary quern and pottery shards indicate the Roman period of occupation.[14]

Very little can be seen today, only faint traces of the linchets or ridges created by the early plough. There seem to be no direct evidence of Roman occupation in the immediate vicinity of present day Hurstpierpoint. However, uncorroborated evidence mentions that large quantities of Roman coins and pottery have been found in Hurstpierpoint churchyard at various times, suggesting it may have once been a Roman temple site.[15]

During the later period of Roman rule in England, Saxon raids from the Continent had become a major problem on the south coast, prompting

Roman defences at Pevensey and Porchester. This factor, plus problems closer to home, persuaded Rome to abandon Britain in AD410, leaving Britain, in the words of Emperor Honorius 'to take care of its own defences'.

This allowed a Saxon occupation, leading to the gradual demise of Romano-Britain culture and a return to more traditional ways. The villas fell into decline and no doubt the building materials were utilised elsewhere. These were the dark ages and there are few historical sources, which shed any light on early Saxon Sussex, let alone Hurstpierpoint. Archaeological information is limited too.

Since the early Saxons built in wood, rather than stone, there are no upstanding building remains as there are for the Romano-British period. Most information is obtained from graveyards found in Sussex cemeteries; such finds as jewellery, weapons, pottery and glass have been recorded at a variety of sites[16] including the Roman cemetery at Stonepound. As mentioned earlier the Hassocks cemetery encompassed a broad continuity of use and although both the Roman and Saxon cemeteries overlapped, the centre of the latter lay to the east of the Roman cemetery. Some of the earliest Saxon burials discovered there appear to have been warrior inhumations interred with spears and shields. The bulk of the burials were however single pot cremations. It is generally accepted that these burials dated to the sixth and seventh centuries from the pottery and cremation urns found upon the site.[17] These discoveries suggest that Saxon settlements existed nearby, although to date only one possibility has been found in the area of Hurstpierpoint that is the site shared by the Roman occupation on the Friars Oak golf course. Here during excavations in 1994, postholes were uncovered revealing a sunken feature building 4 x 2 metres in size and half a metre deep, along with remains of Saxon pottery.[18] Typically Saxon in design, these sunken feature buildings were a type of small hut often associated with craftwork. To support this theory, a clay-baked spindle was discovered nearby. Other settlement sites must have existed but as yet await discovery. Quite recently, in advance of land development to the west of Burgess Hill, in the area of Eastlands Farm formally in the Parish of Hurstpierpoint, further evidence of Romano-British occupation was discovered. The site, it is believed, spanned from the first century to late in the fourth century AD.[19] This was not a high status site but possibly an agricultural settlement as indicated by a large assemblage of pottery from the

Roman period, and the discovery of a flint and sandstone constructed corn-drying oven.

Plant remains suggest that this was once a wooded area of the Weald and that wheat and barley were among the crops grown. This was marginal land where farming would be difficult, compared to the fertile strip beneath the Downs. The fact that people were occupying the margins of the Weald suggests that the better land to the south was already accounted for and that the area as a whole was becoming widely populated even in these early times.

The presence of iron-forging slag suggests small-scale, secondary iron working, more than likely supplying the needs of the settlement itself. When the Roman legions left Britain in 410 the local people were Romano-British, they had been subjects of Rome for nearly 400 years, (as long as from the time of Elizabeth I to the present day) and they would continue to cultivate their fields as before. It was the land that was important; it was essential to feed themselves. Indeed when they were overwhelmed by the Saxon invaders in the fifth century, after Aella landed at Anderida (Pevensey) in 477, the beginnings of the Kingdom of the South Saxons, the new people were also going to need usable land. It might be badly neglected when the original owners were killed or driven out and the Saxons did not require the old buildings and roads; they built their own timber dwellings, but they had to grow their own food. The land of farms such as Randolphs could well have been cultivated now for at least 2,000 years.[20]

We have little evidence as to what the climate was like in those early times and its effect on crops, but famine and disease must have been regular visitors. Recent evidence provided by the science of dendrochronology gives us a brief insight however. From the study of tree rings, the growth of a tree year by year over its life, it is possible to see what the climate was at that time. Research has found that over the period around the middle of the sixth century, the weather was exceptionally cold when the trees hardly grew.[21] The affect on the food supply must have been disastrous. Perhaps this period was one of the causes for the migration of people southwards from Scandinavia and the Baltic.

Although there is no evidence that the Romano-British had a settlement on the ridge where Hurst stands, it is certain that in time the Saxons did so and later built a church there after they accepted Christianity in the seventh century. It is indeed possible it was the site of a Roman temple or shrine.

The original way of life of these Saxons was of small groups of people as opposed to the communal life of the Roman Villa and it may be that their original settlements developed into the number of small farms in the Parish in later years and the derivation of their names gives a clue to them.[22]

In later years in more settled times, the over lordship of the Saxon Earls grew and by the time of the Norman Conquest much of this part of the country belonged to the Earl Godwin, the father of Harold Godwinson, King of England, who died at Hastings.

THE FEUDAL PERIOD – FROM THE NORMANS TO THE TUDORS

William of Normandy never recognised Harold as king and felt he was a usurper. Yet in the Domesday Book of 1086, Earl Godwin, whom we have already met, was still given as a former owner although he had died in 1053.

Hurstpierpoint was, in fact, recorded in two parts, both of which had been given, amongst vast estates, by the King to William de Warenne, a Norman lord: Hurst itself, where Robert de Pierpoint became Lord and a separate recorded entry for Wickham.[23] It is difficult to understand what Domesday means at times, but it seems that 'Herst' had about 2,000 acres in cultivation with 80 acres of meadowland and quite an area of woodland for pigs, to support a population of 51 families, perhaps 200 persons.

There was indeed a church and three mills, which would have been watermills. Ruckford and Cobbs were probably two of them but the third was almost certainly down Langton Lane, not Leigh Mill. Wickham was obviously only a small hamlet.

Rotbrus de Wilto teñ HERST. IN BOTINGELLE HVND.
Goduin tenuit. Tc̄ ſe defd̄ p̄ XL 7 una hida. m̄ p̄ nichilo. q̄a
nunq̄ geldauit. Q̄do receþ:̃ ñ niſi XVIII. hid̄ 7 dimidia.
In rapo comit moritoñ. ſunt. III. hidæ 7 dimid̄. In rapo Wilti
de braioſe. ſunt. XIX. hide. T̄ra. e̅. XXV. caȓ.
In dñio ſunt. II. caȓ. 7 XXXV. uillꝪ 7 VIII. bord̄ cū XXI. caȓ 7 dim̄.
Ibi æccƚa 7 VIII. ſerui. 7 III. molini de. IX. ſoƚ. 7 q̄t XX. ãc p̄ti.
Silua de. L. porc̄.
De hac t̄ra teñ Wilts. III. hid̄. Giſlebt̄. III. hid̄ 7 dim̄. Villi tenueȓ.
T̄oſ T.R.E. ualƀ XXXV. liƀ. 7 poſt:̃ IX. liƀ. Modo. XII. liƀ jn̄t totū.
Vxor Wilti de Wateuile teñ de Wilto CLAITTNE. Azor
tenuit de rege. E'. Tc̄ 7 m̄ ſe defd̄ p̄. VII. hid̄. T̄ra. e̅. XII. caȓ.

27 b

In dñio ſunt. II. caȓ. 7 XXVI. uillꝪ 7 V. bord̄ ſ cū. XIIII. caȓ.
Ibi æccƚa. 7 XXIII. ãc p̄ti. Silua de. XV. porc̄. In Leuues:̃
IX. hagæ de. IIII. ſolid̄ 7 VII. deñ. T.R.E. ualƀ x. liƀ. 7 poſt
7 modo:̃ VIII. liƀ.
De ipſa femina teñ Aluuiñ Wicha̅. Azor tenuit.
Tc̄ 7 m̄ ſe defd̄ p̄. III. hid̄. In dñio. e̅ una caȓ. 7 III. uilli
cū. I. caȓ. 7 in Leuues. III. partes uni hagæ de. XV. deñ.
Wilts de Wateuile teñ de Wilto CHEMERE. Azor
tenuit de rege. E. Tc̄ 7 m̄ ſe defd̄ p̄ XIIII. hid̄. T̄ra. e̅
XXV. caȓ. In dñio ſunt. II. caȓ. 7 XXXVI. uillꝪ 7 XI. bord̄

27 a, b

In BUTTINGHILL Hundred

36 Robert holds HURSTPIERPOINT from William. Earl Godwin held it.
Then it answered for 41 hides; now for nothing, because it never
paid tax. When acquired there was nothing but 18½ hides.
In the Count of Mortain's Rape are 3½ hides; in the Rape of
William of Braose, 19 hides. Land for 25 ploughs. In lordship 2 ploug[hs]
35 villagers and 8 smallholders with 21½ ploughs.
A church; 8 slaves; 3 mills at 9s; meadow, 80 acres;
woodland at 50 pigs.
William holds 3 hides of this land; Gilbert 3½ hides.
The villagers held it.
Total value before 1066 £36; later £9; now £12 in all.

37 William of Watteville's wife holds CLAYTON from William.
Azor held it from King Edward. Then and now it answered
for 7 hides. Land for 12 ploughs. In lordship 2 ploughs;   27
26 villagers and 5 smallholders with 14 ploughs.
A church; meadow, 23 acres; woodland at 15 pigs;
9 sites in Lewes at 4s7d.
Value before 1066 £10; later and now £8.

38 Alwin holds WICKHAM from this woman. He held it himself from Azor.
Then and now it answered for 3 hides. In lordship 1 plough;
3 villagers with 1 plough.
3 parts of 1 site in Lewes at 15d.
[Value...]

39 William of Watteville holds KEYMER from William. Azor held
it from King Edward. Then and now it answered for 14 hides.
Land for 25 ploughs. In lordship 2 ploughs;

ii. Domesday Book facsimile and translation (reproduced by kind permission from the
Phillimore edition of *Domesday Book* (General Editor – John Morris), **2**, *Sussex*, published
1976 by Phillimore & Co Ltd, Shopwyke Manor Barn, Chichester, West Sussex PO20
6BG.

The extent of the Parish would have been determined in Saxon times. There were no maps, of course, but as each community spread, the inhabitants (and the Church) wanted to know where their boundaries were. Mostly they followed watercourses, the remains of old roads, venerable old oak trees, or a bank was cast up and a line of trees or hedging planted on it. Until recent destruction these boundary banks and hedges survived in parts of the Parish, particularly in the north east (now destroyed for the Western Distributor road) and north of West House Farm beyond Twineham Lane.

Plate 3. Parish boundary bank north of West House Farm, Twineham Lane.

Parts of England are fortunate to have old Saxon Charters where the boundaries were described, but none have survived for Hurst. The boundaries were walked every year (preserved in the present Rogationtide) and the small boys had the position of the boundary markers 'impressed on their memory' to ensure the knowledge was passed on.

As can be seen from the map, most of the parishes to the east of Hurst along the Scarp Foot were long and thin with a share of the Downs, woodland and land for cultivation, but Hurst was unusual in that it was much broader, over 2 miles from east to west and with an area stretching out to the west of Sayers Common. Its boundaries were over 15 miles (24.4 kms) in length and that towards the east is more or less a straight line, which suggests an agreed division in very early times of the common lands of Hurst and Clayton.

Plate 4.
Parish boundary marker:
Hurst/Clayton at Crossways.

The parish was part of other earlier divisions of Sussex, the Rape of Lewes,[24] the whole of which belonged to William de Warenne, the Norman Lord who had vast estates throughout England; he was probably one of the wealthiest men of the time. The rape was sub-divided into hundreds and Hurst was in the Hundred of Buttinghill.[25] The focus of the Hundred was certainly the present Ham Farm, just over the parish boundary in Clayton, and it lasted as a unit of administration until Victorian times.

The dispossession of the Saxons and the rule of the Normans began the period of Feudal Tenure of land, which lasted until Tudor times.[26] The basis of this tenure was the manor, and the major portion of this parish was in the Manor of Hurstpierpoint with detached areas to the north. There were, however, at least eight Manors holding land.[27] Pakyns Manor House still survives although radically altered in later times and to the east was Wickham Manor partly in Hurst and partly in Clayton. Between Danny, New Way Lane and Clayton was part of the Manor of Ditchling Garden owned by Lewes Priory and, in the north corner of the Parish, was part of Leigh Manor. The present Pangdean Lane off Malthouse Lane belonged to Pangdean Manor, now just a farm towards Brighton. Sayers Common belonged to Tottington Manor, the Manor House is now a restaurant and hotel.

There was an area around Pookbourne which belonged to Hickstead, itself part of Saddlescombe, where there was a house of the Knights Templar.

There is also evidence that Goldbridge and Court Bushes were parts of Manors.[28] The presence of a small part of a manor did not imply a manor house (there may have been only a farm grange), but Hurst itself certainly had its Manor House which was situated to the north of the Church. Foundations were discovered in the early 19th century when the present houses were built opposite the church.[29]

Danny itself had only been a hunting lodge of the Dacre family, the Lords of the Manor who lived in Hurstmonceux. Simon de Pierpoint had obtained a licence from John de Warenne, Earl of Surrey, to enclose the wood of Daneghithe and in 1343 to enclose 17 furlongs of the wood to form a park and fence it in.[30] Later, in 1571, the Great Park was described as being 2½ miles in circumference and containing '40 deer of antlers, 260 rascals (lean deer) and 40 couple of conies' (rabbits)[31] – obviously not the pest they later became.

The old Manor House had probably fallen into decay by the time the Gorings, the new Lords of the Manor, built the Elizabethan manor of Danny in 1582-93, but the hunting lodge in the Great Park was surveyed in 1571, when it was recorded as being a substantial timber building. The old Manor House was in Herst or Little Park and was 1¼ miles in circumference and contained 80 head of deer and 18 antlers. It also had a pond of two acres, containing 200 carp and tench 'fit for the Lord's House'.[32] Fish was, of course, important in medieval times as part of a limited diet, particularly on Fridays and most manor and religious Houses had their fish ponds or stews

It is difficult now to visualise what Hurst and its community looked like through the majority of the Feudal period. There was the village with its church and Manor House and a scattering of cottages on the ridge to the east and a similar group of cottages around Pakyns forming West Town. Possibly the small Saxon fields had been made into large open fields, some being the demesne, belonging directly to the lord and others cultivated in common by the community, but the extent of this is by no means certain. The names East Field, North Field and Townfield were marked on the earliest maps we have,[33] but any open fields had been enclosed, certainly by the Tudor period, perhaps much earlier. It was also a period of dis-parking and certainly part of Danny Park was divided into fields by 1582 [34] and later, large amounts of timber felled there. Little Park had become a small farm by the 17th century.[35]

Perhaps the Saxon community sites with their surrounding fields had persisted through the years as later individual farms. Those within manors other than Hurst may have been used as their granges.

Like other parts of Sussex, the steady expansion and clearance of woodland for arable continued through the eleventh, twelfth and thirteenth centuries until the devastating period of the Black Death in 1348–9 and recurrent visitations caused a dramatic fall in the population. Land went out of use, some of which undoubtedly not cultivated again until the Tudor period or even later,[36] hence the difficulty now of comparing that Hurst with today. Certainly the Black Death rarely wiped out villages entirely, but many were so weakened that they decayed for other reasons. Hurst was fortunate that it was able to recover and flourish in time, although its population must have been drastically reduced. Life was hard particularly during the Middle Ages. We have seen that during the Saxon period there were times when the climate caused life to be particularly unpleasant. Not unexpectedly any disturbance to the pattern of the growing of food caused distress, the intermittent internal warfare of the Saxons and the trauma of the Norman invasion and conquest in relatively close proximity to us added to the problems of bad weather. There were years of famine from the early years of the eleventh century until its end,[37] though they were unlikely to have led to such a heavy loss of life as William's 'Harrying of the North' where vast areas were left waste. The cycle of famine and plague followed through succeeding centuries, culminating in the Black Death with its appalling mortality. Apparently the climate at least did improve during the fifteenth and early sixteenth centuries and harvests were generally good.[38]

This contributed to a better standard of living under the Tudors, a greater increase in population and prosperity. We find from the Subsidy Rolls [39] a glimpse of the more important landowners who lived in Hurst in the Hundred of Buttinghill in those earlier times. Simon de Perepunt was there, of course, in 1296, and 1327, Simon Pakyn, Walto de Legh, Wilno, later Jone de Eddesle (Edgerley) and others, who are still recorded in the names of farms in the Parish – Willno de Holmwode, (later Grasmere), Godefro

Cobbe, Alic'Relicta (Widow) Walte Randulf, Walto ate Naldrette and many others.

Plate 5.
East Edgerley Barn *c.* 1450:
exterior and interior.

Plate 6.

By the sixteenth century most of the old families had gone, but many names appeared which were to become more important in later years. The Cobbe family were still there in 1524 and were joined by Robert Whytpayn, whose descendants became one of Hurst's well know families, together with the Nortons, Chatfields and Haselgroves, who were also recorded, together with many others.[40] These people would be the more wealthy freeholders who, perhaps, also had land in other parishes and vice versa. The names of copyholders and other poorer inhabitants over the centuries are only likely to be discovered in the Court Rolls of the Manor.

By Tudor times more evidence of Hurst people is given by wills and inventories of their goods, many of which survive, and often give a picture of their farming lives and, as will be seen later, the houses they lived in.

Wills and inventories are, however, confusing at times in that, apart from household articles, those of obvious farmers did not sometimes include horses, carts etc which they must have had. One likely reason was that the descent of property was not to the eldest son, but by the tradition of 'Borough English' peculiar to Sussex and Kent, where it went to the youngest.[41] Most of those making wills were obviously elderly for that period (life expectancy was not high anyway) and such items had been already passed to the eldest son who would have had to run the farm when the owner could not because of age or infirmity, otherwise he would have inherited nothing. There was no pension either in those days! Wills often provided for the widow to have part of the farmhouse and certain rights, known as the 'Widows Bench'.[42]

As will be seen later, the early farmhouses and buildings, as with other houses, were of very basic poor construction by modern standards, walls of wattle and daub, or perhaps flint, with unglazed window openings and roofs of thatch and a beaten earth floor.[43] The remains of such a farm, dating from the twelfth to thirteenth century, were excavated in 1987–9 at Muddleswood.[44]

Following the more stable mode of life in late Tudor times the country became more prosperous and, although the poor still lived in their hovels, the wealthy yeomen began to rebuild their houses, mostly in the form well known today as timber framed and plastered houses, several examples of which from the mid fifteenth century still exist in the Parish. These buildings will be looked at in more detail in a later chapter.

Henry VIII's suppression of the monasteries had perhaps not such an effect on Hurst as other parts of the country. There was surprisingly little of the parish owned by the religious houses: the part east of New Way Lane belonging to the Priory of Lewes, and perhaps a small area belonging to the Knights Templar (later the Hospitallers) of Saddlescombe, and such lands were speedily acquired by the 'nouveaux riches.' People must have been effected by the religious upheaval in their lives but the burning of the Protestant martyrs in Lewes in the reign of Mary had no recorded repercussions in the parish.

The Armada scare of 1588 did impinge directly on rural life, the trained bands being called out and bonfires prepared on such places as Wolstonbury. The French had been often raiding in the past and had burnt Brighton in 1514 and they had landed at Seaford in 1545. The authorities were still really unprepared for a potential invasion by the Spaniards but luckily the Armada stood well out to sea past Beachy Head and there was great rejoicing and the ringing of church bells throughout the country when the enemy fleet was dispersed.[44]

The depreciation of the currency by Henry, with a sharp rise in prices, a threefold increase, and the large growth in population, caused the cost of living to escalate.[45] The higher prices hit the poorest hard and led to the Poor Law of 1601, a far-reaching matter which is discussed later.[46]

Grain was threshed with flails in autumn and winter.

iii. Threshing with flails

APPENDICES

1.   THE MANOR

The ownership or tenancy of land was very important in the feeding of the community.

From the Norman Conquest it was held under Feudal Tenure until this was abolished formally in 1660. In theory it was held directly by the King, the Royal Demesne, or of the King by the Chief Barons or under them the lesser Lords. All owed generally obedience, homage, and fealty and all except the church, military service when called upon. Villagers were required to band together in groups of twelve to be responsible for each other's good behaviour – this was known as Frankpledge.

The Lord had his Manor House and his demesne, land which he exploited directly. There were three important divisions of land tenure – a knight's fee or fief in multiples or parts of 600 acres; his obligations were in time converted to scutage, a money payment.

Socage – freeholders, nominally tenants of land, but rental was often nominal, for example a peppercorn. In later years most were yeomen and often very wealthy men.

Copyhold – the early villeins or serfs became freemen by the 15th century and they held land by the custom of the manor, at the will of the lord, their tenancy being enrolled on the Court Roll. They were bound to provide service to their Lord which could be very onerous. Copyhold could be for a term of years, normally '3 lives' or could be by inheritance which was not necessarily the eldest son (primogeniture). In Sussex generally it was by ' Borough English' – the youngest son.

A large amount of copyhold from the 16th century was converted to leasehold. Many lords found it more convenient to let land out for a money payment, particularly their demesne land, than the often complicated manner of copyhold service. Leases were similar to copyhold for a term of years or by inheritance. Land was often sub-let.

Lastly there were the landless labourers. (The religious houses owned land by what was known as Frankelmoin or 'free alms').

Many manors were extremely large and the lord's steward administered the estate and presided over the manor courts. Depending on local circumstances he could be assisted by a bailiff or bailiffs who supervised the manor(s) and who might have a hayward, beadle, ploughman, shepherd, etc under them.

The manor courts were of two kinds (in practice they were often combined) – the Court Baron which dealt with tenancy and manorial matters, and the Court Leet which dealt with good behaviour (View of Frankpledge) and petty criminal matters.

The tenants were represented by the reeve, elected by them, a headborough or petty constable, usually incorporating the pinder (responsible for the village pound for stray animals) and a surveyor of hedges, ditches and watercourses.

When a tenant died his son or heir had to appear at the manor court and surrender his property and be re-admitted and pay a fine (fee) for his inheritance as well as a 'heriot', usually the deceased's best beast.

The manorial system was beginning to decay by the 16th century and its civil functions were to a great extent taken over by the church vestry. The two often existed side by side even after the abolition of feudal tenure, and copyhold itself persisted until 1922.

2. THE HUNDRED

A division of the County and a grouping of Parishes from very early times which persisted into the 19th century. As a major administrative unit it had disappeared long before Tudor times. The only important officer to survive was the High Constable, appointed by Justices of the Peace at the Quarter Sessions. He was accountable to the Sheriff of the County for the collection of rates and taxes and for the militia. The Hundred Court itself did persist at least until the Civil War and the reputed last High Constable in England, one Phineus Jupp did not die until 1899 at the age of 73.

John Rowe, amongst other things a steward of the Earl of Abergavenny in the seventeenth century, has left us a picture of the Sheriff's Hundred Courts between 1613 and 1621.

Hurstpierpoint was in Buttinghill Hundred and Rowe tells us that this court was a' View of Frankpledge' and gave the names of the headboroughs of the various parishes who had to come with their tithings, the head constables each of a group of parishes, and the Alderman over all, a local gentleman. The court noted those residents who had not paid their contributions and were in default, and went on to record defaulters in the maintenance of ditches and bridges in the Hundred as well as stray animals. The court also included one person who was a 'stamper of leather' and another an 'inspector of leather.'

NOTES AND REFERENCES

1.   Geological data from the British Geological Survey 1984; other references to flints can be found in volumes of SAC.
2.   Young A (1813): *General View of the Agriculture of the County of Sussex*, 6: 'a excessively stiff calcarious loam on a clay bottom . . . very difficult to plough . . . It is a soil that must rank amongst the finest in this or any other country.'
3.   Couchman J E (1925): A Roman Cemetery at Hassocks, *SAC* **66**, 37.
4.   Margary I D (1948): *Roman Ways in the Weald*, 165. Prior to Margary's extensive examinations in 1933, not until 1925 was any part of the road

rediscovered until work by J E Couchman on the Roman cemetery at Hassocks led to the recording by him of that part of the route through Danny and Bedlam Street where it appeared as a fine agger parallel with the modern road. The original pictorial record of the route prepared by Margary is available for viewing in the Sussex Archaeological library at Lewes.

5. Couchman, Roman Cemetery, *SAC* **66**, 37.
6. *Ibid.*, 34–51; Cunliffe B (1973): *The Regni,* 72–73.
7. Couchman, Roman Cemetery, *SAC* **66**, 39–40.
8. *Ibid.*, 35. The greatest period of activity was confined to about 50 years between AD140 andAD190 according to finds collected.
9. The excavation is to be continued during 2000, so no details as yet have been officially published, however, the author (PB)attended many weeks of excavation and collected this information. Dating of the site and duration of its occupancy will, hopefully, be revealed once the analysis of the finds have been completed.
10. Butler C (1994) *SAS Newsletter* **74**, 6–7.
11. Anon (1858): Roman Pavement at Danny, *SAC* **10**, 210; Blencowe R W (1862): Roman remains in the neighbourhood of Hurstpierpoint and Danny, *SAC* **14**, 179; Couchman, Roman Cemetery, *SAC* **66**, 34; Scott E (1993): A *Gazetteer of Roman villas in Britain* Vol 1, 187.
12. Couchman, Roman Cemetery, *SAC 66*, 35 (and map).
13. Holleyman G A (1935): Romano-British site on Wolstonbury Hill, *SAC* **76**, 35– 45; Woodard P (1950): *SNQ* **13**, 131–134.
14. *Ibid.*: the hoard of 21 Roman coins found at the Wolstonbury site referred to has not been confirmed elsewhere.
15. Blencowe, Roman Remains, *SAC* **14**, 178.
16. White S: Early Saxon Sussex *c*.410–*c*.650, in Leslie K & Short B (eds)(1999): *An Historical Atlas of Sussex*, 28.
17. *SAC* **66**, 74–77.
18. Butler, *SAS* **74**, 6–7.
19. Sawyer J (1999):The excavation of a Romano-British site at Burgess Hill, *SAC* **137**, 49–58.
20. Brandon P (1974): *The Sussex Landscape*, 67–78; Brandon P (1963): The Common Lands and Wastes of Sussex, unpublished Ph.D. thesis, University of London
21. British Association Conference report, *The Independent* 9 September 2000, 8; Keys D: Catastrophic Investigations, Channel 4 television programme
22. Eg Edgerley = Eddi's Leigh, Mawer A & Stenton F M (1930): *The Place-Names of Sussex*, **2**, 275.
23. Morris J (ed)(1976): *Domesday Book, Sussex*, 12, 36.

24. Sussex was divided by William into five parts called Rapes: Arundel, Bramber, Lewes, Pevensey and Hastings, each controlled by a Norman baron who erected a castle, of which Lewes is probably the finest.

25. See Appendix 2.

26. See Appendix 1.

27. *Ibid.*

28. *VCH* **7**, 177.

29. A Native, A Minor (1837): *A History of Hurstperpoint*, 26.

30. Ellis WS (1859): Descent of the Manor of Hurst-Pierpoint and its Lords, *SAC* **11**, 65, 66.

31. ESRO/DAN1126, f 192.

32. *Ibid.*

33. ESRO/DAN2096.

34. Brandon, Commons & Wastes.

35. *Ibid.*

36. *Ibid.*

37. Stratton J M (1969): *Agricultural Records AD220–1968.*

38. *Ibid.*

39. Hudson W (ed)(1909): Sussex Subsidy Rolls 1296, 1327 and 1332, *SRS* **10**, 46, 176, 290.

40. *Ibid.*

41. Hey D (ed)(1996): *Oxford Companion to Local and Family History*, 44. The tradition of descent of property to the youngest son was peculiar to Sussex and dated back many centuries, perhaps to the South Saxon Kingdom, and lasted until the eighteenth century at least.

42. Godfrey W H (1928): The Book of John Rowe 1597–1622, *SRS* **34**.

43. Weald and Downland Open Air Museum at Singleton has examples.

44. Butler C (1994): The excavation of a medieval site at Muddleswood, near Hurstpierpoint, West Sussex, *SAC* **132**, 101–114.

45. Goring J (1988): *Sussex and the Spanish Armada*, 16.

46. See Chapter 6

2. THE CHURCH
From Ethelbert to Victoria

SAXON CHRISTIANS

The first documentary evidence we have regarding religious worship in Hurstpierpoint appears in Domesday Book,[1] where, among all the recording of daily agricultural life, taxes and valuation in 1086, is the clear statement *'ibi aeccl[esi]a'* – 'there is a church'. Written as it was only twenty years after the Norman Conquest, it is reasonable to assume that a building dedicated to Christian observances was here in Saxon times. However, it should be remembered that the story goes back further than the previous 600 years, beyond the time when our Germanic forebears started to arrive. Apart from documents we rely on archaeological evidence to trace our story. For example, during the middle of the nineteenth century a ring of baked clay over 4" in diameter, nearly 2" thick, with a central aperture of similar size, was found in the churchyard; it has been variously identified as a stand for a funeral torch, a quoit, or something to do with Druidical worship, or weaving[2]. However, there seems to be some consensus that it dates from the Early to Middle Anglo-Saxon period, with a possible indication of religious activity on the site, whether Christian or pre-Christian, as early as the fifth century AD.

Chapter 1 has related the influence on this parish of the Roman occupation, even to the extent of having a large cemetery only a short distance beyond our eastern boundary at Stonepound. There has also been conjecture that there may have been a Roman temple on our present churchyard site, because of the discovery there of so many coins and pottery fragments.[3] So far as is known, these are references to Roman religious observances, but we do know that Christianity was sufficiently well established and organised for bishops from Britain to attend Continental meetings, and that archaeological evidence indicates that it had become part of life for many of the more educated members of late Roman Britain, having gradually worked its way up the social scale from the slaves and other servants.[4] Moreover, St Alban, the so-called 'protomartyr of Britain', died in the early years of the fourth century, over 100 years before the Romans finally left.

What might be called the re-conversion of southern England began with the arrival of St Augustine in Canterbury in 597 and his baptism of King Ethelbert. The Roman style prevailed over the Celtic tradition at the Synod of Whitby in 664, and by 700 much of southern Britain had Christian devotional practices superimposed on pagan ceremonies and festivals. This was achieved by priests from monastic houses travelling to local settlements to visit the sick, to preach, to baptise and to celebrate mass. For example, St Wilfrid, the somewhat turbulent bishop of York, introduced the Benedictine rule to the monastery he founded at Selsey, from where he taught the South Saxons to fish, an important factor in establishing his ministry. Before the erection of any building, the assembly point would perhaps have been marked with a cross in the open air. Whatever the physical situation might have been, the fiscal one was soon well-established: during the ninth century the Church was requiring payment of tithes and other dues, backed by the force of the law of the land.[5] In addition, parish boundaries had become clearly defined, enabling the authorities to determine which church should be attended for Sunday services, for festivals, and for family occasions such as baptism, marriage and burial. The monasteries often looked on the parishes as merely income. All in all, the Church was clearly determined to be a force in the land.

THE NORMAN CHURCH

The church recorded in the Domesday survey could have been constructed of wood or stone. There are a number of examples nearby of Saxon churches built of stone. Clayton and Wivelsfield both have remnants dating from this period, while Sompting has its tower with its unique (for England) 'Rhenish helm' spire, and Worth has a still untouched Saxon floor plan. It has been suggested that the more complete survivals are an indication of poverty: if the parish prospered, the need for a larger, more substantial building was met from an improved economic situation.[6] If this is so, it provides further confirmation of the evidence in Domesday of a relatively prosperous parish, for the 'Taxation of Pope Nicholas IV' in 1291 assessed Hurst at £13.6s.8d, 'including the vicar's portion'. The incumbent at that time was James de Hastings, the first whose name is known to us.[7] Some substantial building work took place in the Early English period (c.1175-c.1275), items such as the sedilia and piscina surviving to this day. In 1331 Simon de Pierpoint held the advowson or right to present someone to the living.[8] By this time the patron considered the church to be his property. If such a patron, either individual or monastic house, took the great tithes of corn and hay, leaving only the lesser tithes such as milk, eggs, wildfowl or garden produce to the vicar, this depressed the value of the living, and so affected the standard of applicants for the incumbency.[9] This may have been the case in Hurst, for one of the Simons gained a reputation for high-handedness with his serfs, but the parish survived any depredations from its patron. The recumbent effigy of a knight in armour in the vestry of the present church has been dated *c.*1260[10] and has been thought to be that of the Sir Simon who fought as a crusader at the siege of Acre in 1191. Many generations of the Pierpoint family had the same first name, making positive identification difficult, but another tomb effigy at the west end of the north aisle dated *c.*1340 is more likely to represent the Simon of 1331.[11] Whatever the truth may be, there is one thing about which there is no doubt – the close connection between the lord of the manor and the church was well established during the feudal period. The other close link was with the Priory of St Pancras at Lewes.

We find the Priory making a claim on the land and tenements of Peter of Hautboys; Robert de Perpont quitclaiming (releasing from rights) 'all services due from the tenement called Hautboys ... excepting only suit to be done to the court at Hurst'; and Walter de Legh and the heirs of Wycham granting ...'to William de Hautboys all the land which the said William set up on the common pasture called Strodes.' Bishop Rede's register records (from 1396) claims by the Priory of Lewes for tithes from many parishes, including 'At Hurst the tenth portion of sheaves from the demesne of the Manor with the tenth portion of the land called Randulfslonde'.[12] John Gyles (or Gylys) was admitted Rector at Aumbele (Amberley) in 1395, when the patron was a Lady Ela of Hurst. He had some influence beyond the parish, as we find him being consulted when Canon Richard Weston of Michelham Priory was appointed Prior of Hastings. Gyles exchanged the living with that of John Welles, by which time the Norman landlord had appropriated the living to the Prior and Convent of Lewes.[13]

Belief in a continual war between good and evil during the whole period of the middle ages resulted in much grotesque carving based on previous pagan symbols, and powerful paintings like those at neighbouring Clayton. The non-Christian imagery was not always completely absorbed into Church teaching, with the Tree of Life or the Green Man surviving in some churches to the present day. The clergy of this period varied widely in education and ability, but one has to remember that those who came to the attention of higher authority because of some misconduct are the ones whose names are recorded; they were probably a small minority, their fellow priests looking after their parishioners conscientiously. In the first quarter of the fourteenth century they were provided with a practical guide in English, the *Oculus Sacerdotus that* dealt with all their various duties.[14] By this time it had become the norm that the patron or incumbent was responsible for the upkeep of the chancel, the congregation looking after the nave. The absence of pews or any other seats (allowing 'the weakest to go to the wall') gave scope for the greater amount of ritual and ceremonial, which in turn led to the enlargement of many parish churches, by the extension of the chancel or the addition of side aisles.

ST LAWRENCE

iv. St Lawrence Church in 1841.

It may well have been this development that caused John Urry, the then rector, to almost rebuild the church in 1420 at his own expense, retaining only the Norman tower of the earlier structure; and perhaps initiating the dedication to St Lawrence. Urry was allowed to hold another living as well as this one, 'because he had received slender fruit from the said two churches'.[15] The rebuilt church would have been consecrated by the bishop, in addition to his visitations. This is substantially the church which is depicted in the numerous drawings and sketches which were made in the late eighteenth and early nineteenth centuries. It was the church which was assessed at £15.9s.4d. in the *Valor Ecclesiasticus* of 1535, a survey preliminary to the dramatic actions of Thomas Cromwell on behalf of Henry VIII to dissolve the monasteries and break from Rome; incidentally a portion of tithes assessed at 13s4d. belonged to Lewes Priory, showing the continuing influence of the monastic houses on the parishes within their area, the so-called *minster parochiae*. It represented locally the immense influence exerted by the Church on secular as well as religious life, and was the recipient of many bequests from medieval wills. The parish church was the building in which most of the people worshipped for over four hundred years, through successive religious upheavals.

DISSOLUTION AND REFORMATION

The dissolution of the monasteries, and the transfer of much of their property into lay hands, affected parishes significantly. In 1534 the Annates Act empowered the Crown to take over the Pope's claim to the first year's income from the parish, followed by a tenth in subsequent years. The second stage in 1547, that of the dissolution of the chantries and the confiscation of guild funds, added to the financial interest that central government had in all livings, although there is no record of any such chapel or guild in Hurst, nor was much land in the parish owned directly by the Priory. The rector claimed the great tithes which had previously been taken by the monastic houses, still leaving only the lesser to the vicar. One sign of a developing change in individual attitudes can be found in the phrases commonly used in the drafting of wills. The first bequest at this period was that of the testator's soul to God: a Protestant would hope for salvation through Christ's death and passion, a Roman Catholic through the intercession of the blessed Virgin Mary, but the loss of support from the religious houses resulted also in funeral doles and other bequests of money for the relief of the poor being specified.[16]

From Richard Norton in 1509 through to Thomas Croweher in 1547, Hurst wills ask that masses should be said for their respective souls. Richard Savege in 1551 continues this pattern, but also wills 'that the same Daye yr be geven unto the poore as moche bread as can be made of on bushell of wheate meale, a shepe and a vyrkyn of drynk and so in lyke maner to be done at my monethes mynd' (a memorial one month later); and Thomas Cobbe has a similar dual approach the following year. A will drawn during Edward VI' reign by Ralph Beache makes no reference to the saying of masses, but the influence of the Marian return to Roman Catholicism is shown in the words of several legatees, to be superseded once more when Elizabeth I comes to the throne by more practical bequests. Others from 1549 onwards gave to 'the poore mens boxe' sums ranging from 4d to 6s.8d. In 1609 Robert Whitpaine left instructions to be 'buried decently in Hurst churchyard' and 40s. to be distributed among the poor of Hurst. There were also periodic bequests to St Lawrence Church, from 12d to 26s.8d.[17]

As well as the regular Sunday services, the seasonal festivals continued to be observed meticulously; in fact were publicly supported by Henry VII in 1539: ashes on Ash Wednesday, candles at Candlemas and the outdoor procession of the Host at Corpus Christi in addition to the ceremonial surrounding Easter and Christmas with which we are still familiar. In 1541 churchwardens were ordered to obtain a Bible in English, but soon there was a realisation that producing the scriptures in the vernacular had its drawbacks with regard to the continuing control of the authorities. In 1543 the requirement that every church should have its own English Bible was revoked, because of abuse by 'the lower sort'. It was decreed that 'no women, nor artificers, prentices, journeymen, servingmen of the degrees of yeomen or under, husbandmen nor labourers shall read the Bible or New Testament to himself or any other privately or openly',[18] and presumably this attempt to regain the former level of influence applied in Hurst as elsewhere. With the accession of Edward VI, the simplified liturgy of the Church of England involved the banning of much ritual and ornamentation, some parishes being more zealous than others in removing traces of Roman practice. Mary and Elizabeth were to follow with rules on liturgy swinging back and forth. The extremes of Marian persecution, ending in the martyrdom of Sussex men and women at Lewes and elsewhere, did not impact on Hurst to the same extent. It is possible that its position in the middle of the county led to a somewhat 'middle-of-the-road' attitude towards religious observances. During Elizabeth's reign, only an approved preacher was allowed some freedom of expression, the vast majority being required to use twenty or so licensed texts. This led inevitably to boredom, both for the preacher and for his congregation, and could account for the attraction of the more enthusiastic Puritan speakers. The Puritans increased their activities after Elizabeth's death, but the pendulum swung against them when William Laud became Archbishop of Canterbury in 1633 and introduced his 'Thorough' purge of any tendencies towards Calvinism. Visitations sometimes resulted in dire penalties for offending clergy: whipping, imprisonment and physical mutilation as well as fines.

Until the wholesale Puritan approach of the middle decades of the seventeenth century, alongside the annual religious rituals, the church was the focus of much secular jollification. Wassailing, derived from the Old English and Old Norse greeting 'be of good health', is still referred to in some of our carols, but the connection between the drinking bowl and wishing the orchard trees a good harvest has long since been lost. The Hognells or Hogglers raised money during an extended Christmas period which in nearby Bolney lasted until Candlemas on 2 February; Plough Monday in early January raised money for the church by dragging a plough around the streets; Hocktide on the second Monday and Tuesday after Easter involved the paying of a 'ransom' to be released from being bound with ropes; Rogationtide was an occasion for the perambulation of the parish boundaries in addition to its religious connotation of prayers for the harvest; May Day and other occasions for 'church ales' also provided opportunities for parish fund-raising; the harvest itself had, and still has, a communal meal as well as the church thanksgiving. Before the days of pews many of these activities may have been in the nave: dancing, bowling, archery; minstrels, actors; all would have used the empty space to the best advantage. Certainly the churchyard was a centre for all manner of secular pursuits. We have no documentary evidence regarding Hurst, but the likelihood is that neighbouring parishes behaved in similar fashion.[19] As with the purely religious festivals, Edward VI's Protector Somerset tried to put a stop to much of the secular activity, with limited long-term success.[20]

Parish administration received attention from Thomas Cromwell as well. 1538 saw the requirement to keep registers of baptisms, marriages and burials; and to provide a 'sure coffer' (the parish chest) with two locks, thus permitting access to the records only when two persons were present. There seems to have been a somewhat irregular start to compliance with this Royal Injunction in Sussex, the registers for Hurst only surviving from 1558. The next century gives us many more documents which are available for study. From 1601 (see chapter on The Parish and its Poor) the parish, and therefore the church, was required to provide many of the structures for civil control, and the manpower to ensure its management. The incumbent had to urge his people to relieve the poor; to lead the Rogationtide perambulation; to give ecclesiastical sanction to the whipping of rogues and vagabonds by being present when this punishment was inflicted; to prosecute recusants and to take public confessions. Churchwardens, overseers of the poor, surveyors of the highway, headboroughs and constables, were all elected or appointed by the vestry, a meeting of the substantial inhabitants in their role as members of the church. The building itself was sometimes used as a prison, but more commonly as a library containing the only publicly available books, or as a school. This was almost inevitable as from 1571 anyone wishing to teach required a bishop's licence. Often the school's continuing existence depended on the career of the parson/teacher: if he was a curate or awaiting a living elsewhere, there was every likelihood that the school would close on his departure.

A Poor Rate was raised in Hurst in 1629;[21] in 1636 we have evidence of the property belonging to the Rector at that time, Christopher Swale, in an inventory of possessions, particularly land:

> Terriere of Glebe lands and messuages belonging to the Parsonage of Hurstperpoint 1636 Aprill 20th
>
> There is thereunto belonging a howse a Barne and Stable with a close or yard and foure several parcells of Land distinctlie by these names as bounded as followeth.
> 1. The Haselcroft conteyning three Acres of Ground or thereabouts abutting towards the north to a piece of ground of the same name of the lands of William Jordan towards the South to the Mansion house of the said William Jordans towards the west to the Kings highway towards the east to Thomas Luxfords land
> 2. The Goare conteyning 3 Acres bounding to the Long mead towards the South to a piece of land called the west furlong towards the North towards the West to Robert Whitpaine towards the East upon Rich: Whitpaine
> 3. The Reanes conteyning halfe an acre abutting towards the South on Mr Nortons garden towards the North to a meadow of the little parke towards the West to a garden plott of Richard Whitpaines towards the East to the bowling greene

4. A parcell of halfe an acre called the Parsonage orchard bounding on the North and west to the little parke uppon the East to Dr Swales howse called the Matts uppon the South to the high street

Chr Swale   Rector Thomas Butcher   Edward **X** Burtinshaw [22]

The Latin word *'glaeba'* means a clod or soil; the glebe was provided by the landlord for the parson's subsistence. In Saxon times and through the medieval period it would have been worked by the incumbent himself, but increasingly it was rented out to local farmers wishing to extend their holding. By comparison with parishes in other parts of the country the Rector of Hurst received a very small acreage of glebe. In addition to actual ownership of land and property, the incumbent was entitled to a tenth of the produce of the other occupiers of land within the parish, originally paid in kind (hence the great tithe barns which still stand in some parts of the country), and voluntary until King Edmund's reign in the tenth century, but often commuted into money to avoid disputes over the value of particular crops. The original intention was that it should be redistributed to the poor, but gradually the Church encouraged the parson to demand payment for himself. At the Reformation the rights to corn, hay, livestock, wool and non-cereal crops which had been claimed by the monasteries were granted to secular landowners known in this context as lay impropriators.[23] The lord of the manor of Hurst was one such. He had the right to part of the parish's tithes, the great tithes of cereal crops going to the Rector in return for the maintenance of the chancel of the church. Seventeenth century nonconformists refused to pay tithes to landowners; two centuries later their opposition extended to the Church.

The accounts of Thomas Wilford and Richard Marshall, churchwardens in 1685, show how interwoven church and secular affairs had become. The expenses of journeys to church Courts and the cost of bell ropes are listed together with payments for the relief of 'passengers' (paupers passing through the parish) and for 'maimed soldiers'; to be followed by entries for buying bread and wine for communion; 'for gowen after thre fellows to alehouse'; paying the ringers at thanksgiving, mending the church windows and washing and mending the communion linen. In 1702 an entry 'for bere when the Queen [Anne] was crowned' is followed by a short series:

> 'Spent with the shingglers when the work was started   6d
> paid shingglers for shingling steeple   £10. 3s. 6d
> spent with shingglers when I payed them off   1s. 0d'[24]

The activities of the overseers are dealt with in a later chapter, but they too were appointed by the church – in terms of authority church and civil parish were one.

This, then, was the church served by a succession of priests, most of whom were quietly carrying out the pastoral care of their flock, probably recognising the value of a balance between the secular and the sacred, but leaving little or no permanent individual mark on history. But there were exceptions.

ROYALIST RECTOR

Christopher Swale, already mentioned in the glebe terrier above, and to be heard of again later in the book, was inducted and instituted to the benefice and the cure of souls in 1607. As we shall see later, not every rector lived in the parish, but we can be sure that Swale did, although his 'cure of souls' would seem to have been mixed with very strong political views. He was a staunch Royalist, presented to the living by another such, George Goring, and refused to announce publicly the various edicts of the Parliamentarians. In December 1642 the Long Parliament resolved that the episcopacy should be dispensed with and set up a 'Committee of Plundered Ministers', with branch committees in each county, including one sitting at Lewes. Swale had already been heard to 'speak some words against the Parliament', but did not become a target for the Committee's active investigations until February 1645, when he was asked to 'take the vow & covenant & solemn league and covenant' [to accept the abolition of the episcopacy, etc]. His refusal caused the Committee to resolve on 13 March that 'Christopher Swale Doctor in Divinity be forthwith sequestered of and from the rectory of Hurst and all his spirituall promocons in the county of Sussex [he also held the living of Westbourne' – the Elizabethan Canons of 1571 made plurality illegal within 26 miles, and in 1604 this was extended to 30 miles; Westbourne is about 40 miles from Hurst, so Swale was within the law]. There followed some indecision regarding his replacement. Morgan Haine was recommended on 18 March 1645, confirmed on 27th, but two days later asked 'to relinquish all clayme . . . for that there is another minister who hath officiated there & is generally desired'. This was Humphrey Streete, who was recommended to the Assembly on 12 April, on which date the Committee clearly felt that their initial action needed justification, for they resolved that

> Whereas Christopher Swaile Doctor in Divinity Rector of the Parish Church of Hurst in the county of Sussex is a continual practiser of the late superstitious simulacon of bowing at the name of Jesus pressing in his subject the observacon thereof uppon paine of damnacon maintaining the practice thereof by argument & caused the booke of liberty of p[ro]phanacon of the Lordes day to be published in his church highly extolling the same and declared his opinion of the lawfullness of playing the sd day before and after evening prayer [a reference to the Declaration or Book of Sports issued during the reign of James I and reinforced by Charles I [25]] & hath in his sermons reproved keeping private dayes of humiliacon inveighing against such as kept them and hath much neglected the observacon of the monthly fast & hath publikely dissuaded his parishonrs from taking up of armes affirmeing they must beare what ever their Sovraigne please to lay uppon them though to the death And hath said the Parliamt is noe Parliamt And hath refused to publish the order of the House of Commons agt bowing at the name of Jesus saying before his parish it came but from the house of Commons & that it was illegall and other orders of Parliamt laughing at such as read them and hath endeavoured by lies and otherwise to take of divers from their adhering to & assisting the Parliamt and hath otherwise expressed great malignancy agt the Parliamt and it was therefore ordered the thirteenth day of March last. . .[26]

But Streete did not have long to enjoy his incumbency for by 8 November yet another name appeared, that of Leonard Lichfield [Letchford]. He was summoned to 'answer articles exhibited against him'. Apparently James Mathew and Thomas Butcher, acting on behalf of the parishioners who preferred Streete, had denied Letchford access to the rectory. The Committee found Streete, Mathew and Thomas Leney in contempt and ordered each of them to pay £3 costs, and Letchford remained as rector until he died a dozen years after the Restoration. His actions against the Quakers will be looked at in detail in a later chapter.

Amidst all the upheavals of the Civil War and Interregnum, Hurst clearly had its own problems with its ministers, but there is no evidence that the church itself was subjected to the excesses of actual destruction brought about elsewhere by Puritan zeal. Was church life always as exciting as this in the seventeenth century? To some extent, yes. Christopher Swale, although a J P. and parish priest, was disputatious about other matters as well as religious observances. He was presented at the Quarter Sessions for leaving litter in the public highway, and had a public disagreement with a fellow magistrate, Thomas Whatman, ostensibly over some money claimed to be owed to a member of Swales's family, but at a deeper level about status. This was highlighted when the wives brawled in the church on a matter of precedence; the rector preached about sin in a way which was clearly aimed at Whatman, while the latter scoffed at Swale from the pews. The minister claimed that he had been libelled in writing and made 'the talke of men, the laughter of youth and the songe of children'.[27] But this particular incident in church occurred against a background of 'crowded benches, shuffling, talking and ill-behaviour, quarrels which had begun earlier over some secular matter [breaking] out again . . . when the parties found themselves in close proximity. . .'[28]

RESTORATION AND APATHY

The Restoration was the occasion for several measures relating to church observances, and to re-establishing control over a number of secular activities. Visitations by bishops and archdeacons ensured that the church services, the state of the building and its furnishings, the residence of the incumbent and the payment of curates were all kept under some sort of surveillance. The census carried out in 1676 by Bishop Compton shows that Hurstpierpoint had 271 communicants, but also the second highest number of nonconformists in the mid Sussex area (22).[29] The Act of Uniformity of 1662 required that teachers, doctors and midwives as well as clergymen recorded their acceptance of the Thirty-Nine Articles and their loyalty to the monarch in Subscription Books. Loyalty was also expressed in the display of royal coats of arms in the church. In Hurst we have no evidence of such a device dating from this time, the one in the present building being that of Queen Victoria. In this period, the churchwardens were required to 'present' to the authorities the names of persistent absentees from attendance at the parish church, but most of the defaulters were in fact staunch dissenters and as a result this legal action had very little effect, their names being repeated at successive hearings. Other deviations from accepted behaviour were also brought before the courts: in 1675 'Susan Buckwell for not coming to church and for not christening of her children'; in 1677 'Charity Corke, the wife of Edward Corke, for antenuptiall fornication'.[30] A Declaration of Indulgence in March 1672 which allowed Roman Catholics to worship in their own homes, was swiftly followed by the first of two Test Acts which excluded them from public office including parliament. Only the removal of James II and the accession of William of Orange toned down this demand for absolute loyalty, with the Toleration Act of 1689 granting limited freedom of worship.[31]

One can imagine Hurst churchwardens trying hard to keep out of the firing line. Certainly by 1682, they were more likely to have been involved in mundane problems, such as the maintenance of the churchyard wall (there is no Hurst record, but a list of occupiers responsible at Henfield has been preserved [32]). The relative calm of William III's reign gave a chance for the church in Hurst to turn its attention to more decorous things. In February 1699 a diocesan faculty was granted appropriating seats in a singing gallery:

> Whereas by certificate of John Bateman, clerk and curate, William Marchant and John Holden, churchwardens, and other inhabitants, there is a lately erected gallery over the S. aisle adjoining a W. gallery built by the contributions and consent of Rev. Mainard Shaw, rector, Rev. John Bateman, William Marchant, churchwarden, Thomas Beard, sen. and jun., Thomas and John Whitpaine, gents., Richard Wood, and others, for the encouragement and improvement of psalm singing and other devotions. It is decreed that sittings in the gallery be assigned to the principal contributors above named [positions stated], the remainder to be for use of those skilful in singing.

There seems to have been some hiatus, as Thomas Marchant noted:

> 1717. May 9th (Whitsunday) ... The new singers began to sing in the church.[33]

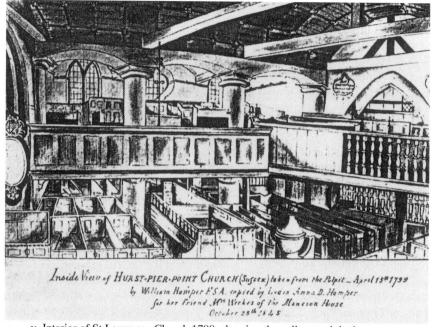

Inside View of HURST-PIER-POINT CHURCH (Sussex) taken from the Pulpit – April 15th 1799 by William Hamper F.S.A. copied by Lucia Anna D. Hamper for her friend Mrs Wickes of the Mansion House October 28th 1845

v. Interior of St Lawrence Church 1799, showing the gallery and the box-pews.

We have no confirmation of any instrumental accompaniment to the singing in St Lawrence, but this faculty was granted just as the eighteenth century was beginning, and the common practice was for this to be the case. Churchwardens' accounts elsewhere show purchases of bassoons, clarinets, flutes, oboes and stringed instruments, to form church bands. Both singers and instrumentalists were positioned in the gallery at the west end, the congregation having to turn to 'face the music' for the psalms and the newly-introduced hymns. It was during this period that rents were paid for occupation of the box-pews. A plan exists showing the names of the major farms and other properties which 'owned' or rented specific pews. A document, the first lines of which have several gaps due to damage, shows a pragmatic approach to the matter:

> ...Condition of an agreement made ...
> of the parish of Hurstpierpoint in the County of Sussex ...
> William Courtness of the same place Mercer as follows

> The said Christopher Dodson dothe let unto the said William

Courtness a pew in the Chancel of the Parish Church of
Hurstpierpoint aforesaid being the first on the right hand going in
the Chancel Dore of the said Church to hold the same in the said
William Courtness for and during the free will and pleasure of the
said Christopher Dodson and his successors Paying yearly and
every year as an [acknow] ledgement for the use of the said Pew
unto the said Christopher Dodson and [his suc]cessors one Pound
of Raisins and one Pound of Currants on the Feast day of the
Annunciation of the blessed Virgin Mary
Witness their hands this Ninteenth (sic) Day of August in the year
of our Lord 1776.

Witness hereto T Marchant   Chris: Dodson   Wm Courtness [34]

Between 1775 and 1784 attention was paid to the casting of six new bells by
William Chapman of London. Two of the new bells, the fifth and the tenor,
were considered unsatisfactory by the parish, and Chapman agreed to cast
new bells in their place. Together with James Exeter, an executor of his late
partner Thomas Pack, Chapman also entered a bond with the churchwardens
to replace the new bells without charge should either become cracked or 'be
otherwise rendered untunable by fair Ringing within one year . . .' in the
event the bond was not executed, so presumably the bells proved to be
satisfactory at the time. Two of the six bells remain in the ring today.[35]
Money was still available three years later, because the south wall (where
the main door was) was built out with flint and brick walls and roughcast
finish, the gallery built at the turn of the century was altered, the whole
extension being roofed with tiles. The work was carried out by William
King, bricklayer, and William Morley, carpenter, at a cost of £167.0s.11d.
At the same time repair work was done on the North side of the church.[36]

By 1673 when Leonard Letchford died the patronage had passed to Sir John
Shaw of Eltham in Kent. Not surprisingly, we find that the next Rector is
one Minhard[es] Shaw. But more obvious nepotism was to follow, for
Jeremiah Dodson, Christopher Dodson, and John Dodson successively
occupied the living from 1701 to 1807. A later member of the family was
elevated to the peerage as Lord Monk Bretton, underlining the common
connection which occurred between the establishment, the gentry and the
clergy, with heredity playing an important part in patronage and preferment.
It was Jeremiah who is the Dodson mentioned on several occasions in
Thomas Marchant's diary.[37] Incidentally, this document shows Marchant's

'carefulness' in money matters, even when dealing with church things:

1715. July 18th.	I went to Bolney, and agreed with Edw Jenner to dig sandstone for setting up my father's tombstone, at 5s. I gave him 6d. to spend in drink, that he might be more careful.
1727. Sept. 18th.	Dined at Mr Hazelgrove's and cheapened a tombstone.

It would appear from the diary that, although he was a churchwarden, his personal attendances were affected by recurrent headaches, often after a previous evening's enjoyment, only occasionally recording that 'Mr Dodson preacht' in his presence. Preaching had become the cornerstone of the Sunday service, the pulpit having two or three tiers, one from which the sermon was delivered, a lower level for the reading of the lessons, the bottom one for the clerk who sang the responses and tried to keep order, striking sleeping men and boys with a knob-ended stick known as a 'sluggard-waker', more delicately tickling the ladies with a fox's brush.[38] Pews were often painted and numbered, or named after the properties to which they belonged (a Sussex example being at West Grinstead). These pews were still being purchased until St Lawrence Church was pulled down. Included in the 'Neat Modern Household Furniture and Effects' for sale at auction on Wednesday 25 January 1837 was

> Also a very Commodious Freehold Pew, in the South Gallery of Hurstperpoint Church; For further Particulars of this Lot Apply to Mr. Muzzell, Hurstperpoint; this Lot will be Sold Precisely at Seven o'Clock in the Evening.

It was sold to Richard Weeks Junior and his brother Frederick for £24, as a receipt dated the following day confirms.[39]

Hurst is not recorded in the diocesan survey of 1686-7, but Bishop Bower's survey in 1724 states:

> The church in good repair, and going to be beautified.
> The Communion table, rails, carpet, linnen, a large silver chalice (lately enlarged by Mr [Peter] Courthop, a pewter flagon, two large pewter dishes given by the Rector for charity collections, the books and surplice, the pulpit, desk, and all belonging to

them, in good order.

The steeple and six bells, one of which a little damaged.

A clock and chimes, a box and chest, but no poor box.

The chancel in good repair; repaired by the Rector.

The parsonage house new built by the Rector; all the rest good.

Families 100, of which two Quakers, one Anabaptist.

Mr [Leonard] Letchford, sometime Rector, gave £100 to purchase land, the rent of which is to be divided yearly between ten industrious persons with large families. The parishioners who are trustees distribute the interest accordingly, no land being yet purchased.

An annuity of £4 per annum given by Mr [Henry] Smith, alias 'Dog' Smith to the poor.

. . .

[Value of the of living in] King's Books £15 9s.4 1/2d; not discharged from first fruits, the yearly value exceeding £50. A portion of tyth granted to the priory of Lewis, now in the hand of Mr Richard Whitpaine of Hurst; present value, about £24 per annum.

Divine service and sermon twice every Lord's Day in the summer, once in the morning and service [alone] in the afternoon in the winter. Divine service all the year on holy days, Wednesdays and Fridays in the morning; supplied in the winter by the Rector, in the summer by the curate, Mr Edward Martin.

…

The Holy Sacrament administered twice at each of the three solemn festivals and the first Sunday in every month. At each of the former about 100, and at the latter about 25, communicants …. The glebe about 5 acres, including the parsonage garden.'[40]

The Rector also joined in the local round of hospitality, for example providing on Easter Monday 1715 three bottles of claret to be consumed by his close friends.[41] Even the small glimpses that the diarist gives of the activities of the Hurst parson indicate some parallels with those of James Woodforde half a century later: a fairly regular social round with the local gentry, but whether he cared for his parishioners when the need arose in the same way we have no record.[42] However he was mean when it came to claiming his tithe: in 1716 Dodson decided to go to court 'to secure the grain that fell to the ground from the bottom of the tithe cocks'.[43] Mr Marchant was more assiduous in the administrative side of his duties, dealing with the distribution of charitable money (both the Letchford and Smith bequests being mentioned in the diary) or goods, settling parish accounts or appointing officers such as overseers and surveyors. He was very definite in his views about certain appeals for money. The church authorities from time to time sent a 'Brief' commending an appeal from some other parish in need, particularly after some major damage had occurred to the church structure:

> January 9th 1715 . . . Mr Dodson read a Brief for the repair of a church, to which I gave nothing.'[44]

A century later John Dodson's name appears in the diary assumed to have been kept by Richard Weekes, the local doctor and the Rector's next-door neighbour, between 1800 and 1823, and in his letters to his sons at the beginning of this period. The Weekes's house was then called 'Matts' (now Norfolk House – the Dodsons' Rectory was what is now Church House, but John Dodson moved to Chantry House and his successor had it rebuilt to face Little Park in 1808). We shall see later that John Dodson was not always popular, but he was also unable to carry out any church duties for three months due to illness, going to Staffordshire in April 1802, much to the apparent relief of Weekes:' We do not regret thier (sic) absence at all,' although the empty house three months later made Hurst 'quite a deserted place'. By the end of July 'Jno. Dodson is returned and is a little more chatty.'[45] Apart from the less than neighbourly relations and the fact that Weekes does not record his own attendance at church in either diary or letters, the impression is left that John Dodson relied on his curate for the care of his parishioners:

> For the well-paid, beneficed clergy the Church offered an attractive career, with comfortable living and a minimum of duties, and it became a popular choice for the younger sons or close relatives of gentry families, especially if the family controlled the patronage of one or more benefices.[46]

As will be clear from the preceding paragraphs, we have very little direct information about the church in the eighteenth century. What we can glean indicates that Hurst was largely following the pattern throughout the country, one of lack of enthusiasm:

> In its flight from fervour the Church adopted a somnolent round
> of services, sermons and moral teaching which emphasised the
> importance of social harmony and the maintenance of the
> established order, but which was unlikely to inspire deep
> commitment among the majority of people.[47]

One material benefit which was of concern to the Rector was that of the
tithes mentioned earlier – a system which persisted until the Tithe Act of
1836. The value of the tithes was not inconsiderable: at Michaelmas 1808
the rector collected over £830 from the land occupiers (and just over £6 from
the smaller householders). At least three cases of dispute between the
Rector, Jeremiah Dodson, and individuals in Hurst reached the courts: in
1716 and 1719 Mr [Thomas] Norton of Edgeley had 'reaped and carried
away' crops without setting aside a tenth, and had kept livestock without any
recompense to the Rector.[48] Such legal action was not uncommon,
particularly when commutation to a fixed money payment had taken place,
and arose from 'the desire of a parson to break out of the straitjacket of a
modus decimandi which had not kept pace with inflation.'[49] Even in the
1870s there were men who could recall the central part played in the harvest
by this church tax:

> When the hay was in cock or the wheat in shock, then the
> Titheman come; you didn't dare take up a field without you let
> him know. If the Titheman didn't come at the time, you tithed
> yourself. He marked his sheaves with a bough or bush. You
> couldn't het over the Titheman. If you began at a hedge and made
> the tenth cock smaller than the rest, the Titheman might begin in
> the middle just where he liked.[50]

Each Dodson in turn asserted his right to tithes most assiduously. Moreover,
as we have seen, he could afford a curate, particularly during the summer,
allowing him to go away on holiday, apparently expecting the harvest to
provide him with his dues in his absence. In fact, John Dodson, the last of
the three successive rectors, was non-resident, being also Vicar of Eltham in
Kent. Non-residence and pluralism were widespread at this time, incurring
much opprobrium, although one of the possible explanations lies in the
difficulty of attracting suitable educated entrants to the profession in a period
of inadequate incomes. In more than a third of all livings, the income was
less than £50 per annum; the glebe and tithes together often made the
difference to an incumbent's standard of living. It would appear that the

living of Hurst was a relatively desirable one.[51]

One further aspect of this period is the alienation of the craftsmen and labourers from the church. To some extent this may have started with the Chantries Act of 1548 which prohibited many gilds and fraternities, but this piece of legislation is more likely to have been a factor in the towns. Also, the incumbency was now being occupied by university graduates, thus creating a gulf, perceived or actual, between the pastor and his flock. In any event, many of the secular activities which had been centred on the church building and land were now frowned upon by respectable folk, particularly those with Puritan leanings. Those who felt that their religious needs were not met by the established church probably became active dissenters. For others it is evident that the alehouse emerged as an alternative venue for ritual, with many of the seasonal celebrations taking place there. It may be significant that the earliest date on a Hurstpierpoint pub is 1591.

The right to the advowson remained with the lord of the manor for over four hundred years, with only one exception: in 1545 the King is recorded as patron, presumably because Thomas Dacre was a minor and therefore a ward of court, his father having been executed four years earlier for murder (see the chapter on Law and Order). However, in 1778 the advowson passed from the lord of the manor when Sir John Shaw bequeathed it to the Winningtons, who presented in both 1784 and 1807. It later reverted to the Shaws, the Rev. Robert Shaw being patron in 1835, during the incumbency of J Kenward Shaw-Brooke, who succeeded John Dodson, but was also Rector of Eltham in Kent. He was a late example of the pluralism which was rife in the eighteenth century. William Cobbett estimated that some 832 parsons held over 3,000 parishes, and that nearly two-thirds of all the livings in the country did not have resident incumbents.[52] Shaw-Brooke only visited Hurst twice a year, thus continuing the practice of leaving his curate to look after the parish on a day-to-day basis. This was the last time that Hurst had a 'sinecure' rectory (an incumbency without the 'cure' of souls). Soon afterwards it was acquired by Nathaniel Borrer of Pakyns, who presented his son Carey Hampton Borrer to the living in January 1841. Later still, the right returned to the lord of the manor of Hurst by purchase, and remained with successive members of the Campion family.[53]

CANON BORRER AND HOLY TRINITY

The Reverend Carey Hampton Borrer (see Colour Plate 2) came to Hurst as a curate at 26 years of age. On the death of Shaw-Brooke he was presented to the living and brought about a dramatic change in the local church: in its buildings, its worship, and its involvement in the life of the wider parish. The revival in worship instigated by the Oxford Movement which sought to re-establish the Church's own authority as a divine institution, was gathering momentum. Its leaders were John Keble, Edward Pusey, John Newman and Richard Froude; they issued a series of Tracts for the Times, becoming known as Tractarians. Not without opposition, they emphasised ceremonial and sacrament, championing High Church practices. Borrer was inspired by this, and his great energy and determination would prove to be crucial in implementing reforms. There was then, and has been since, much criticism of the over-zealous removal of the past in the contemporary enthusiasm to provide churches worthy of new standards of worship and pastoral care.[54]

When he came he lost little time in getting his superiors on his side. On 11 September 1841 the Rural Dean told the churchwardens that essential repairs to St Lawrence Church should be completed in the following three months. Also, a week later the Archdeacon wrote:

> it was a great delight to find a Parish under the care of a Minister so devoted to his duties and so zealous for its welfare in every point of view . . .it is indispensable that your church should be able to contain a far greater number of persons. . .it is a miserable patchwork and there is hardly any thing in it worth preserving . . .
> I would therefore earnestly exhort you to consult your Parishioners on the propriety of building an entirely new Church . . .[55]

By 2 October a Vestry meeting had agreed to ask for opinions regarding the alternatives of enlargement or rebuilding. Charles Barry, the architect of the new Houses of Parliament, maintained that enlarging St Lawrence was impracticable, and the following June the Vestry announced its decision, accepting the report of the Building Committee, a document which reflects the general revival of enthusiasm in just eighteen months:

> That the present Building contains room for barely one fourth of the Inhabitants whereby three fourths are deprived of the comforts and advantages of Church going. That this is a state of

things in a populous Parish that calls loudly and plainly to every Man for immediate remedy. That having had an accurate survey made of the Church by an eminent architect it has been declared to be unsound and at the same time incapable of any good or effectual enlargement. That taking this into consideration, at the same time the Archdeacon and Rural Dean insisting on very considerable and expensive repairs, they recommend an entire rebuilding of the Edifice. That a substantial and handsome Building capable of containing one thousand People can be erected for a sum not exceeding £5,500, including every expence.'[56]

The die was cast. Of course there were objections, some showing genuine concern about the loss of an old and much-loved church, others only about the cost, particularly to property owners by way of rates. But the money was raised (the £5,500 almost inevitably becoming £7,500), the Church rate lending £1,700 to be repaid by way of mortgage at £100 per annum with interest. Individuals also contributed, ranging in status from the Dowager Queen Adelaide to the local gentry and other inhabitants: the Rector himself gave £1,000, Mr William John Campion (who was the lay impropriator of part of the tithes as well as being the lord of the manor £1,200), and the patron £500 (eventually £3,000) plus stone from his quarry at Pickwells at the north end of the parish. Campion and the Borrers, father and son, indemnified the parish of all liabilities over the £1,700 already raised through the rate. On 29 September 1843 the Bishop of Chichester laid the foundation stone (because of later extension, this can now be found inside the St Lawrence Chapel), returning on 28 May 1845 to consecrate the completed building, one of 759 new churches built during that decade.[57] So a 'large and prosperous' church replaced 'a sweet villagey one' – although how Ian Nairn, writing in 1965, could be so definite is unclear.[58] In the 1851 Census of Religious Attendance, against a national figure of only 21 per cent of the population attending an Anglican church, in Hurstpierpoint on 31 March there were no less than 1,200 attendances at Communion and Evening Prayer, of which 200 were Sunday School pupils at both morning an afternoon classes, plus about 100 at St John's College and almost 80 at Sayers Common (before a church had been built)' out of a total population of 2,219 according to the 851 census.[59]

Although the old church was destroyed, not all links with the past were lost. The Norman font was reworked by Sir Gilbert Scott in 1863 and painted, and a number of funeral monuments were preserved.[60] Those relating to the Dodson family are in the Sanctuary; the seventeenth century memorials to the Courthopes were placed in the Chancel floor and (later) in the St Lawrence Chapel; those of Campions of the eighteenth and early nineteenth centuries in the Campion Chapel, permitted by a faculty later in 1845 on the north side; with a few recording the lives and deaths of members of other gentry families in the walls of the nave. The Borrers' memorials now adorn the south chapel. Other earlier incumbents such as Christopher Swale and the Dodson have their plaques in the chancel.[61] As was normal, no memorials to lesser families were allowed inside the building, the lives of the farmers and other substantial inhabitants being recorded in stone in the churchyard. Depending on the quality of the stone, the depth of the carving, and the weather, these are often less than completely decipherable. Among those that have been lost is one referred to as 'Brand's Dial', a stone pillar erected by the eponymous mason; his epitaph was alleged to have read:

> Here lies the body of William Brand,
> Who worked through life in lime and sand,
> And 'cause he would not be forgotten,
> He built this tomb for his bones to rot in.

Thomas Marchant found that this particular edifice came within his responsibilities as churchwarden:

> 1722. Octr. 14th   (Sunday). Had a meeting about old Brand's dial.
> Octr. 29th.   *My Lord Treep* [local tinsmith] here with Mr. Pointin's draught of a dial for old Brand's tomb, and carried it way again.[62]

William Hamper, who left £100 to the poor of the parish in his 1829 will, is recorded on 10 June 1815 as 'twice painting over Brand's Monument & drawing the 3 dials', and is reputed to have added:

> But where he's gone no one can tell,
> Some say to Heaven, but some to Hell,
> For that's the place where Atheists dwell.[63]

For the most part, the churchyard contains records of ordinary folk who lived and died in Hurstpierpoint, but there were some who ventured further afield: two standard War Graves Commission headstones, and one to a man who returned to Hurst after serving as a Colonel in the American War of Independence; the grave of an Indian Mutiny holder of the Victoria Cross is also there, but unmarked by any headstone. One exception to the convention of allowing only gentry memorials within the building is the headstone to George Greenaway, who died in 1770 at the age of 21, now against the wall of the north aisle – but this is because it shows a representation of St Lawrence Church; it was for this reason that it was brought inside to preserve it, not for any claim to fame on the part of George!

So Carey Hampton Borrer had achieved all this in less than five years. Together with his introduction of what were considered to be High Church practices, he was bound to meet much opposition, but he overcame this with a mixture of zeal, determination, private means, and unfailing diplomacy and good temper. William Wood, a local farmer, wrote:

> I never saw him lose his temper, or his pleasant cheerful manner. .
> [presiding] at meetings where he alone preserved a calm demeanour,
> his opponents meanwhile in a state bordering on fury . . .[64]

This remarkable man was Rector of Hurstpierpoint for 57 years, and was not merely instrumental in providing the present parish church and later extensions, as well as the installation of furniture and fittings and the introduction of new aspects of worship: the clock and five new bells in 1846; a new hymnal in 1852; St Lawrence Chapel and a new organ in 1854; the 'Durer' glass medallions in 1861; the South Chapel in 1874; 'new warming apparatus' in 1875; the copies of the Chichester Cathedral iron grills; the chancel floor dedicated on the fortieth anniversary of the consecration, and so on.[65] Not content with looking after the spiritual needs of the centre of the parish, he was responsible for the building of Christ Church, Sayers Common in 1880. He was also active in other spheres of village life.

He was actively involved in no less than three schools in the parish: what is now St Lawrence School, not only in its transfer from its original premises, but also taking part on an almost daily basis, with his family and his curates, in the religious aspects of its teaching and its administration, entertaining the children on special occasions, and presenting books to its library; the building of a school at Sayers Common in 1842-3; and the invitation to Nathaniel Woodard to establish St John's College on land owned by his father. He was much involved in the building of the Parish Rooms in 1891; assiduously administering a clothing club for the poorer people, visiting the sick frequently and comforting the dying. Beyond the parish he became Rural Dean, a Prebendary of Chichester Cathedral and its Treasurer, a Proctor in Convocation (an elected member of the precursor of the present-day Synod), on the Committee of [Bishop] Otter College, etc., etc.

We have the testimony of William Wood regarding his equanimity, but he was a man of great determination and it was perhaps inevitable that differences of opinion would occur. Mention has been made of one property owner who objected to the cost of Holy Trinity; this was Charles Sharood, who lived at St George's. By 1852 this house was owned by Colonel Charles Hannington, who had a difference of opinion sufficiently deep (at least to Hannington) that he left the Church of England. He had the means to build a chapel in the corner of his grounds (incidentally not facing east in the traditional way) and this became a nonconformist place of worship known as Little Park Chapel (he had recently bought Little Park from the Marchants). In 1867 Hannington rejoined the Church, the chapel was licensed, and eight years later his son James was appointed Curate-in-Charge, attracting increased congregations. He became a missionary and the first Bishop of East Equatorial Africa, eventually being martyred in Uganda. The local directory of 1887 recorded the news in typical contemporary style:

> The principal event to disturb the serenity of the everyday life of the town during 1886 was the alarming rumours, and later on, sad news of Bishop Hannington, who was so beloved there. With the first day of the year arrived tidings from Zanzibar, announcing the seizure of the Bishop and his men by order of the King of Uganda (near whose dominions he was prosecuting missionary labours) and that the monarch had ordered the prelate's execution. Other news tended to confirm the original tidings, and they were on the whole believed to be correct. In March arrived the authentic information that on October 31st, 1885 the Bishop was, with his cook, shot, and others of his followers were speared. Thus the Bishop exchanged an earthly mitre for a heavenly crown.[66]

James's brother Samuel presented the chapel to the Church of England in 1892 and it was consecrated by the Bishop as a Chapel-of-Ease.[67]

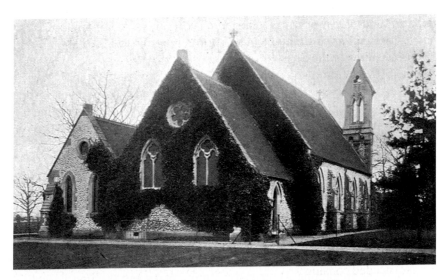

Plate 7. St George's Church, showing the original bell turret.

Borrer had a succession of conscientious and hard-working curates, at least one other becoming a bishop. Henry Montgomery was in Hurst in 1871 before going to St Mark's, Kennington, having married Maud, the daughter of Dean Farrar of Canterbury (the author of *Eric, or Little by Little*). He returned to Hurst to officiate at the funeral of Canon Borrer's wife in 1887. Two years later he was promoted to be Bishop of Tasmania. His other claim to the notice of twentieth century readers is that his fourth child, born in 1887, was the famous World War II soldier, Field-Marshal Viscount Montgomery of Alamein.[68]

Carey Hampton Borrer stoutly defended church property, and what he considered to be church propriety. In 1853 a Burial Act empowered local authorities to run cemeteries, and vestries appointed Burial Boards for this purpose. By 1875 the need for further ground for this purpose resulted in the conveyance of a portion of Church Field to the south of Holy Trinity to the

Board for £650; the retaining wall was built at a cost to the Board of a further sum of £205.15s. The government regulations required that not less than a quarter of the grave plots should be unconsecrated. Borrer's response was to demand free access for himself and his family through the ground to the field beyond, and that nonconformist burials should only take place from the south, that is not through the 'old' churchyard. Twenty years later, yet more ground was needed, but Borrer's asking price was too high for the newly-formed Parish Council, who then went instead to Mr Campion, who sold three acres of the Snashalls site for £800 to become the South Avenue cemetery.[69]

The Marchant referred to above was one of Borrer's churchwardens, but not in favour with the Rector, who wrote in his diary for 27 January 1852:

> Hannington said to have bought Little Park Estate of the Marchants, a respectable old family reduced to nothing by irreligion, and on 25 March: The infamous N Marchant resigned his office of Churchwarden.[70]

Borrer married Elizabeth (Lizzie) Orr in 1837, and she bore him fourteen children, of whom twelve survived to adulthood – the rectory (Chantry House) needed considerable enlargement! His family life was clearly a very happy one, in spite of the frequent references to ill-health. It was also one of constant concern for the children's progress, both at school and beyond. But he also enjoyed his local outings with his wife and children, his holidays, his shooting, his natural history and archaeological interests.[71]

It might appear that a disproportionate amount of this chapter has been about one man, but the clear evidence is that his influence on the Church and the parish was indeed historic. On his death, the local press voiced the feelings of all:

> . . . a singularly attractive personality has been removed from the religious and social life of Sussex . . . an ideal parish priest . . . the placid life of his parish [having] the first place in his affections . . . and the attachment was mutual.'[72]

Apart from the large brass plate, recessed in a sedilia, in the Borrer Chapel, and the tombstone surmounted by a cross in the churchyard, the pulpit which is still in use was built in his memory.

THE LAYMAN IN THE CHURCH

The story told so far has been about the buildings, the patrons and the incumbents. But, even in the relative 'doldrums' of the eighteenth century, the church has engaged the attention of the laity throughout. Attendance at services (by both rectors and people) may have been variable, but the duties imposed on the parish by higher authority, both secular and ecclesiastic, have been attended to with a considerable degree of dedication.

We have seen that Thomas Marchant was one such – less than regular in his appearances on Sundays, but always carrying out his churchwarden's tasks punctiliously. There was a succession of men like him – wardens, overseers, and surveyors – who took their responsibilities seriously. Some will appear in later chapters, involved in poor relief, education initiatives, maintaining law and order. They are too numerous to name here. One of them, William Wood, gave a layman's view of the church:

> The Church of England was in a very slack condition some one hundred years ago [1830s], it sadly needed revival . . . [Canon Borrer] ministered in the parish near sixty years . . . a shining example of courtesy . . .[73]

There were sometimes those who did not maintain the expected dedication. An assistant overseer, Henry Muzzall, ran off in 1841 with rates he had collected. When his successor, Richard Davey, was appointed, a security of £500 and two sureties were demanded.[74] In the event, this was unexpectedly possible, for Richard Davey had returned from the Peninsular War with enough money to buy land opposite the church on which he built two houses. (His name is perpetuated there by 'Frank Davey, Funeral Director'). Apart from being collector of rates, he became Parish Clerk or Sexton, with duties which ranged from grave-digging to Crier.[75] In contrast to his predecessor, he remained a faithful servant of the church for many years.

NOTES AND REFERENCES

1. Morris J (ed)(1976): *Domesday Book,* 12, 36.
2. Catalogue of Antiquities, *SAC* **8** (1856), 297; Welch M G (1984): *SAS Newsletter* **43**.
3. Blencow R W (1862): Roman Remains at Hurstpierpoint and Danny, *SAC* **14**, 176–81.
4. Bettey J H (1987): *Church and Parish*, 11.
5. Friar S (1996): *Companion to the English Parish Church*, 447.
6. *Ibid.*, 28.
7. Historical notes by Canon C W G Wilson (assistant curate 1893-7) in undated guide by J L Denman.
8. *SAC* **7**, 178.
9. Bettey, *Church & Parish*, 30.
10. *VCH* **7**, 178.
11. *Ibid.*; *SAC* **11**, 76–8; Norris J (1973): *Notes on Holy Trinity Church*, 10; Norris J: personal communication.
12. Salzman L F (ed) (1934): Chartulary of the Priory of St Pancras, Lewes, Part II, *SRS* **40**. 31–3; Deed C (ed)(1910): Bishop Robert Rede's Register, Part II, *SRS* **11**, 373-82.
13. *Ibid.*, 217, 238–9, 268.
14. Pantin A W (1962): *The English Church in the Fourteenth Century*, 195–202, quoted in Bettey, *Church & Parish*, 37.
15. Friar, *Companion*, 447.
16. Bettey, *Church & Parish*, 85-8.
17. Godfrey W H (1938): Transcript of Wills up to 1560, Vol III, *SAC* **43**; ESRO/A28/32.
18. Paxman J (1998): *The English*, 111-2.
19. Bettey, *Church & Parish*, 62.
20. Hutton R (1994): *The Rise and Fall of Merry England*, passim.
21. WSRO/SAS/OR/325.
22. WSRO/ Par 400/7/1.
23. Friar, *Companion*, 447.
24. WSRO/ Par 400/9/1/1–9.
25. PRO/SP/16/442/137.
26. Sawyer F E (1880): Proceedings of the Committee of Plundered Ministers Relating to Sussex, *SAC* **30**, 121–3.
27. Fletcher A (1975): *A County Community in Peace and War: Sussex 1600– 1660*, 55-6.
28. Bettey, *Church & Parish*, 91.
29. Cooper J H (1902): Religious Census of Sussex in 1676, *SAC* **45**, 143–5.

30. Johnstone H (1949): Churchwardens' Presentations (17th Century), Part 2, Archdeaconry of Lewes, *SRS* **50**, 16, 56.
31. Coward B (1980): *The Stuart Age*, 267, 318–20.
32. WSRO/SAS/OR/326.
33. WSRO/ Par 400/4/1; Turner, Marchant, *SAC* **25**, 181.
34. Bettey, *Church & Parish*, 119; WSRO/ Par 400/6/2/f2r.
35. WSRO/ Par 400/4/2–10.
36. WSRO/ Par 400/4/2/11–14.
37. Turner, Marchant, *SAC* **25**, 168-95.
38. Goodenough S (1983): *The Country Parson*, 101.
39. Bettey, *Church & Parish*, 115; WSRO ADD MSS 27333–4.
40. Ford W K (1994): Chichester Diocesan Surveys 1686 and 1724, *SRS* **78**, 133–4.
41. *Ibid., 172.*
42. Atkinson R (ed)(1985): *A Country Parson: James Woodforde's Diary 1759–1802.*
43. Goodenough, *Parson*, 68.
44. Turner, Marchant, *SAC* **45**, 170.
45. Ford J M T (1987): *The Weekes Family Letters*, 136, 152, 175, 201.
46. Bettey, *Church & Parish*, 112.
47. *Ibid.*, 109.
48. WSRO/ Par 400/6/2; 'A Native, A Minor' (1837): *A History of Hurstperpoint*, 40–1.
49. Gibson W (1994): *Church, State and Society, 1760–1850*, 28.
50. Lucas E V (1903): *Highways & Byways in Sussex*, 19.
51. Gibson, *Church*, 21–3, 29–30.
52. Goodenough, *Parson*, 36.
53. *VCH* **7**, 178.
54. Bettey, *Church & Parish*, 142.
55. WSRO/ Par 400/4/15, 44.
56. WSRO/ Par 400/4/15.
57. WSRO/ Par 400/4/38, 42(a), 46; Bettey, *Church & Parish*, 129.
58. Nairn I & Pevsner N (1965): *The Buildings of England, Sussex*, 541.
59. Vickers J A (1987): Religious Census of Sussex 1851, *SRS* **75**.
60. *VCH* **7**, 177.
61. For a complete list see the inventory compiled by R A Packham in 1989.
62. Turner, Marchant, *SAC* **25**, 191, 192.
63. A Native, A Minor, *Hurstperpoint*, 54 (there is no evidence that the words were actually on the monument itself); WSRO/ Par 400/9/3/1.
64. Wood W (1938): *A Sussex Farmer*, 184–5.
65. Norris, *Holy Trinity*, passim; *Sussex Agricultural Express* 4 November 1854; WSRO/ ADD MS 17737.

66. Charles Clarke's *Mid Sussex Directory 1887*.
67. *Notes on St George's Church* nd.
68. *Dictionary of National Biography*.
69. WSRO/ Par 400/55/1, 49/1.
70. WSRO/ ADD MS 17736.
71. WSRO/ ADD MSS 17734–42.
72. *Sussex Daily News* 5 August 1898.
73. Wood, *Farmer*, 181.
74. *Ibid.*, 192–3.
75. Woodward W A (ed)(1928): A Sussex Soldier of Wellington's, *Sussex County Magazine* February 1928, 48.

3. GENTRY AND YEOMAN FARMERS

THE SEVENTEENTH CENTURY AND THE CIVIL WAR

We have seen how the way of life was altering by the Tudor period and by the turn of the century, into the 1600s, it continued to do so to a much greater degree, for better or worse, depending on one's status and wealth. The feudal system was formally abolished in 1660[1] but had mostly perished long before that. The land use itself was changing. Where there had been open fields, which everyone farmed with his neighbour for subsistence, enclosure had brought farming for profit where food was surplus to immediate requirements. It was traded at the local markets such as Lewes, and, despite the dreadful roads, as far away as London which was growing rapidly, requiring more food for its increased population.

Queen Elizabeth I died in 1603 to be succeeded by James I, the first of the ill-fated Stuarts, and the major part of the century was certainly not a joyful one. The weather was apparently exceptionally poor with severe winters when the River Thames froze over several times.[2] Bubonic plague and smallpox were endemic.[3] The great plague of London of 1665, preceding the great Fire of London in 1666, is well documented; one eighth of its population died of smallpox in 1674. There was also great mortality in sheep and cattle.[4]

The religious intolerance in the Tudor period left a legacy of bitterness, fuelling the Civil War from 1642 until 1651, when a fugitive Prince Charles escaped to France from Shoreham. Hurst itself was not the scene of strife, the nearest being an excursion from Bramber Bridge of Royalist forces to Haywards Heath in 1642 where they were soundly beaten.[5]

Those in power were however affected. The Rector, Christopher Swale, a Justice of the Peace, was strongly Royalist and ended up by being ejected from his living in 1644/5,[6] and George Goring, created 1st Earl of Norwich by Charles 1st in 1641, had to sell Danny in 1652, the house built by his grandfather in 1582, to the Courthopes. He died in 1663. Discovered in the Danny Archives [7] are what appear to be rough notes to calculate the value of George Goring's Estate which show the not inconsiderable total area of 820 acres. Danny itself, including the Great Park of 135 acres, with arable, meadow and pasture amounted to about 420 acres. A large amount of the woodland existing in 1571 had been felled. The rest of the Estate included Little Park of 136 acres,117 acres of Willcombe (south of Danny on the edge of Wolstonbury), and 128 acres of the Lyemead, Breache, Rushy Ham, and the Great and Little Hams (now Washbrooks Farm Centre). The 420 acres about Danny were being costed at 10/- an acre.

Plate 8. Peter Courthope (1577–1657).

Plate 9. George, Lord Goring (1608-1657).

Plate 10.
Henry Campion and Barbara, his wife, daughter of Peter Courthope (1639–1725).

Most of East Sussex including Lewes was strongly for Parliament and also the area around Horsham. The centres of Royalist families[8] were mainly around Steyning and northeastwards to Hurst, Albourne (Juxons), Slaugham

(Coverts), and Wakehurst (Culpeppers). Dr William Juxon was Bishop of London at the time and he had the melancholy duty of accompanying Charles I to his execution in 1649. His brother John lived at Albourne and there is a tradition that William was later hiding there and disguised himself as a labourer when a party of Parliamentary troopers came searching for him – luckily unsuccessfully. At the Restoration he became Archbishop of Canterbury.

We do not know what effect the two strong Royalists in Hurst had on the local people. Perhaps some, from an initial spirit of adventure, followed their lead. Further research into that period may tell us. There are glimpses of the landowners in the early part of the century with Tax Returns 'Temp Elizabeth' around 1600,[9] and again in 1615 [10] and the Poor Rate of 1629.[11] The Nortons, Luxfords, and Chatfields were prominent but we have little information on Hurst during the Civil War period.

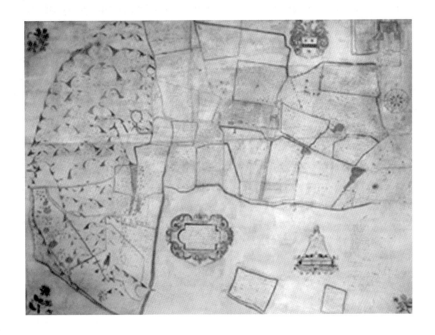

vi. Danny Map 1666 (ESRO/DAN 2097).

In 1658 and 1666 the first fine maps of the copyhold lands of Hurst Manor and of Danny were produced by Robert Whitpaine.[12] These, linked to the Rental of 1663[13] and Hearth Tax of 1662,[14] give a much more detailed picture. The 1666 map of Danny shows the house with its dovecot and park, now divided into fields, and the 1658 map shows a large part of the Parish and also land to the north, actually in Cuckfield (Pickwell, Horsemanshoad etc). The map is not totally comprehensive, of course, as freehold farms such as Wortleford were not shown nor lands belonging to other Manors such as Pakyns. Its pattern of roads and field boundaries can, however, be related to those of the first Ordnance Survey maps of the 19th century and what are left of the old hedgerows can be found today. There is a theory that it is possible to actually date many existing hedgerows in the country to this period or even earlier by counting the number of shrub species in a length of 30 yards of hedgerow but there have recently been strong arguments against it.[15]

The enclosure of the fields meant that it was possible to improve the quality of livestock. By separating animals from their scabby neighbours and preventing haphazard interbreeding, distinct strains, particularly of sheep and cattle, evolved in different localities.

The land itself was improved by the enfolding of livestock, to better manure the fields. There were, of course, no artificial fertilisers yet and experiments with all sorts of materials were tried including rotten offal and fish as well as marling and denshiring.[16] It could truly be said 'Many and strange must have been the country scents in those days'.[17]

Cultivation itself had altered little, ploughing and harrowing were mainly by oxen, six or eight at a time which could plough an acre a day using a heavy two wheeled plough called the Kentish turn-wrest.[18] Corn was still sown broadcast, not in drills as today. Apart from wheat and oats, barley was grown for brewing and hops had been introduced in the late 16th century. Most farmers, as well as innkeepers, brewed their own beer as everyone drank it, even children, water quality being poor. At the end of the century vegetables such as cauliflowers, peas, beans, root vegetables, including potatoes were grown in gardens rather than the fields.[19]

Plate 11. Oxen plough-team (at Saddlescombe: their last day's work).

Surprisingly the actual amount of tillage in the parish was small bearing in mind the population had probably regained its pre-Black Death figure of around 600. The acreage of each of six farms in Hurst[20] was more or less the same in 1840 as in 1582 but the arable proportion was only about a quarter of the whole rising to over half more than 250 years later in 1840.

vii. Kentish turn-wrest plough.

viii. Broadcasting seed by hand.

Cattle rearing seems to have been important. (The officials who attended the meetings of the Hundred Court included a 'Stamper of Leather' and an 'Inspector of Leather'.[21] An inventory in May 1660 on the death of John

Lindfield [22] showed that he sowed only 11 acres of wheat and 20 acres of oats and pulses out of 120 – 135 acres. The crop value was only 30% of the total crop and livestock valuation and cattle represented 74% of the total value. Thomas Marchant records that most of the oats and pulses would also have been animal feed.[23]

Sheep rearing on the Downs was important and was often in the charge of a communal shepherd,[24] the name Tenantry Down occurring locally in several places. As well as animal hides, wool was an important product; an Act of Parliament of 1666 requiring burial in wool was not repealed until 1814.[25]

There was also a trade in timber from the Weald, principally for shipbuilding. The iron industry there was flourishing, with activity as near as the southern part of Cuckfield around the Pond of Leigh. There was concern at national level over the destruction of woodland.[26] In a Court case to which Peter Courthope was party in 1674,[27] when he was accused of obstructing a highway, evidence was given that in the 1620s 'waggons laden with wood and faggots out of the wild of Sussex crossed Danny Park bound for Pyecombe and Brighton'. This was undoubtedly a summer trade as the Weald was impassable to heavy wheeled traffic for most of the year.[28]

It was not until late into the next century that the coming of turnpike roads enabled easier travel by coach and wagon. Indeed nearly all travel at that time was on horseback or by the use of packhorses – otherwise one walked!

Most farms had their farm hands and maids living in. Their hours were long,[29] starting sometimes before sunrise when the ploughman had to see to his oxen, or sometimes horses, until late at night when he bedded them down. Indeed it was not practical with such early rising and long hours to live any distance from work.

Despite the difficulty of travel and transport the influence of London with the courts of Charles II, William and Mary, and Queen Anne affected the more important local gentry. The old timber framed houses became unfashionable and the rebuilding in brick of mansions with 'Dutch Gables' such as Little Park in 1677 [30] and Randolphs (both of which have medieval timber cores)[31] spread into the countryside and their interiors with stylish furniture, silver and glassware reflected the new taste.

THE GEORGIANS – FROM GEORGE I TO VICTORIA

We have seen previously how Sussex had slowly changed over the centuries from an insular, deeply rural community, to one looking outwards towards developments in other parts of the country, particularly the influence of London. Communications within the country and abroad had become easier, although the roads were still appalling, and life was still hard and at times dangerous. Well into the next century men still went armed when travelling and punishment for crimes was severe – public whippings of both men and women were common and so were public hangings. Knowledge was however more freely available both from newspapers and books, particularly relating to farming, informing of new methods, new varieties of seed and new food which had started to be imported, and could often be grown in this country.

One of our best pictures of life in the 18th century comes from the diary of Thomas Marchant (1676–1728)[32] of Little Park. Apart from being a landowner he dealt in fish, the two acres of ponds which almost certainly date from medieval times still exist and were recorded in 1571 as being stocked with 200 carp and tench. He was related to or friendly with Jeremiah Dodson the Rector, and many of the local gentry, including Campion of Danny and Beard of the Mansion House, with whom he often dined. Other cameos of life at this time were the papers and account books of the Stapley and Wood families of Hickstead[33] and letters of the Weekes family,[34] medical practitioners of Hurst. There had been Marchants in Hurst in the early 17th century and in 1629 Thomas Marchant (presumably the grandfather of the diarist) was at West Edgerley,[35] one of the two farms just north of Little Park which was acquired by the family in c1670.[36] By the early 18th century they also owned Wanbarrow and lands around, and by the end of the century they had acquired East Edgerley (Big Edgerley as it is now known), Breems in Hurst Wickham and the Black Lion in the High Street, now Boles delicatessen. Their holdings by 1801[37] and still in 1842[38] were over 250 acres, one of the largest landowning families in the Parish. There is an original map of the estate of his relative Ralph Beard dating from 1736[39] which comprised Washbrooks and the Townfields south of the Mansion House where he lived. In one corner is the drawing of a little man and his dog out shooting almost the same as one on the 1666 map of Danny.

At one time there were perhaps 60 identifiable farms in the parish. By 1801[40] there were about 50 landowners of whom five had over 2,000 acres between them, including, of course, Campion who had over 723 acres and William Borrer (see Colour Plate 3) with 471, and four others with over 100 acres each, totalling 532 acres. Thus nine people owned 2,612 acres between them, over half the parish. By the time of Tithe Survey of 1842[41] Campion's holding had increased to 948 acres; 6 people had each over 200 acres totalling 2,686 acres, and 10 had between 100 and 200 acres totalling 1,304 acres – nearly 4,000 acres altogether out of a total area of 4,840 acres!

Many were farmed directly but the majority were tenanted. Most farms were in fact quite small, of 50 acres or less. Members of the Avery family were some of the earlier landowners – as usual difficult to individually identify as most of them were called Thomas or Nathaniel! They first appeared in 1610 when Thomas bought Leigh Manor in Hurstpierpoint which remained in the family until c.1725 when Nathaniel (see Colour Plate 4) sold it to Daniel Beard.[42] By 1629 Thomas was in the top band of payers of the Poor Rate[43] and in the 1662 Hearth Tax he had obviously a fairly large house with 4 hearths[44] (two others, Richard and Nathaniel had only two each). In 1663 Thomas owned Little Danworth;[45] by 1703 Nathaniel owned Great Danworth[46] and by 1780 their holdings had increased still further. Nathaniel, who was a miller, owned Ruckford Mill which for many years was known as Avery's Mill, Latchetts – just south of Ruckford in Hurst Wickham, Cophall (the site is now Hurstpierpoint College), and he was a tenant of Tott farm. To the west he had Knowls, Knowls Tooth, and abutting them to the east, Court Bushes and Minepits.[47] To round it off brother Thomas had Bridgers to the north. Not content with these, Nathaniel also had Stroods, Shinnings, and Little Stuckells near Sayers Common, all part of the Manor of Tottington.[48] We are however all mortal and in 1788 both Nathaniel and Thomas died. Nathaniel had no male heir and in his will[49] left part of his lands in the western area to his daughter Elizabeth. He also left Latchetts, Ruckford Mill, Cophall, and also a freehold – Brickhouse, otherwise Beals (now Beildside) in the High Street to his daughter Lydia who was married to John Pelham Roberts. Alas Lydia died in 1801;[50] her youngest son Henry aged ten who inherited[51] died in 1817 leaving his brother William. J P Roberts,[52] their guardian, described in 1801 as a landowner of 244 acres, including Court Bushes, Knowles Tooth, Bridgers, Stroods, Latchetts, Cophall and Ruckford – a fortunate man indeed, one of the top five landowners. By 1842 [53] a descendant, Avery Roberts, had 240 acres – still one of the top 6 owners. Another major landowner of 1801 was William Lindfield, who owned 385 acres.[54] We have already mentioned his ancestor John in 1660. William had acquired Great Danworth from Nathaniel Avery by 1719,[55] and lands in the detached portion of the Manor in Cuckfield, including Pickwell. By 1780 another John Lindfield [56] had also acquired Little Danworth, Grubbs, Longs (Pickhams), Ebbutts (Horns), Dean House, Pellings, West Town land and Cobbs Mill, and by 1798 [57] the lands around the present Washbrooks from Marchant. The family apparently lived in Dean House which had been taken down by 1873 [58] and a new house built on the site. By 1842 the family had gone and their lands dispersed.

A new 'empire builder' had arisen in the person of Sir John Dodson who became the second largest owner with 550 acres. The Dodsons, father, son and grandson had been Rectors of Hurst from 1701 to 1807 and had confined their holdings in the parish to the modest six acres of glebe plus Cobbs and Thorne Crofts. Not so their great-grandson Sir John Dodson, who became an M.P. His son was elevated to the peerage in 1884 as Baron Monk Bretton of Hurstpierpoint and Conyborough, where he actually lived,[59] and where the family still lives. Apart from the glebe which in 1842 belonged to Cary Hampton Borrer the new Rector, he bought the Manor of Leigh in Hurst of 60 acres and Danworth Brook Farm in 1840 from Richard Weekes; Westend in Clayton and Floods in Hurst of 89 acres; South Holmwood (now Grasmere) of 60 acres; and Wortleford Farm. By 1841 he had acquired Dumbrells of 122 acres, and by 1851 he had Gatehouse Farm of 33 acres; part of High Hatch of 60 acres, Dean House of 117 acres; and finally Rickmans and Kents Farms of 100 acres. All in all, together with lands in Clayton, this comprised the grand 'Hurstpierpoint Estate of Lord Monk Bretton' which he finally sold in 1918.[60]

What influence then did this transfer of land have on the community? In general it was certainly to the advantage of the small farmer who, by selling and staying as a tenant, could have the financial backing of a wealthy owner. Directly perhaps it had very little effect on most of the workers. The weather had the greatest effect for the century did not start very well. 1703 was a very wet year and on 26th/27th November there occurred the 'Great Storm' which swept across England and was responsible for the loss of a fleet of ten warships and 1,300 men and the destruction of the new Eddystone Lighthouse. Much damage was done to buildings in its path, to roofs, chimneys and particularly to thatched buildings as many of the barns were so roofed, and several thousand people were drowned in flooding of the Thames and Severn.[61] It was apparently the equivalent of the 1987 hurricane which thankfully did not result in a heavy loss of life. In the first years of the 18th century life on the farms would have been much as earlier times. The slow, laborious plodding of the ploughman would still only achieve an acre a day with his oxen, and everyday life would be monotonous and hard. The Kentish turn-wrest plough was still in use – it was described as having 'as much timber as would build a Highland cart'[62] – but better more efficient iron and steel ones were being designed and acquired.

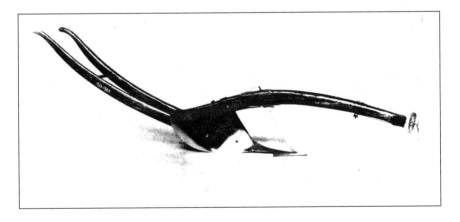

ix. Later model plough.

More mechanisation, however, was on the way and the earlier tentative experiments into the betterment of the agricultural scene progressed rapidly in the eighteenth and nineteenth centuries. It was the Agricultural Revolution. Some of the improvements were not so welcome including the threshing machine, and also the seed drill and horse hoe invented by Jethro Tull.[63] The former invention and its development sparked off riots characterised by the smashing of the hated machines which the farm workers feared would rob them of their traditional winter employment of threshing in the barns with a flail.

x. Drill plough with seed and manure hoppers.

The main impetus nationally was the spate of enclosure of the commons and open fields. This did not affect Hurst which was already enclosed but small areas of waste did persist into this period, often occupied by squatter's cottages on the verges of roads. There were still areas of common unenclosed in Clayton and Keymer, including St John's Common. Some outstanding landowners in the country were responsible for major improvements in agriculture .One was Viscount Townsend who from 1730 developed the four course rotation of the fields – he used turnips, hence his nickname Turnip Townsend.[64] The development of this rotation allowed feed for the livestock over the winter and it was no longer necessary to slaughter most of them and salt the meat down. Another pioneer in the latter part of the century was Thomas Coke of Holkham in Norfolk, whose estate was a model of the new ideas which, when followed, vastly improved the land, and, of course, the tenant's income.[65] Obtaining an increase in the fertility of the soil without the use of chemicals is a lesson being re-learned by many farmers today, and organic farming is on the increase. Seeds of wheat and other crops were carefully selected and improved.

Plate 12. Horse plough team.

Thanks to the work of Robert Bakewell of Dishley in Leicestershire,[66] from 1760 stock was greatly improved by the careful breeding of cattle and sheep, while a local man, John Ellman of Glynde [67] was prominent in the development of the Southdown breed of sheep. Cows and heifers were being shipped from the Channel Isles, and Shorthorn cattle were established by the end of the century. The heavy warhorse was no longer needed and the main breeds of the Clydesdale, Shire and Suffolk Punch were developed. The local landowners would certainly not have ignored these improvements in land and livestock, particularly with the better communications. The increased demand for food from London meant the input there of immense herds, flocks and droves of livestock some of which were driven from as far away as Wales and Scotland, as there was no other way of getting them there before the coming of the railway. Large flocks of sheep were on the Downs, many owned by local farmers, and they were driven to St John's fair in Burgess Hill and other fairs until very recent times. Findon Fair, near Worthing, is one of the last. In other parts of the country even flocks of geese were driven, some of them actually being shod by dipping their feet in tar.

National events probably had little impact locally. The rising of the Stuart pretender in 1715 would hardly cause a flutter and that of 1745 was probably of little more concern. The loss of the American Colonies and the wars on the continent were events to be read about in the newspapers by the more literate and passed on by word of mouth. The nineteenth century, like the previous one, began however with a period of trauma for the people. This time it was not the elements which caused the problem but their neighbours across the Channel. They had to take serious notice of events. Britain had been at war with France since 1793 following the French Revolution of 1789, and after a brief period of peace for two years, it had broken out again and in 1803 there was a very real threat of invasion by Napoleon. Earlier, plans had been made for what was, in fact, a scorched earth policy along the south coast. In Hurst these plans had been prepared by 1803 in some detail.[68] An 1801 Rental of the Parish [69] gave some guidance regarding the population. (The first National Census was in 1801 when there were 1,104 inhabitants in Hurst; in 1811 there were 1,184 in 225 families).[70] In 1803 much more detail was required. It was planned that the fitter younger men would defend the coast, Campion of Danny raised a troop of horsemen, about 40 of them, mostly young farmers and John Roberts was captain of a company of infantry of about 60 men.[71] All the sick and elderly, the women, children and the livestock would be evacuated northwards towards St Leonards Forest. Not only were wagons required to transport the families but animals to pull them (mainly oxen); drivers and supplies of food, not only for the people but the animals. Each person was allocated a wagon from either Randiddles (New Way Lane), the Church, Goddards Green or Sayers Common, and they were only allowed to bring one bundle of clothing each. The elderly, sick and very young children were allocated places but the older children and fit women would have to walk. Detailed schedules of the wagons were prepared [72] and they give a unique picture, not only of the well-off inhabitants, but the children and the very poor. What a cavalcade it would have been, travelling slowly northwards, and what an undertaking! Thankfully it never needed to be put into operation as the invasion was postponed several times (shades of 1940!), and Nelson's defeat of the French fleet at Trafalgar in 1805 removed the danger. A major effect of the Napoleonic War was the need to grow more food, imports were severely restricted and some land was used which had never been ploughed up since the Black Death. (A similar pattern of increased ploughing was repeated in 1914 and 1939.) An unwelcome affect on the farm labourer was that the price of food inevitably rose.[73] Some landowners made huge profits – not so the farm labourer! We have seen that the price of wheat was a measure of the economy. Bread was the staple food and 'Hodge' saw its price increase from 49/3d a quarter in 1793 to over 100/- and reaching a peak of 119/6d in 1801.[74] Most certainly the workers did not benefit from these prices, their standard of living got worse. Their cottages were still poor hovels and they were hungry. There had been discontent amongst the poor since the beginning of the war, food was scarce and the new ways of dealing with the poor, discussed later, in fact, led to the pauperisation of many.[75] Arthur Young, indeed, commented in 1813 about the totally inadequate wages.[76] Against an average annual wage of £28 to £29, just over 11/- a week, the rent of a cottage was 1/-, leaving 10/- a week to feed and clothe a family. Food alone for a family of two adults with 4 children would absorb that, and the minimum of new clothing for a family cost just over £8 a year, 3/- a week. Parish relief was a necessity. Some labourers earned much less with most of their income restricted to harvest time, when women and every available child had to help. The gulf between the rural gentry and wealthier farmers and the farm labourer grew wider. The government did nothing and many were on the verge of starvation, not in third world countries in Africa but here in England, here in Hurst.

When prices started to topple after the war a parliament largely composed of rural landowners and hidebound aristocracy tried to keep the price of corn artificially high.[77] The phenomenal increase of population, particularly in London and other towns and a succession of bad harvests (that of 1816 was one of the most disastrous known)[78] meant that the country was unable to produce enough food and many agricultural labourers were unemployed. We have mentioned earlier the rural discontent. The Swing Riots which swept through the South in 1830 started in Kent but soon affected Surrey and Sussex with burning of ricks, machine wrecking and general disturbance.[79] The discontent of the farm worker was not totally ignored; the authorities, both national and local were alarmed. The basic problem was really the increase in population with less work being available for the lesser skilled workers. Although farming was still labour intensive for many years, mechanisation could not be halted. It was the beginning of the Industrial Revolution and the Age of Steam and, like the present day, made those who worked with their hands no longer required in the same numbers.

The population of Hurst had risen to 2,118 by 1841 [80] compared with 1,104 in 1801 and after the coming of the railway to Brighton through Hassocks Gate in 1841 it rose steeply again. In the local return for the 1821 Census, when the population was 1,321,[81] the enumerators stated that the 'remarkable difference' in the number from that of 1811 'was due to no particular causes further than that marriage had been earlier'. The number of houses had also risen from 245 in 1831 to 359 in 1841; in 1811 there had been only 168.[82] The protests of the labourers were only part of a national desire for a change and reform of the system of Government. The price of corn did drop, prosperity slowly grew and there were sweeping changes, despite the rooted objection of the old guard and their harshness in dealing with what they regarded as trouble by the lower orders. The reform of criminal law under Robert Peel came in 1823, with the beginnings of the police force. In 1832 came the great Reform Act when the rotten boroughs (the nearest of which was Bramber) which had few if any inhabitants but returned members to Parliament, were disenfranchised. Many more lost one member thus allowing unrepresented towns to have members. The power to vote was given to freeholders, copyholders, and holders of long leases, so that farmers and yeomen ruled the poll instead of the landed gentry (the poor still did not get the vote for over 50 years). The period of the Georges really carried over into that of William IV, to the accession of Queen Victoria in 1837. It was the beginning of a new era: the coming of the railways, penny postage in 1840, the Tithe Commutation Act of 1836 getting rid a hated imposition, or at least converting it to a money payment, and the first Census of the Population in 1841 which survives in any detail.[83]

The story of Hurstpierpoint takes a new turn with the comprehensive information now available on maps from the Ordnance Survey, Fisher's map of 1841 of the village itself, the Tithe Map of the Parish (with its inset map of 'Hurst Town') showing for the first time the land and houses in detail, and by written and printed documentation now much easier to read. We shall see in the next parts how this information enables a better picture of life in Hurst to be obtained. With the coming of the railway the trading aspect developed but it was still a farming orientated community for many years to come.

NOTES AND REFERENCES

1. Feudal tenure was legally abolished in 1660, long after it had ceased to operate in practice: Hey D (ed)(1996): *Oxford Companion to Local and Family History*, 179.
2. Stratton J M (1969): *Agricultural Records AD220–1968*.
3. *Ibid.*
4. *Ibid.*
5. Fletcher A (1975): *A County Community in Peace and War: Sussex 1600–1660*, 262.
6. Sawyer F E (1880): Proceedings of the Committee of Plundered Ministers relating to Sussex, *SAC* **30**, 121–4.
7. ESRO/DAN326-9.
8. Howard M: Civil War, in Leslie K & Short B (eds)(1999): *An Historical Atlas of Sussex*, 59.
9. A Native, A Minor (1837): *A History of Hurstperpoint*, 23.
10. WSRO/SAS/OR/324.
11. WSRO/SAS/OR/325.
12. ESRO/DAN2096.
13. ESRO/DAN1118.
14. Sussex Genealogical Centre 3.
15. Hooper M D (1976): *Hedges and Local History;* Muir R (2000): *Reading the Landscape*, 84–6.
16. Seebohm M E (1976): *The Evolution of the English Farm*. Denshiring was the practice of skimming off the turf, burning it and turning in the ashes as a manure.
17. *Ibid.*
18. *Ibid.*
19. *Ibid.*
20. Brandon P (1963): Common lands and wastes of Sussex, unpublished Ph.D. thesis, University of London.
21. Godfrey W H (ed)(1928): The Book of John Rowe 1597–1622, *SRS* **34**; Renshaw W C(ed)(1916): The Hundred of Buttinghill, *SAC* **58**, 13, 15.
22. ESRO/AMS2212.
23. Turner E (ed)(1873): The Marchant Diary, *SAC* **25**.
24. Brandon, Commons & wastes.
25. Tate W E (1983): *The Parish Chest*, 67–9.
26. Armstrong J R (1974): *A History of Sussex*, 102.
27. ESRO/DAN2071–81.
28. Brandon, Commons & wastes.
29. Seebohm, *English Farm*.

30. WSBG site report 1997.
31. *Ibid.*

The next section made considerable use of: Hammond J L & B (1911): *The Village Labourer 1760–1832.*

32. Turner, Marchant, *SAC* **25**.
33. Turner E (ed)(1849): Extracts from the Diary of Richard Stapley, *SAC* **2**.
34. Weekes R: Glimpses of the Past, Extracts from a Hurst Resident's Diary, *Mid Sussex Times* (nd, pre–1912).
35. WSRO/SAC/OR325
36. Indicated by a rainwater head dated 1677, with the initials WMM for William and Mary Marchant.
37. ESRO/MOB633.
38. WSRO/TD/E39.
39. WSRO/ADD MS28783
40. ESRO/MOB633
41. WSRO/TD/E39.
42. *VCH* **7**, 177.
43. WSRO/SAC/OR325.
44. Sussex Genealogical Centre 3.
45. ESRO/DAN1118.
46. ESRO/DAN1119.
47. WSRO/MF 639, 1780 Land Tax; WSRO/Par400/30/1.
48. WSRO/ADD MS 27053. (Court Book of the Manor of Tottington alias Woowood 1606–1850)
49. WSRO/MF1321.
50. WSRO/ADD MS 27053.
51. *Ibid.*
52. ESRO/MOB 633.
53. WSRO/TD/E29.
54. ESRO/MOB633.
55. ESRO/DAN 1123.
56. WSRO/MF 639, 1780 Land Tax.
57. WSRO/MF 639, 1798 Land Tax.
56. Turner, Marchant, *SAC* **25**, 167.
59. ESRO/Monk Bretton 1173.
60. WSRO/SP 615.
61. Stratton, *Agricultural Records.*
62. Seebohm, *English Farm*; Whitlock R (1983): *The English Farm.*
63. *Ibid.*
64. *Ibid.*

65. *Ibid.*
66. *Ibid.*
67. *Ibid.*
68. WSRO/Par400/36/8–49.
69. ESRO/MOB 633.
70. WSRO/Par400/37/74,75, 76–86
71. WSRO/Par400/36/8–49.
72. *Ibid.*
73. Young A (1813): *A General View of the Agriculture of the County of Sussex.*
74. *Ibid.*; Stratton, *Agricultural Records.*
75. *Ibid.*
76. *Ibid.*
77. Woodward L (1964): *The Age of Reform*, 60–1.
78. Stratton, *Agricultural Records.*
79. Hobsbawm E J & Rudé (1969): *Captain Swing*, passim.
80. National census 1841.
81. WSRO/ Local census returns.
82. *Ibid.*
83. National census 1841.

4. CRAFTSMEN AND THEIR TRADES

Working life was deeply rooted in the Hurstpierpoint soil, as the village has always been predominantly a farming community. Labourers worked the crafts especially connected with the land: ploughing, sowing, reaping, hedging and ditching. The work was seasonal, and there was a demand for more specialised crafts such as hurdle making and thatching the hayricks.

In 1700 there was a basket maker living in Hurstpierpoint called Factor Corbell. He would have played quite an important part in the life of the village, as basket-ware was very necessary before the invention of plastics. Anything from straw to hazel and willow could be used. Basket making is an ancient craft, and for many centuries the hazel and willow trees were coppiced in the woodland around the village, some of which still survives although it is not managed now. Willow in particular grows quickly. It was coppiced in springtime when the sap was rising, sorted into different thicknesses, then bundled up and stored to dry out. It was soaked again before being woven into the many different types of basket, some of which have not changed for thousands of years. In Sussex there are trugs, still much loved by many gardeners today; made of willow and sweet chestnut and first made in Herstmonceux by Thomas Smith, who entered them in the Great Exhibition of 1851, where they were noticed by Queen Victoria and won an award. By 1881 the local basket maker was Alfred Willett, living at Shaves Cottage.

Bee skips (hives) were formerly made of straw bound tightly with split strands of hazel or willow, then an entrance was cut for the bees. Beehives were kept, as honey was an important source of sweetening, indeed the only one before the arrival of cane sugar from overseas. Bees were notified of births, marriages and deaths in the family, because people believed that unless this was done they would either die or fly away. 'Telling the bees' was undertaken by a member of the family knocking on the hives three times with the back-door key and chanting 'the master is dead', or whatever was appropriate. This custom was still carried on in Sussex within recent years.[1] Honey production still continues in the village, not only in several private gardens, but also at the Bee Farm off Wickham Hill.

Plate 13. A coppiced wood: young shoots in the foreground, more mature growth behind.

Harvest time involved whole families, with children taking time off from school to help with haymaking and fruit gathering, including acorns for animal feed. They were also employed as rook-scarers and stone-pickers, making important additions to the family income. The chapter on Education shows how often school attendance was affected by these activities.

Women worked in many ways: spinning, weaving and sewing clothes – most homes except the poorest would have a spinning wheel, sometimes two, as shown in the inventory of William Webb's goods in 1711: 'one woollen wheele, one linnen wheele'. 'The only music heard in the cottage, the farm-house, or even the manor-house, was that of the spinning wheel'.[2] Women worked as midwives, did the 'laying-out' as Betty Cheale did in 1721 for Francis Osbourne, 'laying and washing for burial';[3] and were also the washerwomen and wet-nurses, and many villagers worked in the larger houses scrubbing floors and doing other 'rough work'.

Ale was brewed at home, fruit preserved as jams or cordials, vegetables pickled or salted in large jars for eating in the winter months. Many families would keep a pig for fattening, the meat being salted or smoked in the chimney and anything to spare taken to the market on the Lamb Platt (at the top of Cuckfield Road) for sale or exchange for other goods.

Anthony Stapley of Hickstead Place wrote in 1741:

> . . . had of George Luxford of Hurst 12 nailes [a nail was 12
> pounds] of beef which I have since repaid him.[4]

Villagers also worked for the gentry, at Danny, Little Park or Pakyns,
learning trades such as carpentry, masonry, gardening or forestry, working
with the horses as stable-lads or coachmen, or in the house itself, starting as
kitchen girls and some working all their lives with the families.

APPRENTICESHIPS

Boys were apprenticed to a trade for six to eight years, to learn the craft
under a master who was responsible for them. The object was quite as much
social and educational as it was economic. 'Until a man grow into twenty-
three years, he for the most part, though not always, is wild, without
judgement, and not of sufficient experience to govern himself.' After the age
of twenty-four, having served his apprenticeship, he was at liberty to marry,
and either to set up a business of his own or to become a journeyman for
hire.[5] During that time he would live and work with his master and be given
'sufficient wholesome and competent meat, drink, lodging, washing,
apparell and all other necesaryes meet and convenient',[6] and when the
apprenticeship was ended he was given two sets of clothing, one being for
Sunday. Indentures had as a rule to be enrolled by the Town Clerk or similar
official, and an Act of 1710 made stamp duty payable.[7] Masters had the right
of correcting their apprentices with the rod, within reason. There were no
inspectors and no checks on ill usage, so the system was often abused,
sometimes forcing children to abscond. However, it was important not only
for learning a skilled trade, but also for the continuation of education for a
child whose school years finished before his 'teens', as a certain amount of
general teaching was usually stipulated in the indentures.[8] As a journeyman,
the tradesman was hired by the year and lived in his employer's house, either
after his apprenticeship or after picking up his skills in other ways.

In the eighteenth century Hurstpierpoint boys were apprenticed to a
cordwainer and a tailor, as well as in husbandry. On 12 November 1701
'William Illman, a poore boy of the parish' was apprenticed to Mr Richard
Luttman 'until Michaelmas next ensuing', to the trade of tailor. The officers

and inhabitants paid Luttman 'Thirty and five shillings' which were to be returned if 'the said Richard Luttman shall turn the said William out of his service or refuse to keep him'.[9]

xi. Pauper Apprenticeship of William Illman to Richard Luttman, tailor, 1701
(WSRO/Par 400/33/2)

This was a common means of reducing the costs to the parish of maintaining a pauper child. However apprenticeships were not confined to the lower classes. Many gentlemen's sons who did best in later life were those who had been apprenticed to craftsmen and merchants.[10] In the next hundred years the range of trades became much wider, including a shoemaker, a weaver, a hairdresser, a blacksmith and a plumber and glazier. Millers' apprentices and journeymen feature prominently in the nineteenth century census returns: in 1871 George Cooley and in 1881 John Whiting were at Ruckford Cottage working for Robert Broad at the mill; in the same year journeymen Stephen Harris and Philip Henty were living at Goldbridge and working at Cobb's Mill.[11]

THE MILLS

We in Hurstpierpoint are used to seeing windmills on the Downs whenever we travel southwards out of the village. In the eighteenth and nineteenth centuries almost every town had its windmills, and few villages would be out of sight of at least one or two. This was due to the rapid increase in population which resulted in the exploitation of wind power to the fullest extent, as all available waterpower had long been fully utilised and steam power was not yet in sight.[12] Sadly most have been taken down and the ground used for building.

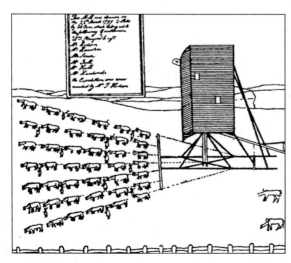

xii. Removal of 'Jill' windmill
to Clayton

Jill, a post mill, was built in Brighton in 1821, towed up Clayton Hill, probably in sections, and re-built on the site. Earlier another mill was moved bodily from one site to another:

> In 1797 a miller of Brighton, in the presence of many thousands of spectators, removed his windmill whole, and literally as he worked her, with the help of 36 yoke of oxen and a number of men, across the plains to a brow near Withdean, a distance of more than a mile, where he fixed her without the smallest accident.[13]

Jill worked alongside Jack, a tower mill built on site in 1876, until they stopped grinding by 1909.[14] We can still see Jill's sails working on Sunday afternoons during the summer months. Hurstpierpoint had a post-mill at the west end of the village, standing to the south of the Albourne Road on the Pakyns manor estate. In 1817 the miller was William Peskett. A map of 23 years later shows the site, the owner being listed as William Borrer and the occupier as Thomas Wickham.[15]

> In a high field just beyond this house [West Town House] is a windmill, a conspicuous object in the distance and the only one we have nearer than Clayton.[16]

The mill did not work for many years and had disappeared by the turn of the twentieth century. When the ground was being prepared for the new A23 no trace of it was found.

Domesday Book mentions 163 mills in Sussex; these were not windmills, but either watermills or those worked by cattle. There is no known record of windmills in England before the middle of the twelfth century. The Hurst entry in the 1086 survey says there were three mills valued at 9s. Two of the sites were still occupied by mills in the nineteenth century:

> . . . Cobb's Mill occupied by Mr Unwins, Ruckford's by Mr Mitchell and the other by Mr Peckham. These are all watermills and they stand at the extremities of the Parish on the north, west and east.[17]

Cobb's Mill stands at the north end of Langton Lane. It was shown as 'Jobes Myll' in 1587, when the miller Jerrard Vinall was buried. By 1663 in the Manor of Hurstpierpoint Rentals it was called Cobb's Mill, in the ownership of Leonard Letchford the Rector 'in the right of his wife Anne, widow and relict of Christopher Swale, deceased', and occupied by Richard Hatton at a yearly rent of six shillings. In 1780 Nathaniel Avery was the owner, living at Knowles Tooth in Langton Lane. The mill at that time was referred to as 'Knowles Tooth Water Mill'. Antony Ede was the miller in 1804. A newspaper advertisement later in the century shows that:

> Mr Drawbridge will sell by auction on 24th November 1865, by order of the Trustees of the late Mr Edward Pickett . . . Lot 4. A brick and timber built Water Corn Mill, known by the name of Cobbs Mill, driving 3 pairs of stones, standing upon a stream with a fine supply of water and close to the high road, with residence and farm buildings and large gardens. It is now in the occupation of Charles Packham. .[18]

For fifty years, from 1841 to 1891, Kelly's Directory shows the occupier as Charles Packham, employing seven 'hands' in 1871 and adding corn merchant to his activities.[19] The family, together with their hands and the journeyman millers, lived at Goldbridge in Langton Lane. Cobb's was one of the last watermills to close, grinding corn until 1966.[20]

Ruckford Mill stands on the same Herring Stream as Cobb's, originating in the Downs, running from Spitalbridge in Hassocks and serving Hammond's Mill in Clayton parish before meandering through Twineham to Henfield and the River Adur. Ruckford is situated off Malthouse Lane, and was shown in the 1663 Rental as 'a messuage, barn, garden, orchard and watermill', owned by Susan Brooker, widow, and occupied by Edward Harraden. By the 1703 rental it was held by John Oliver who continued in possession for the next 50 odd years. A century later George Bishop was the miller, to be succeeded by James Mitchell, also a farmer, by 1841. Robert Broad was there five years later, and by 1871 he was employing four men, showing how the trade increased in prosperity during Victoria's reign. His occupation was not without its drama, as a local newspaper reported:

> Ruckford Mill, Hurstpierpoint which is in the occupation of Mr Robert Broad, junior, had a narrow escape from destruction by fire on Monday afternoon, June 5th. As it was the roof was burnt, and only by the utmost exertions was the fire stayed from

spreading over the whole roof, the wind being favourable to help
on the conflagration. It appears that about 5 o'clock the engine
house burst into flame on the north side, and the whole was soon
enveloped in flames past recovery. The mill, thanks to those
present, was saved. The origin of the fire is a mystery, as the
engine had not been worked since Friday evening. Valuable help
arrived from the College and Mr Matthews of Locks Farm. Mr
Broad is insured in the Sun Fire Office.[21]

We are lucky to have these mills still standing, albeit as houses. There are
some mills still grinding corn, but mainly those restored by preservation
societies, such as Jill windmill and watermills at Michelham Priory to the
east and the Weald and Downland Museum to the west.

xiii. Pond Lye Mill.

Leigh or Lye Mill was to the north of the parish, off the Cuckfield road
beyond Goddard's Green. It stood by a fairly large stretch of water called
Pond Lye which is reputed to have been the site of an old ironworks.[22]
Benjamin Packham milled there from 1841 to 1881, when he was employing
two men and his son.[23]

The third milestone (from Hurst) is near Mr Packham's watermill
and Leigh Pond, a line through which is the north boundary of the
Parish.[24]

Leigh Mill was last worked as a corn mill in 1913-14 by the Packham brothers, one of whom went to Cobbs, and it was pulled down around the time of the last war and a house built on the site. Mills were also used for fulling cloth, and the land tax of 1780 shows William Peskett's fulling mill owned by Mr Rickman. The milling function has added to our language: 'bringing gryst (or grist) to the mill', 'we are only grysting now' both referring to inferior corn for cattle feed, not for flour.[25]

In the eighteenth century specially designed granaries made for safer storage of corn. These were relatively small buildings raised from the ground on mushroom-shaped 'staddle stones', often now seen lining the drives of houses, and which protected the grain from rising damp and vermin.[26] However, thrashed corn was often stored on an upper floor in barns or in farmhouse attics.

Corn merchants or chandlers dealt with the local mills – indeed some of the millers, like Charles Packham, were also chandlers. Stephen Crosskey in 1839 was a dealer in marine stores, in 1845 and 1855 a corn merchant, and in 1871 a coal merchant living at Ribbetts.[27] In the late 1800s John Leppard lived at Wickham House in the High Street. In Kelly's Directory of 1874 he is classed as a corn and seed merchant, and in the 1891 census as a corn and lime merchant, many traders branching out into selling other goods. High in the east wall of the house is a doorway opening into the attic, probably used for a hoist to pull the grain sacks up for storage.

In 1891 William Wood was a corn merchant, miller and farmer, living at Stanhope Villa in Western Road. We have already seen that Charles Packham, the miller at Cobb's, was also a corn dealer. Henry Unwins was another corn dealer living in 1841 in the High Street, possibly the son of Thomas, who was a miller in 1814. Sixty years later William Alwin added bakery to corn dealing, as by Victoria's reign bakers' shops were to some extent replacing home baking in the bread oven in the side of the main fireplace.

CLOTH AND CLOTHES

Wool has always been important to the wealth of England, as is shown by the Lord Chancellor sitting on the 'Woolsack' in Parliament. It has been said that London Bridge was built on bales of wool, referring, of course, to the vast revenues which came from the taxes on the trading of wool, it being the main source of revenue to the Government from the Middle Ages onwards. In Magna Carta of 1215, there is a section fixing the breadth of 'dyed cloths, russets and halbergetts' at two ells (90 inches) 'within the lists' (the selvage at the edge of the cloth). Infringement of the 'assize of cloth' could sometimes lead to the cloth being forfeited.[28]

Over the years sheep have been bred for their different types of fleece as well as meat. The local breed in Sussex is the Southdown, one of the oldest British breeds, growing a medium wool. John Ellman, who farmed at Glynde in the second half of the eighteenth century, was famous for the great improvements he made to his Southdown flock, and in 1786, with the Earl of Sheffield, founded the Wool Fair at Lewes.[29] In the early fifteenth century the production of broad cloth in England was trebled, and its export increased ninefold. Thanks to our changeable weather England had an enormous advantage over other countries as a feeder of sheep and producer of best quality wool. This gave her the opportunity gradually to win command of the world's cloth market.[30] The importance of the cloth trade has also found its place in our language, with many phrases and metaphors borrowed from the manufacture of cloth. We 'thread a discourse', 'spin a yarn', 'unravel a mystery'; we talk of the 'web of life' and of being 'fine-drawn' or 'home-spun'; and we 'tease'; while all unmarried women are 'spinsters', and we are often on 'tenterhooks' (the hooks on which dyed cloth is stretched).[31]

In the fourteenth century a law was passed which forbade anyone below the rank of the nobility to wear cloth not made in England, Wales or Ireland, in an effort to protect the wool trade. However, expert workers from Flanders were encouraged to settle in England; indeed, they were given special protection, as naturally they were not popular with the native weavers.[32] By the mid-seventeenth century Parliament banned the import of foreign cloth and the export of raw wool – and ordained that everyone should be buried in wool.

'Odious! In woollen! 'Twould a saint provoke'
Were the last words that poor Narcissa spoke.
Pope – 'To Lord Cobham' in *Epistles to Several Persons.*

Thomas Marchant records in his diary:

1727. Octr. 9th   . . . discharged all that was due at Rusper on
account of my mother [in-law] Stone's
funeral . . . Paid James Chapman 50s forfeited
to the poor for burying her in linen.[33]

Wool went through many processes before it became cloth.

Cloth that cometh from the weaving is not comely to wear
Till it be fulled under foot or in fulling stocks
Washen well with water, and with teasels cratched,
Towked and teynted under tailors hands.
Langland – Piers Plowman

Wool is very greasy when it is first shorn, so it must be cleaned. Originally
'lye' (water and vegetable ashes) was used; then the wool was washed in
running water. In Hurstpierpoint, Pond Lye or Leigh, alongside the site of
the old Lye Mill was possibly used for this purpose. Later lye was replaced
by a formula of a mixture of human urine and water. After washing any
necessary dyeing took place. The wool was carded to separate the fibres,
then spun, dyed and woven into cloth. The carding and spinning was mostly
done in the home. Marchant, as one of the parish officers, made use of this:

1718. May 11th   Pd. Widow Webb 2s. For spinning 6lb. of
tow for the parish.[34]

Weaving was mostly done by men, strength being needed to pull the shuttle
through tightly. John Bourton was working as a weaver in Hurst in the mid-
1660s. There is also a sad entry in Thomas Marchant's diary:

1719. Augst 21st   Richard Patching, the weaver, had his leg cut
off this morning, per J Snashall. He died the
following afternoon.[35]

Fulling took place after the cloth was made. This process scoured, cleaned and thickened the cloth by beating it in water. Originally this was done by men trampling upon it in a trough or a stream, an activity known as walking (hence the name Walker).[36] Later this was carried out with huge wooden mallets or hammers, worked by the use of watermills called fulling mills. Finally, after being washed it was stretched out on to racks to dry and brushed with teasels to get the nap to rise – quite a process! Again it is Thomas Marchant who confirms that this was happening in Hurst:

> 1719. Augst 12th   . . . Paid Ellis, the fuller, 13s. 6d. for dressing 27yds. of Irish lincey.
>
> 1720 Decr. 26th   . . . . Pd. Ellis, the fuller, 27s. For dressing and dying the blew cloth for a bed at 1s. Per yd., and he carried home a cloath waistcoat to dress and scour.[37]

Sometimes, if the cloth belonged to the fuller, there was a temptation to overstretch to gain extra yards. This greatly impaired the strength of the cloth. 'Guildford Cloths' which were made in Surrey, Sussex and Hampshire, lost their reputation in the Middle Ages, and measures had to be taken to restore their good name by forbidding fullers or other persons to buy cloth in an unfinished state. [38]

Richard Hazelgrove was a flaxman living with his wife Anne and his family in Hurstpierpoint in the early eighteenth century. Flax was a crop grown widely in Sussex, producing a carded thread called 'tire' which was then spun into linen, forming one of the more important local industries. Much care was needed in its preparation; gloves were to be worn to pluck the plants as cutting damaged the fibres. Any damaged fibres were called 'tow' (such as Widow Webb was paid to spin) and made a much coarser linen.[39] Spinning flax was a common workhouse activity and mention of it occurs frequently in the parish accounts (see chapter on The Poor).

In the probate inventory of cloth worker Abraham Muzzell's goods (see also next chapter), dated 27 September 1712, there is listed, among many other things, 'a chest with linen in him', valued at £4; a parcel of fine linen valued at £1-10-00; two blankets, 5s. each; new cloth, 12s. 6d; and some linen yarn.[40]

Thomas Marchant's inventory date 2 October 1728 [41] showed a separate section for the linen:

Twenty pr of fine sheets	£20-00-00
Thirty pr of coarse sheets	£10-10-00
Three dozen Damask napkins	£4-10-00
One dozen Huckerback do.	12s. 0d
Two dozen tow do.	12s. 0d
Three Damask tablecloths	£1-10-00
Four Huckerback do.	£1-00-00
other small linen	£2-02-00

This shows what a difference there was in the value of the different qualities of cloth, Huckerback being a coarse linen or cotton with a raised surface used for towels. Incidentally it also shows the difference in social status between Marchant and Muzzell.

The sale of the goods of Francis Osbourn on 14 June 1721 gives us some idea of the value of second-hand items:

Mrs Coulstock, a tuck apron	8d
Mr Beadle, a pair of sheets	4s. 0d
Eliz. Cheal, two shifts and an odd sheet	3s. 10 ½d
Goody Pierce, an apron	1s 2 ½d
Goody Lashmer, 3 aprons & 3 kerchiefs	3s 6d.
Goody Lashmer, one handkerchief	6s ½d.
Goody White, a head & kerchief	6d.
Goody Buckwell, a white apron	1s. 9d
Mrs Norton, headcloths	1s. 3½d.
Goody Lashmer, 3pr of sleeves & caps	11d
Dame Walnut, a pr of shoes	1s. 9½d.
. . White, a pr of gloves	1s.
Wm Lashmer, a coverlet, a blanket & 3 feather pillows	8s. 8d.

There were other pieces of household furniture sold, but 'left unsold ye day of publique sale – ye wheel, and old chair, woollen clothes & a black hat'.[42]

Eighty years later, Hampton Weekes made a gift of his old clothes to his servant. Also he wrote from St Thomas's Hospital to his brother Dick in December 1801:

> Dick I mean to send you my black silk breeches for they are a great deal too small for me – I wear my boots and pantaloons now.

Dick replied the following month:

> Your silk breeches exactly fit me, and I can tell you I cut quite a dash in them and black stockings.[43]

The Weekes family wrote regularly for Hampton to buy things to be sent to Hurst from London:

> . . . a nice warm shawl, very fashionable now, made of silk and cammels hair, 9s. was the price . . . A Second-hand, Wilton; Carpet for our common, large, Sitting parlour, we have measured it, . . . We should like to have one as soon, as you can conveniently get it. . . Grace [sister] begs you also . . . to buy a Muff for her . . . I [Mary Ann, another sister] like my lace very much indeed.[44]

Mercers were the traders who sold cloth. In the late seventeenth century Thomas Dunstall and his wife Elizabeth lived just to the west of the church, in a house still called 'Dunstalls'. He issued a 'tradesman's token', a metal coin with a wool comb on one side and 'Thomas Dunstall – Mercer of Hurst' on the other.[45] He clearly was successful as he financed a brickfield on St John's Common (now part of Burgess Hill).

Tailors, of course, made the cloth into clothing. We have already met Richard Luttman in 1701. Others in the earlier records of Hurst were Thomas A Moore who lived in the middle of the seventeenth century, and Christian Smith, whose occupation of premises is recorded in the 1703 Rentals of the Manor of Hurstpierpoint. He lived with his wife Elizabeth and several children in 'a small passage and garden platt with use of well'.[46]

Women mostly made their own clothes, the wealthy engaging the services of a dressmaker or seamstress. For the working man smocks were the usual form of dress. Sussex women were very proficient at the craft, and their intricately worked white round frocks became prized possessions for Sunday and holiday wear. The name 'smock' was a shortened form of 'smocked round frock' and took more time to make than the workaday round frocks which were grey or natural-coloured, and, although smocked to some extent, were not worked sufficiently to merit the name 'smock'.[47] (see Colour Plates 5 & 6).

William Cobbett, writing about Horsham in 1822-25, said:

> The people are very clean, the Sussex women are very nice in their dress and in their homes, men and boys wear smocks more than they do in some counties.[48]

With the smock 'half-high' hats were worn. These were hard felt hats with crowns which, when painted, were shiny and kept out the rain; shepherds usually painted theirs grey.[49]

Including those already mentioned, we know of a number of people in Hurst in the seventeenth century who were working in the cloth trade: one flaxman, one flax-dresser, one fuller, one weaver, one cloth worker, two mercers and three tailors. One of these, James Holder, was taken to the Court at Lewes on 12 January 1659 'for refusing to assist Thomas Luxford, yeoman, constable, in carrying of one Overington Wood to the common gaol house', whence he was committed for felony.[50]

In the nineteenth century, the Hurstpierpoint Vestry Book has an entry dated 23 December 1823 regarding the rules for dress at Chichester House in the High Street:

> It is agreed that all girls who come into the House pregnant with child shall immediately be clothed with grey linsey gown and yellow stockings as a mark of disgrace those that will not submit to have such clothes and attend to the Regulations of the House shall be turned out of the House.[51]

By Victoria's reign there were many more traders employed in the clothing industry: mercers, drapers, tailors, seamstresses, hosiers & shirt makers, milliners, bonnet and straw-hat makers, glovers, a furrier and feather-dresser – and there was a commercial laundry to keep the clothes clean.

LEATHER AND TANNING

Leather has been in use ever since man first wore animal skins to keep out the cold, after carefully cleaning them with flint-scrapers such as the one found in Weald Close in 1984 (see page 3).[52] They must have dried and been very uncomfortable to wear before the discovery that soaking the skins in a mixture of tree bark and water change the skins into supple leather.

Although the barks of many trees have tannin – willow, larch, spruce, birch and elm – in England oak bark was used, presumably because of the great forests of oak which covered so much of the land. The trees were usually felled in April, when they are full of sap, and the bark can be stripped off more easily. There is a Sussex saying: 'The Devil cannot creep between oak and its bark'. The bark is then stored until it is dry, then pulverised for use in the tan yard. This had a series of pits and vats, where the hides were first soaked in lime to loosen the hair, then washed to remove all traces of lime and scraped to remove any fat from the inside; and finally soaked in a solution of bark and water ('wooze'), being constantly turned and transferred into progressively stronger mixtures. This process took about a year for ordinary leather, but longer for that used for soling boots. Finally, the hides were hung in sheds to dry. In Sussex in the 1700s oak bark was costing about £1 a load (about £75 now), and a hide about 16s. 6d.[53]

Trevelyan writes in his social history:

> The great quantities of cattle in England helped all leather industries. The southern English walked on leather and disdained the 'wooden shoes' that foreigners were fain to wear. Clogs, however, were very generally worn in the thrifty north.[54]

The stock-in-trade of the tanner was simple: hides, oak-bark, and a number of vats and tubs, plus various tools such as 'schapyng knyfes' for the tan. [55] The skins were sold by the fellmonger, such as Thomas Rooke who lived in Hurst in the 1820s, and the tanner would take care to see that they were all in good condition. There were two main types of leather: hides came from cattle, skins from sheep and goats.

Leather-dressers settled where they might have plenty of water in brooks or streams – to dress their product, and complaints of fouling of the water supply were not unusual.[56] Tanneries were usually outside the village because of the smell.

In Hurstpierpoint one tannery was in Langton Lane, on the west side of the road, south of Knowles Tooth. It was owned at different times by William Hart and Mrs Soale, whose tanner was named Prior. There is evidence that another tan yard was situated just to the south of Tott Farm, presumably using the water of Cutler's Brook. The earliest tanner we can trace was Henrie Standrye who was buried in Hurst in 1582. Later there was John Vine living here with his family in the early seventeenth century.

A number of trades used leather: glovers, saddlers and collar-makers, purse-mongers and bottle-makers. The best of these were called 'cordwainers', the name deriving from the fine leather which originally came from Cordoba in Spain.

But the most important were shoemakers. Shoes were made with both feet the same. We have George IV to thank for being one of the first to insist that his shoes were made for a left and right foot, and were not left for the wearer to shape these for himself. [57] Richard Davey, a staff sergeant in Wellington's army, wrote to his wife Sarah in Hurstpierpoint regarding the employment of his son Richard:

> I don't like Richard to be a shoemaker, but if he likes it I don't much mind. I likewise think it will be rather too much to board him a year if he is working for nothing, but I cannot think of his having half what he earns to be bound for 7 years. That will not keep him, by no means. It would be better for him to go for a soldier than starve himself that way. If he had minded his learning he might have got to be a clerk by this time![58]

However, in spite of this, Richard did become a shoemaker, and later followed his father to become parish clerk, both living in the two houses opposite the church – one now Davey the undertakers. There was a William

Davey who was in the trade in 1841, living at 'Old Magpie' at Goddard's Green – perhaps a relation?

Robert Barnes of Hurstpierpoint, labourer, was indicted for grand larceny on 20 January 1597. He stole 4 pairs of shoes (4d), a knife (2d), a pair of gloves (2d) and 2 girdles (4d) from John Brooks.[59]

In the nineteenth century the parish had a long list of boot- and shoe-makers. They were a vital part of the community, the majority of whom walked everywhere. Shoes and boots were usually made and repaired by the same craftsman. A travelling cobbler was called a 'snob' in Sussex.[60]

In saddlery the leather is stitched with waxed hemp, using two needles at each end of the thread, both going through the same hole in opposite directions to make a 'saddle stitch', giving greater strength. George Courtness was a collar-maker in the early nineteenth century, together with Thomas and William Bartley, who were listed as collar-makers and harness-makers. Until quite recently we had a saddlery in the village.

Leather has also been used for 'bettles' (bottles) and 'bombards' (big jugs) and tankards because, although there have been glass bottles for holding liquid of one kind or another since antiquity, in England they were still rather a novelty as late as the mid-seventeenth century.[61]

THE HORSE AND CARRIAGE TRADE

The Fisher map of 1841 shows that there were then two blacksmiths' shops in Hurstpierpoint. One in Church Lane (the row of buildings to the west of the church) was owned by James Burchfield; the other, just to the east of the New Inn, in what is now Pit Road, belonged to Joseph Chandler, who had a house, yard and blacksmith's shop.

The Chandler family were blacksmiths in Hurst for at least two generations. In 1837 Joseph & George Chandler had a draft lease for 99 years for 'Part of Townfield in Hurstpierpoint to erect a shop for their own use, rent 5s'.[62] Joseph was there for about twenty years, becoming also an ironmonger by 1855. George Knight was apprenticed to him on 1 December 1835.[63]

Plate 14. Interior of smithy in Pit Lane *c*. 1930,
with Charlie Diplock and his assistant Arthur Norkett.

Horses were a very important part of the life of the village from very early times, being the main means of travel. In Tudor times 'the English were already notorious for their devotion to horses and dogs . . . but the horse was still a cumbrous animal . . . still bred to carry a knight in his armour'.[64] The breeding of horses had to keep pace with an ever increasing demand, as the horse was replacing the ox at cart and plough, although the process was very gradual;[65] oxen were still in use in some places in Sussex right into the early years of the twentieth century.

The condition of the roads varied according to local soils. Sussex roads were well known for their dreadful state, highways often being impassable for even wagons or carts. In winter months especially the only way people could visit one another was on horseback, the women having to ride pillion behind their menfolk. As the highways improved during the eighteenth century the transport of goods progressed, and the wagon took the place of the packhorse. One of the commonest sounds upon the roads was the chiming of bells announcing the approach of a wagon drawn by four great horses, from whose collars the music was suspended.[66] The parish was responsible for the upkeep of the roads, every householder having his own section to maintain. This, of course, was not popular, and many were taken to the Hundred Court at Buttinghill. In September 1614:

> Richard Butcher of Stuckells to amend a 'gutterlogge' in Hurst near the lands called Cuckfildes by Pentecost next under penalty of 5s.

And the following month:

> The parishioners of Hurst are to repair a 'gutter bridge' the King's highway between Stocker's field and Isaak's field [south of Wanbarrow farm] by the Feast of St. John Baptist next under penalty of 5s.[67]

Many of the roads were mainly used by travellers passing through, so it was inevitable that some way of passing these costs on to the users should be found, and in the eighteenth century the turnpike system with its tollgates was introduced. By the middle of the century the stagecoach had appeared, but travelling was very uncomfortable as there were no springs and the wheels, with their metal tyres, would bump over every rut in the road. Private coaches were much more comfortable and elegant, many being sprung. As horses could be changed at 'posting inns', travelling was much faster, there being no need to wait for the horses to be rested.

We have all received Christmas cards showing the delightful pictures of coaches and horses travelling through the snow-covered countryside, but, especially through muddy mid-Sussex, it was not always as pleasant as that. During the great snowstorm of 24 December 1836 the Brighton up-mail coach fell into a snowdrift near Stonepound. The guard set off immediately to get assistance, but when he came back no trace could be found of the coach, coachman or passengers, three in number. After much difficulty the coach was found, but could not be extracted from the hollow. . . the passengers, coachman and guard slept at Clayton.[68]

After the building of the turnpikes and the imposition of tolls for both men and animals, many travellers tried to find ways of bypassing the tollgates, even mis-counting their herds or flocks to cheat the tolls man. In 'A History of Hurstperpoint', written in 1837s, its author says:

> . . . East and West, North and South (with the exception of the latter whither you may go about a mile before you meet a gate) you cannot stir out of Hurst for half a mile without a tax on your advancement.[69]

Another writer (assumed to be Dr Richard Weekes) said in 1818:

> This spring the tolls were doubled on our Hurst turnpikes.[70]

Horses were valuable assets, and consequently fairly well cared for. Thomas Marchant records:

1714. Dec. 10th.	My wife, Grey, Willy and May went to Lewes, and staid all night, because Willy's horse was taken with the gripes.
1715. April 19th.	Ned Penfold went part of the way to Lewes with butter, but the wind was so high it blew him off his horse. So he came back again.
1717. Decr. 11th.	Mr. Snashall [doctor as well as vet] was here twice to see the bay horse that was sick.
1719. July 15th.	Bought a bay horse of John Smith at £7. 13s., and 100 faggots. He is 6 or 7 years old.

Of course, there were accidents, recorded by Thomas Marchant, Richard Weekes and James Hannington in their respective diaries or letters:

1722. July 22nd.	Mrs Dodson [Rector's wife] got harm by a fall from her horse yesterday, near Saddlescombe.
1801. Sept. 21.	Frank Gander [servant to Burtenshaw of Painsfield Farm near Henfield] fell off his horse Saturday Evening & was Kill'd on the spot just by Danny.

1866. Nov. 3rd.   Riding over from Brighton to shoot, my
horse fell and rolled over with me on my leg.
I never said anything about it, lest I should
be forbidden to strain the leg by going out
shooting – killed eighteen brace of
pheasants.[71]

Wheelwrights were in constant demand while horsepower was the principal
form of transport. A well-crafted wheel, once encased by a metal tyre, could
withstand years of jolting across fields and along rough country roads. The
hub of a wheel was mostly made of elm, the spokes of oak, and the felloes
which form the outside of the wheel of ash or elm. Each part was precisely
measured and shaped, then closely fitted to give the tightest of joints,
without the use of any glue or nails.[72] The design varied with the type of
work and with the district:

The waggons of the Weald as most deep-rutted districts, are tall
and large with a wide grasp, or span, between the wheels   . . . I
have measured ruts of a broad-wheeled wagon, full six feet from
out-to-out.[73]

xiv. A Sussex wagon.

John Mitchell was a wheelwright in Hurst in 1841, with a shop at the eastern end of the High Street by 'Trumpkins' (from the narrow part to opposite South Avenue). At about the same time there were four other 'wheelers' living in Hurst with their families: John Young, John Penfold, James Ford and English Corney. Wheelwrights often worked alongside the blacksmiths, sharing their shops. From the early Victorian years more and more parts of a wagon were made of iron instead of wood.

While the farrier did the shoeing of horses, the blacksmith, with apprentices and journeymen, made everything of iron: chains, nails and hammers, the latches for doors, windows and gates – the gates themselves for the wealthy – through to pot-hangers, gridirons and pots, fire-dogs and fire-backs. These last constituted a traditional Sussex craft dating back to the 1600s. The smith protected himself from flying sparks by wearing a chamois leather apron.[74]

In Sayers Common in the mid-1800s Thomas Hole had a blacksmith's shop and lived at the Duke of York. Edwin Hole had taken over by 1891, although he was not the publican, whilst Amos Hole of the same address was listed in the census of that year as a higgler (huckster, so-called from higgling over his bargains).[75]

There were many other traders in Hurst connected with the horse. There were six horse-keepers in the 1830s who had animals for hire. Isaac Nye was a flyman, driving a one-horse hackney carriage, who lived in the 1830s in a cottage with stable near St George's. Harness, saddle- or collar-makers were all making leather harness; one of these was Henry Brown who owned a shop at Trumpkins which had passed to his wife by 1841 and to his son George by 1867.[76] Ostlers like John Edwards, who was in the village in the early nineteenth century, were stablemen at inns. Young stable lads were taught how to look after horses, eventually becoming grooms like David Elley, who lived at Poplar Cottage in 1828. Coachmen, many working for the local gentry, drove the carriages and coaches. Even the undertaker needed horses to pull the hearse. Among the charges paid out for the funeral of Francis Osbourn in 1721 is 'some plumbs [plumes] for ye funeral'[77] These would have decorated the horses' heads and would, of course, have been black.

After the opening of the London-to-Brighton railway, a horse-drawn omnibus travelled between Hurstpierpoint and Hassocks Gate Station and on to Ditchling. This was owned by Mr C L Ellis who ran the service from a base in Hassocks. At the end of the nineteenth century part of the business was sold to William Cherriman, who had been a driver for Mr Ellis. He moved it to West Furlong Lane before the First World War, passing the business to his son Laurence, who in 1925 brought the first motor-bus to Hurst.[78]

BRICKMAKING

The importance of the carpenter has been recognised in the chapter on timber-framed houses, but, with the gradual introduction of other methods of construction, he became just one of a number of tradesmen involved. Not least among these were brickmakers.[79]

The raw material for making bricks can be found all over Sussex apart from the chalk downs: brick earth, clay and sand form much of the subsoil, so that the rapid expansion of house-building in the nineteenth century was served by local brickyards and tile-yards in almost every parish. The clays of Sussex vary enormously and almost every parish contained a brickyard by the middle of the eighteenth century, where the bricks were made, often as a part time or seasonal occupation. The Weald Clay in our own district is of a type which can be used to make pottery, facing bricks and tiles as well as ordinary bricks. When clay was dug by hand the pits would be shallow but widespread; machinery reached lower levels, but the earth then had to be weathered before use. In Hurstpierpoint we can trace the history back to Roman times with the discovery of a tile-kiln in Danny Park.[80] The use of bricks was not reintroduced to this country until the fourteenth century, and in significant quantities only over 100 years later.

By the nineteenth century there were premises at three sites within the parish: at Reeds Lane, Sayers Common, where Richard King, William Ashdown, members of the Page family, followed by Walter Lynn and W Allfrey ran the business from 1808 until the middle of the twentieth century; on Little Park farm (where Fairfield Crescent is now) Stephen Gander made bricks, tiles and pottery from 1855 to 1874; and in the immediate area of the

Sportsman at Goddards Green the Hurst Brick & Tile Company was functioning just before the Second World War.[81] Two of these potteries were on waste adjacent to commons, close to brushwood for faggots to heat the kilns.

These were themselves brick-built, often into an earth bank to increase the heat insulation, with a firing tunnel at the bottom. The bricks, having been cut and left to dry, were spaced in the chamber to allow the hot gases to rise as the temperature slowly increased over several days. A temporary roof was sometimes put in place as protection from the weather. After this, cooling had to be allowed before the bricks were removed and the whole process started again.   As demand rose a second kiln would enable continuous production to be achieved.

HIGH DAYS AND HOLIDAYS

Of course it was not all work – mostly, but not all! First and foremost was the fair. For centuries all over England the annual fair was a time to look forward to for weeks before the event, and to remember for months afterwards.

In some places there were hiring fairs at Michaelmas at which labourers and other servants offered themselves for hire for the coming year. If a man was dissatisfied with the work he was doing or, more often, with the employer he was doing it for, he would dress himself up in his best clothes and present himself at the hiring fair. A carter would carry his long carter's whip, a ploughman a 'shining stick', a shepherd a piece of sheep's fleece either in his hat or pinned to his coat or smock – each to signify his willingness to work.

There were horse fairs, sheep fairs like the one at Findon, goose fairs, fruit and other produce fairs. At all of these the main object was to sell and buy things. Farmers and villagers came from miles around and caught up with all the local gossip.[82]

In Hurstpierpoint the right to hold a fair was granted by King Edward II on the 23rd day of July 1313, by a charter signed by the King allowing:

Our beloved and faithful John de Warenne, Earl of Surrey to hold
[among similar events at his other manors in Surrey and Sussex] .
. . One fair at his Manor of Hurst in the same county each year for
one day's duration in the day of St Laurence [the patron saint of
Hurstpierpoint at that time].[83]

xv. Charter of 1313, giving the Earl of Surrey the right
to hold an annual fair in Hurst (among other places).

This charter is now in the Public Record Office at Kew.

The fair has continued ever since, with only a short gap, although the date
has changed. The Feast of St Lawrence is in August, but about 1775 the fair
moved to May and stayed there for many years. In the twentieth century it
has been called 'Hospital Saturday'. Violet Morley, who was born in 1901,
recorded her 'Memories of Hurstpierpoint' for her family:

> A Carnival took place each year to raise money for the hospitals.
> A hurdy-gurdy would go round the village in the morning,
> playing tunes to let people know the fun had started. Adults and
> children would get into fancy dress, and there would be prizes for
> these, and for sports in the recreation ground in the afternoon. As
> it got dusk, there would be a lantern procession round the village.

I don't know who owned these lanterns, they were collected from
the New Inn, and when returned we were given a bun. These
small lanterns, and also the large ones carried by the grown-ups,
were gaily coloured Chinese ones lit by candles, but I never saw
any catch fire.[84]

Plate 15.
A float ready for Hospital Saturday outside Woolgar's smithy, now Harper & Eede's.

Later the fair was called 'Hurstpierpoint Carnival', and now it is St
Lawrence Fair again, but at the beginning of July. Kelly's Directory for
1855 says ' there is a Pleasure Fair on 1st May'.

There were other pastimes. Thomas Marchant recorded:

> 1718. Janry. 24th.   A mountebank [quack doctor] came to
> our towne to-day. He calls himself
> Dr. Richd. Harness. Mr. Scutt and I
> drank tea with the tumbler. Of his
> tricks I am no judge; but he appears to
> play well on the fiddle.

1721. June 16th.   The mountebank in the town; a smock
race in our field.[85]

Some sixty years after Marchant, and in another village, John Burgess of
Ditchling, whom we hear about in the chapter on dissenters, was writing his
diary:

August 1st 1785.   There was a cricket match at Lingfield
Common between Lingfield and Surrey
and all the county of Sussex, supposed
to be upwards of 2,000 people.

March 14th 1788.   Went to Fryersoake to a Bull Bait to sell
my dog. I sold him for one guineay
upon condition he was Hurt, but as he
received no Hurt I took him back again
at the same price.[86]

Guy Fawkes Day was a holiday. Richard Weekes anticipates the occasion
on 5th November 1802:

There is to be a great display of sky rockets to night by Messrs.
Weekes Ellis Borrer & Marshall Juniors on the Church Green
they have bought as many as came to £0. 12. 6 . . .[87]

Guy Fawkes day was celebrated with a peal of bells and general rejoicing,
and the firing of cannon. A special service was held in all churches, and this
service remained in the English Prayer Book for more than two centuries,
not being deleted until 1859, thirty years after the Catholic Emancipation
Act of 1829. Children still chant the traditional rhyme, while collecting 'a
penny for the guy':

Remember, remember the Fifth of November
Gunpowder, treason and plot.
I see no reason why gunpowder treason
Should ever be forgot.

May Day was celebrated with dancing around the Maypole. This was
decorated with flowers and garlands, and watching was the May Queen,
chosen as the prettiest girl in the village. Many villages had a permanent
Maypole which stood in position all year round, to be freshly painted and

adorned when the great day came round. In 1644 Maypoles were forbidden throughout England by the Parliamentarians. Nearly all the standing poles came down, but with the Restoration in 1660 many came back, to be used either on May Day or on Oak Apple Day, the 29th of May, chosen to commemorate Charles II's return to the throne. The chapter on education shows that the custom was still alive at the village school in Hurst in Victorian times, and into the twentieth century.

At Harvest time corn dollies were made from the last corn that was cut, to ensure the fertility of the following year's crop. They were carried home in triumph to the farmhouse where they presided over the Harvest Supper in the kitchen or barn, and were kept there until replaced by the corn dolly from the next harvest. There was a great feast for all who had worked at the harvest, after which there were toasts to the farmer and his family, singing of old traditional songs, and dancing. The making of corn dollies has now become a country craft, and they are made in many shapes and sizes.[88]

In 1802, apart from the Guy Fawkes fireworks already mentioned, there was great excitement at the signing of the Treaty of Amiens between England and France. Grace Weekes wrote to her brother Hampton on 31 March:

> . . . Dick says we are going to have illuminations at Hurst to night if we are we shal have 3 candles in each of our windows [at Matts, now Norfolk House, in the High Street] Mr Campion is carrying faggots up the hill [presumably Wolstonbury] and has ordered 10 cheeses to be carried up and I don't know what all on account of the peace. Mrs Cripp's house at Stantons was illuminated last night from top to bottom and Lewes was all in a blaze. . .

But it was merely a truce and only lasted until May of the following year. In any case, Grace was bored in spite of the entertainments:

> . . . Hurst is so dull and there is no amusement going forward nothing but business here. . .

-    poor Grace – she was only eighteen!

When Napoleon abdicated in 1814 there were more celebrations:

> . . . great rejoicings at Hurst. Suspended . . . above the top of the
> spire, consisting of 43 yds calico cut asunder so as to make two
> breadths, and being a strong wind to extend it, it had a good
> effect. All the principal inhabitants dined at the New Inn, and we
> collected 20 guineas for the poor. Mr. [Nathaniel] Borrer gave
> another treat for them at West Town [Pakyns].[89]

Hurst boasted several clubs and societies: a Friendly Society formed in
1777; a Union Society instituted in 1825; the Sparrow Club and the
Cricket Club; a Burial Club; a Horticultural Society; and the Hurst Penny
Club, established by the Reverend Mr Tufnell:

> . . . for the encouragement of Industry and Prudence among the
> young unmarried men in the labouring and working classes. The
> end which the Society has in view, is to restore if possible those
> habits of industry and prudence for which the labouring and
> working classes were so much distinguished; and its immediate
> object is to induce the young men to make a periodical deposit of
> some part of their earnings in the Savings Bank, and not bring a
> burden on themselves and the Parish, by unreasonably early and
> improvident marriages . . . . In 1833 there were ninety-six young
> men, boys, and girls, who deposited £150. 6s. 5d; in 1834, one
> hundred and twenty three, who deposited £174. 14s. 6d; and
> 1835, one hundred and eighteen, who deposited £162. 10s. 8d.[90]

There were, of course, the celebrations of Christmas and Easter, and hunting
for those who could afford to keep a horse. The Southdown Hunt was
established in 1843, and many of the villagers would have been involved in
beating or following the hounds across the countryside. But for the majority
of villagers there was not much time nor money to spend on amusements.
The hours were long, from dawn to dusk, and wages were small. It was not
until the railway started in the mid-nineteenth century that people were able
to go from place to place cheaply. Then the pleasure gardens, such as the
Chinese Gardens mentioned in the chapter on public houses, sprang up all
round the district. On the whole, most people made their own
entertainments at home, and, if there was nothing else to do, they could
always meet up with friends to enjoy the gossip and have a pint at the local
inn.

AND NOW?

As the village grew, so more and more trades appeared. Thomas Marchant mentions a butcher, a tinker, a farmer; a farrier, a smith and carrier; a spinner, a fuller and a weaver; a midwife, a barber and a surgeon; a schoolmaster and a dancing master. However, he went to Lewes to buy gloves, silver lace (for mourning?) and cloth, and travelled to Horsham to have the cloth made into a coat.

A hundred years later the local traders had grown to include bakers and grocers, a watch and clock maker, and a milliner. You could buy lace and cloth from a draper, and have your coat and gloves made in the village. There was also an attorney, a registrar, a printer and a bookseller. The doctor no longer had to attend horses as well as humans, as there was a veterinary surgeon; the tinker had progressed to an ironmonger; and commercial brewers were making the beer, as shown in the chapter on the High Street traders.[91]

Alas, we don't have all these skills in Hurstpierpoint nowadays, but they do still exist. Members of the Guild of Sussex Craftsmen exhibit and sell their work at craft fairs throughout Sussex.

NOTES AND REFERENCES

1. Candlin L (1985): *Tales of Old Sussex*, 67.
2. ESRO/W/FNV265; Fleet C (1883): *Glimpses of our Sussex Ancestors*, Vol 1, 296.
3. WSRO/ Par 400/37/12.
4. Fleet, *Ancestors*, Vol 2, 20.
5. Trevelyan G M (1944): *Illustrated English Social History*, Vol 2, 104.
6. WSRO/ Par 400/34 (apprenticeship of John Bignall, Hurst 1718).
7. Hey D (1996): *Oxford Companion to Local and Family History*, 21.
8. Salzman L F (1923): *English Industries of the Middle Ages*, 341–2.
9. WSRO/ Par 400/33/2.
10. Trevelyan, *Social History*, Vol 1, 157.
11. WSRO/ Par 400/33.

12. Armstrong J R (1974): *A History of Sussex*, 136.
13. *SNQ* 1886, quoted in Meynell E (1947): *Sussex*, 238.
14. Darby B (1975): *A View of Sussex*, 90–1.
15. WSRO ADD MS 17683A: Fisher Map 1841.
16. 'A Native of this Village' (1826): *A Slight Sketch of Hurst*, 14.
17. 'A Native, A Minor' (1837): *History of Hurstperpoint*, 14.
18. *Sussex Advertiser* 7 November 1865.
19. Censuses 1841-91.
20. Cox D: Wind, Tide and Steam Mills, in Leslie K & Short B(eds)(1999): *An Historical Atlas of Sussex*, 109.
21. Bower A (2000): Census database 1846; census 1871; *Sussex Advertiser* 14 June 1871.
22. Census 1871.
23. Census 1881.
24. A Native, A Minor, *Hurstperpoint*, 71.
25. Hall H (ed)(1957): *W D Parish's Dictionary of the Sussex Dialect*, 52.
26. Armstrong, *History*, 141.
27. *Pigot's Directory 1839, Kelly's Directories 1845, 1855;* census 1871.
28. Salzman, *Industries*, 198.
29. Meynell, *Sussex, 208.*
30. *Trevelyan, Social History*, Vol 1, 84.
31. *Ibid.*, 87.
32. Salzman, *Industries*, 205.
33. Turner E (ed)(1873): The Marchant Diary, *SAC* **25**, 194.
34. *Ibid.*, 183.
35. *Ibid.*, 185.
36. Salzman, *Industries*, 221.
37. Turner, Marchant, *SAC***25**, 185, 186.
38. Salzman, *Industries*, 224.
39. Beswick M (1985): *Leather and Cloth*, 22.
40. ESRO/W/FNU354.
41. ESRO/XA26/20.
42. WSRO/37/12.
43. Ford J M T (1987): *The Weekes Family Letters*, 94, 102.
44. *Ibid.*, 74, 89, 224.
45. Caldecott J B (1943): The Penfold Bequest, Coins and Tokens, *SAC* **83**, 112.
46. ESRO/DAN1123.
47. Hall, *Dictionary*, 179.
48. Armstrong, History, 131.
49. Hall, *Dictionary, 53.*

50. ESRO/QRS/5; see also chapter on Law and Order regarding reluctance of inhabitants to assist constables.
51. WSRO/ Par 400/12/11.
52. Ditchling Museum catalogue number 94. 1980. 1a.
53. Beswick, *Leather & Cloth*, 4.
54. Trevelyan, *Social History*, Vol 2, 32.
55. *VCH* **2**, 259.
56. *Ibid.*
57. Dale A (1950): *The History and Architecture of Brighton*, 32.
58. Woodward W A (1928): A Sussex Soldier in Wellington's Army, *Sussex County Magazine* February 1928.
59. *Calendar of Assizes, Elizabeth I.*
60. Hall, *Dictionary*, 124.
61. Davis D C (1972): *English Bottles and Decanters 1650–1900*, 14.
62. ESRO/DAN1612.
63. WSRO/ Par 400/34/3/1–7.
64. Trevelyan, *Social History*, Vol 1, 260.
65. *Ibid.*, Vol 2, 32.
66. *Ibid.*, Vol 3, 164.
67. Renshaw WC (1916): The Hundred of Buttinghill, *SAC* **58**, 12.
68. Harper C G (1906): *The Brighton Road*, 397.
69. A Native, A Minor, *Hurstperpoint*, 65.
70. *Mid Sussex Times* (nd, pre-1912): Glimpses of the Past, Extracts from a Hurst Resident's Diary.
71. Turner, Marchant, *SAC* **25**, 169, 172, 191; Ford, *Weekes*, 41; Dawson E C (1914): *Lion Hearted*, 19.
72. Ward S (1991): *The Countryside Remembered*, 50–1.
73. Marshall (1798): *Rural Economy of the Southern Counties*, Vol 2, 136, quoted in Sturt G (1923): *The Wheelwright's Shop*, 205n.
74. *Ibid.*, 210n.
75. *Kelly's Directories* 1855–74; Hall, *Dictionary*, 52.
76. Fisher Map 1841; *Kelly's Directory*.
77. WSRO/ Par 400/37/12.
78. Packham R A (1997):*Hurstpierpoint in old picture postcards*, Vol 2, 51–3.
79. Beswick M (1993): *Brickmaking in Sussex*, 3–29, 202.
80. Armstrong, *History of Sussex*, 120: Couchman J E (1925): A Roman Cemetery at Hassocks, *SAC* **66**, 34–61.
81. *Kelly's Directories* 1845–1938.
82. Bignall A (1986): *Tales of Old Kent*, 81–2.
83. Harrison F & Sharp J (1937): *Old Brighton, Old Hove, Old Preston*, 94–6.
84. Morley V (nd, 1990s): Memories of Hurstpierpoint, 8.
85. Unpublished Marchant Diary

86. Burgess D F (ed)(1989): *No Continuing City, the Diary and Letters of John Burgess*, 7, 54.

87. Ford, *Weekes*, 23.

88. Hole C (1976): *British Folk Customs*, 84, 93–4.

89. Ford, *Weekes*, 149-50, 192; *Mid Sussex Times*, Hurst Resident's Diary

90. A Native, A Minor, *Hurstperpoint*, 55–6.

91. *Pigot's Directory* 1839.

5. BUILT TO LAST

Within Hurst parish there are over 80 houses, which are officially listed as being of architectural or historical importance, so we are fortunate to have a number of examples to help us trace their development as they were altered to reflect changes in the way society evolved.

A thatched cottage, with roses round the door, and a garden full of flowers, for many a dream home.

In the fifteen and sixteen hundreds the reality was somewhat different. Some cottages were single-storey, divided into two, one half with an open fire in the centre for cooking and heating. The floor was of beaten-down earth, so there would be damp rising from the floor, and a rather smoky interior. Medieval and early Tudor cottages were often made of simple wooden frames with a mixture of clay, straw, animal hair and dung as an in-fill, the so-called wattle-and-daub. By their very nature they were not expected to last long, perhaps only for a single generation. Not until after 1600 were more permanent materials used for these humbler dwellings, and, of course, only the most substantial still survive. The original total living area, perhaps divided for day use and sleeping, would probably have been significantly less than a modern 'mobile home' with low roofs, tiny windows and single fireplace for both heating and cooking. Very occasionally an upper floor reached by a ladder would be built, but extra accommodation was more often achieved by extending outwards. They were occupied by peasant smallholders living off the produce of a few acres, both crops and livestock. Later a requirement that the land should be not less than four acres in order to ensure a level of self-sufficiency brought many a squatter before the justices for illegally erecting a cottage.

Many of the more substantial houses started as medieval open halls with central hearths, used by masters and servants alike. Some degree of segregation of function and social standing was achieved by dividing a service area at one end and private rooms at the other. The introduction of brick for chimneys eliminated the sooting of roof timbers, while the desire of the master for greater privacy resulted in further sub-division of the house, including the provision of a full upper floor and perhaps attics, and the gradual decline of the practice of having live-in servants. The heavier timber large-frame construction of fifteenth century houses gave way to close studding, in part as an expression of increasing affluence. Framed buildings continued to appear until 1700, well after brick had been re-introduced for domestic architecture. The spaces between the timber were filled with wattle-and-daub both inside and outside, or brick-nogging, and as the vertical timbers rotted over time brick or stone was introduced below the framing to produce the mixed result so often seen today. This transitional period was followed by a steadily increasing number of houses built of brick from the start or a combination of brick and stone or flint. Roofs were covered with thatch with a pitch of 45 degrees to shed the rain, especially some of the smaller dwellings. Alternatively tiles or stone were used, the local example being Horsham stone; a clear indication of relative wealth. Local refinements resulted in the Wealden house, with its jettied (overhung) first floor wings either side of a recessed central part. This is not the place to expand on the techniques involved, merely to emphasise that a knowledge of the methods and styles used enables experts to date both original buildings and later additions and alterations with considerable accuracy.[1] What we can do is to look at some of the buildings in our parish, and try to show, very briefly, how they have altered as the owners or occupiers changed their perceptions of both their domestic needs and their social aspirations. It may be helpful to group these houses by periods: first, the time when timber construction predominated; then a second wave which reflects the more intense development of the centre of the village.

TIMBER-FRAMED HOUSES

Hurstpierpoint, like many villages, has grown tremendously over the years, particularly since the Second World War, but fortunately it has retained a number of its earlier buildings, some hidden behind more modern exteriors. Anyone who lived in the parish in the seventeenth or eighteenth centuries could return today and walk along the main road from west to east and find that many of the houses they knew are still here.

Entering the village at the Albourne boundary we first come upon Pakyns Manor. (see Colour Plate 7). As this holding was a sub-infeudation its records are not included with those of the manor of Hurst. The manor land was originally quite extensive, including a large part of Langton Lane, as well as various properties in Albourne, and it was not until 1953 that it was divided by sale into smaller lots. The manor house is described as an L-shaped sixteenth century timber-framed building, which has been much altered over the years. The earliest known owner was Paganus who was Sheriff of Sussex in 1157. It appears as Pakyns when it came to William Pakyns in 1216, and the last of the Pakyns owned it in 1509. In 1629 William Burtenshaw paid 4d towards the Poor Rate, but it is difficult to believe that this represented a major part of the holding, when others in the parish were rated at over 30s. The Poor Rate of 1663 gives the owner of Pacon or Pakyns as Mrs Soale; mention is made of a tan yard, which would have been sited near water and outside the village because of the smells. It was located in Langton Lane near Blossoms Cottage or Blossams Well.[2]

On the opposite side of the road, at the corner of Langton Lane was Crouch House, now divided into two cottages called Pigwidgeon and Spotted Cow. (see Colour Plate 8). This is the most visible and attractive example of a Wealden House, a style that evolved from the fourteenth century. Under a single roof, the jettied ends with the resultant recessed hall not only provided more space on the upper floor, but the more sophisticated construction also acted as a status symbol, particularly with the dragon beam at the south-east corner providing a jetty on two elevations. This particular example has a single bay hall with close-studding, dating it c.1500, with an inglenook (Gaelic for fire-corner) fireplace and a timber-and-plaster chimney having a brick flue at ridge level supported by collars, a rare survival from c.1600. The introduction of chimneys in the late sixteenth century allowed the flooring-over of the main hall, provided more living and storage space whilst heat from the chimney-breast would warm the upper rooms. This was recognised by contemporaries as a major advance in domestic building:

> There are old men yet dwelling in the village where I remain which have noted three things to be marvellously altered in England within their sound remembrance. . . One is, the multitude of chimneys lately erected, whereas in their young days there were not above two or three. . . but each one made his fire against a reredos in the hall, where he dined an dressed his meat.[3]

The inglenook also improved cooking arrangements: fire-dogs, fire-irons, jacks and spits, together with various pots and pans, and a bread-oven often to one side above the main fire. A dripping-pan could collect fat which could be used to soak rushes to make rush lights, candles being very expensive and only used by the merchants and gentry. Probably the most important item of furniture was the bed; apart from the very poor families, this would have been a four-poster, with ropes stretched across the base and covered by a mat to support the straw or flock mattress. Sheets and pillow-cases were of unbleached linen; curtains would be hung to keep out the draughts. As many beds were high off the ground, a smaller trundle or truckle bed could be stored beneath. Most beds, although solidly built, could be easily dismantled for removal. Like many other household items, they were passed down through families, and lasted a good many years. Wooden chests stored clothes and linen, while better homes also had cupboards of various sizes.[4]

The 1663 Rental states:

> William Colby owns and occupies a messuage barn and orchard in West Town called Crouch House former occupiers were John Coulstock and then Thomas Luxford.[5]

Bullfinch Lane runs south from the present Pakyns Lodge. In 1837 Nathaniel Borrer moved the entrance to the lane from its original position directly opposite Langton Lane.[6] About 200 yards down the lane, on the east side, are Bullfinch Cottages, clearly timber-framed, and in the 1703 Danny Rental occupied by Abraham Muzzall[7] He was baptised in Hurst in 1677, and has been easily confused with Abel Muzzall, who was baptised in Albourne nine years later. Abel's 1703 rent for Neeves near West Town was 'a garland of red roses at Midsummer's Day in the morning'. The probate inventory of Abraham's goods a few years later indicates that, in common with others, he was able to achieve a level of self-sufficiency in addition to any income from his trade of cloth-worker:[8]

> September 27th Day 1712
> The true & perfect Inventory taken of all & every ye Goods, Chattels & all other ye personal estate whatsoever, of Abraham Muzzall Senr of ye pish of Hurstppoint Clothworker lately Deceased: by John Box of ye pish of Albourne, and John Stone of ye said parish of Hurstppoint in manner following (viz.)
>
> | | £ | s | d |
> |---|---|---|---|
> | or ffirst his purse & Apparel | 68 | 00 | 00 |
> | It[em] his books | 02 | 10 | 00 |

Five Cows at	18 00 00
Hay at	03 00 00
a Mow of White Pease at	07 00 00
Grey Pease Winnowed	01 05 00
Wheat Thrashed & unthrashed	03 00 00
a Mow of Barley	04 00 00
Oats unthrashed	02 00 00
five sieves & a Winnower	00 13 00
a half Bushel, Gallen & Shallow [tray]	00 04 00
Ten sacks	00 10 00
A Hay-Cutter & 5 prongs	00 05 00
a Gate	00 10 00
A Hog, Sow & nine Pigs	03 17 00
Wood, Fagots & a Wheelbarrow	02 00 00
A Shop of Tools as Saws Axes &c	00 12 00
two Spitters, a Shovel & Ladder	00 07 00
In the Kitchen	
A Table & a firm [form]	00 10 00
another Table	00 02 06
A Cubberd & Glass Cage	01 03 00
five Iron & Brass Pots a kittle, Morter & Pestle	01 04 00
two skillets, Grid-Irons, Slice, Tongs Fire-Pan,	00 10 00
Treft [triffet or trivet] Cleaver &c	
five Pewter Dishes, 9 Porengers & other small	00 12 00
things	
A Watch, Warming Pan, skimer & bras spoon	00 16 00
six Chairs a firm & stool	00 07 00
A Gun & other small things	00 10 00
a pare of Bellow & Pot Cubberd	00 02 00
A paire of Pot Hooks & spit	00 02 06
In the Middle Room	
A Cheese Press, hoops & fallows	00 10 00
Tubs & keelers	02 00 00
A Quarn [quern]	00 05 00
three Meal Bags & other small things	00 06 00
In the Milkhouse	
Nine Barrels	00 18 00
a Bacon Iron	00 10 00
A Table, frame & a Threelegg [stool]	00 07 00
A Tub	00 05 00
two Buckets & a Churn	00 06 06
three brass Kittles	01 05 00

three Trays	00 02 00
Pots, Crocks, Bottles & Pans	00 14 00
forty Cheeses & a Crock of Butter	03 19 06
A Lid[ded?] Pan & a Paire of Scales	00 04 00
a frying Pan	00 03 00
three meal sieves, Dishes & other small things	00 08 06
In the Sink	
five Buckets	00 04 00
in the Schoole & Chamber over	00 10 00
In the Milkhouse Chamber	
A Cheast & Linen in him	04 00 00
A Bedstead & Tester	00 05 00
A Close Stole & other things	00 05 00
In the Middle Chamber	
A parcel of fine Linen	01 10 00
A Bed with the furniture as he stands	03 00 00
A Trunk	00 05 00
three Cheasts	00 12 00
In the Kitchen Chamber	
A ffeather Bead with the furniture	04 10 00
A Trundle Bead & furniture	01 15 00
two Blankets	00 05 00
New Cloth	00 12 06
two Cheasts & boxes	
In the Closett	
Linen yarn, a Desk & box	00 12 00
two Silver Spoons	00 07 00
Debts due on his Book	06 10 08
unsite & unseen	00 10 00
Summa totalis	162 13 02

In today's money this would be something well in excess of £10,000.

Most cottages had a plot of land on which to grow vegetables, herbs and fruit; to keep a pig and some hens, and perhaps some beehives for honey, the normal sweetener before the first imports of sugar. In 1589 an Act was passed requiring such a plot to be at least four acres, the object being to encourage self-sufficiency and reduce the risk of the occupants becoming a charge on the parish. Mention has already been made of the temporary nature of some of the earlier, simpler dwellings. There is a suggestion that, if such a structure could be erected within one day, squatters' rights would have been established. It is certain that many such cottages were built on waste ground, away from the eyes of parish officials. Here, many of the wild plants that grew in the hedgerows, such as Fat Hen, Wild Orache and Hedge Garlic, were used to make potage, a stew thickened with oatmeal. Plants were also constituents of medicinal remedies, like comfrey roots used in the treatment of bruises and broken bones.

xvi. A skillet, a gridiron, a trencher and a tripod

Continuing down the lane, passing the two Victorian cottages, once known as Pokers Hole, close to the stream, a slight rise brings us to Wanbarrow Farm (called at some periods Swan Barrow). This provides an example of how a house could be enlarged, improved and embellished as the fortunes of the owners improved over the decades. The double range building is in fact two, as there is separate framing internally for each. There is evidence to suggest that the eastern portion was built *c*.1600, and may have originally had a hipped roof at both south and north ends. Within a generation the western range was added, but its earlier, heavier timber construction indicates that it was moved from elsewhere. In the first half of the eighteenth century a partition allowed the insertion of a fine staircase serving both ranges; a rear outshot was added; and the roof rebuilt to accommodate attics, where the living-in servants slept, separate stairs giving access to the men's and women's quarters. Much of the timber framing is visible inside the building. The roofs are mainly of Horsham stone, and while the north and south elevations have been tile-hung or brick-faced, the east front – the one first seen by a visitor – is faced with mathematical tiles.[9] By 1663 George Luxford had inherited the property from his father Richard and, with 40 acres, it was rented by Henry Scrase for £1 8s 4d, a sum which remained the same through subsequent rental records: in 1703 when the owner was William Marchant; in1719 when Peter Marchant had taken over; and in 1759 by the tenant James Harmes. Thomas Marchant frequently visited his widowed mother there.[10]

Plate 16.
Wanbarrow Farm.

Retracing our steps to Albourne Road and travelling east we come to Policeman's Lane. Until 1777 this was the continuation of the High Road, turning left at the bottom and then continuing east towards West Furlong Lane, and thence into the High Street. On the right-hand side of the bend is a delightful cottage called Cowdrays. Originally a much humbler building, parts of it date from *c.*1600. Thomas and Cordelia Cowdry lived there in 1631, and Richard Cowdry paid for one hearth under the 1662 Hearth Tax. By 1703 the occupier was Richard Cowdry, while the 1759 Rental record has an indecipherable surname after the first name of Mary, possibly a descendant of the Cowdrys. It was in the early eighteenth century that major alterations were recorded by Thomas Marchant in his diary:

1717. May 6th   Cowdry's old house was pull'd down. I was there several times during its demolition.

May 8th   . . . put the framing of Cowdry's old house to Tho Hamper at 3/-d per square out of the old timber and 3/-d per square for laying the floors and to fell, hew and saw what new timber is wanting into the bargain and to cleave, hew and put up the stantions or studs for the saddle walls. Mrs Beard is to pay for sawing the boards and he is to be paid for making the doors and putting up the partitions by the day.

Plate 17. Cowdray's.

The results of this work were probably extra flues to the chimneystack and the raising of the roof of the outshot to accommodate a staircase to a first-floor passage.[11]

On the eastern corner of the lane, and facing the High Street, is Treeps, surrounded by a high wall. In 1719, John Treep lived there; he was listed as a locksmith, but he appears to have been a man of many talents in metal, as recorded by Marchant:

1714. Dec. 24th.	Paid *my Lord Treep* [apparently a jocular term for a skilled artisan – he also referred to *my Lord Burt*, a farrier] 1s. Per week about Willy's gun.
1717. Janry. 16th.	Paid *my Ld. Treep* for new brazing a screw.
1719. Decr. 5th.	*My Lord Treep* put a ferral and pick to my stick.
1722. Octr. 29th.	. . . *My Lord Treep* here with Mr. Pointin's draught of a dial for old Brand's tomb, and carried it away again.

The archaeological evidence dates an original L-shaped structure, probably in three occupations, at *c.*1700-25, so Treep may have been the first occupier of just part of the building. A late Georgian up-date, which added a door-case and introduced sashes was carried out when two of the cottages were combined, and a Victorian addition, was followed by the twentieth century inclusion of the last cottage. Treep's interest in metal extended to his will dated 15 May 1729:

> I give unto six good ringers belonging to the parish of Hurstpierpoint 10/- for ring a good peall with the bells belonging to the said Parish Church, at least one hour long; so soon as my body is buried in the earth, my will is that the 10/- as soon as the peall is over should be spent on for them to drink together in a good and sober manner.[12]

Almost next-door is Home Cottage, the first in a line of cottages once known as Church Row. Its clapboarding hides a timber-framed building *c.*1550-1600 with an inglenook fireplace at its eastern end. Another peculiarity is the chalk walls in the cellar which may link its date to Tott Farm at the eastern end of the village which has chalk foundations and is estimated to date from the early 17th century. As Home cottage was probably not its original name, it cannot be traced in the rentals of that time, and previous owners in its early life are unknown.

Plate 18. Home Cottage – note the steep roof pitch, perhaps indicating earlier thatch.

A few yards further along the High Street is Dunstalls, and an old photograph of the rear of the house shows its timber frame. A 1662 Rental shows 'cottage and garden next the Church' occupied by Edward Hollingham, the rent being one shilling; by 1703 Thomas Dunstall, a mercer and a substantial enough tradesman to issue his own tokens, had 'one small cottage at the Churchyard.'; and the1719 rental showed John Dunstall, clerk, as the occupier.[13]

At the southeast corner of the churchyard, partly hidden from view, is Church House, in Queen Anne style. It has been said that the Reverend Jeremiah Dodson lived in London in 1666 and had suffered greatly losing some of his family in the Plague, and then his parish and his possessions in the Great Fire. Much distressed, he wrote to his relatives, the Courthopes of Danny, and was granted the living of Hurstpierpoint. He found the old rectory so unfit for habitation that the family lived over the stables for several decades until he was able to build on the foundation of an old farmhouse. As he did not become Rector until 1701, this story implies that he waited 35 years before taking up the living, and then lived a further 35 years before his son succeeded him in 1736. At least part of the present building is timber-framed, the front being hung with mathematical tiles; a large inglenook fireplace and a bacon loft still remain.[14]

On Church Green stands the coach-house built later by the Campions to accommodate the Danny coach while the family attended church. This open space was much larger than it is today and was used as a livestock market, with the village stocks, lock-up and pound all situated there.

Across the Brighton Road, the first house to be encountered in the 1700s would have been Bank House (now West End Cottage) set back from the line of the present street. Its size, shape and steep roof pitch all indicate a timber-frame behind the brick and tile. The rent-roll of 'The Manor of Hurstpierpointe' dated 8th April 1703, and already referred to in respect of several properties, gives the following information:

> Marchant Widd[ow], the only daughter and heir of Thomas Whitpaine, holdeth a Cottage called Banke in the possession of Charles Smith and pays £00-00-02.[15]

In line with Bank Cottage a few yards to the east is Chichester House, thus indicating the original building line before the Victorian built shops. It was originally called The Brick House as perhaps one of the earliest to be built of this material from the start. It has had many alterations over the years, and now extends along West Furlong Lane as Bieldside, previously Beals. The roof-space still has the old chimneystack in place, and a queen post in splendid isolation, its original function of roof support long gone. The house was part of the Pakyns estate sold in 1783 to Nathaniel Avery for £430 by the trustees of James and Henry Wood. In the late nineteenth century Chichester House provided accommodation for girls being trained in domestic service.

On the north side Down House which has wings projecting at right-angles to the front range. This was the Swan Inn at the time Thomas Marchant was writing his diary:

> 1716. Feby. 28th. Spent 2s. With Mr Pointing, the exciseman, at the Swan in the evening.[16]

The garden of the Mansion House is hidden behind high walls, its street frontage being a good example of brick facing to a timber-framed building. The 1636 Glebe Terrier describes some church land as:

> . . . abutting towards the north to a piece of ground of the same name of William Jordans the south to the Mansion House of the said William Jordan.[17]

but later maps indicate an area further to the south as being part of the glebe land, so this is unlikely to have been the building we now know by that name. It seems to have been part of the Pakyns estate, as it is listed in the Court Book of the Manor of Packens or Pacons in 1765, occupied by Thomas Bartley who paid

> Rent of a Capon on New Year's day in lieu thereof 2s 6d on the feast of St Michael the Archangel.

By 1773 Philip Soale, gentleman, was the owner of Pakyns, and the Mansion House was occupied by William Sayers; fourteen years later these two had been succeeded by William Borrer and John Sayers of Twineham respectively.[18] The foundations have been reported to have been built on tree trunks. If this is so, the first house on the site could have been erected in the middle of the twelfth century, as this method was not used after the reign of Stephen. Wattle-and-daub walls were still to be seen in the 1950s as infilling in the timber-frame construction. The house has been brick-faced on both its north and west elevations. The actual windows are sashes, first used in this country in the 1670s at Chatsworth, but not widely installed in lesser houses for some years. Like several other properties in the centre of the village, it later came into the ownership of the Weekes family:

> Hurstpierpoint Oct.28 [1801]
> . . . Mrs Beards house is repairing but goes on very slow, have put in new sashes, stopt up 2 in front & made a large window west end for a drawing room above stairs.[19]

Here is confirmation that the 'stopt up' windows had nothing to do with avoidance of the window tax introduced in 1697 (and not abolished until

1851), but were a direct result of the improvements made by Richard Weekes, the local doctor.

Nestling against the eastern wall is Mansion House Cottage, with a large sitting-room on the ground floor with an inglenook fireplace and a separate bread oven; hooks on a central beam and wide doors originally leading to the Mansion House and its cellars, and further hooks on a beam on the upper floor suggest a kitchen and storage space belonging to the main property.

Seen through the iron gate of the Mansion House Cottage is the west wall of the New Inn (see Colour Plate 9), showing timber-framing and early windows that may originally have had rabbit skin stretched over the openings to let in some light. This building, behind the rendered frontage, is a 4-bay Wealden house *c.*1500 with a single bay hall, the joisting for the upper floor being of seventeenth century style. It did not become an inn until the early nineteenth century, when the justices finally ordered the closure of the Royal Oak on the opposite side of the street. A drawing by Thomas Henwood in the 1830s (see page 303) shows stables extending to the east, essential accommodation for riding horses and the carriage trade of the period.[20] The church vestry meetings were at one time at the New Inn, the advantage of having liquid refreshment on hand for thirsty talkers must have been an incentive to attend.

Plate 19. Wickham House.

On the opposite side of the street is Wickham House, like Wanbarrow a double-pile and faced with mathematical tiles, possibly made at the Keymer Brick Company, in an eighteenth century embellishment, similar to many examples in Lewes. The 'quoins' are of wood, in contrast to the actual cornerstones of the Mansion House. The rear elevation is in brick, displaying the date 1739 in two places, but the interior timber-work indicates that the southern range is slightly earlier. A high-level door in the east wall suggests storage for some commercial enterprise, probably with a hoist for raising goods from ground level.

The centre of the village would have been where the various traders would have set up their stalls in medieval times. Each would have had his own allotted space for a trestle table, with perhaps a canopy over to protect goods from the weather. Eventually these stalls became part of more permanent buildings with plots of land at the rear, known as burgage plots. The average frontage was 16 feet – one rod, pole or perch in old measurement. The occupiers were known as burghers or burgesses and became involved in the running of village affairs. The present Post Office and its neighbours, together with the three shops opposite, may well have been the original burgage plots; No 103, at present a greengrocer's, has a low ceiling and a floor below street level, and a large roof timber was removed after damage in the 1987 gale. All of these properties have frontages of about 16 feet, and the Fisher map of 1841 shows land behind each, now taken up with other buildings.

A few hundred yards to the north of the High Street, via the twitten to Trinity Road, lies Little Park (see Colour Plate 10), originally part of the demesne lands of the Manor of Hurstpierpoint, the Great Park being what we now know as Danny. There is evidence that the original Pierpoint manor house was situated near the church (probably where the terrace of cottages on the north side of the High Street now stands), while a survey of 1570 records that the park was one and a half miles round and contained 80 deer and a large pond for carp and tench 'fit for the lord's table.' [21] Parts of the double-pile house we can now see show evidence of late fifteenth century construction, with an open hall extending southwards beyond the present frontage. In 1664 Little Park was sold to Mrs Anne Swayne by Sir William Juxon, the executor of his uncle's estate. This uncle was the Archbishop of Canterbury who, when Bishop of London, had received the last words of

Charles I on the scaffold. The Archbishop had died the previous year, so there is a possibility that it may have formed part of his estate; his brother John owned Albourne Place at the same period, further evidence of family interests in the neighbourhood. The transaction is also an example of the developing financial strength of the 'middling sort', as they became increasingly able to purchase properties of this size and quality.[22] It was purchased from Mrs Swayne's son Richard by Thomas Marchant of Albourne, yeoman, for his son William in or just before 1677, as on the west elevation, with its Dutch-style double gables and sliding upper storey windows, a rainwater head bears this date and the initials W M M – for William and Mary Marchant.

Plate 20. Little Park: dated rainwater head; note also the fire mark to the left of the downpipe.

Their son Thomas was our celebrated eighteenth century diarist, who has proved to be such a valuable source of contemporary information for almost every chapter of this book. The present entrance is through an archway in an elaborate nineteenth century stepped chimneystack, while earlier brickwork is evident on an eastern extension to this south front. Inside there is a large inglenook with a bread oven, and a Jacobean privy on the first floor with a visible outlet at ground level.[23]

The house was insured against fire in 1723, the Sun Fire Office mark 26884 being displayed on the premises. The dwelling itself was covered for £200, the contents for £100, and the barns and their contents for another £300, a clear indication of the relative value of his farming operation. We are dealing here with a different stratum of society from the cottager. The poor had simple furniture: stools, benches, and a trestle table, with perhaps the prized possession of one chair. The yeomen, merchants and gentry had their furniture made by craftsmen, much of it enhanced with delicate carving. Their principal rooms were often panelled, again with carving, an example being the stylised carp in which Thomas Marchant traded in one of the rooms at Little Park.

Plate 21. Jacobean privy *en suite* with the kitchen chamber (the room above the kitchen).

Thomas often consulted Timothy Burrell, a barrister who lived at Ockenden House, Cuckfield. His journal, covering the thirty or so years before the Marchant diary, gives insights into the social activities of this group of people. His Christmas guest list in 1707 contains several Hurst names:

> Walter Gatland, G and J Savage, Rt Chatfield, T Uwins, Mrs Luxford.

A typical menu during the festive season included:

> calves head and bacon, goose [twice during the meal], pig, roast beef (sirloin), veale (a loin), boiled beef (a clod)[the cut at neck and shoulder] and plumm pottage [three times]; two baked puddings, three dishes of mince pies; two capons; two dishes of tarts; two pullets.

The recipe for plumm pottage was given in the editorial notes:

> Take of beef-soup made of legs of beef, 12 quarts, if you wish to
> be particularly good, ad a couple of tongues to be boiled therein.
> Put fine bread, sliced, soaked, and crumbled; raisins of the sun,
> currants and pruants, two lbs. of each; lemons, nutmegs, mace,
> and cloves are to be boiled with it in a muslin bag; add a quart of
> red wine, and let this be followed, after half an hour's boiling, by
> a pint of sack. Put it a cool place and it will keep through
> Christmas. This was the national dish for the happy season of
> Christmas.

Another popular dish was firmity, eaten on Refreshment Sunday in mid-Lent
to recall the gospel of the miracle of the loaves and fishes: the corn of wheat
deprived of its skin was gently boiled, and the yolks of eggs, with sugar and
flour, currants, raisins and grated cinnamon were added. It was a great relief
after severe fasting.

Plate 22. Little Park: two bread ovens in the kitchen.

Like the cottagers, presents of food were exchanged regularly, but they went
beyond eggs and vegetables. In 1712 he received:

a noble dish of trouts; a leveret; a fine goos; a noble hare;
13 pigeons; and a number of oatcakes [from Mrs Dodson].[24]

Plate 23. Little Park: salt box.

When Thomas Marchant died in 1728, his probate inventory showed him to
be financially of much greater substance than Abraham Muzzall sixteen
years earlier. Marchant had ten oxen, five carthorses and four riding horses,
and 130 other farm animals. The corn and hay in his great barn alone were
worth more than all Muzzall's goods and chattels together; he had much
more furniture, including leather-covered chairs and a long-case clock, a
considerable quantity of linen and some silver. He also owned a 'towne
house,' clearly a separate property, and his whole estate was valued at just
under £1,000, more than £70,000 today.[25]

Shopkeepers were increasing in number and prosperity, indeed challenging
the yeoman farmer in this respect. William Courtness was a dealer in cloth
and other items in the early eighteenth century and featured in the same 1703
Rental as holding three acres, part of Hatches, land two or three hundred
yards to the south of the village. His shop may have been there or more
centrally placed in the High Street. His probate inventory in 1721 recorded a
total value of £639 12s 10d. So, not just a mercer, but a grocer, spirit
merchant and hardware retailer as well – and certainly more prosperous than

the cloth-worker Abraham Muzzall. For comparison we find that Edmund Buckwell, a smallholder with cattle and pigs and at least two acres of arable land, left goods and chattels valued at £57 12s 9d in March 1710; and a year later William Webb, a thatcher, had worldly goods worth less than £19.[26]

Near the High Street end of the twitten we come to Upper Trumpkins (now Hamilton Lodge Interiors). This delightful building has had its timbers on the ground floor exposed by the present owner for all to see. The inglenook is still in place, and was at one time double-sided, suggested by the lay-out of the rooms, one each side of the chimney-stack. The original entrance may have faced the street. There are signs of an outshot at the rear to the eastern side, indicated by an old doorway. At some time part of the eastern side of the building was incorporated into its neighbour. The staircase to the first floor has long gone, but that to the attic appears to be original, complete with its newel post, much worn by many hands, perhaps an indication that the original house was built on three floors. Among the visible internal timbers is a dragon beam like that at Pigwidgeon, again providing jetties on two elevations, but this time at the south-west angle of the house, and on the first floor the wide floorboards run diagonally over this beam. Like many buildings of its age it was enlarged on the ground floor to occupy the space below the jetty on the west. Sliding windows on the first and second floors, all visible from the High Street, are evidence of seventeenth century alterations. The 1663 Rental lists a West Trumpkins owned by Thomas Moore, who had to pay tax on two hearths the previous year; by 1759 the owner was William Borrer, and in later times the Woolgar family.

There is some confusion over the separate parts of Trumpkins, a holding that extended from the present narrow part of the street eastwards to the land opposite South Avenue. By 1703 Upper Trumpkins, including a garden and an orchard, was owned by Robert Smith, but the same document states:

> Stephen Byne holdeth a cottage and garden called Lower Trumpkins and pays 02d, also another garden platte parte of Upper Trumpkins and pays 01d.[27]

Immediately opposite Upper Trumpkins was a row of timber-framed cottages known as Hardings, very modest dwellings, but considered valuable by their owner Richard Herriott, a mason, as he, like Thomas Marchant, took care to insure them against fire. In 1703 a man called Jeffery was 'the holder of a tenement in Hurst Town in the possession of Thomas Westover and two widows . . . called Hardings'.[28] When Richard Bevan became Rector at the turn of the nineteenth century he found the cottages to be so dilapidated that he bought them and adjoining properties in order build Card's Place.

Plate 24. Hardings, now Card's Place.

At least two more timber-framed houses on the north side of the High Street are disguised behind rendered facades. Grape Vine Cottage was originally Trumpkins, a name which included the Poacher public house next door and the premises of Harper and Eede, both the yard and the small building used as a shop window. Like many houses of a similar age, it has lost some of its original shape and gained some modern extensions. Originally there was probably one large room, a passage running from front to back, and two smaller rooms on the eastern side. The inglenook fireplace retains its old bressumer beam with two hooks still in place. There may have been a passage between the chimney wall and the pub next door, as the back of the bread-oven is filled in. A cupboard under the stairs has old floor tiles, perhaps the floor of the old kitchen – the present one being a rear outshot under a cat-slide roof. The first floor shows much of its timber framing, the chimney diverted into an outside stack and the floor extended over the space behind the fireplace. The rental of 1663 lists the building as copyhold to Henry Fowle and occupied by Thomas Moore. By 1719 Thomas Hamper had one part and William King another. Forty years later John and Thomas Hamper were the tenants. In 1839 Henry Brown, a saddle-maker, is listed; two years later the Fisher map shows Jane Brown as a saddler and harness-maker. The Poacher part of the property was owned in 1841 by John Spratley, a maltster, while wheelwright John Mitchell was also listed – evidence that two trades have continued on the site to the present day, albeit in modified forms.[28]

No.157, for many years a shop, but identified as Lower Trumpkins, is set back slightly from the row. As with Grape Vine Cottage, the large ground-floor room is dominated by a huge inglenook fireplace, with a bread-oven on the side. High on the wall above is an ornate carved door, about eighteen inches square, opening for an old spice cupboard, popular in better houses around the 1670s. The East India Company's ships which were bringing the currants and spices made a great difference to the flavour and variety of food, life gradually becoming more comfortable for those fortunate enough to be able to afford such things. The timber-framing suggests an earlier date, and again the main room may have been divided by a cross-passage from two service rooms on the eastern side. The staircase has been moved at least twice, the first time probably when a second range was added to the north. On the second floor an ornate door, of the late 1600s, with an old wooden latch, leads into a room with wooden panelling of similar date. The upper section of the chimney warms the room above the fireplace, and has a panelled cupboard with ornate 'cock's head' hinges, a type made from 1628 onwards. The attics of the two ranges are still separated by the original walls, but doors now connect them. These attics were sometimes let to single tradesmen as workshops; during repairs in 1990 the floorboards were removed to disclose mats of felt built up by cotton threads falling through over the years, so the tradesman in this case may have been Jesse Knight, listed as a tailor in the 1841 schedule to the Fisher map – again evidence of some sort of continuity, as for many years of the twentieth century Miss Woolgar sold all manner of items connected with this type of activity. In the garden there is a Victorian wash-house, complete with its copper and large sink, and a separate privy about ten feet from the house.

Continuing east along the highway, Tott Farm (see Colour Plate 11) lies just to the south on steeply sloping ground, with the north end of the building actually cut into the slope, the whole structure supported on a chalk base. The name has a similar derivation to Knowles Tooth to the northwest of the parish, and means 'look-out', an example of an entirely appropriate title. The house, probably dating from the early seventeenth century, is much larger than most farmhouses, being three storeys high with a central group of six chimneystacks and an enormous cat-slide roof to the rear covering a two-storey outshot. Each floor of the main range has two principal rooms, with a further number on each floor of the outshot. The southern room on the ground floor has a large cooking hearth, while the northern part was ideally cool enough to be a dairy until recently. Robert Whitpaine held Tott early in the seventeenth century, dying in 1662. His son, also Robert, was a minor, and it would appear that in 1663 Tott may have been rented by John Smith, until Robert came of age. In 1715 Thomas Marchant records:

> April 30th. Let the house at Tott to James Burt, reserving the tan yard.[29]

Early maps show a Tanner's Field to the south of the farmhouse, but the precise location of the tanyard has not been established.

About two hundred yards north of the highway, in College Lane, is Wickham Farmhouse which demonstrates an earlier means of providing more headroom in the roof space, that of dropped-tie construction (as suggested at the beginning of this chapter, technical details should be sought elsewhere). This method does not appear until c.1580, continuing until c.1700, the proportions of the house suggesting a date of c.1625. This was a property of some status, and this is confirmed by documentary evidence of the name de Wykham occurring as early as 1296 in tax returns, supporting other evidence that it was part of Wickham manor before the Conquest.[30]

This one walk has shown us many of the timber-framed houses of the parish, but even with the diversions by no means all. As well as Wanbarrow, several of the outlying farmhouses have their own stories to tell of changes in fortune over the years.

To the south of the village, off the Brighton Road, lies Randolphs Farm which was originally a late fifteenth century 4-bay open hall, with door-heads still indicating the entrances to the buttery and pantry. Probably in the second half of the sixteenth century an external chimneystack was built and a floor inserted to provide rooms in an upper storey.

This was followed in the middle of the next century by adding more stacks, re-roofing the gables, encasing the house with a brick skin, inserting stone mullion windows, and creating a new attic floor. This was an exercise showing considerable investment and much pride in status, indicated by the date 1643 and the initials TL (for Thomas Luxford) on the studded door. Further extension took place in Victorian times, consisting of a large northwest wing and a small dairy. All this is evidence of a continuing rise in prosperity for the owners over a long period.[31]

Plate 25. Randolphs Farm.

To the north of the village are several more farmhouses. In Malthouse Lane Kents Farm was originally a 3-bay house of the second half of the seventeenth century, indicated by square framing and the lack of bracing in walls or roof. At least one, possibly two, external contemporary chimneys tend to support the later dating. However, much of the timber shows evidence of re-use, perhaps coming from an earlier house on the site. An outshot to the west was not original, as the west wall of the main range is weathered. It was raised to two storeys in Georgian times, thus obscuring clues to earlier work. As it stands at present the east facade is symmetrical, but this may date from the period when the house was furnished with a brick skin and tile hanging. Further along the same road is Grasmere, identified as another example of a Wealden house.

Stuckles, near the north-western boundary of the Sayers Common part of the parish, was in the middle of the seventeenth century the residence of Richard Butcher, who incurred the displeasure of the courts over his maintenance failures, but when he died it became the subject of an indenture entered into by no less than eight individuals, indicating the importance of the farming land around it. Nearby New House Farm is yet another example of substantial properties arising from increasing agricultural prosperity.[32]

There are many other timber-framed houses worthy of mention, but space does not permit individual descriptions. Perhaps one out of all of them will underline the processes of extension, alteration and adaptation that have gone on over the centuries. Bearstakes, down New Way Lane, started as a hall house, probably early in the sixteenth century, with a roof hipped at each end. The hall was floored over, and an eighteenth century two-storey extension was added at one end with a gable to provide extra space on the first floor. In Victorian times a wing was built out at a right angle to this extension. In the mid-twentieth century the central floor was removed to return to the interior hall design, exposing the original down-braces and roof-timbers, as well as three early windows of the type already seen at the New Inn.

BRICK AND STONE

Mention has already been made of the gradual introduction of complete brick and stone building, as opposed to the earlier practice of infilling a timber-framed structure. Although some timber framing may have continued into Georgian times, there is evidence that in Hurst most substantial houses built from the reign of Queen Anne onwards were of brick or stone or a combination of the two. It was probably the advent of the new buildings that prompted the cladding of existing houses to give the appearance of modernity. Bricks of about 2 ¼ inches in thickness were the norm until improved methods enabled slightly larger ones to be made, but a major increase to three inches occurred when in 1784 a Brick Tax was levied on numbers, irrespective of size. In 1803 a change in the law claimed double duty on extra large bricks, so the thickness eventually stabilised at about 2 5/8 inches.[33]

Of course, our earliest house with an all-brick exterior, and also our best-known, predates this period by two hundred years. In 1570 there was a

> fair mansion house of timber work lying within the Park of Dannye whereat the keeper lyeth who hath the custody thereof; the same being moated about, two parts of the said moat being always with water, replenished with roach and carp. . . the house and scyte within the same mote containing 180 feet long and 80 feet broad. . .the hall lyeth on the south side containing 43 feet long 24 feet broad having no other storye and at the higher south end thereof a faier parlour containing 28 feet long and 20 feet broad of two storyes; the lower storye having two fair bay windows. . .'[34]

George Goring built the one we see today, starting *c.*1580 and completing it *c.*1595. It followed the common design of large Elizabethan mansions in the eastward facing E-shape (see Colour Plate 12). The structure is of stone, with brick facing. Narrow Tudor bricks were made in the grounds, the normal practice at the time. A reflection of earlier times may be conjectured in the presence of a great hall – certainly it was one of the last to contain such a large room. The failure of the Royalist cause meant that Peter Courthope was able to buy it from Commonwealth speculators in 1650 for £550. Just over fifty years later Barbara Courthope married Henry Campion, and they altered the south wing by facing it in Queen Anne style (see Colour Plate 13), demonstrating that it was not only timber-framed houses that were adapted in line with current fashion.

For most of the next two and a half centuries the family lived the quiet but influential life of country squires. It did, however, achieve national importance briefly: in 1918 it was used by David Lloyd George when he was Prime Minister, and several War Cabinet meetings were held, culminating in the drafting of the terms of the Armistice which ended hostilities on 11 November. In 1947 it became a school, and is now divided into apartments for retired people.

A more modest example is Abberton, just to the east of the High Street. Built in Queen Anne style, it was later in the eighteenth century occupied by Peter Morfee, steward of the Manor of Hurstpierpoint, and was known as Morfees until Dr Henry Holman bought it in 1823 and renamed it Rose Hill. The conveyance of the property was couched in lengthy legalistic terms with much repetition; one can only hope that the parties to the agreement understood it all. One thing is certain: the price was £450, and included the purchase of

> . . . all that Pew or Seat Room in the Parish Church of Hurstperpoint aforesaid marked with No.1 situate in the South Gallery of the said Church and full and free Liberty of Ingrese Egrese and Togrese in to and from the same at all convenient times of Divine Service and all other reasonable times. . .

After Henry Holman's death his brother Constantine sold it in 1881 to William Wood, a Clayton miller, for £1800, Constantine Holman paying 'succession duty' at 3% of the £63 annual rental value, £1 17s.10d. Ten years later Wood conveyed it to a Miss Willett at the same figure, perhaps an indicator of the stagnation of the property market during a period of agricultural recession.[35]

Almost at the northern boundary of the parish is Oaklands Park, also known from time to time as High Hatch Manor or Gothards Green Farm, built at about the same time to replace an earlier building of which no record remains. It is a triple-range building of stone with brick cladding and stone mullion windows. In the 1850s a serious fire destroyed the central portion, which was rebuilt in typical Victorian style, complete with turret

The surrounding farms being already long-established, it is to the rising professional and trading classes that we must attribute the next phase of new building. They came into prominence with the increase in population and the significant reduction in subsistence food production. As will be seen in a later chapter, William Courtness's business was succeeded by many and varied shops serving the wider demands of the people. Throughout the nineteenth century a number of family villas was erected, most of them in the centre of the village. One family in particular gave impetus to the trend.

Richard Weekes was a successful doctor who not only undertook substantial alterations to the Mansion House as we have seen, but rebuilt the house in which he lived, Matts (now Norfolk House) in the High Street, and owned 150 years earlier by Christopher Swale. He also owned Dene House (the present Rectory in Cuckfield Road), Norton House two doors from Matts, and later Hampton Lodge at the eastern end of the High Street, named after one of his doctor sons. Interestingly, Howard Lodge at the western end of the street has a facade, which is the mirror image of Hampton Lodge, so they were probably built at about the same time in 1832.

Carey Hampton Borrer used what is now Chantry House as his rectory, and made major alterations to the property. Not only were there twelve children to accommodate, but he also reversed the aspect of the house in order to be able to look out over Little Park rather than the High Street.

When Richard Bevan succeeded Borrer as Rector, he had the Red House (now Furlong House) built with a view towards the Downs, and this remained the Rectory until 1954.

Charles Smith Hannington founded the successful Brighton store, which still bears the name, and in the 1840s purchased St George's as his family home.

There are many other dwellings in the parish with interesting architectural features, some original, some later alterations and embellishments that provide evidence of changes of life style through the centuries. While some new houses are designed to be as up-to-date as possible, others hark back to earlier times – Braky Platt along the Cuckfield Road was built in 1926 – so we need always to look for the tell-tale features which indicate the origins of each house and its extensions.

NOTES AND REFERENCES

For further reading see: Harris R (1993): *Discovering Timber-Framed Buildings*; Powell C (1996): *Discovering Cottage Architecture*; Brunskill R W (1985): *Timber Building in Britain*; Brunskill R W (1990): *Brick Building in Britain*; Mason R T (1964): *Framed Buildings of the Weald*; Johnson M (1993): *Housing Culture*.

1. ESRO survey 1951; ESRO DAN 1115.
3. Harrison W (1587): *The Manner of Building and Furniture of our Houses*, in Furnivall F J (ed)(1877): *Harrison's Description of England in Shakespeare's Youth*, Part 1, 233–42.
4. WBSG (1997): site visit notes.
5. ESRO/DAN 1118.
6. Unpublished diaries of Carey Hampton Borrer, Vol 2: 7, 13, 16 January 1837
7. ESRO/DAN 1119.
8. ESRO/WINV354.
9. Martin D (1992): Survey 1992/69, Field Archaeology Unit, Institute of Archaeology, University College London; Hughes A (1997): site visit report.
10. ESRO/ DAN 1118, 1123; ESRO Adams MS 554; Turner E (ed)(1873): The Marchant Diary, *SAC* **25**, 172, 173.
11. Burchall M J (1980): *Sussex Hearth Tax Assessments 1662*, 12; ESRO/ Adams MS 554; Turner, Marchant, *SAC* **25**, 181; unpublished Marchant Diary; Hughes A (1997): site visit report.
12. ESRO/DAN 1123; Turner, Marchant, *SAC* **25**, 170, 186, 192; Hughes A (1997): site visit report; Manchester V (ud, ?1976): *Memories of Hurst*, 14.
13. ESRO/DAN 1118; ESRO/ Adams MS 554; Caldecott J B (1943): The Penfold Bequest: Coins and Tokens, *SAC* **83**, 112.
14. Herbison V (1979): Hurstpierpoint: kind and charitable, *Sussex Life*, June 1979, 22.
15. ESRO/DAN 1123.
16. Turner, Marchant, *SAC* **25**, 175.
17. WSRO/Par 400/7/1.
18. *Ibid.*; WSRO/ ADD MS 32,970.
19. *Guide to Hurstpierpoint – Festival of Britain Edition* (1951); Ford J M T (9187): *The Weekes Family Letters*, 57.
20. WBSG (1997): site visit report.
21. Turner, Marchant, *SAC* **25**, 165.
22. WSRO/ ADD MS 22,155.
23. WBSG (1997): site visit report.
24. Blencow R W (ed)(1850): Journal and Account Book of Timothy Burrell Esq, *SAC* **2**, 152–3, 164.

25. Guildhall Library MS 11,936/14; ESRO/ MF XA26/20.
26. ESRO/W/FNV265.
27. ESRO/DAN 1118.
28. Sun Fire Policy 350155; ESRO/DAN 1119.
29. WBSG (1997): site visit report; ESRO/ DAN 1118.
30. Hughes A (1999): site visit report; Turner, Marchant, *SAC* **25**, 176.
31. Hughes A (1999): site visit report.
32. WBSG (1997): site visit report; WSRO/ ADD MS 21,251.
33. Brunskill, *Brick Building,* 37–8.
34. British Library MS 5638, f 185.
35. WSRO/ ADD MSS 35,872–8.

6. THE PARISH AND ITS POOR

In this chapter we shall be looking into the lives of the poorest in Hurst during the period (1601-1834) when the parish itself, through its own officers, was legally responsible for their care, and for the cost of that care. To make more sense of this, we shall need to remind ourselves of the national picture, and glance both forwards to when control was taken out of the hands of the parish in the later nineteenth century, and backwards to the less formal arrangements of earlier times.

Communities have long recognised that their poorer members need support. Before 1500 the monasteries, fraternities and guilds provided networks from which help could be obtained. At a local level stocks of materials were maintained in order to provide work for the able-bodied, while almshouses and church poor-box collections attempted to give shelter and succour to the very young, the very old, and the infirm. In contrast, the state, influenced by humanistic attitudes, was interested only in controlling labour and eliminating idleness, dirt, disease and indiscipline by punishing beggars and vagrants. The problems had always been there, and measures were introduced to tackle vagrancy, death and plague, but the Dissolution removed the main charity framework, the problems increased, and so did the legislation. Between 1531 and 1834 no less than 51 Acts of Parliament were directly concerned with these matters.[1]

> Laws grind the poor, and rich men rule the law.
> Goldsmith: The Traveller (1764)

In 1536 the Council's concern with public order led Thomas Cromwell to require parishes to provide work for vagabonds and to put poor children out to service. For the rest of the century piecemeal legislation further established the parish as the unit of administration, and these laws were consolidated in the last years of Elizabeth I's reign. Much of the money raised from rates and doles by the Vagrancy and Relief of the Poor Acts of 1598 and 1601, and administered by the churchwardens and overseers, was given to paupers living at home, although almshouses did already exist. Further Acts were passed during succeeding decades, until the Poor Law Amendment Act of 1834 dramatically changed the system under which the poor of this country existed.[2]

'Books of Orders' in the reigns of Elizabeth I, James I and Charles I attempted to deal with bad harvests and outbreaks of disease by regulating the sale of grain stocks to the poor, but also by requiring reports of numbers of vagrants punished, alehouses closed and poor children bound as apprentices. The theory was that poverty spelled danger – deal with drunkards, bastard-bearers and other idlers, and poverty would be eradicated. On the other hand, it was accepted that the genuinely poor needed help. One way of establishing entitlement was to ascertain everyone's home parish – where they were born, where they had lived and worked, or where they came after marriage. The formal expression of this notion came eventually in the Settlement Act of 1662, leading to many disputes between parishes, many representations in the Courts, and much bureaucracy.[3]

THE PARISH HAS TO PAY

In rural parishes the adoption of poor rates took effect only slowly, with about a third doing so by 1660. Hurst was in the forefront of this activity, with evidence of a rate being raised for this purpose in 1629.[4] The document refers to 'the later p[ar]te of the year', so may we assume that at least two demands were made within the year? Some 80 occupiers of land and property were rated for a total of £28. 3s, equivalent to almost £2,000 in today's money. There is no indication as to how many paupers were relieved by this rate, but a generally accepted dole in the early 17th century was 6d a week, rising to 1s by the 1660s. If we take the former figure, it implies that about 43 out of an estimated total population at that time of 660 were in need of financial support, some 6.5%. These figures do not match the national ones that started to become available some 70 years later and showed only 3.6% of the population being relieved. There may have been some other local factor not revealed in the document. Certainly the 1629 rate compares very unfavourably with that for 1780, when £203. 17s 8d was raised for the whole year from 147 ratepayers out of a population nearing 1000, although by 1834 the figure was £731. 4s 4d.[5] This last period was one of apparently inexorable rise over much of the country, provoking eventually the Poor Law Amendment Act of 1834 and the building of the large Union workhouses, such as ours at Cuckfield which abolished out-relief and segregated men from women and children.

This was only the latest in a number of attempts over the years to deter claims for relief. In 1697 every pauper 'shall wear upon the shoulder of the right sleeve . . . a large Roman P together with the first letter of the name of [his] parish . . .' (although this edict was soon abandoned).[6] In 1723 parish officers were authorised to buy or rent workhouses and deny outdoor relief to those who refused to enter them. This helped to stabilise matters for a while, but population and price rises after 1760 brought inevitable increased unemployment, exacerbated by poor harvests and after the end of the Napoleonic Wars, when poor relief costs went spiralling out of control.[7]

To underline the full horror of the 1723 Workhouse Test Act look at George Crabbe's poem 'The Village', written in 1783 – a poem, yes, with a degree of poetic licence, maybe, and certainly with a political axe to grind, but describing vividly the kind of small poorhouse then in use:

> Theirs is yon house that holds the parish poor,
> Whose walls of mud scarce bear the broken door;
> There, where the putrid vapours flagging, play,
> And the dull wheel hums doleful through the day;
> There children dwell who know no parents' care,
> Parents, who know no children's love, dwell there;
> Heart-broken matrons on their joyless bed,
> Forsaken wives and mothers never wed;
> Dejected widows with unheeded tears,
> And crippled age with more than childhood-fears;
> The lame, the blind, and, far the happiest they!
> The moping idiot and the madman gay.
>
> Here too the sick their final doom receive,
> Here brought amid the scenes of grief, to grieve;
> . . .
> Here sorrowing, they each kindred sorrow scan,
> And the cold charities of man to man.[8]
> . . .

Even a writer with a less polemical approach was unhappy: 'All about it is solid, substantial, useful – but so dreary! so cold! so dark! . . . I always hurry past that place as if it were a Prison'.[9]

CHARITY

Was Hurstpierpoint as bad as this? We may find out as the story unfolds. Before 1629, the date of the Poor Rate mentioned above, there is no evidence of parish-controlled relief. Wills of the 16th and early 17th centuries show that personal charitable bequests were not uncommon, and were still being made after the Elizabethan legislation came into force. These were usually in the form of funeral doles, sums of money distributed at or soon after the funeral at the discretion of the executors. A few examples from many will suffice: in 1580 Thomas Whitpaine provided that 6s 8d should be given to the 'poore of the parishe'; Richard Chatfield in 1603 increased the amount to 40s; and both Thomas Luxford in 1620 and his widow Mary in 1625 gave similar sums.[10] There may be a slight suspicion that these distributions not only helped the poor a little, but also shed a favourable light on the testators, particularly those who believed that their souls would be judged on their earthly actions. A century later, what appears to be a somewhat lower level of charitable thought – more likely an avoidance of financial penalty – is found in the diary of ThomasMarchant of Little Park. On October 9th 1727 he arranged for the distribution of 50s 'forfeited to the poor for burying [his mother-in-law] in linen' during the period (from 1678 to 1815) when an Act of Parliament required woollen shrouds.[11]

> Then the great man helped the poor,
> And the poor man loved the great.
> Macaulay: Horatius (1842)

However, 40 shillings in the early 1600s would be nearly £150 today, so the bequests were not insignificant.

Of greater long-term importance were several major bequests, some of which are still bearing fruit today. Henry 'Dog' Smith was a wealthy member of the City of London Salters Company who was concerned about the paupers who had lost the help given in earlier centuries by the religious houses. Before his death in 1627 he had already given large sums to a number of causes, including 'impotent and aged poor' who were to be given 'apparel of one colour and badge' as a sign that it was Smith's gift (a forerunner of the 1697 Act!) or '. . . bread, flesh and fish'. Part of his estate was a farm at Tolleshunt D'Arcy in Essex, worth in the mid 17th century £140 a year, and this income was clearly wisely invested, as a number of parishes in various counties have been beneficiaries ever since.[12] Hurst is among them, receiving in 1642 £8 and in 1996 over one hundred times that amount; when adjustment has been made for the difference in purchasing power, the current distribution has over twice the value of 350 years ago.

A century after 'Dog' Smith, Leonard Letchford gave £100, the interest to provide 10s yearly to '10 poor aged people or having great charge of children', while in 1875 Samuel Hannington set up a trust to provide help for seven poor parishioners, and later still St Christopher's Home was built a hundred years ago.[13] Other benefactors include William Hamper in 1829 and Dr Avery Roberts in Sayers Common in 1862. The churchwardens and overseers were responsible for the distribution of most of these funds – Thomas Marchant refers to both Smith and Letchford in his diary in the early 18th century,[14] in 1789 the Henry Smith distribution 'was delivered out in Beef by John Burry the 16 Nov', the amounts ranging from 1 stone [14lbs] to 2 stone 4lbs [15] – and, with the Parish Council, this still continues, although the meat changed to fuel at some time in the past, and is now in the form of vouchers.

CONTROLLING THE COST

In spite of these examples of individual concern, from the time of the Tudor legislators onwards it became increasingly apparent that statutory support would be needed for the large numbers of paupers in many parishes. So far as Sussex is concerned, this problem was, and would remain, more obvious in the 'open' Wealden parishes than in the smaller Downland villages under the close control of resident squires (for example, Stanmer was never troubled with the raising of a Poor Rate). Hurst has its southern boundary touching the Downs, its northern one well into the Low Weald, so we might expect to find an intermediate situation arising. But we know already that a great deal of money had to be raised in 1629, so there can be no doubt that a serious problem existed. After that date we have no documentary evidence until the last quarter of the 18th century. From then until 1835 we can follow the rising cost of poor relief being borne by those occupiers of land and property who were not themselves in need.

In 1776 the Poor Rate produced £367, but the cost was £472. In the next few years matters improved temporarily, the average expenditure from 1783-85 reducing to £376, while the books were less accurately, if more happily, balanced with an average of £594 raised from just under 100 occupiers. But it was a relative calm before the storm. Twenty years later costs were four times greater, a rate of ten shillings in the pound producing £2456 to cover outgoings of £2419. In the first years of the 19th century no less than 22.6% of the population of Sussex were receiving relief in one form or another. By the 1830s the rate had rocketed to more than £1. 6s in the pound.[16] With those figures in mind, it is small wonder that the officers made strenuous efforts to keep the parish commitment to the minimum.

Apprenticeships were arranged whereby poor children were removed from parish liability to acquire some skills, either in a specific craft such as shoemaking, tailoring or weaving, or more generally in husbandry or housewifery. For example, we find an

> Agreement between Mrs Laugham & Wm Acton Overseer of Hurstperpoint for Ann Farncomb to be put Aprentice to A Mantuamaker for one Year from the 12th of July 1790 to the 12th of July 1791 Mrs Laugham to be alowed three Shillens per week for her board & Lodging and One pound one Shillen for Aprentice & two Shifts & one pr of Shues
> Mary Laugham

On the same day 'Mr Gower Agrees to pay the Overseer of Hurstperpoint 6d pr week so Long as Michael Farncomb Works for him'.[17]

If this was not appropriate, 'putting-out' could be adopted. In 1790 a Mr Picknall of Wivelsfield agreed 'to keep Lucia Farncomb for 2s per week and her clothes [presumably the same family but probably at the Easter Vestry meeting], Mrs Sam Wood to keep Eliza Hazelgrove 1s pw, Mr Goddard to take Elizabeth Wicks 9d pw & allow him 1 guinea for clothes & the girl 1pr stays'. This last placement was also outside the parish, at Shermanbury, for we read in Overseer Stephen Croskey's disbursements for May 1 'the expences of Elizabeth Wicks's going to Shermonbury & horse 4s 6d, paid Wm Wicks [? father] for going to Shermonbury 1s 4d'; and Stephen Croskey paid himself £1 for keeping John Holden for 20 weeks. And the bald entry in the Vestry Minutes: 'Agreed to take away 4 of Jenner's children & send them to the Poorhouse'.[18]

xvii. Indenture apprenticing Leonard Haselgrove
to John Newland of Chailey, shoemaker, 1700 (WSRO/Par400/33/1).

Money in the form of weekly or monthly doles, sometimes for a short period but more often permanently, was allocated by the Vestry to those considered to be in need. In 1789-90 some 33 names are listed in the vestry book: 21 adults ranging in age from 83 to 28, of whom 10 were widows, 2 absent militiamen whose wives and children were left for the parish to look after, and 10 bastard children aged from 10 years old down to 1 month; unnamed 'dependents' comprised 8 wives and 25 other children – a total of 66. Apart from them all being categorised as 'poor', two of the men were 'lame' and one was 'blind'. The militia wives, each with one child, received 6d a day, while the rest were given weekly amounts ranging from 1s to 8s. The payments each month varied between £10. 18s and £17. 12s 3d, and totalled £160. 17s 9d for the vestry year which ran from Easter to Easter. Rents too were paid, some 28 varying from £1. 1s to £4. In 1826-27 at least 82 individuals were being assisted financially (the number is probably significantly higher as the numbers of children in large families were not indicated) at an annual cost of £687. 6s 10d.[19]

Some of the entries for 1826-27 show that being an overseer, or indeed an ordinary member of the vestry, was not without its physical risks: AB applied for [parish] work – refused in consequence of having a gun [presumably because he was a potential poacher], ordered to bring gun and receive necessary relief, refused relief, threatened in Vestry room to run away and leave his wife and family and to get a gun and kill same, ran away not leaving any of his earnings, refused relief, threatened to leave his wife and child chargeable on the parish; CD refused in consequence of keeping a dog and gun; EF ordered to work, threatened to knock all in the room down. Other comments indicate the miserable states which brought applicants to the Vestry: unable to work; to be allowed the doctor to his wife; to have a pair of shoes; wife and family ill and child dead; to bury his child; to pay for son's coffin; to be taken to Lewes [House of Correction] pregnant of a bastard; bad leg; bad eyes; just left prison for bastardy; refused work on account of being idle and being discharged from [working on] the road [Ditchling turnpike]; ran from her place [of service], to come into the [work]house. . .[20]

THE POORHOUSE

The workhouse referred to was situated at the corner of Pit Lane in the centre of the village. 'An Acct of Interest, Rent & Tithe due (Yearly) to the Revd Doctr Dodson' refers to interest of £6. 6s on £140, presumably advanced by the Rector for the purchase of the property. An inventory of the contents taken in 1790 itemised some 14 bedsteads, but gave no indication of size, so we can only hazard a guess as to the number of inmates. The management of such establishments was often farmed out to an individual contracted to provide food and lodging, employment where possible, and sick care. Here in 1790 'Dame Gander at the Poorhouse has taken the Poor at 2/3d each the Parish to clothe them & the said Dame

Gander is to have her flour at 6/- Bush[el]'.[21] Later there were some 100 inmates, sufficient to warrant a schoolmaster and mistress in addition to the workhouse master himself and the beadle to keep order.

Plate 28.
Aerial view of Townfield Cottages (centre), converted from the workhouse in 1845.

Dame Gander's name was Ann, and she presented her monthly bill to the Officers of Hurst. She seems to have carried out her dressmaking duties assiduously, as in one month she made 1 Round frock, 2 Short frocks, 6 Shirts and 3 pairs of Hose for the various identified inmates, in addition to Boarding at the agreed rate. The number boarded varied from 18 to 24 in the vouchers still preserved. But, perhaps because she was too autocratic or perhaps she was indulging in taking more than was her due, in 1802 she is 'turned out of the Work House'.[22] In the year 1810 the Churchwardens and Overseers contracted with John Purvis, a Lewes yeoman, that he should maintain the poor at 2s 6d and the price of one gallon of flour per head per week, the parish paying for a minimum of 30 inmates. The reason for stipulating flour and not merely increasing the monetary sum lies in the rapid inflation which was occurring at that period; in 1793 a gallon of flour in this area cost 11d, but high price rises in 1795-6 and 1800-1 had probably made the parish officers realise that there might be a risk of the inmates being underfed, even by the standards of the workhouse. The contract had 16 clauses covering work both in the workhouse and outside, religious instruction, medical care, the rate of out-relief and so on.[23] The accounts become increasingly detailed, dealing separately with men's and boys'work, weekly doles, other relief, admissions and discharges from the workhouse, purchases of flour and bran and of shop items, lists of paupers receiving faggots, and 'flint books' showing work done in digging, cleaning and carrying flints for the roads, continuing in this manner until 1842. These account books were supported by the individual vouchers obtained by the successive overseers.[24]

Plate 29.
Narrow entrance to Pit Road; the workhouse master's house was not on the corner as originally thought, but next door; both now replaced by flats and modern shops.

Those poor who, like Richard Smith in 1686, 'doth receive common & publick Almes of the parish of Hurstperpoint' had their goods distrained. In Smith's case, the inventory lists the expected simple beds and bedding, kitchen and brewing utensils and 'also a Gold Ring', and is signed by Abraham Muzzall as Churchwarden and by William Berwick (with his mark) as Overseer.[25] In the same year an inventory was also taken 'of the goods at the workhouse when Abraham Muzzall came in [to office]'. [26] This was a very simple listing on one sheet of paper; by 1807 the regular annual appraiser, George Tester, covered ten sides of foolscap, very carefully itemised, including a valuation of the clothes being worn by the 43 named inmates to a total value of £58 9s 8d. [27]

The earlier mention of flour leads to another aspect of the way in which the fortunes of the parish and its paupers were closely intertwined.

> The Churchwardens, Overseers and the Majority of the Inhabitants of the Parish of Hurstpierpoint agreed that the Millers are to serve the Poor in Rotation: Mr Lindfield April, August, December; Mr Peskett May, September and January; Mr Borrer June, October and February; Mr Kennard July, November and March.

This sort of arrangement would have applied to the other retailers of basic food and other requirements, but they were all paid for such provision. [28] The range of goods supplied covers domestic utensils and tools, food, clothes, and shoes. There is further evidence of sharing out to a number of traders the income derived from supplying the parish for its paupers. For example, at least four men, Francis Spratley, Richard Wood, John May and Hilman made shoes for either inmates or those receiving out-relief. The materials for the dressmaking activities of Ann Gander and others were provided by William Courtness, who also supplied household goods such as buckets and brooms, and John Gard among others. Some of the individual entries make interesting reading to our twentieth century eyes. Both Worsted and thread were supplied by weight rather than length; linsey and woolsey are itemised separately, although linseywoolsey is defined as a mixed fabric of wool and linen used for clothing for the poorer classes; John Gard sold '14 nail of Chekque' (a nail was 2 1/4 inches); [29] Russian sheeting was a durable leather popular for chairs, while Prunella was a strong material for clergymen's and barristers' gowns. [30] One wonders about the use of the last in a workhouse – could it be that someone else in the parish was using this account? [31] For the 19th century, in the remaining years of parish responsibility, all of the activities of the Overseers and the workhouse were detailed separately in small notebooks and collections of papers. [32]

Small cottages on outlying commons were acquired or built in many parishes. In 1769 the accounts show an entry for tithes for Sandfield House (down New Way Lane), and for Standings House in 1790, as well as the regular one for the workhouse.[33] In addition Hurst took over another such property, known as Peters's house, on St John's Common (now Burgess Hill) in 1790.[34] This would appear to have been in the farmyard of West End Farm (today's Woolpack pub). Peters had clearly fallen on hard times, as the parish agreed to take the cottage and pay his debts. It is open to question as to whether this building was technically a poorhouse, but William Edwards had taken occupation on Lady Day 1790 at £2. 2s 0d a year, and an Overseer's inventory of his goods was taken a week later:[35]

1 1-galln Iron Kettle 15d 1 stolledge 1s 1 keeler 1s	3	3
1 Barrell 2s 2 Wood Bottles 1s ½doz chairs 1s	4	0
1 good Pott 3s	3	0
1pr Andirons 1pr Tongs Fire Pan 1 Bellows		
1pr Pothooks	3	0
Shelves in Kitchen, 1 Rack & Tabl	1	0
Cupboard & Table in Kitchen	2	0
1 Warmng Pan 18d a Clock 15s A Bedstead 4s	1 0	6
3 Crocks 2 Boxes		6
1 Spitter [small spade] 1 Hand bill	1	6
allow		9
	1 18	0

about £85 in today's money.

Any such goods, which fell into the hands of the parish officers, were a potential source of income. Here we find George Verrall Jnr's bill:

Two Journeys and selling Goods	1	1	0
Auction Duty		10	9
Expences at Hurst		3	9
Crying [announcing the sale]			6
1 Bottle Wine		2	6
	1	18	6
Produce of Goods	18	9	3
Bot by Mr Ellis	7	15	3
Paid Cash to Mr Ellis	8	18	0
	18	9	3
Expences	1	18	6
To Parish	16	10	9

The amount realised would indicate that this account does not relate only to William Edwards's goods.

Stephen Croskey claimed 4s expenses conveying the property to Mr Henry Davey two months later, on 20th May 1790, but the cottage itself was in bad shape and clearly remained the responsibility of the parish, at least for some months, as in January 1791 William Greenaway presented a bill including:

February the 16 and 17 for 2 days my man	7 4
and & to 125 bricks and 4 bushall of morter	
and haire for bilding oven at the Common house	7 3

which may have referred to work carried out in 1790, but continues:

1791
for Repairs at Saint John Comon materials
from Hurst morter and tilesfor 38 bushalls

of morter	19 0
& to 125 plain tiles	3 9
Do paid Mr Taylor for 500 bricks 200 tiles	17 0
January the 11 a day my man and labourer	3 8
the 12 a day my man and labourer	3 8
the 17 a day my man and labourer	3 8
Do paid Mr English for 200 of laths	5 6
the 22 a day my man and labourer	3 8
the 24 to the 30 for 4 days man & labourer	14 8
& to 1 day my selfe to bundell laths	3 2
for 1 paper and a quarter of nails	3 0
& to 2 bushall of haire	2 0
for 2 new glass lights	2 4
paid for the Carrage of all materials	12 6 [36]

Like any other property, the central workhouse also needed maintenance, and bills for repairs occur at fairly frequent intervals.

Apart from distributing the weekly doles to those paupers on out-relief, the Overseers had direct responsibility for providing food, clothing and work for the inmates of the poor house, and were required to present detailed accounts of their disbursements to the Vestry, with the supporting vouchers discussed above.

Thus, in the Poorhouse accounts for 1769 [37] we read repetitive entries such as:

Jan 2	Dame Mitchell for 1/2 day tyer spining & winding	5	0
	Dame Weeks 5 wks pay	5	0
7	Ann West 1 wk & for spinning 2lb tyer	2	4
	Wdw Jacket 1wk	4	0
	Ann West spinning 1lb tyer		8
13	Ann West spinning 1lb tyer & 1 wks pay	1	8
	Wdw Jacket 1 wk	4	0
	Hannah Holden 1 wk	1	0
	Wdw Godman 2 wks	8	0
	Richard Walket for a pr of shoes for John Standen	5	0
19	Ann West 1wk	1	0
	Wdw May 6lbs tyer	4	0
. . .			
Feb 4	Master Wile a bill for tyer	16	0
5	Mr Pilbeam for making the poor books	3	0
	& signing the books	2	0
	Henry Wood for Barley	2 11	0
	Thomas Hampers bill	1	8
	Nathaniel Naylors bill	1 9	0
	James Nye	7	6
	Wm Wicks	7	6
	John Burtenshaw	2	6
	Abraham Muzzells bill	3	0
	Mary Wears spinning	4	0
	Mary Wears pay	12	6
	Mr Averys bill	1 13	9

Wm Bakers bill	2	9
Ann West	4	0
Mary Bonniface spinning	3	0
Mary Bonniface pay	7	6
Philip Cards bill	14	1

. . .

	Dame Stonehams bill	6 8	11
	Richard Pockney coal & carriage	18	0
	Thatch White 2 bush barley	4	0
	Mrs Courtneys bill	1 1	4
	John Ashfields bill	1 16	0
	"	2 9	10
	"	1 2	1
Mar 26	Mr Marchants bill for doctoring	7 17	6
	Dame Davey 2 faggots	3	0
April	John Lindfield 1 bush beans 3 oats	8	3
	William Harland for Mary Vallances child	6	0
	Samuel Gear 2 wks for Sary Jennings girl & 1s for making a coat	5	0
	Richard Herriot for Pilbeams schooling	3 15	0
	Richard Heryot mending the workhouse	2	2
July 3	Richard Pockney 1 load wood	17	0
	Hannah Holden 1 wk	1	0
	James Holden 1 load wood	17	0
Oct	Work done on ye highways by Jsph Coulstock Mr Avery Lucrey Ashfold J Huggott	12 2	3
	Dame Wicks stitching Frances Pilbeams stays	4	0
	Workhouse tithe	2	0
	Sandfield House tithe	2	0
Nov 3	Dame Bonny spinning	2	0
	Mary Bonny 4 wks	4	0
	Dame Packham spinning	4	0
	John Ashfold work on highways	18	9
	Grovers bill for coal	7 8	0

and on, and on, and on – those were only a small selection from one year's accounts; even so they give us a flavour of what life was like for the Overseer and those in his charge.

> With fingers weary and worn,
> With eyelids heavy and red,
> A woman sat, in unwomanly rags,
> Plying her needle and thread
>
> Hood: The Song of the Shirt (1843)

There were the regular weekly pensions, some 31 individuals during the year; the purchase of clothes including shoes; the provision of fuel – coal, [cord]wood and faggots; education and health; and the wherewithal to work. In the case of the women this was the spinning of tyre (flax) or occasionally tow (waste flax trimmings) to earn a small supplement to their doles.

Although we have looked at length at one year, this activity had been going on for a long time, for we find Thomas Marchant 'pd Widow Webb 2s for spinning 6lb of tow for the parish' on May 11th 1718.[38] Here in Hurst the going rate in the last quarter of the 18th century seems to have varied between 4d and 8d per lb, whereas in Wivelsfield at about the same time the spinners always got 5d – perhaps they were spinning different quality thread. This activity went on monotonously week after week. The 1790 Poorhouse Inventory lists only two spinning wheels, so the women must have taken turns using them – and they are recorded as having been in the men's chamber! The men on the other hand seem to have been employed only occasionally, mainly on the making and repair of the roads. Perhaps the lack of regular employment for idle hands accounts for the occasional hint that life inside was not always calm and placid. In 1801 a warrant was issued against Thomas English for a breach of the peace in the workhouse – presumably the beadle came up against someone beyond his control.

Inevitably, sickness and death occurred in the Poorhouse as elsewhere, and the accounts record all this as well. The diarist's grandson, also Thomas, was a surgeon:

> 1769
> May 26 Mr Marchant's bill for doctering   7 17 6

He was still doing the same twenty years later:

> 1789   Hurst Parish Dr to Tho Marchant
>   Cure of Bennet's Fractured Thigh   3 3 0

Jun 19	Delivering Dame French	5 0
30	Do Dame Simonds	11 6
Sep 29	Do Dame Mitchel	10 6
Nov 7	A Journey Mast Fillary	6 0
26	Med & Attendance Ganders Family	1 5 6
1790		
Feb 15	A Journey Mast Farncomb	6 0
	Do	6 0
23	Delivering Mary Terry	10 6
	Med & Attendance on ye Poor	8 8 0
		18 11 6

Paid the Widow Gander One Guinea for Boarding Wid
Howard at the Pest House 4 July 1790.

(where William Greenaway did repairs during the previous February to April
at a cost of 7s 4d).[39]

In 1807 the parish agreed to pay Dr Weekes £35 for looking after the poor as
usual, indicating a well-established arrangement; in 1827, Weekes & Co,
Boddington & Morgan surgeons agreed to supply the poor with medicines
and attendance for £40 a year.[40]

At the end, the carpenter and the grave-digger:

April the 13 1790
A Cofen for John Simons
By the Order of Mr Croskey   11 0

The Overseers' accounts confirm:

August 7th 1790
Thomas Nye His Bill for buring of Elizabeth Simons   2 6
Aprill ye 21 1791
Thomas Nye his Bill for Burin of Thomas Ockenden   2 6
May 1 Mary Howard for laying J Simmonds forth   5 0
June the 11 A Cofen for John Simons Child   6 0
1791 A Cofen for Wiliam Ethards Child   4 0
Feb the 19 A Cofen for Sarah Rendfield   11 0
April the 18 A Cofen for Ockenden Child   8 0 [41]

> Rattle his bones over the stones;
> He's only a pauper, whom nobody owns!
>
> Noel: The Pauper's Drive (1841)

The Vestry would seem to have kept a strict watch on the Overseers, requiring specific undertakings from them on occasion when deemed necessary:

> I Stephen Croskey one of the Overseers of the Poor of the Parish of Hurstperpoint in the County of Sussex do acknowledge to have disbursd by the consent of the Churchwardens & Overseers the Sum of Two pounds for Slabbs, Nails & Workmanship to make a Coal-Pen for the use of the Inhabitants & benefit of the Poor of the said Parish and do hereby promise to deliver over to the Person who shall succeed me in Office or to the Inhabitants of the said Parish either in the year 1790 or 1792 all the Slabb Nails &c belonging to the said Pen on demand.
>
> Witness my hand this 26th Day of May 1789
> Stephen Croskey [42]

Understandably, the parish made every effort to keep the cost of poor relief to the minimum, and we find that in 1790 a single woman and another family were refused; in 1792 a total of 25 individuals in five families, although some names are the same as those having received relief in earlier years; and in 1795 no fewer than 120 were denied help by the officers and vestry.[43] These refusals were presumably on grounds of insufficient need, as there is no suggestion that they were incomers from other parishes.

SETTLEMENT

While managing the relief, limiting the cost and keeping the accounts were major activities within the parish for the Overseers, there was another factor which occupied a great deal of time and used a great deal of paper – that of Settlement. The Act of 1662, already mentioned, enabled the parish officers to limit the numbers receiving relief to those who could prove entitlement. Any newcomer not occupying a tenement with a rent of £10 a year or more and who, in the opinion of the parish officers, was likely to become chargeable, was brought before a JP and examined as to his place of birth, apprenticeship if any, and marriage. If this examination resulted in establishing a home elsewhere, contact would be made with the other parish. Sometimes the situation would be resolved quickly, either bowing to the inevitable or effecting a 'swap':

xviii. A pauper family being evicted from the parish (Bill Parrott).

> April the 16 1759 We the Churchwardens and Overseers and Inhabetants of the parish of Ditchiling do Acknowledge Isaac Blinck and Ann his wife to be our perrisheners of our parish of Ditchaling and as your parish of Hurstpierpoint has Tho White and his family in our parish of Ditcheling we will take the same Acknowledgement from your parish for them.[44]

Sometimes, the parish became involved because of temporary, but urgent, problems. Thomas Marchant on December 3 1720

> Lent a traveller, whose wife was lying in at the inn, 50s on the parish account. He stated that his name was Hobbes, and that he belonged to St George's parish in the borough of Southwark; that he was born there, and apprenticed to one Adds a packthread spinner in that parish, and never had gained a settlement elsewhere.[45]

All too frequently, matters were not resolved so easily, and appeal was made to either the local magistrate at the Petty Sessions or to the Quarter Sessions, usually for us held at Lewes. 105 contested cases involving Hurst were heard between 1750 and 1835, some only being finally resolved with Removal Orders after several Court appearances.[46] In 1784 a warrant was issued to bring George Huggett before the court for returning to Hurst without a certificate of settlement.[47] There were several instances within Mid Sussex where the children in a large family were sent to different parishes, and different parishes from their parents, in accordance with their places of birth.

xix. Removal Order sending Jane Nye to Hailsham 1802 (WSRO/Par400/32/2/17).

Legal representation was considered necessary on many occasions, with inevitable additional cost. In 1790, part of Peter Morfee's account reads as follows:

Xmas Session [1789]
Hurst Appellants & Twineham Respond[an]ts

Fee tak[in]g instr[uc]t[ion] to quash the Order forthe removing of Sarah Terry from Twineham to Hurst	6	8
Notice of Appeal and fair copy thereof	6	8
to Draw[in]g & Ingr[ossing] Brief & fair copy for Counsel	13	4
To Mr Hurst therewith	2 2	0
To his Clerk	2	6
To ingrossing fair copy of Brief & Examination of Pauper for Junior Counsel	10	6
To Mr Curteis therewith	1 1	0
To his Clerk	2	6
Fee attending Court	1 1	0
Paid expences self & Horse	17	6
Bill of costs & copy	1	0

Presumably the parish thought that £6. 14s 8d (roughly £300 today) was money which had to be spent in an attempt to shift the maintenance of one pregnant single woman to another parish. In this case it would appear to have been in vain as Ann Gander's bill for April includes £2 for Sarah Terry's lying-in.[48]

The Hurstpierpoint documents for 1820 and 1821 include those relating to the Tidy family. Stephen Tidy had left the parish, ostensibly to look for work, leaving his wife Sarah with her two children Mary and Elizabeth chargeable. It is possible that Stephen was not the father, as the girls were also known as King. The examination and subsequent Removal Orders sent Sarah to Cowfold, the children to Bolney, but this was appealed against. In order to establish the facts more accurately, authority was given on 6 March 1821 to pursue Stephen; doubt was expressed as to whether he was using his own name, and he was not found at his last known address at Plaxtol near Tonbridge or at work at Cobham near Rochester; further attempts were to be made to find him, but tantalisingly there are no continuing references to the search. In the absence of more information, the Removal Orders were confirmed by Quarter Sessions at Lewes on 4 May 1821. In all this, there is no indication of the ages of Mary and Elizabeth, but the whole exercise cost money.[49]

Concerned less perhaps with cost than with the continuing worry about disorder, Jane King was, in 1821, removed from Hurst to East Grinstead as a 'Rogue and Vagabond, wandering abroad in the open air and also lighting fires under hedges'.[50] By the very nature of their lifestyle, such individuals were of concern beyond the particular parish. From 1767 onwards a tax was levied to defray the costs of controlling this problem, and Hurst's demand was for £10. 9s 8 ½d each year.

BASTARDY

Another major area of activity for the parish officers was that of bastardy, for obvious financial reasons. Not only would the mother be chargeable until her settlement elsewhere could be determined, but the illegitimate child born within the boundaries would acquire settlement, and continue to be chargeable thereafter. Thomas Marchant records:

> 1717. June 7th. . . . Mr Whitpaine and Mr Burry were here in the forenoon, and Thos Norton, sr., of Edgeley, about a woman that had a child born in our parish. Her name is Mary Davis, alias King.
> June 30th. . . We had a meeting about King, the travelling woman.[51]

There are no subsequent entries which tell us the final outcome. Rates of illegitimacy increased dramatically in the second half of the eighteenth century, but not solely due to lack of moral restraint. As farms were enlarged the intentional destruction of tenements and cottages prevented the poor from occupying them. The labourer was forced to find casual work where he could, and live where he could, often in grossly overcrowded conditions. As a contemporary political observer put it: 'the poor abhor [living with parents or lodging] as much as their betters and certainly in many cases run into licentious amours mainly for want of a cottage or a certificate'.[52] The alternatives of 'knobstick weddings' (the parish equivalent of 'shotgun weddings', so-called from the Churchwardens' staves which were used to persuade unwilling couples to the altar), or physically and often forcefully bundling the pregnant single woman over the border to become the problem of a neighbouring parish, were exercised on numerous occasions by the churchwardens and overseers.

Whenever possible, the father was persuaded into signing a maintenance bond, frequently with the agreed financial support of his father. For the period 1713-1800 seventeen such bonds have survived relating to Hurst, such as the one in 1758 relating to Mary Herriot. At her bastardy examination she swore that Thomas Nye the Younger was the father. He and his father Thomas Nye the Elder, both husbandmen, were

> held and firmly bound to the Church-wardens and Overseers of the poor of the said parish of Hurstpierpoint. . . they or either of them; And their successors and either of them; in the sum of Two hundred pounds of good and lawfull money of Great Britain; to be paid to the said Church-wardens and Overseers they or their successors. . .[53]

xx. Bastardy Bond for the support of the child of Mary May, 1774 (WSRO/Par400/34/12).

If no agreement to enter into a bond was possible, the magistrates could issue Maintenance Orders against known fathers, followed by warrants for their arrest where necessary. Some 27 such examinations, orders and warrants have survived for Hurst, covering the years 1734–1827, the father (when brought to Court) being required to provide an initial lump sum or a weekly maintenance, or both. [54] Sometimes this needed careful monitoring, and again involved legal fees, as the rest of Peter Morfee's 1790 account shows:

Mich[aelm]as Sessions 1789

Fee for Draw [in]g & Ingr[ossing] instr[uc]t[ions] for Mr Steel to move the Court to recommit Timothy Brigden to the House of Correction 'till Mary Thompsett be delivered of a Child of w[hi]ch she has charged Timothy Brigden as the reputed father thereof   10   6

Xmas Sessions

Fee for Draw[in]g & Ingr[ossing] instr[uc]t[ions] for Mr Steel to move the Court that Timothy Brigden may be continued on his recognizances &c   10   6
To Mr Steel therewith   1   1   0

Desertion of fathers resulted in the parish being left with the cost of feeding, clothing and housing the family, so strenuous efforts were made to apprehend such men. If this failed, the settlement of the wife was checked rigorously, in the hope that some other parish would have to foot the bill. The parish officers of St Margaret's, Westminster returned Elizabeth Lloyd Eldridge to Hurst in 1823 pregnant; she was admitted to the poorhouse, where she presumably had her baby, but both she and her son William were dead by the following June. In July 1828 we find Sarah, the deserted wife of William Fuller, and her 4-month-old son John returned to Nuthurst – presumably William was off as soon as there was another mouth to feed. Was Sarah the same woman from Nuthurst who, over six years later, was told twice to return 14 miles to apply for relief for her 7-year-old son, because there was nobody locally who had authority to grant or deny help? The Poor Law Commission, sitting to discuss the national situation just prior to the enactment of the New Poor Law, approved of this inaction. [55]

WARRANT, B. B.

SUSSEX ⎱ To the Constable of the Hundred of *Whalebone* ——
TO WIT. ⎰ in the County of Sussex, and to all other Officers of the Peace whom these may concern, and also to *John Comstock* ——
—— especially appointed for this Purpose.

WHEREAS *Ann King* —— of the Parish of *Hurstpierpoint* in the said County, single Woman hath by her voluntary Examination, taken in Writing upon Oath, before me, one of his Majesty's Justices of the Peace in and for the said County, this present Day, declared herself to be with Child, and that the said Child is likely to be born a Bastard, and to be chargeable to the said Parish of *Hurstpierpoint* —— and that *James Penfold* of *Brighton* —— in the said County, *Bricklayer* is the Father of the said Child.

AND WHEREAS *John Comstock*, —— one of the Overseers of the Poor of the Parish of *Hurstpierpoint* aforesaid, in order to indemnify the said Parish in the Premises, hath applied to me to issue out my Warrant for the apprehending the said *James Penfold*

I do therefore hereby command you immediately to apprehend the said *James Penfold* —— and to bring him before me, or some other of his Majesty's Justices of the Peace for the said County, to find Security to indemnify the said Parish of *Hurstpierpoint* or else to enter into Recognizance with sufficient Surety for his Appearance at the next General Quarter Sessions of the Peace, to be holden at Lewes, in and for the said County, then and there to abide and perform such Order or Orders as shall be made, in Pursuance of the Statutes in that Case made and provided.

Given under my Hand and Seal, this *eleventh* —— day of *October* —— in the year of our Lord, one thousand, eight hundred, and *twenty one*

E.S.R.O.
PAR. *400/34/2/12*. ⟵ *Harrison*

xxi. Bastardy Order to apprehend James Penfold, alleged father of Ann King's child, 1829 (WSRO/Par400/34/2/12).

GONE FOR A SOLDIER

One further group concerned the overseers, the dependents of soldiers or militiamen. During the time of the Napoleonic Wars, the families had to be cared for in accordance with allowances set by the magistrates. Often, substitutes were agreed, but support had to be provided in any case. William Hobden as one of the Overseers in 1790: 'Paid the Substitute for Militia and expences going to Lewes £2. 9s 9d'. Even though these were hardly desertions, when there was doubt regarding the settlement of the wife or children the whole machinery was brought into action again, Isobel Goodman with two very young children being removed to Henfield, while

Elizabeth Arkney and Frances Golds came here from Clayton and Brighton respectively. The name Golds appears on Hobden's account as one of four who received wood at a cost of 16s 6d.[56] After their period of service, the men themselves were likely to return to minimal employment opportunities, thus increasing the burden on the Poor Rate payers.

LOSING CONTROL

Was none of this foreseen? In 1782 an Act of Parliament introduced by Thomas Gilbert recognised that workhouses were ineffective and should only take in those incapable of work, at the same time providing employment outside for others, with wages supplemented from the rates if necessary. In 1795 a careful analysis of the earnings and expenses of labouring families was published, and we have already noted one contemporary's opinion that lack of work and housing contributed to one aspect of pauper dependency through bastardy.[57]

The 1782 Act required overseers to be supervised by Guardians (parish priests, £30 freeholders and magistrates) as a first step towards the eventual transfer of responsibility from the parishes. However, between then and 1834 the existing arrangements became increasingly burdensome, and various local efforts were made to alleviate the situation, for both the poor and the ratepayers. The Society for Bettering the Condition of the Poor was set up in 1796 with the aim of making 'the promotion of their happiness a science'. This philanthropic approach was not likely to find an immediate response in those directly concerned with the practical problems on the ground. In Berkshire the Speenhamland magistrates in 1795 based their allowances on the cost of bread, while elsewhere other methods were devised to enable employers to avoid paying a minimum earned wage, such as the parish making up the difference, or farmers taking on able-bodied paupers in turns in the Roundsman system.[58] In Sussex the Speenhamland system was adopted, costing in 1832 the highest amount per capita of any county in the country. Hurst was right in line with this policy, in 1803 laying out £1855 on out-relief and only £229 in the workhouse.[59]

In his report to the Poor Law Commission on 1 March 1835, Mr W H T Hawley, the local Assistant Commissioner, stated that in Hurst single men could earn 6/- per week, but the work was done in three days; married men could get relief whether they worked or not, a wife and child attracting a further 3/-, with extra children 1/- each, plus rent and fuel; the old and defenceless had the 'screw of economy' applied, receiving only 2/6d per week with 'shop tickets' redeemable for goods supplied only by local traders, who were often members of the Vestry. He found that there were 630 paupers (out of a population of less than 1500); that there was an 'excellent and extensive workhouse' providing employment; that the overseers and ratepayers were anxious to change, but 'fearful and unwilling to be first', although the Vestry clerk maintained the advantages of the system, with all being supplied equally. His most damning comment was that there was 'sad gentry mismanagement' but some sense of shame. His conclusion was that the parish was in favour of the Cuckfield Union, under its Board of Guardians.[60]   Mr Hawley was quoted as saying that 'the poor have no claim to relief. . . all that is received by them ought to be considered in the shape of a gratuity'.[61]

It is unlikely that the inmates of the workhouse were asked their opinion. While they were housed here in Hurst their standard of living can only be described as 'breadline', but at least they had been where visits to and from their neighbours were possible. Now they had to accept separation, in what to them must have seemed a huge building, and in a place too far away for family or friends to reach easily on a daily basis. The regime was intended to be harsh – enforcement of strict silence was considered, but it might have been 'driving the screw rather too close' [62] – but often the officers were as tightly controlled as the inmates; it was the carefully calculated monotony and the more subtle deprivations and degradations which were most repressive. Inmates lost their dignity and, until 1918, any right to vote that they may have had previously.[63]

There were those who felt that Gilbert's Act of 1782 sapped the English labourers' spirit of independence, relieving them of the necessity to get work, and at the same time setting the farmers in competition with the parish regarding wages. The Poor Law Amendment Act of 1834 was 'among the greatest achievements . . . Parliament, [working] a gradual improvement in the character and prospects of the agricultural labourer', restoring 'the virtues of prudence, thrift and self-respect', and eliminating 'improvident marriages' which gained financially from the old system.[64]

Whatever the final verdict, the fact is that from 1834 the days of the direct involvement of the parish in caring for its poor were numbered. Locally, feelings ran high, and the arguments against the Union were publicised in sections of the press. Mr Hawley was accused of undue influence on the Guardians, particularly when it came to disposing of the parish poorhouse, claiming in effect that it was the property of the Commissioners, and should be valued in order to sell it. A Vestry meeting in July 1835 voted that 'the appointment of a valuer [would] be giving sanction to an unjust and injurious system of treating the poor',[65] but it was to no avail. The best parish representatives were able to do was to help some individuals avoid the workhouse:

> 13.11.1840
> Proposed and unanimously carried that the sum of Twenty Pounds be offered to Thomas Knight for the purpose of Allowing himself, his wife and family to Emigrate to Sydney in New South Wales – provided he can make up his mind to accept the same.[66]

Once the Union had been established, there was no longer any accommodation for paupers in the village, and the workhouse was eventually sold in 1845. Even as soon as September 1835 the bailiffs called on John Hazlegrove, a long-term pauper with a wife and six (soon-to-be seven) children, to distrain on his so-called furniture for non-payment of rent on a six-foot square shed in the backyard of some premises behind the main street, containing only bedding (some lent by neighbours), no bedsteads, tables or chairs, valued at £1. Rent had previously been paid by the parish, but now the landlord had to recover this from the tenant, a clear impossibility. A local resident, Mr G Faithfull, attempted to raise a subscription, but this realised only two shillings, so he paid out of his own pocket. William Lewry, more industrious than Hazlegrove, was also in danger of losing his furniture, and his wife was advised by the clergy to leave her husband, saying that she got a family too fast. Mr Faithfull again intervened, and was ostracised by the clergy for his pains.[67]

> Few, save the poor, feel for the poor.
> Letitia Elizabeth Landon (1802–38): The Poor

Official reports during the first years of the new regime ran to many pages, including statistics to justify the change, at least on financial grounds. While the average expenditure for the years 1831 to 1834 on the poor in Stanmer was 8/3d and in Falmer 14/5d, that in Ardingly was £2 8s 10d and in Slaugham £2 1s 5d. These figures give support to the view that the 'close' Downland villages, with tighter control of their labour needs, did not suffer from the problems of the 'open' parishes in the Weald. Not surprisingly Hurst, extending from the foot of the Downs northwards to the Low Weald, had a figure between the two ends of the spectrum, £1 6s 10d. Sussex as a whole spent more per head on poor relief than any other county in England and Wales, but the Union system had reduced the cost significantly. In 1834 the county cost was set at 18s 1d per head, the next year 15s 6d, and in 1836 11s 10d.[68]

The Cuckfield Guardians took over, and Overseers became mere rate-collectors. In 1886 George Rawlinson, the master of the boys' school, was also the Assistant Overseer, living at Rectory Villa (now Rectory Cottage), and forms were printed for a demand at 10d in the £. This function continued until abolished in 1925, while Poor Law Guardians survived four more years.[69]

Local concern remained, and private charity continued. St Christopher's Home for the Aged was built in 1898 with money given by Miss Harriet Gurney for those 'who may otherwise have to spend their last days in the workhouse'. There is an echo of the religious dimension of centuries earlier in the dedication of the building 'in the fear of God'.[70] Park and Manor cottages were built in the 1850s and 60s, but the 'deplorable state' of the latter led to the Rector buying the properties and a group of Hurstpierpoint gentlemen forming a trust to improve them, providing extensions to each house containing WC and wash-house to replace the two shared blocks for the 126 residents listed in the 1891 census.[71]

NOTES AND REFERENCES

1. Tate W E (1983): *The Parish Chest*, 323–7.
2. Slack P (1990): *The English Poor Law 1531–1782*, 17–21.
3. *Ibid.*, 22-9.
4. WSRO/SAS/OR/325.
5. WSRO/Par 400/30/1/4.
6. 8 & 9 W&M c. 30.
7. Workhouse Test Act. 9 Geo I, c. 7; Slack, *Poor Law*, 29–34; Marshall J D (1985): *The Old Poor Law 1795–1834*, 23–30; Baugh D A (1975): The Cost of Poor Relief in South East England 1790–1834, *Economic History Review*, 2nd Series, 28, 50–60.
8. Edwards G (ed)(1991): *George Crabbe, Selected Poems*, 9–10.
9. Mitford M R (1824): *Our Village*, 50–1, Folio Society 1997.
10. ESRO/A7–285, A12–3, A19–39.
11. Turner E (ed)(1873): The Marchant Diary, *SAC* **25**, 194; 22 Car II, c. 3.
12. WSRO/ Par 400/24/1–4, 7.
13. WSRO/ Par 400/4/87, 90–4.
14. Turner, Marchant, *SAC* **25**, 170, 175.
15. WSRO/ Par 400/12/1.
16. ESRO/ Abstract of Returns relative to the Expenses and Maintenance of the Poor (43 Geo III A 1803)
17. WSRO/ Par 400/31/58, 33.
18. WSRO/ Par 400/12/1/1.
19. WSRO/ Par 400/12/1, 17.
20. WSRO/ Par 400/12/17.
21. WSRO/ Par 400/12.
22. Ford J M T (1987): *The Weekes Family Letters*, 137.

23. Young A (1813): *General View of the Agriculture of the County of Sussex*, 412; WSRO/ Par 400/37/73.

24. WSRO/ Par 400/31/20–121.

25. WSRO/ Par 400/37/2.

26. WSRO/Par 400/37/32.

27. *Ibid.*

28. WSRO/ Par 400/12/1/1.

29. Bristow J (1994): *The Local Historian's Glossary.*

30. Milward R (1989): *A Glossary of Household, Farming and Trade Terms.*

31. WSRO/ Par 400/31/58.

32. WSRO/ Par 400/31/21–48.

33. WSRO/ Par 400/30/8.

34. WSRO/ Par 400/12/1.

35. Matthews H (1989): *Burgess Hill*, 70; WSRO/ Par 400/12/1/1.

36. WSRO/ Par 400/31/58.

37. WSRO/ Par 400/31/13.

38. Turner, Marchant, *SAC* **25**, 183.

39. WSRO/ Par 400/31/58.

40. WSRO/ Par 400/37/120, 12/17.

41. WSRO/ Par 400/31/58.

42. *Ibid.*

43. WSRO/ Par 400/37/62.

44. WSRO/ Par 400/32/1.

45. Turner, Marchant, *SAC* **25**, 187.

46. ESRO/QO/EW19–54.

47. WSRO/ Par 400/37/106.

48. WSRO/ Par 400/32/2, 35/1.

49. *Ibid.*

50. WSRO/ Par 400/32/3.

51. Turner, Marchant, *SAC* **25**, 181.

52. Young A (1774): *Political Arithmetic*, 93–4.

53. WSRO/ Par 400/34/4/6.

54. WSRO/ Par 400/32/3/34, 34/1–3.

55. ESRO/QO/EW19–54; PRO/MH12/12829.

56. ESRO/QO/EW19–54; WSRO/Par 400/31/58.

57. 22 Geo III, c. 83; Davies D (1795): *The Case of Labourers in Husbandry.*

58. Marshall, *Old Poor Law*, 13–14.

59. Abstract of Returns 1803 (see note 16).

60. PRO/MH12/12829.

61. *Brighton Patriot* 6 July 1835.

62. *Ibid.*

63. Reid A (1994): *The Union Workhouse*, 3.

64. Broderick G C (1881): *English Land and English Landlords*, 217–24.
65. *Brighton Patriot* 13 July 1835.
66. Hurstpierpoint Vestry Book, 48.
67. *Brighton Patriot* 15 September 1835.
68. Rating and Valuation Act 1925.
69. *First Annual Report of the Poor Law Commissioners for England and Wales* 1835, 377–9; *Second Annual Report* 1836, 564.
70. *Clarke's Local Directory and Yearbook.*
71. Deeds deposited with Castle & Co, Solicitors, Hurstpierpoint.

7. IN SICKNESS

As we enter the third millennium AD with life expectancy beyond the biblical threescore years and ten, we should perhaps remember that this situation has developed only recently. Drugs to control both limited and epidemic infections, together with continually improving techniques to manage many other actual and potential health problems, may make us forget how hazardous life was in the past. Add to this the annual dependence on a good harvest of basic foods to avoid starvation which itself would have increased susceptibility to disease, and we can begin to understand why a child born at any time between 1550 and 1800, even if he or she survived the extra risks attached to childbirth and infancy, had at best a life expectation of 45 years, with significantly lower chances during many of the intervening half-centuries.[1] The other side of the coin is that until there were settled communities there was no transmissible disease. The hunter-gatherers who left the Mesolithic tool mentioned in Chapter 1 may have suffered from arthritis and dental abscesses; they may have suffered individually from the parasites of wild animals, but their lifestyle ensured that infectious diseases made isolated appearances without passing on from one to another. What is more, there is evidence that these people had better nutrition than their farming successors. The recent outbreaks of salmonella, E coli etc, and the implications for humans of BSE, have shown all too clearly how domesticated animals have provided us with both food and the potential for infection. Some cases are beyond even the power of modern medicine. Add overcrowding and limited hygiene to this, and it is easy to see that 'community' equalled 'disease' in times past.

Nowadays we assume that we will be healthy; illness comes from outside and the doctor is expected to solve all our medical and surgical problems. In earlier times greater care was taken to maintain the body's normal functions in balance; illness was a manifestation of an individual's failure to achieve this. In spite of this positive attitude the home or work environment was often antagonistic, with overcrowding, poor sanitation and injurious materials loading the dice against remaining fit. 'Ague' (malaria) was prevalent in marshy areas; lung disease or paralysis was accepted as inevitable if you were working with dust or lead. Beyond these obvious practical equations was the religious assumption that disease was due to man's disobedience, even to the extent that a few fanatics felt it would be wrong to attempt to avoid or treat sickness; that childbirth must be painful for this reason; and death was a release.[2] To add to the confusion, resort to magic, although declining through the 17th and subsequent centuries, still had considerable power. Founder members of the Royal Society believed that bleeding could be stopped by applying blood or powder to the weapon, not the wound, even at a distance of thirty miles; village 'wise men' thrived in times of inadequate orthodox medicine; prayers and charms were devised for the cure of specific ailments; healing by touch, such as for the tuberculous swelling of neck lymph glands known as the King's Evil or scrofula, was a royal attribute although George Fox and other religious dissenters claimed similar powers. Passing a child under a donkey was still thought to cure whooping cough well into the 19th century; an outbreak of diphtheria in Lewes as recently as the 1930s was 'prevented' by a wise woman tying a hazel twig to the child's throat or by swallowing stewed mice. Sudden loss of muscle power, or irreversible weight loss would today be diagnosed as a stroke, or cancer or tuberculosis; in the 17th century they could result in a woman being charged with witchcraft; mental illness would inevitably have been considered the work of demons.[3]

One of our problems when we try to look at the past comes from changes in language and meaning, and nowhere is this more apparent than when we are dealing with disease. While both we in the late twentieth century and our forebears will understand what is meant by 'smallpox' and 'measles', things become more problematic when terms such as 'malignant fever', 'autumnal fever', 'ague', 'spotted fever', 'bloody flux', 'contagious fever', 'vernal fever', 'sweating sickness' are used. They were common currency in the 16th, 17th and 18th centuries, but at this distance in time we may have difficulty in equating them with modern terminology. We may, therefore, have to make some assumptions when describing how people suffered, both in Hurst and elsewhere.

ARRIVALS

Let us begin at the beginning. Normal childbirth may have been no more risky than it is today; when we take in account the active and hardy life style of any rural women it may even have been easier on occasion. However, although unbaptised persons formed the majority of omissions from the burial registers, dual entries show that slight deviations from normal delivery greatly increased the hazard to both mother and child:

> 1638. Apr 5   stillborn daughter of William Piercie
> May 27   stillborn daughter of Thomas Reaue
> Sep 6   stillborn daughter of John Linfield
> Sep 8   Mary wife of John Linfield.[4]

four out of a total of only 15 entries for a six-month period.[5]

Experiences elsewhere confirm this. The wife of the Vicar of Earl's Colne in Essex had ten live births and five miscarriages between 1642 and 1663; her first daughter Mary lived eight years, but two sons, both called Ralph (it being common for a new arrival to be given the name of a dead brother or sister), survived for ten and 28 days respectively, in 1648 and 1649. Nationally, for the period 1550-1850 infant mortality, that is death within one year, varied between 135 and 171 per 1,000, boys always being more susceptible than girls.[6]

The registers do not reveal how many mothers died from puerperal fever, but it was still considered a great scourge in the late 18th and early 19th centuries, and discussed several times in letters between Hurst and St Thomas's Hospital:

> I am sorry to hear of the death of poor Tom Wadg's wife . . . the Puerperal Fever is certainly a terrible disease – October 1796; I lost two young women last year they had both very easy & natural labors, in good health . . . – November 1802.[7]

Another eighty years and we find James Hannington writing in his diary:

> Visit Mrs Clark dying under painful circumstances. Given birth to 2 stillborn children. . . she is now quite unconscious and will probably not last 12 hours; in fact she lingered for a week, only for Hannington to find 'her relatives behaving very badly, gave advice'.[8]

Not until better understanding of the importance of asepsis, starting with Lister's use of chlorine water or carbolic acid, and developing in the twentieth century, did its widespread occurrence diminish.

The midwife was only one of several women, both family and neighbours, present at the birth of a child; her skills were acquired from experience rather than books or formal training.   By the 17th century physicians were sometimes called if complications were anticipated or encountered. Once safely delivered, the care of infants was largely controlled by the experience of generations of women. Swaddling, to keep limbs straight or prevent an animal posture on four legs, was adopted for up to three months. There was another, very practical environmental reason for this practice: a swaddled baby could be propped up by a hook in an overcrowded cottage away from the dangers of an open fireplace and rumbustious siblings. Breastfeeding was expected by the Church and advocated by lay experts, but upper class women often employed wet-nurses, with reduced chance of survival through the first year, only the socially conscious allowing themselves to be influenced by the stress laid on the emotional needs of infants in Jean-Jacques Rousseau's 'Emile'.[9] For the children of the poor breastfeeding was the only viable option. Thomas Marchant's diary entries on the subject of childbirth are laconic in the extreme:

> 1715. Sept. 7th.   Mrs Dodson [Rector's wife] brought to bed of a son. My wife supt at Mr Dodson's.
>
> Sept. 24th.   My wife brought to bed of a girl.

CHILDHOOD FEVERS

This was another Ann, followed by Katherine in 1717. Her arrival is not mentioned, although her christening is, on June 3rd. Katherine was ill enough three years later for the visit of the doctor to be recorded, while in August 1722 she contracted measles, along with at least three other members of the household. It is difficult for us in these days of mass vaccination to think of measles as a serious illness, although it still claims its occasional victim, and the Latin 'morbilli' translates as 'little plague'. But until the early years of this century it could be a killer on a grand scale, particularly among the poor and ill-nourished, but also in better-off families. Three months after the Little Park infection, Thomas was recording:

> 1722. Novr. 30th.   My brother Box's two girls were buried
> both in one coffin in Albourne
> churchyard. My wife and the two girls
> were there. The younger died yesterday
> morning, and the elder the day or night
> before, both having had the measles.

By December 8 the girl's mother, Marchant's sister was 'very ill'.[10]

We must assume that she recovered eventually, as there is no further reference to the crisis. Half a century earlier Thomas Sydenham, among his many accurate observations of epidemics, had written about the ordinariness of the disease, but his dispassionate medical viewpoint was no consolation to the families affected. Eighty years after the Marchant diary entries, in the letters of the Weekes family, there is no mention of it occurring in Hurst, and only one in London, but it is inconceivable that the disease had ceased to be a problem – its management was probably better understood, but it could still be a killer of the vulnerable ill-nourished.[11]

Thomas Marchant's wife survived several deliveries and other illnesses to outlive him by twenty years, but the deaths of his infant children are mentioned in what seems to us to be a very matter-of-fact manner, reflecting the contemporary acceptance of the frequency of early death:

> 1715. Sept. 5th.   Paid William Nicholas 1s. 6d. for raising the
> graves of my four deceased children.[17]

Ann, Mary and James all died within the first year, and Thomas only reached his fourth birthday, all in the space of eight years between 1703 and 1711. And remember, this was the family of a man who could afford to call in the best available help and advice.

Another 'childhood' fever, which we hear little about in these days of effective inoculations and antibiotics, was scarlatina or scarlet fever. It is not mentioned in the Marchant record, but a hundred years later it was certainly a scourge. Richard Weekes writes in January 1802 that

> The Scarlitina is a very prevailing Complaint just now ... we are
> very full of business indeed.[13]

William Wood, who farmed at Washbrooks until 1931, was born in 1857; he remembers three of his brothers dying from scarlet fever between the age of two and five years in an outbreak in which not less than thirty or forty children died, due to the well water, the only source. Hurstpierpoint College had its home in the Mansion House from 1850 to 1853, and three boys died of scarlet fever during that time, in spite of a new cesspool costing £10. One effect was that Wood's father and others raised the money for a new water company to pump water from the Downs. Weekes and Wood also thought that this cleaner supply helped to limit the ravages of diphtheria, mentioned by both at a time when its epidemiology was not properly understood.[14]

Not only the water supply was suspect. Main drains and sewage disposal did not reach the area until the turn of the century, and the parish was exposed to the inevitable hazards. In August 1862 another epidemic of scarlet fever started at the College and some boys were sent to properties in the village, leading to complaints about spreading the disease. In September the Bishop of Chichester, who had a son at the school, wrote a stiff letter to the parish officers '. . . that the prevalence of fever . . . [is] attributable to the imperfect and bad drainage' and gave warning that he would report the matter to the Registrar General if expert advice was not sought quickly. His opinion was reinforced by that of the local doctors, but they were sacked by the College in 1863 for failing to attend and for lack of skill, in spite of charging high fees, so their comments may not have had any great influence on the discussion. The Vestry noted that of 38 deaths in a recent twelve month period only two were caused by fever, and felt that the existing Nuisances Act was sufficient to control the problem; they would arrange for expert inspection of the parish; and the Bishop should be informed that the inhabitants could be trusted to manage their own affairs, and there was no need for him to inform central authority. The following year two cesspools were constructed in the Lime Mead, and by 1866 the Sewage Acts provided for money to be borrowed and rates to be levied for more efficient drains to be installed. In 1870 a more comprehensive drainage system was instituted. Nevertheless, as late as 1893 the Medical Officer of Health for East Sussex was still concerned about the sewers which he felt would be ineffective if an outbreak of typhoid occurred.[15] In 1876 another outbreak of scarlatina seems to have resulted in the recently extended burial plot in the churchyard being used more than anticipated.

Other childhood infectious fevers, such as chickenpox or German measles, are not mentioned by either Marchant or Weekes, probably because they caused only comparatively minor problems and were not considered to be important. Important or not, the whole range of childhood illnesses resulted in mortality rates between 1600 and 1800, for ages 1–4 years of 8–10%, and for ages 5–9 of 3–4.5%.[16] Of course these ailments were not experienced by children exclusively, and when adults contracted them the effects were often more severe, but children were most frequently susceptible.

ENVIRONMENTAL INFLUENCES

A number of illnesses were liable to infect anyone of any age and were no respecters of class either, except to state what is, to us in the late 20th century, the obvious, that the poorer-nourished living in overcrowded dwellings with lower standards of sanitation were most at risk. It could be said that Poor Law relief, in warding off destitution, gave a rudimentary health service to many. Among these potential (often actual) killers were smallpox, typhoid and typhus fevers, malaria and cholera. Here in Sussex it has been found that diffuse Wealden parishes were less affected by epidemics than nucleated Downland villages. Mortality increases due to epidemics were of two types, widespread without severe peaks and isolated intense local attacks which did not affect adjacent parishes. In either type, malnutrition would be expected to expose individuals to greater risk of succumbing, but this has not been proved in this area.[17]

Smallpox could spread by contact or inhalation, but one of its worst features was the relatively long period of incubation, during which those already infected could travel considerable distances. In November 1714 Thomas Marchant notes that a letter from his mother-in-law at Rusper gives news of a member of the family being infected.[18] It has never been treatable, only avoided, either by escape from the affected area or by immunisation. Those who recovered were often scarred but subsequently immune and, of course, it was this which led to the deliberate exposure of the young to cowpox or to grease, the similar disease affecting horses. Richard Weekes refers to a specific case of grease involving two 'young men John Ball & John Hider at Knowls Tooth [who] used to rub Chamber ley into his greasy heels every day or two' and later proved immune to smallpox. In the latter part of the

18th century direct use of inoculation developed, first with the smallpox virus itself and later with the virus of a much milder illness, cowpox. This process was publicised by Edward Jenner in 1798, after some twenty years considering the problem. During that time others had been experimenting with using a vaccine, among them a local individual named Cooper Samson. We first find mention of him in the area in 1742 in Henfield, when he and two others obtained permission for a seat to be placed in the church, and then ten years later when he and his wife moved to Hurst and sold their interest in the seat. By 1760 he had moved again, to Ditchling and in 1766 to Wivelsfield. Here he certainly practised vaccination, patients coming from as far afield as Ashford in Kent.[19] Its increasingly successful use can be illustrated here in Hurst.

If we go back to October 1716, Thomas Marchant records the infection of Master Jervis, Sarah Grey and Widow Gun and a meeting called to discuss the epidemic, the only known solution for the community as a whole being isolation of the victims. There is still no indication of more precise measures in either 1720 when 'the small pox came out on Mr Dodson (the Rector)'s man, and he was moved to Broadwater towards night' or in 1727 when Mr Campion's teenaged son Henry was infected in London, surviving to die in India in the 1740s; while in 1728 his own son John Marchant died from the disease while a student at Oxford. But by 1750, the realisation of the importance of isolation led to Henry Campion leasing for 999 years a piece of land in the corner of a field called Haselcroft [south of the village], with the consequent expenses for building a small pox house.[20]

Less than 80 years later the picture had changed radically. Smallpox was still the disease most frequently causing concern, but Richard Weekes writes from Hurst to London on many occasions asking his son to send vaccine, and he clearly believes in the efficacy of inoculation, while admitting that it was not always successful. In November 1801:

> Old Strong is dead & we have got 7 more of the family to have caught it & 3 inoculated, but Barrett had Inoculated them all with Cow pock matter very early none of which took or at least came to nothing;

a month later: '3 of our patients out of 5 in the Natural Small Pox are dead', but by March 1802:

> Mrs Burt was taken in Labour just as the Small Pox was making
> its appearance but the Child had no marks of Small Pox nor has it
> now altho: it was 6 days ago that it was born I have inoculated it
> its arm rises well and the Woman altho: she has a great crop of
> pustules is doing very well.

The need for isolation was still accepted, for in July of the same year both the Hurst Pest House in Bedlam Street to the south of the village [now a private house but still with the name] and Nailards [a private establishment at Bolney] received patients. It was then that the requests for vaccine become ever more frequent, not to say desperate:

> Send us some Cow Pock matter down directly as we cannot wait
> longer . . . . send it by the Coach to Stonepound, in haste . . . .[21]

By 1853 smallpox vaccination had become compulsory, even against much opposition from religious and liberty groups. The Pest House was felt to be unsuitable and was sold in 1877, during a period when national attention was being directed to means of control, the proceeds of nearly £180 being credited to the account of Hurstpierpoint Small Pox Hospital.[22] Perhaps this was somewhat premature, as only four years later James Hannington was alarming the parish with his pastoral activities:

> . . . all over village that I went into all the houses with small pox
> and people seemed greatly enraged the relieving officer called to
> order me to go no more. I told him that if the law was on the side
> of the sanitary officers it was open to them to use it but where
> duty called I must go . . . Letter from Medical Health Officer
> asking me if I went to be very cautious as [it was] most virulent . .

The Isolation Hospital at Goddard's Green was not functioning in time.[23]

Once man began to establish fixed settlements he required a supply of water, but his very presence in one place ensured that the water would become contaminated with the typhoid bacillus. This has both human and animal hosts, although the clinical disease appears only in man. Often confused with typhoid fever is typhus, a disease with similar symptoms of fever, diarrhoea, abdominal pain and exhaustion, but in this case transmission is via rat fleas or lice. Improved sanitation since the middle of the 19th century means that in this country we have now controlled the problems, but we still see on our television screens reports of virulent outbreaks in underdeveloped areas of the world. Such epidemics were common here in earlier times. A survey of epidemic diseases in southeast England from 1601 to 1800 uses 165 parish registers as its database, including those of Hurstpierpoint. The incidence of annual disease was analysed in two main ways: to determine how virulent any epidemic was by means of the mortality level; and to assess how widespread any outbreak was. During that period mortality rose more than 10% above normal in 37 years, more than 20% in 12 years and more than 40% in three – four out of ten individuals died as a result of a specific outbreak. It helps us to put matters in some sort of perspective to read that smallpox was the villain in 77 of those 200 years, typhus 29, (bubonic) plague 23 (virtually all before 1665), while typhoid, scarlet fever, measles and the rest were singled out for mention to lesser degrees. Hurstpierpoint was also one of 404 parishes used to plot mortality crises throughout England between 1557 and 1763. In this survey Hurst had burial rates significantly above average in two periods, from October 1596 to June 1598 and from July 1678 to June 1681. Of the six other Mid Sussex parishes whose figures were analysed, Cowfold and East Grinstead also had crises in the first period, East Grinstead in the second. For the whole of the two centuries under review there were two further crisis periods in East Grinstead, together with three in Worth and two in Woodmancote, but none in Ardingly or Bolney. One should remember that this latter survey does not differentiate between disease and death as the cause of the rise in death rates, although it is obvious that malnutrition will make for lower resistance to illness.[24]

Typhus was still endemic in the 19th century. Along with other diseases connected with contaminated water and ineffective sanitation, it only became an increasing rarity in the present century. Cholera, epidemic rather than endemic, also responded to the efforts of such pioneers as John Snow, with his observation of the causal relationship between incidence of the disease in the City of London and the use of the Broad Street pump by the local inhabitants, and Edwin Chadwick, who persuaded the authorities to deal with the problem. Not everyone approved of the 'nanny state' even then. In 1848 The Times had a leading article asserting that it would rather chance death by cholera than be bullied into health, but gradually large towns, followed by smaller settlements, were cleaned up under legislation following that for vaccination. Hurst, with a population of just over 2,000, appointed a committee to report on sanitary nuisances in November 1848, action being taken the following year, so not too much attention was paid to the views of 'The Thunderer'.[25]

Tuberculosis was largely a disease of urban overcrowding, and so one would not expect to hear of it as a major problem in Hurst. Certainly Thomas Marchant does not mention it, but Richard Weekes recorded three fatal cases between May and July 1802:

> Chas Goldsmith is dangerous with Ptysis pulmon: . . . Chas Goldsmith is dead. died of Typhus attendd. with Inflamn. of the Lungs he was ill only 15 Days . . . Thos Tabb Randidles is dead died of Ptysis Pulmons . . . Mrs Welber Locks is dead died of idem.[26]

Weekes also refers in 1801 to 'the Yellow fever [continuing] about here, Chs Weller has got it', but it is unlikely that he means the virulent viral infection which killed so many slave traders and other colonials, as it seems that he was confident that '2pd of Lent Figs' sent from London would cure his patient. Dysentery was causing concern in 1802, with a number of sufferers including William Campion, of little surprise to us in view of the likelihood of contaminated water.[27]

The evidence regarding the incidence in Hurst of the worst scourge of all – bubonic plague – is almost entirely circumstantial. The most devastating epidemic was the one in 1348-50, called The Black Death, brought into the country on a ship bearing a victim at Melcombe Regis (now part of Weymouth) at the end of June 1348. It swept rapidly through the West Country before invading the rest of southern England. During 1349 almost every town and village was afflicted, Sussex being assailed from the west, from London and by independent entry at half a dozen Channel ports. Its arrival at Appledram near Chichester and soon after at Wartling, inland from Eastbourne, has been documented; so too is the decimation of the Priories of Michelham and Malling, near Lewes. At the latter

> . . . the plague carried off so vast a multitude of people of both sexes that nobody could be found who would bear the corpses to the grave . . . There was so marked a deficiency of labourers and workmen of every kind . . . that more than a third of the land . . . was let to lie idle.[28]

It is inconceivable that Hurst could have escaped, but burial registers were not required for another two hundred years, and so we have no clear evidence. Attempts to control the spread were limited to isolation, but were largely ineffectual. On the Continent extreme measures were sometimes taken – walling-in, enforced closure of town gates. Alongside these were other less certain methods used by individuals such as phylacteries and amulets, alcohol and fire. Many subsequent outbreaks occurred over the next three centuries, the parish registers of our next-door neighbours in Pyecombe showing that it lost 15% of its population in 1603. The last major occurrence in this country was that of 1665, so vividly recorded by Pepys, Evelyn and Defoe, and the year in which the Derbyshire village of Eyam undertook voluntary isolation. Naturally, concern was widespread, and we find the Easter Quarter Sessions in Lewes in 1666 expressing this at somewhat tedious length by issuing a series of orders:

> Whereas the Court is informed that there is greate default made within this County by those who ought to keepe watch and ward according to the statutes in such case made and provided And whereat this time is more necessary than formerly by reason of the visitation of the pestilence within this Kingdom of England And whereas diverse disorderly persons doe travell up and down this County under pretence of selling goods and wares as chapmen and hodlers contrary to the lawes in such case made and provided It is hereby ordered by this Court that all constables and headboroughs and other his Majesties Officers and Ministers within this County of Sussex doe from henceforth keepe due watch and ward in all towns and parishes within this County And that they shall take all travellers chapmen and hodlers and other persons which shall travill contrary to the Law And all other persons comeing from London and all other places infected with the plague And convey them by passe to the place of their legal settlement And if that cannot be found or knowne then to the place of their birth And it is further ordered that the Bayliffes Criers and other Officers of all towns and places within this County where any faires have been usually kept doe ymmediately uppon sight hereof make all such proclamation att such places for the publique notice and for prevention of such conventions and faires by reason of the present visitation aforesaid And every Constable of each Hundred where any such faires are usually kept shall cause the day before and the dayes when the faires should be best to keepe a sufficient guard to keepe out all chapmen

> whatever from soe conveaning as aforesaid Except all growers
> graziers and buyers and sellars of cattle And if any person shall
> confound this order it is desired that he be bound by some one
> Justice of the peace for this County to appeare at the next
> Sessions to answeare his contempt concerning the same.[29]

– all very understandable if typically long-winded, except for two points: it
was only the lower orders who were subject to this edict, and returning them
to their own parish did nothing to help control the spread of infection. Fire
at any rate proved effective in London the following year. Even so, sporadic
episodes continued into the 18th century, and we find Thomas Marchant
recording 'a publick fast on account of the plague, &c' on 16th December
1720, and another one a year later.[30]

At the same time that Jenner was developing his vaccination theories to
control one of the great killers Thomas Malthus was expounding his
'Principles of Population' and would have argued that disease was one of the
'positive checks', along with war and famine which limited population
growth, and so was an inevitable necessity until such time as food
production could be guaranteed to sustain increased numbers. Such an
attitude would have been small consolation to Thomas Marchant's
neighbours in Hurst in the early 18th century, or to Richard Weekes's
patients in the early 19th.

INDIVIDUAL CURES

So far, we have been looking at diseases, which potentially affected
significant numbers of people. But there were also other health problems,
not perhaps so lethal to the community as a whole, but no doubt of great
concern to the individual affected. In Tudor and Stuart times life expectancy
may have been under 35 years, the young being especially at risk, and
medicine patently had no answers, relying on expelling toxins from the body
by purging, sweating, vomiting and bleeding, and a few drugs such as
Peruvian Bark or quinine for fevers and opium as a sedative and for bowel
disorders. The individual's dominant 'humour' was basic to any diagnosis,
but astrology also helped to the extent that the position of the stars could be
blamed not only for a patient's failure to respond, but also for epidemics.
John Gerard's vast *Herbal*, extolling the virtues of willow-bark for cornes,

Solomon's Seal for broken bones, crane's-bill for hernia, even saffron against smallpox or measles and angelica against plague, among hundreds of remedies, was published in 1597.[31] It was certainly used not far away at Wiston,[32] and could well have been consulted by the more literate here in Hurst, along with such other books as *The Queen's Closet Opened* and *A Choice Manuall of Rare and Select Secrets in Physick and Chirurgery*, both printed some 70 years later.[33] Close by, at Hickstead Place, Richard Stapley entered a prescription in his diary:

> To cure the hoopingcough: – get 3 field mice, flaw them, draw them, and roast one of them, and let the party afflicted eat it; dry the other two in the oven until they crumble to a powder, and put a little of this powder in what the patient drinks at night and in the morning.[34]

xxii. Page from a 15th century herbal.

The remedies detailed in such books used such diverse ingredients as frogs and frog-spawn, lice and centipedes as well as the large number of herbs still incorporated in many modern preparations. Others recommended angelica stalks eaten like celery for a mad dog's bite, rue for that of a snake, and mandrake for sterility. Arguably the most famous of the early works of this type was Nicholas Culpeper's *The Complete Herbal*, published in 1649 in English and recommending indigenous plants, largely because Gerard had written in Latin and used imported drugs. Modern chemical analysis has confirmed the rationale behind many of these natural medicines.   For example Culpeper wrote that comfrey 'will meld flesh together' after injury; it contains allantoin which is used by the body to repair tissue. What is certain is that the housewife not only had to find the herbs; they had to be stored satisfactorily for use outside the growing season, and then made up into potions and salves, often through a process of distilling. A private 'clinic' using the products of herbs grown at the foot of the Downs was still providing cures for a wide variety of ailments well into the 20th century.[35] At a more official level pharmacopoeias were published on behalf of colleges of physicians with instructions for preparing simples, tinctures, pills and powders, ointments and balsams and so on, together with recommendations for the use of each, seen for example in the display of herbs and other remedies in the old St Thomas's Hospital operating theatre open to the public in London.[36]

xxiii. collecting herbs.

Crude surgery, including the frequently necessary setting of broken bones following falls from horses on rutted roads, was undertaken without even rudimentary cleanliness, or anaesthesia.[37] Samuel Pepys was one of the lucky ones who survived lithotomy at the age of 24,[38] living 46 years until 1703, about ten years before our own diarist started his personal record in much less exuberant style. This particular problem was still in evidence over two hundred years later. James Hannington records the death of his father on 7 June 1881, followed two days later by a post-mortem (which he observed) showing acute inflammation of kidneys and bladder caused by multiple stones – 'any attempt at an operation [would have proved] both useless and fatal'.[39]

So far as Marchant's brief medical entries are concerned we have to remember that diagnosis was often doubtful and in any case he was not a doctor. He 'paid John Snashal 30s for setting Ned Grey's leg' [a servant] on 9th November 1714. In May 1718 Capt Whitpaine died within two days of being taken ill, while in 1727 Marchant was sick with ague [? malaria] 'of which I had several fits', and in 1728 two friends were also ill 'with an ague'. He himself was bled on several occasions by R Patching, probably the local barber, but he gives no specific reason, seeming to be more concerned at being charged 1s for the privilege. It was the normal thing to do, along with purges and emetics – January 13th 1717: 'Mrs Beard and Mrs Kettleby were here in the evening to see Willy [son, then aged about 16] take a vomit'. Even when the event is more dramatic he records it fairly laconically:

> 1719. Sept. 21.   Richard Patching, the weaver, had his leg cut off this morning, per J Snashall. He died the following afternoon.

xxiv. bleeding.

Barber. surgeon 1804

Snashall seems to have been the vet as well as the surgeon, as Marchant records his visits to 'see the bay horse which was sick', and a late entry in the diary, on June 26th 1728 reads: 'John Snashall here, and made two issues in my neck'.[40] Whether he was a member of the Barber Surgeons Company of London is something we cannot know, as the Surgeons did not separate from the Barbers until 1745, and the first register was not published until 1779.

On the other hand, there is no evidence either that he was merely a blacksmith or farrier going in for a little diversification as was often the case. We do know that William Bryan was a barber-surgeon in Hurst some sixty years earlier, not because of any record of success or failure in his practice, but because he appeared before the Quarter Sessions in Lewes accused of illegal gaming and assault.   In the absence of someone like Bryan or Snashall villagers relied on self-help and home-made medicines, supplemented by a belief in religious healing or magic.   The treatment offered or suggested by the clergy and the gentry to their tenants and servants was reinforced by a succession of publications on home medicine (for example, John Wesley's 'Primitive Physick' of 1747), drugs sold by grocers and pedlars, and the miracle 'cures' of quacks and travelling mountebanks, such as the one who came to Hurst in February 1716. Patent and proprietary medicines such as Dr James' Powders, the 18th century equivalent of paracetamol, were in well-stocked homes alongside herbal remedies, while drugs like opium and poisons could be bought over the counter. This last trade was increased considerably when plate glass was introduced in the 1830s, allowing displays of patent medicines and sick-room requirements, together with the large coloured carboys and jars which became almost the trademark of the chemist.[41]

The Weekes were trained at London teaching hospitals, Richard at Guy's, Hampton across the road at St Thomas's, Dick at Guy's, and Hampton's son Richard at St Bartholomews, and they tended to look down on old-fashioned surgeon-apothecaries such as Charly Morgan of Henfield.[42]   Because they were writing to each other about the problems of their own profession, there is inevitably more detail in the 1800s, including some insight into the advances in treatment.

> Mrs Cripps has a slight attack of Inflammatory Rheumatism, a
> complaint pretty general in this neighbourhood at present, Charly

> Morgan gives bark [quinine] during the high inflammatory stage
> of the disorder neglecting the Lancett in Robust habits & country
> situations, this is horrid practice, nothing but evacuations will do.

Weekes himself suffered from rheumatism to a degree which made him feverish.

> Grace's Eye has been bad again but by applying the Leaches [still
> in use in ophthalmic surgery] twice it is now nearly well . . . two
> girls out of three [with hydrocephalic fever] completely recovered
> the other had frequent fitts of Epilepsy . . . and died . . . I treat by
> bleeding & other evacuants together with blistering the head &
> back, after which bark & mercury is the most to be depended on,
> the Digitalis is now much looked up too, but between you & I, I
> have seen medicines fail so often & nature do so much, that I hold
> it a matter of great niceness to discriminate between the operation
> of medicine & the natural cure, in short I do not look up to
> medicines as I used to do.[43]

Accidents were commonplace, and Richard and Dick Weekes comment on many in the letters to Hampton. Woolven's teenaged son had shattered his hand when a gun burst, a girl was terribly burned after setting her clothes on fire, a man shot through the liver with a pistol, a 13 year old boy with a very bad compound fracture of the leg and another at Henfield, a sprained wrist when a chaise overturned, fractured ribs, a dislocated hip, compound fractures of both arm and leg of a boy run over by a roller, plus his own sprained ankle falling from a horse. On other occasions his services were of no avail: a fall from a horse, a child drowning by falling into the water closet, death from concussion after being overturned in a chaise; often the coroner's inquest seemed to blame the poor animal for the tragedy. All of these were deemed to be of sufficient importance to be mentioned in letters covering a period of less than a year. The dental problems of prehistoric man were still around: Mrs Marchant had been very ill with toothache in January 1727; Dick Weekes removed six teeth in May 1802.[44]

One area of ill-health which has remained a 'taboo' subject until recently is that of mental disorders. The more overtly disturbed were often treated with ostracism, if not outright fear. Those less dramatically affected, but who still failed to conform to 'normal' behaviour, were cared for discreetly by their families; where they could not cope, arrangements were made for committal to an asylum. Here is another instance of the burden placed upon parish officers, for it was the overseer who had the unenviable duty of dealing with lunatics. For obvious reasons, some paupers became a charge on the parish precisely because of their mental deficiencies, and the description 'lunatic' often appears against an inmate's name, both in Hurst and later at the Cuckfield Union workhouse. Sometimes the condition was such that only an asylum could deal with the patient. In 1844 Jane Gow was sent to Bethlem Hospital in London, as at that time there was no equivalent establishment in Sussex (the Sussex County Asylum, later St Francis Hospital, did not open until 1859). In order to keep the cost to the parish to the minimum she was moved to cheaper institutions on two occasions. In the end Hurst had to pay for her funeral – £2.[45]

Later in the nineteenth century Henry Holman became prominent in the medical life of the village. From 1823 it is recorded that he lived in the house occupied earlier by Peter Morfee, steward of Hurstpierpoint Manor, and known as 'Morfees' until renamed 'Rose Hill' by Dr Holman (the property is now known as 'Abberton'). He was joined in the practice by his son Henry Martin and the name Holman was synonymous with caring medical practice in Hurst until the son's death in 1881.[46] Henry's sons and daughter dedicated the drinking fountain and horse trough which used to be on the Church Green to his memory, recording that he practised in the area for nearly sixty years; Henry Martin's brother Constantine, also a doctor, gave Hurst its first fire engine after the 'Great Fire of Hurstpierpoint' in 1882 in his memory.[47]

So, from a period when Thomas Marchant and his fellow parishioners adopted a philosophical attitude to accident and ill health, we travel on less than a century to the time of active medical practice. Heroic and often successful efforts were made to control the spread of disease and its effects on the individual patient; bones were broken and needed setting; gunshot wounds were treated, gout endured. From abortion, abscesses & amputations to tumours, ulcers and 'yellow fever', the Weekes practice was kept busy covering on horseback a radius of about five miles. As John Ford, the editor of the letters, says 'it would be a brave local who did not consult the Weekes'. Richard senior's 'success was founded mainly upon his skill, but also on his readiness to visit patients regularly, his availability, and his willingness to care as well for the parish pauper as his social superior'.[48]

Fifty years further on, and we find the community playing its part, through the implementation of legislation, in changing attitudes once again. And yet the inevitability of personal tragedy was still accepted when James Hannington was recording in his diary the local events of the 1880s.

NOTES AND REFERENCES

1. Wrigley E A & Schofield RS (1989): *The Population History of England 1541–1871*, 252.
2. Porter R (1987): *Disease, Medicine and Society in England 1550–1860*, 24–7.
3. Hill C (1972): *The World Turned Upside Down*, 88; Porter, *Disease*, 26–7; Thomas K (1971): *Religion and the Decline of Magic*, 210–34, 639; Moore J (1996): *Sampling Sussex, Old Country Recipes and Remedies*, 124.
4. Turner E (ed)(1873): The Marchant Diary, *SAC* **25**, 174.
5. WSRO/ W H Challen Transcripts.
6. Macfarlane A (ed)(1976): *The Diary of Ralph Josselin*, quoted in Hughes A (ed)(1980): *Seventeenth-Century England, Vol 1 Primary Sources*, 121–2; Laslett P (1983): *The World We Have Lost*, 112.
7. Ford J M T (1987): *The Weekes Family Letters*, 13, 30, 33, 228–31.
8. Hannington J: Diary 30 March, 8 April 1881.
9. Houlbrooke R A (1984): *The English Family 1450–1700*, 129–34.
10. Turner, Marchant, *SAC* **25**, 173.
11. Ford, *Weekes*, 246.
12. Turner, Marchant, *SAC* **25**, 173.
13. Ford, *Weekes*, 118.
14. King P (1997): *Hurstpierpoint College 1849–1995*, 12; Wood W (1938): *A Sussex Farmer*, 53.
15. King, *College*, 61, 73–4; Vestry Minute Book 1862–1984.
16. Wrigley & Schofield, *Population*, 249 (figures much simplified from Table 7. 19).
17. Brent C E (1974): Devastating epidemics in the countryside of eastern Sussex between the harvest years 1558 and 1640, *Local Population Studies* **14**, 42–8; Dobson M J (1987): A chronology of epidemic disease and mortality in southeast England 1601–1800, *Historical Geography Research Series* **19**, 23, 25; Nelson I (1991): Famine and mortality crises in mid-Sussex 1606–40, *Local Population Studies* **46**, 39–49; Hay D & Rogers N (1997): *Eighteenth Century English Society*, 82.
18. Turner, Marchant, *SAC* **25**, 168.
19. Ford, *Weekes*, 104; WSRO/ Par 100/4/1; ESRO/ Par 308/30/1–3; *Sussex Weekly Advertiser* 14 September 1761.

20. Turner, Marchant, *SAC* **25**, 176, 187, 195, 197; Wooldridge J A (1966): *The DannyArchive*, xvii; ESRO/DAN2201.
21. Ford, *Weekes*, 10, 83, 96, 104, 191–2, 196, 249.
22. WSRO/ Par 400/24/88–9.
23. Hannington, Diary 1 & 2 November 1881.
24. Dobson, *Epidemic*, passim; Wrigley & Schofield, *Population*, 671–84; Wood, *Farmer*, 53.
25. WSRO/ Par 400/13/3.
26. Ford, *Weekes*169, 175, 201.
27. *Ibid.*, 96, 175–6.
28. Ziegler P (1991): *The Black Death*, 127 and passim.
29. ESRO/QO/EW5.
30. Turner, Marchant, *SAC* **25**, 187, 190.
31. Woodward M (1927): *Leaves from Gerard's Herbal*, 51, 90, 73, 161, 258.
32. Pennington J (1987): Red Herrings, *West Sussex History* **37**, 11.
33. Fraser A (1989): *The Weaker Vessel*, 49–50.
34. Lucas E V (1904): *Highways & Byways in Sussex*, 205.
35. Moore, *Recipes*, 113–4.
36. Shaw P (1753): *The Dispensatory of the Royal College of Physicians of Edinburgh*.
37. Porter, *Disease*, 14–16.
38. Bryant A (1947): *Samuel Pepys, The Man in the Making*, 41–3.
39. Hannington, Diary 7 & 9 June 1881.
40. Turner, Marchant, *SAC***25**, 168, 171, 179, 182, 192, 198.
41. *Ibid.*, 175; Porter, *Disease,* 18–19, 21, 28–30; Jackson W A (1981): *The Victorian Chemist and Druggist*, 5–7.
42. Ford, *Weekes*, 2–5, 25.
43. *Ibid.*, 105, 229.
44. *Ibid.*, 41, 54, 95, 118, 136, 141, 149, 175–6, 201, 212.
45. Wood, *Farmer*, 194.
46. WSRO/ ADD MS 17683A: Fisher Map 1841.
47. *Sussex Agricultural Express* 2 May 1882.
48. Ford, *Weekes*, 8.

8. FRIENDS AND CHAPEL-GOERS

'A specially dangerous man'

In 1648 on the fells of Westmoreland a young boy was on his way home from school. He came to a stop as he heard a loud rumbling boom echoing around the mountains. It must be the cannons sounding from Carlisle Castle, he thought; for this was the time of the Civil War.[1]

The struggle between King and Parliament, State and Church had come to a head. Families had become divided and strong allegiances to one side or the other were evident. Towns and villages from north to south and east to west were affected. In general the King and the Church were supported in the rural regions and market towns furthest away from London. Puritan and Parliamentary sympathies were strongest in London and the developing commercial towns.[2]

In January 1649 the boy in Westmoreland was as shocked as the rest of the country by the news from London that the King had been executed. What, you might ask, has Ambrose Rigge, for that was the boy's name, to do with the history of Hurstpierpoint? To find out read on!

The turmoil of the Civil War had seen a huge rise in the number of radical religious sects. Dissent in religious matters had been growing since the 14th century. England had welcomed many groups from the Continent fleeing from persecution, only to find the same in England. Henry VIII's quarrel with the Pope and the subsequent establishment of the Church of England did nothing to stop the growth of more and more groups who grew dissatisfied with the newly established Church; Puritanism grew. Many Puritans intended to stay within the Church and purify the worship from within but gradually found that this was not practical and they began to break away from the Established Church. The State started to pass Acts in order to suppress these groups which were seen as enemies of the State; imprisonment or even execution were penalties for not conforming. Many dissenters, therefore, did not advertise their disillusion. Some even attended worship at the Parish Church and then attended their own meetings.

The Conventical Act of 1593 had set out a series of fines payable for holding services other than at the Parish Church. Continued refusal to attend services for one month could result in imprisonment and for three months absence exile or death. In the seventeenth century imprisonment, death or exile were still in evidence.[3]

What was happening in Hurstpierpoint during these upheavals?

The Goring family were in residence at Danny. They were supporters of King Charles I. George Goring was Member of Parliament for Lewes between 1620 and 1628. He held many important positions at Court as well as commanding Royalist forces in Kent and Essex. He spent much of his wealth supporting the Royal cause. This resulted in his bankruptcy and the subsequent sale of the Danny Estate.[4]

As we have seen in the chapter on the Church, in 1607 Dr Christopher Swale was instituted to the Rectory of the Parish under the patronage of George Goring. Dr Swale came from a Yorkshire family who had lived in Swaledale for many generations. He graduated from Cambridge in 1598, took a BD degree in 1605, and a DD in 1612. He was tutor to Prince Henry and chaplain to James I and then to Charles I. His sympathies were wholly to the Royalist Cause. There is a report that he was one of the loyal Sussex Clergy who each furnished a musket for the King's Defence. In 1625 he was appointed a JP for the county.[5] Dr Swale was married three times. His second wife Rose was the daughter of John Sackville of Chiddlingly. She had four children in 1619, 1620, 1623 and 1624 – 2 boys and 2 girls. In April 1624 Rose and her baby daughter of three days were buried. Dr Swale's third wife was Ann West daughter of Lord Delawar. She had two children. These first seventeen years in Hurstpierpoint were not happy ones for Dr Swale; unfortunately his life was not going to improve.[6]

By 1642 the King's insistence on his Divine Right to rule was being opposed by more and more of his subjects, including many of his once staunch supporters. The Long Parliament resolved that the Government of the Church of England by Archbishops, Bishops etc was an impediment to Reformation and prejudicial to The State of the Kingdom and that the same should taken away. In 1644 an Ordinance was made that every man over the age of 18 years should be directed to take the Solemn League and Covenant and the following year another Ordinance abolished the Prayer Book and a directory for Public Worship was established. This was a signal for the many dissenters' groups to report clergymen who refused to follow the directive.[7]

In February 1644 such a report was made to The Sussex Committee of Plundered Ministers by a group of Quakers in Hurstpierpoint. Dr Swale was asked by the Committee to take the vow and covenant by a certain date. This he obviously refused to do and he was 'sequestered of and from the Rectory of Hurstpierpoint and all his spirituall promocons in the County of Sussex.' On April 12 1645 the indictment was made that 'Christopher Swale DD Rector of the Parish Church of Hurstpierpoint, had, among other things continued the practice of the superstitious simulacion of bowing at the name of Jesus.' He was also accused of saying that the Parliament is no Parliament' and he had refused to publish the order of The House of Commons against bowing at the name of Jesus.[8] While the investigation into Dr Swale's actions was being made two more of his children died. His incumbency of the Hurst Living proved to be an unhappy one. Just six months after he left the Rectory he also, was to die.

The success of the group of Quakers in Hurstpierpoint was an impetus to their faith and witness. Their belief was that every individual had direct communication with God who would guide them in the ways of truth. Their disagreements with the church were expressed in many ways. They refused to pay tithes to the church or support it in any way. They refused to take the Oath of Allegiance. They were determined to meet for worship wherever and in what manner they chose. Their refusal to pay for and bear arms is well known.

In 1645 Leonard Letchford became Rector of Hurstpierpoint after two other priests had refused the appointment. He must have had a reputation as to his attitude towards the Quakers as two of them tried to keep him from the Living. James Matthew and Thomas Leaney were committed to Horsham Assizes and ordered to pay £3 in costs. Letchford took up the appointment and proved a scourge to the local Quaker Meeting for many years.[9]

The Danny Rental of 1663 records that Leonard Letchford, held copyhold lands of 65 acres called East Edgeley and Farnefield and one water mill called Cobbs Mill in the name of his wife Ann. He and his wife set up a charity by which a hundred pounds was given to purchase land, the rent of which was to be divided yearly among ten industrious persons with large families.[10]

The first recorded Quaker Meeting in Sussex was at Horsham in 1655 when John Slee, Thomas Laycock and Thomas Lawson spoke in public in the market square. Meetings had to be held in private houses to avoid the public disturbances that often took place. Soon Lawson and Laycock began to travel to neighbouring villages 'declaring the Truth.' Hurstpierpoint appears to have become the centre of the Society in this part of Sussex. The Hurst Meeting took in the villages of Twineham, Woodmancote, Bolney, Slaugham, Cuckfield, Clayton and Keymer. Lawson and Laycock visited the house of Humphrey Killingbeck in Twineham and from then on dissenters in Twineham and Hurstpierpoint in particular allowed their houses to be used for meetings.[11]

George Fox, the founder of The Society of Friends, had been travelling the country spreading 'The Word' and in 1655 he visited Sussex for the first time speaking at a meeting in Horsham. He then moved on to Steyning and spoke at a meeting 'where many were convinced'. His Journal goes on to record:

> And several; meetings I had thataways. And there was a meeting appointed at a great man's house. And he and his sons went to fetch several priests that had threatened to come and dispute but when the time came none of them would come, the Lord's power struck them . . . [This would indicate, perhaps, that Leonard Letchford was not the only local priest against the Quakers]. Fox went on to record . . . And Nicholas Beard and many others were convinced that day that came to hear the dispute.[12]

It is probable that members of The Hurstpierpoint Meeting would have attended. From 1655 onwards Horsham Assize Court was committing more and more Quaker prisoners to gaol. Their crimes were mainly of sedition and non-payment of tithes due to the Church. Thomas Avery, 'at the suit of Leonard Letchford,' was committed for two years and likewise Thomas Luxford in 1660 for the same offence of non-payment of tithes. Luxford was a retired sea captain who had become a farmer. He was the leader of the Hurstpierpoint Meeting.[13] The 1663 Danny Rental records him as being the copyholder of various lands and tenements as well as of a messuage garden and orchard named Matts. The former owner of this property (roughly where Norfolk House is today) was the sequestered Rector Christopher Swale. (It is unlikely that Thomas Luxford the Quaker and Thomas Luxford of Randolls were one and the same.) The year 1662/1663 was a milestone in the history of the Hurst Quakers. Thomas Luxford's house was used regularly as a meeting place not only for local members but for members of Societies from surrounding areas such as Lewes and Brighton. As such it is probable that visiting preachers stayed there. What is certain is that a young man from Westmoreland who had been travelling the country spreading 'The Truth' had visited the family in 1656 on his journey through the south. After much suffering and imprisonment in Wiltshire and Hampshire he came to Hurstpierpoint again – his name was Ambrose Rigge.[14]

In May 1662 officers arrived at Luxford's house while a religious meeting was in progress and arrested eight men; Henry Scrase, Richard Scrase, Nicholas Beard, William Holben, Richard Webb, James Matthew, Ambrose Galloway and Ambrose Rigge.[15] All had been arrested before. James Matthew was a resident and Henry Scrase occupied Wanbarrow. Ambrose Galloway came from a well-known Lewes family all of whom were prominent Quakers. Nicholas Beard was one of the most eminent of Sussex Quakers and came from a Rottingdean family. Members of the Beard family lived in Hurstpierpoint, at one period in the Mansion House. The eight men were committed to Horsham Assizes and then to terms of imprisonment. Letchford published a tract in which he charged Quakers with having a devil in ten particular forms:

1. An irreligious Devil
2. A seducing and erroneous Devil
3. A proud, supercilious, uncharitable, censorious Devil
4. An uncivil, unmannerly Devil
5. A covetous, fraudulent, sacriligious Devil
6. A rebellious, traytorous Devil
7. An absurd, senseless, stoical Devil
8. A trifling, peddling, ridiculous Devil
9. An atheistical Devil
10. A discontented, blundering Devil

Rigge was offered the Oath of Allegiance at Letchford's instigation. Ambrose refused and he too was tried at the Assize Court, Letchford being his chief accuser. The latter described him as 'a jugler, a mountebank, a lyer, a locust and a specially dangerous man.' Rigge was committed under the Statute of Praemunire, which meant he was unprotected by law and out of the protection of the King and his goods and chattels forfeit forever and all his lands and tenements during his life. He was to be imprisoned during the King's pleasure. This in fact lasted for ten years.

Ambrose did not waste his time while in prison. In 1663 he petitioned the King for the release of prisoners 'to whome the gaoler is cruell.' This was granted and all but Rigge were pardoned.[16] In 1664 in Horsham Gaol he married Thomas Luxford's daughter Mary. Nicholas Beard, James Matthew, Richard Webb and Richard Scrase were among the witnesses.[17]

Mary was Letchford's next target. She had inherited property in Hurstpierpoint and so was liable for tithes – she refused to pay. Letchford did not recognise Mary's marriage to Rigge as they were not married at the parish church. The process to exact tithes was issued in her maiden name. She was arrested at her father's house and joined her husband in prison. Mary was able to furnish their room in the gaol. In 1666 their first child Ambrose was born there. He died the following year. Two more children were born – Mary in 1667 and Thomas in 1670.[18] When Letchford could not exact his tithes from Mary, the bailiffs were sent to the gaol with an execution order to obtain goods to the total of tithes due; 'they brake and spoiled, robbed and carried away all proper goods leaving not so much as a bed to lie upon.'[19]

Ambrose finally left gaol in 1672. The family lived in Horsham for a time and then moved to Gatton. There he was soon in conflict with the local priest. He was prosecuted and the family excommunicated. Mary's health began to deteriorate and she died in 1689. Ambrose married a family friend who was a widow. He died in Reigate in 1705.[20]

The group of Quakers persecuted by Leonard Letchford were, in the middle of the seventeenth century, the most high profile members of the Hurst Meeting. Many of them came from other parts of the county. There were others in the surrounding villages, who had been convinced by the travelling preachers. The names of these appear in the Quaker records of marriages births and deaths. Just as Anglican Parishes kept records so too did the Quakers.

Marriages would take place in the houses of Members. In Hurstpierpoint the houses of John Grover, Thomas Luxford, Frances Randall and Constance Best were used. The names of the bride and groom, their places of residence and the names of the witnesses were all recorded. The number of witnesses varied from three (at the marriage of Robert Johnson and Kathleen Langley both of Hurstpierpoint in 1660); to forty-six (at the marriage of Jon Snashall, widower of Hurstpierpoint, to Elizabeth Bradford, widow, of Wartling in 1706).

There are many names recorded in these registers. We can only guess that the majority were Quakers. A large number of them are names familiar to the history of Hurstpierpoint including the Scrase family, the Beards, the Averys and the Grovers.[21]

The first mention of the Grover family was in 1655 when John the Elder became 'convinced' during the visit of Thomas Laycock and Thomas Lawson to the house of Humphrey Killingbeck in Twineham. In 1658 he was fined 20 shillings for non-payment of tithes to Edward Hind, priest. John the Elder died in 1666.[22]

His son John, who was a cooper, married Ann Killingbeck and it was at his house in Hurst that meetings and some marriages took place.[23]

Leonard Letchford was still the priest and he continued his persecution though not apparently on the same vicious scale as with Ambrose Rigge. On one occasion it proved rather embarrassing.

Informers entered John Grover's house to take the names of those present at the illegal meeting. Unfortunately the Headborough (constable) could not write and no one would do it for him. A Justice was approached and he levied a fine of twenty pounds five shillings on goods of John. The goods were seized but not taken away. John appealed at the next Assizes, the jury was discharged but eventually some of his stock was seized.[24]

Leonard Letchford died in December 1673. The Records of the Society of Friends Suffering state that:

> The said Leonard Letchford went to bed but was found dead in the morning and Soe Ended that wicked persecutor who was a constant persecutor of the people of God not onley for the tithe wch he claimed of them but allso Tooke all other occasions to Stirr up persecution against them and wrott a very falce and Lying Pamphlet against them stuffed full of Grosse abuses to render them as unfitting to live upon the earth which was answered by Ambrose Rigge.[25]

It must be remembered that the constant persecutor of the people of God had more charitable thoughts towards his other parishioners. The charity founded by him and his wife was still paying out sums of money to deserving villagers in 1714. Thomas Marchant made several references to it in his diary.

The death of Letchford did not end the misery of the local Quakers. They still refused to pay tithes and refused to attend Divine Worship at the Parish Church.

In 1677 John Grover and his wife with members of other families were excommunicated.[26] John's continued absences from Divine Service finally resulted in seizures of more goods including such items as a warming pan, pewter platters, porringers, a spade and one iron kettle taken from the fire with water in it for use. This final sentence proved too much for his business which he could not then carry on. He died in 1689.[27]

His son John was twelve years old at the time of his father's death. As a shepherd boy he began to support the family. In turn he became a maltster, a schoolmaster and a skilled mathematician.

The Minute Book of the Friends at Brighton show that John Grover and Elizabeth Harrison were married at West Blatchington in 1697.[28] He was appointed master at the Free School in the Lanes in Brighton in 1702. From there he went to teach navigation at a Charity School for the education of 20 poor boys also in Brighton. Sometime before 1730 a Mr Haylor described John:

> As being famous for his mathematical skill. He was descended
> from mean parentage and was bought up illiterately but he had an
> inquisitive genius which stirred him up to the aquirement of arts
> and sciences. His skill in mathematics without one day's
> instruction but his diligence proficiency was as great as any in his
> time.[29]

He taught there until 1750. At his death in 1752 the following
obituary appeared in the Lewes Journal:

> He obtained a considerable knowledge of the law in which
> capacity he was highly useful, he practised it with uncommon
> honesty and moderation in his demands.[30]

The Toleration Act of 1689 meant that Dissent was no longer a crime.
Dissenters were able to apply to the Quarter Sessions for a licence for a
Meeting House. The Hurstpierpoint Meeting obtained such a licence.[31] By
the end of the 17th century the status of Quaker families in the community
had risen and neighbours and local persons of note would be invited to and
attend marriages.[32]

In 1706 when John Snashall, a well-known local Quaker, married for the
third time many well-known non-Quakers were among the witnesses. Sarah
Courthope, Richard Whitpaine and Mary Marchant were just three from
local wealthy families. One of the signatories was William Penn, the
founder of Pennsylvania. For 10 years he lived at Warminghurst Place near
Horsham.[33]

Those not of the Established Church were refused burial in the Parish
graveyards so dissenters had to find land for their last resting place, possibly
outside the boundaries of their village or town. The Hurstpierpoint Meeting
were very lucky to be granted a plot of land at Twineham Parish Church. It
is thought that the Rector, the Reverend Killingbeck allowed the local
Meeting this part of the churchyard as his daughter had married a Quaker.
(Ann Killingbeck married John Grover snr). The plot was bought by The
Society in 1694 and about sixty interments took place – the last being in
1732. The plot can still be seen marked by four boundary stones.[34] The
names of those buried there are recorded in the Quaker Registers.

These registers have one or two interesting entries. In July 1661 George Fox jnr was buried. On closer investigation it transpires that this was not the son of George Fox who, in fact, had no children. The person referred to was George Fox the younger who was no relation to the Founder of the Quaker Movement but who did have similar views. In 1651 he had joined the movement and become a preacher and writer of pamphlets. He visited Hurstpierpoint in 1661 and it is thought that he died at the house of Thomas Luxford.[35]

A rather sad event is to be found recorded in 1663. In May, June and July of that year five members of the same family were buried: Sarah Hogg, her three daughters Mary, Sarah and Jean and finally Richard her husband. Ambrose Rigge the son of Ambrose and Mary died in April 1667, he was one year old.[36]

The rectors who followed Leonard Letchford appear to have left the Quakers to worship in peace. The few references to the rectors were in Thomas Marchant's diary and they were not of a spiritual nature.

The eighteenth century saw a decline in the number of Quaker adherents throughout the country as the numbers of other non-conformist groups rose.[37]

We can only assume that those of the Hurstpierpoint Meeting continued to meet in the premises licensed in 1689. There appears to have been no attempt to build a Meeting House as many groups through the country had done.

The years of persecution had presumably dampened the faith of the younger members of those families who had incurred the wrath of the Reverend Letchford. The impetus gained by that persecution and by the fervour of Ambrose Rigge perhaps decreased with the death of Letchford and Ambrose's move to Horsham.

The boy from Westmoreland who had set out on a pilgrimage so many years ago had for a short time made a profound impression on a small Sussex village.

METHODISM

'I look upon the world as my parish'
John Wesley's journal

In the bedroom of a house in City Road, London an old man lay dying. The thoughts and prayers of thousands of people throughout the country were focussed on that bedroom and its occupant. His name was John Wesley; the date was March 2nd 1791. He died surrounded by his family, Methodist preachers and two Anglican priests.[38]

Born in 1703 John was a child of the Rectory. His father became the rector of Epworth in Lincolnshire. John and his brother Charles were both ordained as Anglican priests. In 1727 he became a curate to his father. Charles attended Christ's College in Oxford and while there he and a group of friends joined in a strict method of religious observance which earned them the name of Methodists. When visiting his brother, John joined in the meetings and in 1729 he became leader of the group. Some historians judge this to be the beginning of the Methodist movement. The general consensus however is that the movement began in 1739.[39]

In the mid-eighteenth century the parson was becoming more and more identified with the wealthy members of his flock and consequently the rural workers and those in the expanding industrial areas felt that the Church had abandoned them. Although the brothers were part of the High Anglican tradition they were being drawn to a more humanitarian spirit in their preaching. The atmosphere at the Rectory in Epworth had been one of religious observance, self-discipline and work for others.
Like the Puritans of the 17th century Wesley wanted to revive from within what he saw as a static Church. He worked to improve the evils of the Poor Law, penal code, prisons and public hangings. He published pamphlets on social and political issues but he forbade his preachers to meddle in politics.[40]

John Wesley's revivalist style of preaching deeply moved the vast numbers of the population who had felt neglected by the established Church and the State. Singing formed a considerable part of his services and he wrote many hymns. His first hymnbook was published in 1737 in America while he was a missionary in Georgia. Many of the hymns were translations from German writers.[41] Although he wrote a large number of hymns it was his brother Charles who was our greatest hymn writer. His output was prolific, over five and a half thousand, many of which were based on the scriptures and in language easily understood. An example is 'O for a heart to praise my God' taken from psalm 51. The coincidence of the growth of Methodism and the Industrial Revolution had a profound effect on England for many years.[42]

Wesley and his itinerant preachers travelled hundreds of miles throughout the country. He organised his followers into local societies, which were then united into circuits and the circuits into districts under a superintendent Minister. The first Annual Conference was instituted in 1744. In the early days of the movement ministers were moved from circuit to circuit each year but to keep a sense of continuity a great reliance was placed on lay preachers. To this day ministers are still moved on after a statutory length of time.

Apart from London the most important societies were in the mining towns of Cornwall and Yorkshire and the commercial centres of Bristol, Manchester and Birmingham. Much of the rest of the country including Sussex was not swayed by the preaching of John and his travelling preachers.

At the time of Wesley's death Methodism had 70,000 members and a possible 500,000 sympathising adherents. The Society had neither Ministers nor Sacraments. Those wishing to take Holy Communion did so at their Parish Church unless Wesley or other Anglican priests who had joined him were preaching in a nearby town or village. His intention still was to revive the Established Church from within. By the time of his death, however, he had been moving towards creating a separate denomination. After the Conference of 1795 splits were beginning to appear. Those who had begun to disagree with Wesley's views felt able to speak out. Methodists became Bible Christians, Primitive Methodists, the Methodist New Connexion and Wesleyan Methodists to name but a few; the latter being those who still followed John and Charles Wesley's teaching.[43]

The Methodist story for Hurstpierpoint has to begin in Brighton.

There are no records of John Wesley preaching in Brighton or Mid Sussex. He was, however, a frequent visitor to Rye. In 1773 he recorded in his diary his disgust at the smuggling activities of the inhabitants. Rum and other spirits from the Continent were the smugglers' main trade. It was in Sussex at Winchelsea in 1790 when he was 87 years of age that he preached his last outdoor sermon under an ash tree outside the parish church.[44]

A group of Calvinist Methodists had existed in Brighton since 1759. In 1780 Edward Beves came to the town from Fareham. He was of the Arminean Methodist persuasion. They, like the Wesleyans, rejected the Calvinist doctrine of predestination. Beves worshipped at the Parish Church of Saint Nicholas but gradually a group of Wesleyans gathered round him and a class meeting of nine was established. They met in a house in Middle Street. The numbers increased when the North Yorkshire and South Gloucestershire Militias were stationed at Preston barracks in 1804. Preachers were invited from the Lewes circuit and in 1807 the Lewes and Brighton Circuit was formed. In 1811 it was renamed the Brighton Circuit. In 1816 Cuckfield was the first village in Mid Sussex to have a meeting place.[45]

On 18 November 1830 a licence was granted for 'an Assembly of Protestant Dissenters in a messuage in the occupation of Henry Hider Farmer in the Parish of Hurstpierpoint in the County of Sussex.'[46] The society does not seem to have been formed until 1833.[47]

In 1851 a religious census was taken of congregations at all places of worship on the 30th March. This records that a Wesleyan Methodist Chapel was built in Hurst in 1834. It had seventy-six free seats and fifty-five others. At the morning service there were seventy in the congregation and in the evening ninety-one. Mr George Batchelor was the Steward. There was no mention of a Minister.[48] This chapel was built on land at the bottom of Chinese Lane (Western Road) given by Henry Hider. The farmer owned a lot of land in the Courtbushes, Fairfield, Eastfield and Copthall areas. Unfortunately the premises were badly built and the front had to be rebuilt in 1848. A sketch of the layout of sewers and drains made in 1870 shows a chapel next to the gas works in Western Road.[49]

In 1836 the membership of the society was twenty. The leader was William Batchelor. Others were Thomas Bowyer, Jane Crookery, Richard Davey, John and Mary Gorringe, William and Mary Harmes and their two children, Henry and Mary Hider, John Noble, Henry Sayers, James and Susan Talmey, William Standen and son, Thomas and Mary White.[50] Some of these names appeared in the schedule to the Fisher Map of 1841; only an assumption can be made that they were people in the group.

Thomas Bowyer a bricklayer occupied a house with garden opposite Churchfields. The Davey family were long-time residents of Hurst. In 1841 Richard Davey snr was the Parish Clerk living at Prospect Place where the funeral director's is today. There were two properties listed and Richard Davey jnr owned the other one with a tenant living there. He was a shoemaker and apparently lived in Brighton. Was he one of the members mentioned above? John Gorringe was also a shoemaker. He lived in North Cottages (Ribbetts Cottages). Thomas White, a saddler lived next to the Church. The leader William Batchelor was perhaps the labourer living at Clerkenwell Cottage, (down the Brighton Road south of Church cottages near Policeman's Lane).[51]

Henry Hider, farmer, was a member of the Sparrow Club whose activities were extensively reported in the local press. In 1845 a newspaper report indicated that he had died.[52]

Small societies would have relied on visiting Ministers from the Brighton Circuit and elsewhere and on lay preachers. In 1846 The Rev Theophilus Woolner of Worthing was engaged to preach at morning, afternoon and evening services and administer the sacrament. He left home at 5.00 am, walked to Hurst and then walked home arriving there at midnight.[53]

An intriguing remark was made by the Rev Carey Borrer in his diary of 27 January 1852:

> An exceedingly wet day. Tidings of a sad division among the Wesleyans.[54]

Unfortunately the Rev. Borrer did not elaborate on this division.

The next milestone was in 1868 when the Society bought a chapel in Manor Road for £400 (Wellesley House). This had been erected by an Independent Minister named Lambert.[55]

In December 1876 the following report appeared in the East Sussex News

> The Wesleyans at Hurstpierpoint held a Service of sacred songs on a Monday evening when connective readings from Pilgrim's Progress were given and on the following evening 'An Illustration of Bunyan's Christians' was the title again with connective readings.[56]

By 1889 the membership had risen to twenty-seven.[57] Membership of the Methodist Church is a renewal of the promises and vows made in one's name at baptism by godparents. In the Anglican Church this is Confirmation.

Plate 31. Methodists outside Manor Road Chapel sometime between 1868 and 1908.

Sunday Schools were an important part of most Methodist Societies. Some large chapels had their own day schools. Many children and adults learned their three R's at Sunday School or in adult classes at their local chapel. Many were too poor to pay the half penny (or whatever) a week to go to the National School.

Violet Morley who was born in 1901 remembers going to the Sunday School and Chapel in Manor road. On summer evenings the harmonium would be taken outside and open-air services held.[58]

In 1908 a New Trust was formed with the intention of building a new chapel. In August 1909 the stone-laying ceremony took place and on Easter Monday the following year the new Chapel in Cuckfield Road was opened. The names of some members of the New Trust will be remembered by many in the village today. Messrs Boxall, Boyling, Buckingham, Bundock, B Bunker, Griffin, Eleazar Harvey, Ernest Harvey, H Hoad, P A Izzett, H King, Rusden, Townsend, W H Voyce and T White snr and jnr. sixteen men and their families who continued the tradition set by the twenty members who first met in Henry Hider's farm house. Eleazar and Ernest Harvey were two of the many Cornish Methodist farmers who migrated to the southern counties at the beginning of the twentieth century. Their leadership encouraged the growth of the Society in Hurst.

In 1928 after long discussions permanent accommodation was built for the Sunday School. It had a slow combustion stove for heating.

In 1932 the various strands of Methodism were united under one denominational title. The Church had been served for many years by supernumerary ministers, many of whom were in office for only a year or even months due to age. In 1938 Mr Eleazar Harvey died. He had served the Church for many years. In his will he left a sum of money for the purchase of a house for a Minister to reside in the village. In 1939 the first Minister took up residence.

In 1963 the long association with the Brighton and Hove Circuit ended when a transfer to the Sussex Mission Circuit was agreed. New arrangements meant that younger and fully employed ministers were appointed instead of supernumeraries. There was a case of 'déjà-vu' in autumn 1966 when the west wall was in need of repair. Many changes have been made to the building, some being necessary repairs but some like the replacement of the front porch by the vestibule, ministers vestry and upper room have improved the facilities.

In 1968 a truly memorable occasion took place. Lord Soper, the well-loved twentieth century Methodist who followed closely the hopes and ideas of John Wesley, preached to a packed church – a highlight in the history of any Methodist Society.[59]

THE BAPTISTS

The Baptist Movement in England predates the Methodists by about two hundred years. It stems from Separatists of the early 16th century who were influenced by Anabaptists from Holland and by Calvinistic Puritans who were disillusioned by the Church of England in Elizabeth I's reign.

As with the Quakers many of them were persecuted and even burnt at the stake for heresy, sedition and failure to follow the prayer book. Many fled to Holland. Some settled there, some returned to England and some sailed for the New World as the Pilgrim Fathers. One who returned to England was Thomas Helwys. In 1612 he was to establish the first General Baptist Church at Spitalfields.

As with the other non-conformist denominations, splits occurred. There were three main groups – Anabaptists, General Baptists and Particular Baptists.[60] Anabaptists were those who had been baptised in infancy and then again as adults on a confession of faith.[61]

Bishop Sheldon's review in 1669 recorded an Anabaptist Group in Ditchling. A leading member of the group was the vicar the Reverend Edward Lulham. In 1672 he and his churchwarden, Robert Marchant, were given licences to hold meetings in cottages in the area. The congregation soon linked itself to the General Baptist Assembly. Gradually they began to question orthodox belief and took up more liberal views and by the end of the 18th century became Unitarians.[62] The Unitarians of the seventeenth century denied the Trinity. They accepted God as the Father but rejected the divinity of Christ. Now they identify with more liberal beliefs, the movement to world peace and a more Humanist point of view.[63] A chapel was built, the trust deeds dating from 1740. In 1851 the Minister was Thomas Gilbert of Hurstpierpoint.[64] One could speculate that people of like mind in Hurstpierpoint journeyed those few miles into Ditchling.

The Baptist cause in Sussex gradually succeeded the Quakers throughout the 18th century. The first registered meeting in West Sussex was at Handcross in1775. John Burgess who lived in Ditchling began writing a diary in 1785. He was a glover by trade and apart from recording everyday events he made many references to visiting the Baptist Meetings in villages around Ditchling. He made no mention of Hurstpierpoint with regard to religious meetings. He did however visit Mr Randall a shoemaker and twice had to fetch Doctor Weekes to assist at the birth of two of his sons.[65]

In Hurstpierpoint there is evidence that a Meeting aligned to the Strict Baptists was established in1829.[66]

The next documentary evidence of a Baptist chapel was in the Fisher schedule in 1841. It records houses, yard and Baptist Chapel owner Mrs Lampriere of Brighton. The whole property was called Uttica House and was situated behind the Royal Oak opposite the New Inn. The site is now occupied by Alldays. Was this the house where Pastor John Grace of The Tabernacle, Brighton preached in 1846? [67]

What we do know is that in the 1851 Religious Census there is the following entry:

> Providence Chapel east end of the Town of Hurstpierpoint, Independent Calvinist built about 1833. Seats – all free for 160 adults attendance (last Sunday in March) am 100 afternoon 140. Supported by Voluntary Contributions
> John Banks, Lahore Cottage, Minister.

A word here about Little Park Chapel.

In 1852 Colonel Charles Smith Hannington lived at St George's House. The rector of the time was Carey Hampton Borrer. At some point a disagreement occurred between the two men. In 1942 an explanation about the split was given to Mr A H Gregory author of 'Mid-Sussex through the ages' by Major C H Hannington JP. It appears that the Colonel did not like the way he was being treated by Canon Borrer and he told the Rector so. The Canon retaliated by preaching at the Colonel who promptly left the Parish Church. Mr Hannington is reported to have told Borrer 'not to come the High Priest over me.' The Colonel built a Chapel in the grounds of his house, the Rector opposed the appointment of an Anglican curate.[68] The Chapel was known as Little Park Chapel. Between 1852 and 1867 many of the well known Baptist Pastors from Brighton and other parts of Sussex were invited to preach in the Chapel, Messrs Banks, Grace and Vivall among them.[69]

The Bishop eventually acted as mediator between the two men and in 1867 the chapel was licensed for public worship by the C of E. In 1892 it was made over to the Diocese of Chichester and became known as St George's Church.[70]

At some point a chapel had been built at the beginning of Manor Road. In 1875 this became too small. Some land at the top of Western road became available and in 1876 the present Hope Chapel was built (see Colour Plate 14). Among the original trustees were Henry Hide, Charles Stevens and Henry Miles. Henry Miles was the first pastor.[71] A Henry Hide is mentioned in the 1874 Kelly's directories as occupying Danworth Farm and in the 1894 directory as being the surveyor of highways, assessor and collector of highway rates and Queen's taxes. Was this the same man? Was Charles Stevens, the tailor mentioned in the same two directories?[72] The chapel continues to have two services a month.

THE MEETING HOUSES MYSTERIES

It has already been mentioned that in the seventeenth, eighteenth and nineteenth centuries licences had to be sought in order to hold religious meetings that were not of the established Church. There were several of those pertaining to Hurstpierpoint after that granted to the Quakers. In all but one of the licences granted between 1765 and 1842 we do not know which particular denomination was concerned, about the first in 1765 a speculation can be made:

Feb 1765   A meeting or assembly for Religious worship of
            people called Protestant Dissenters to be held at

the house of John Wakear situate in the parish of
Hurstpierpoint in the County of Sussex at the
request of Henry Beach and Richard Harman.[73]

In 1757 Selina the Countess of Huntingdon went to Brighton. She was not impressed with the Anglican ethos there and decided there was a need for evangelical religion in the town. George Whitefield an evangelist had aroused great interest with his preaching, mainly in the open air. He inspired the Countess to the extent that she built a chapel on land behind her house in North Street. She gathered round her a group of ministers who were ordained Anglicans. These were her missioners who travelled around the neighbouring villages and towns. She finally established herself in Wivelsfield living at Great Ote Hall. Her chaplains became well known. One of her chaplains visited Hurstpierpoint in 1769 where he held an open-air meeting. He was accompanied by friends from Ditchling, Ote Hall and Brighton. He had expected opposition and in the end was shouted down. After the meeting and inspite of the reception he commented that 'many were deeply attentive and much affected and he was impressed by the fervour shown in the small villages.' Several applications were made for registration of meeting places in the district, perhaps that made in 1765 for a place in Hurstpierpoint was one of them.[74]

Who was William Cotton? Where did he live? In December 1816 an application was made for meetings to be held at his house.[75]

Most applications gave us little information. In 1817 however we learn a little more as a Court Baron was needed:

Court Baron of W J Campion esq Lord of the Manor of
Hurstpierpoint
13.5.1817 surrender of all messuages or tenements lately erected
and built upon part of a certain tenement called Lower
Trumpkins. To the use and behoof of the Rev George Bennet of
Hurst, Clerk.

The licence was issued in September 1817. The chapel has been attributed to the Methodists [76] but the return in the Religious Census of 1851 refutes this. Who then was the Rev George Bennett and what denomination did he represent? There was obviously not a large congregation for the Rev

Bennett, as in 1819 the building was sold to William Borrer for £460. With the chapel went all fixtures and the free right to water. In April 1820 the land with chapel was released to William Borrer and eight other gentlemen to be converted into a National School House.[77]

In 1868 the new church school was built in Cuckfield Road (now St Lawrence School). The National School building was sold to Mr Henry Sendall, grocer at a public auction. A covenant was attached to the sale that the premises should not be used as a place of public worship.[78]

xxv. Chapel at Trumpkins, later the National School, now the Player's Theatre.
(Bill Parrott, after a sketch made in 1826).

The entries in the Parish registers on the above transactions tell us quite a lot about the area known as Lower Trumpkins. This is the area from east of Grapevine Cottage (Trumpkins) to the end of Hampton Cottages. Three tenements belonged to Thomas Herriott. In his will of 15 March 1810 he bequeathed 'all effects to his widow and executrix Sarah while she remained his widow with provision otherwise for his children'. In May 1817 the Rev George Bennett acquired these premises. The need to sell these properties was to pay costs and the redemption of the mortgage. In October 1819 the Rev Bennett then sold the tenements to John Geering, farmer of Twineham.[79]

The chapel is now the Players Theatre. A drawing was made in about 1826, which shows the building and cottages surrounding it.[80]

In 1820, 1832, 1839 and 1842 more applications were made.[81]

In 1820 William Pierce lived at Pookbourne. Pookbourne Lane runs north from Cobbs Mill to Jobs Lane, an area where there are few houses today. William was possibly a carpenter.[82] He and other like-minded people did not wish to worship at the Parish Church but in premises of their own choice.

In 1832 John Ashfold of Sayers Common applied for a licence for a congregation of Protestants to worship in his house. The Ashfold family had lived in the area since the seventeenth century. William Ashfold was one of the first Quakers of the Hurst Meeting in 1655.[83]

After 1833 there were two recognised places of worship for dissenters so one wonders why William Randall and James Vallance applied for registration for their premises to be used for worship.

The Randall family is quite well documented in the middle of the nineteenth century. The schedule to the Fisher map of 1841 records William with several properties, including a garden at Prospect Row and Prospect Place (opposite the Parish Church) Blackford House on the High Street, Amwell Cottages and Amwell Place (his residence). William, who was a shoemaker, fly proprietor and the postmaster died in 1844.[84] The tombstone of him and his wife is outside the St Lawrence Chapel porch door.

The trade directories of 1839, 1845 and 1867 include James Vallance Esq. of Kingsland, Sayers Common (where the Priory is today). There are three gentlemen by the name of Vallance listed in the 1841 census, one of them a farmer and two of independent means. Which of them wanted to use the entrance lodge for worship? [85]

Between 1839 and 1855 the Antinomians came to Hurst. They were a sect that had been in existence since the Reformation. In England the sect developed during the Commonwealth. Their general belief was that Christians are, by grace, set free from the need of observing any moral law.[86] During that period there was a chapel somewhere in the village. There was no mention of it in a later directory.

In 1894 the 2,883 inhabitants of Hurstpierpoint and Sayers Common had a choice of seven places of worship. There were a total of seventeen services on a Sunday, with some weekday services as well. Added to the three Anglican churches and the Wesleyan and Baptist chapels, were the North End Mission Room at Oaklands Park and Hampton Lodge Mission Room (unsectarian).[87] The latter was possibly the chapel built in 1833 by the Independent Calvinists. In 1937 it was reported that Miss Bristowe and Miss Cowley, joint superintendents of the Hurstpierpoint Mission, had retired after thirteen years service. In 1938 the name was changed to The Evangelical Church.[88] The North End Mission Room was opened in 1887 as a gift from General Alexander of Burgess Hill. It was next to the Sportsman at Goddards Green.[89]

A century later the Methodist Church, the Hope Baptist Chapel and the Evangelical Church are the only three non-conformist places of worship left in Hurstpierpoint.

In 1676 the Compton census recorded the religious allegiances of those over the age of 16. In Hurstpierpoint there were 217 Anglicans, 22 dissenters and no Roman Catholics. Sussex Catholicism was centred on large estates like Cowdray, Arundel and others mainly in the far west of the county.[90] In Hurstpierpoint the Catholic Church was not established until 1925. It has no resident priest.

The mystery remains. The attraction of independence may have been the initial driving force for the need to worship differently from the Church of England and the recognised Non-Conformist societies. That independence was, perhaps, not enough to keep the small house groups alive and mainstream non-conformism became the answer.

NOTES AND REFERENCES

1. Kohler C (1990): *Soldier in the Lamb's War*, 1.
2. Trevelyan G M (1972): *English Social History*, 256.
3. Watts M R (1996): *The Chapel and the Nation*, 9.
4. ESRO/ DAN 276–310.
5. Sperling J H (1870): Parochial History of Westbourne, *SAC* **22**, 103n.
6. WSRO/ Par 400/1/1/1.
7. Watson D R (?date): *The Life of King Charles I*.
8. Sawyer F E (1880): Proceedings of the Committee of Plundered Ministers relating to Sussex, *SAC* **30**, 121, 122.
9. *Ibid.*, 123.
10. Turner E (1873): The Marchant Diary, *SAC* **25**, 183, 186.
11. Figg W (1854): Sufferings of the Quakers in Lewes, *SAC* **16**, 87.
12. The Journal of George Fox.
13. Albery W(1947): *A Millennium of Facts on the History of Horsham and Sussex*, 412.
14. Kohler, *Soldier*, 20
15. Albery, *Millennium of Facts*, 419.
16. *Ibid.*, 424, 434.
17. WSRO/MF677/RG6/1205.
18. *Ibid.*
19. Albery, *Millennium of Facts*, 435.
20. Kohler, *Soldier*, 29, 36–40.
21. WSRO/MF677/RG6/1205.
22. Figg, Lewes Quakers, *SAC* **16**, 87.
23. WSRO/MF677/RG6/1205.
24. Clayton C E (ed)(1888): Some notes on the history of John Grover, *SAC* **36**, 77.
25. Sawyer, Plundered Ministers, *SAC* **30**, 124.
26. Churchwardens Presentments 1675, *SRS* **50**, 16, 56.
27. Clayton, Grover, *SAC* **36**, 75, 76.
28. *Ibid.*, 75.
29. Farrant J A (1984): The Brighton Charity School in the Early Eighteenth Century, *SAC* **122**, 143.
30. Clayton, Grover, *SAC* **36**, 81.
31. Albery, *Millennium of Facts*, 451.
32. Figg, Lewes Quakers, *SAC* **16**, 87.
33. WSRO/MF677/RG6/1205.
34. *Twineham Parish Church Guide*.
35. *Dictionary of National Biography*.
36. WSRO/MF677/RG6/1205.

37. Watts, *Chapel & Nation*, 19.
38. Davey C J (1955): *The Methodist Story*, 11.
39. *Dictionary of National Biography*.
40. Trevelyan, *Social History*, 375, 376.
41. Davey, *Methodist*, 13.
42. Preface to the *Methodist Hymn Book 1904*.
43. Davey, *Methodist*, 13, 14, 25.
44. Brabant F G (1938): *The Little Guide to Sussex*, 232, 237.
45. Griffin Rev E (1957): *A Pilgrim People, The Story of Methodism in Brighton, Hove and District 1807 to 1957*.
46. WSRO/ EpII/25/3 f22.
47. Griffin, *Pilgrim People*.
48. Vickers J A (1989): Religious Census 1851, *SRS* **75**.
49. Maps 1834, 1842, plan of drainage 1870, held in Hurstpierpoint Library.
50. Griffin, *Pilgrim People*.
51. WSRO/ ADD MS17,685A: Schedule to Fisher Map 1841.
52. *Sussex Agricultural Express* 1845.
53. 75th Anniversary Newsletter (1985) Hurstpierpoint Methodist Church.
54. Diary of Rev Carey Hampton Borrer, transcribed by R A Packham.
55. Griffin, *Pilgrim People*.
56. Caplan N (1979: The Calvinist Methodists and the work of the Countess of Huntingdon, *The Sussex Genealogist and Local Historian*, June 1979, 4–10.
57. Griffin, *Pilgrim People*.
58. Morley V (nd, 1990s): *Memories of Hurstpierpoint*.
59. See note 53.
60. Watts, *Chapel & Nation*, 9, 10.
61. Brewer E C: *Dictionary of Phrase and Fable*.
62. Peacock A (1967): Parish Churches of the Opposition, *Sussex Life Magazine*.
63. *Philips Millennium Encyclopaedia*.
64. Religious Census 1851, *SRS* **75**.
66. Burgess D (ed)(1989): *No Continuing City, Diary and Letters of John Burgess 1785–1819*.
67. Hope Chapel Centenary Leaflet 1976.
68. Packham R A: The Hannington Family.
69. Hope Chapel Leaflet.
70. Packham, Hannington Family.
71. Hope Chapel Leaflet.
73. WSRO/ EpII/25/2 f 53.
74. *Sussex Genealogist* 1979.
75. WSRO/EpII/25.3 f 10.
76. WSRO/Par 400/25/5.
77. WSRO/Par 400/25/6.

78. WSRO/Par 400/25/12.
79. WSRO/Par 400/25/15.
80. 'A Native' (1826): *A Slight Sketch of Hurst*, 15.
81. WSRO/EpII/25 ff 12, 23v, 28, 29.
82. Bower A (2000): unpublished database of Census Returns.
83. Figg, Lewes Quakers, *SAC* **16**, 87.
84. *Kelly's Directory*.
85. Census returns.
86. Oxford Dictionary of the Christian Church.
87. Kelly's 1894.
88. Gregory A H (1938): *Mid Sussex Through the Ages*, 249.
89. Hurstpierpoint Parish Magazine April 1960.
90. See note 53.

9. LAW AND ORDER

THE CONCERNS OF SOCIETY

We have seen in the chapter on the poor that the authorities were principally concerned with maintaining order – if control was not effective, anarchy would swiftly follow. This understandable attitude was present in the management not only of those who were unable to support themselves, but also throughout the whole spectrum of disorder, from the sincere conviction of religious consent, through the petty squabbles of neighbours and perceived affronts to 'normal' behaviour, to actual attacks on property and individuals. It was a natural outcome of the stratification which had developed in society, by birth, wealth, occupation or life style. It was also a matter of dealing with the problems of the poor, the weak and the vulnerable as well as controlling the actions of the violent, the quarrelsome and the irresponsible.[1] We have looked at the first group already, but, although we cannot avoid some further mention, we are now concentrating on those whose clashes with their neighbours or with the community in general took more explicit action.

The 'rich man in his castle' could feel secure so long as the lower orders accepted their place 'at his gate', so long as deference was balanced by paternalism in an intricate web of patronage and neighbourhood ties. Order was achieved in the family and at work, where relations between spouses, children, dependants and servants were essential cogs in the machinery of society. By 1600 the gentry were beginning to see their relationship with those below them clearly, almost solely, in terms of management. One contribution to this change has been referred to in an earlier section on timber-framed houses. The open hall gave way to family privacy and backstairs for servants, with a steady increase in the proportion of living-out labourers. While deference remained this development was fairly innocuous, but we shall see that, as these ties loosened, the picture became more complex. By the eighteenth century the gentry in their role as justices thought of themselves as arbiters of agricultural employment relationships and the rulers of rural society, custodians of its peace. The parish priest played a role in trying to maintain this hierarchical structure, even as recently as the end of the nineteenth century:

God, in His infinite wisdom, had appointed a place for every man,
woman and child on this earth and it was their bounden duty to
remain contentedly in their niches.[2]

Among the factors which contributed to this gradual evolution were new
thinking about God and man, about science and nature, the waning influence
of magic, the spread of education, and also the national standards of
administration and culture which penetrated even local communities. For
example, the church's rituals and holidays were reinforcements of popular
culture, giving authority to feasts, fairs and sports, while country folk had
little concern with the deeper meanings of Christianity. While the parson
was an intimate member of the community, not significantly better educated
than his flock, ecclesiastical control was acceptable. As livings were
increasingly given to university graduates from outside, the clergy joined the
gentry in life style, and on the bench. Seventeenth century chapbooks
peddled by itinerants dealt with repentance, prophecy and judgement, and by
so doing provided some external yardstick for behaviour. But when these
promoted more radical ideas, as during the 1640s and '50s, with the 'world
turned upside down', the gentry felt that other methods of control would be
necessary. We have seen in the chapter on health how the law was called in
to control the movement of travellers in times of plague,[3] but these methods
were available to deal with the spread of perceived subversion as well as
actual infection. Like many other parishes, Hurst reflected these changes,
while in more recent times its relative proximity to London and the coast
ensured that some of them were adopted here sooner than in more remote
areas. Such unstable times tended to blur the dividing line between protest
and crime, increasing the concern of the gentry and other men of property.
In 1772 Tom Paine was only a few miles away at Lewes, putting his radical
ideas into print, so it is likely that rumours of his activities reached Hurst;
the Rights of Man was published in 1790. Reaction was inevitable,
particularly against the background of the French Revolution. In November
1792 a national movement was started for the formation of Loyalist
Associations, and a meeting was held at the Royal Oak in January 1793 to
form such an association against Republicans and Levellers, a document
signed by 64 of 'the inhabitants of Hurstpierpoint . . . [who] perceive with
the deepest concern the [circulation of] seditious and mischievous
publications and opinions subversive of our rights and privileges as
Englishmen'.[4]

Throughout the centuries there has been an acceptance by all strata in society that law has evolved out of custom, at any rate in rural areas. The parish boundaries were perambulated regularly in order to provide evidential support in cases of dispute over fishing or timber rights; any perceived encroachment might be dealt with by demolition of either buildings or fences. Gleaning was a customary right of the poor in many areas, and denial of this right could lead to court proceedings. Commoners claimed customary rights of pasture, of estovers (small wood) and turbary (turf and peat for fuel), while the landowners encroached on the same land to increase the size of their holdings, a situation which could lead to dispute, both civil and criminal, at any time between the thirteenth and eighteenth centuries. These customs were reinforced by the manorial court baron and court leet. The former dealt with matters of copyhold and payment in lieu of services, the latter with petty law and order problems by means of a system of mutual responsibility known as a 'view of frankpledge' in which representatives from each tithing in the area acted as jury. For example, the legal right to take rabbits was jealously guarded, but the development of commercial coney warrens encouraged poaching. Actual enclosure of common land, whether by mutual consent of local landowners in a process of rationalisation of holdings and engrossment or by parliamentary edict, frequently gave rise to popular protest of an acrimonious nature, such as affrays between commoners and loyal estate servants, but also to delays and compromises which ameliorated to some extent the adverse effects. In all this the gentry realised they were also bound by the law, in earlier times administered by the manor and later by centrally inspired legislation, but they had a longer view of such matters, and tended to act together with their friends in county and national society.[5]

Alongside these concerns about ownership and property there were other matters which, if not carefully managed either by the gentry or by a common acceptance of 'normal' behaviour, could lead to disorder. We have already looked at the cost considerations which influenced decisions about the support of the poor. In addition, community attitudes to atypical habits, even when they did not involve potential charge on the rates, could result in ostracism in one way or another. For instance, bastardy may have involved a breach of custom or the law, or both; one illegitimate birth might be tolerated, repetition was outside the community norms, and unofficial action could be taken alongside the punishment of the courts. Adultery triggered public humiliation by the display of rams' horns, ducking or noisy demonstrations known as rough music or charivari, often led by the constable as a way of defusing problems without recourse to official action which in earlier times would have involved the archdeacon's court meeting in the local area of the deanery.

xxvi. ducking a witch.

Theft, violence and vagrancy were other misdemeanours where the courts had the support of the community, but profanity and frequenting of alehouses found less unanimity between the social classes. Thus, although there was technical rigidity in the system, with nearly a hundred capital offences in the eighteenth century, mainly for crimes against property, in practice there was a large element of flexible common sense as convictions depended on the testimony of witnesses.   Justices realised that the cooperation of the general population was essential if a higher degree of disorder was to be averted.   In effect there were two categories of crime: 'real crime' such as murder, rape and theft; and 'social crime' which could include poaching, smuggling and riots about food costs, enclosure, militia recruiting, turnpike tolls and so on. Legal language can sometimes blur an understanding of the actual offence.   On the one hand 'trespass' often included theft of growing crops, although illegal gleaning was often tolerated when harvest labour was needed, while on the other hand 'forcible entry' such as hedge-breaking could have been a protest against enclosure. This last activity did not affect Hurstpierpoint during the active period of parliamentary legislation, but there were earlier examples of piecemeal enclosure.

In 1674

> Richard Butcher of New House in Hurst took out of ye highway
> well nigh an acre of land, and made an enclosure of it, and set up
> a wean [wagon] gate and horse gate. .

The tone of the record indicates that the appropriation was illegal, but there is no evidence that Butcher was penalised in any way.[6]

THE FRAMEWORK OF JUSTICE

At parish level the vestry, so named because its members met in the only appropriate public place, was a fusion of religious and secular control by a local elite with limited parochial horizons, while the sheriff (shire-reeve) was responsible for a wider area, subdivided into hundreds, each with a headborough or constable responsible for maintaining order over several parishes. Henry II's legal innovations such as assizes were fitted into a framework of court, county and parish which already existed. Even when we move to the nineteenth century and the Sturges Bourne Acts of 1819 which established voting (one vote for a rateable value of £50, one extra for each additional £25 to a maximum of six votes) and written minutes of regular meetings, the 'select' vestries were to remain the focus of local control until parish councils came into being in 1894.[7]

The sheriff or his agent held courts at stated intervals within each hundred. For our parish these matters were dealt with in the Hundred of Buttinghill. Buttinghill is situated at Ham Farm, just over the boundary in Clayton Parish, and it was here that the view of frankpledge was held twice a year, in spring and autumn. In Domesday Book the Hundred comprised Hurstpierpoint, Clayton and Keymer; by 1296 Cuckfield and Crawley had been added; and in the fourteenth century it also included Worth and Slaugham, tithingmen representing the most northerly parishes travelling some distance to present their problems to the court. Fines were payable by individuals and by tithings, bringing revenue for the lord of the hundred. In 1274 this was the earl of Surrey, who was also lord of Barcombe, Fishersgate, Poynings, Streat and Younsmere hundreds. The proceedings were recorded on parchment in the Hundred Rolls, including complaints about the increases in the customary payments.[8]

Justices of the Peace have been appointed since the twelfth century, taking on the responsibilities previously held by the sheriff and his officers. In effect they ruled the English counties from the reign of Elizabeth I until 1888 when their administrative powers were transferred to the newly-formed councils. They were appointed from the ranks of the gentry: in the seventeenth century in mid Sussex, the Stapleys of Patcham (with long-standing family connections in Twineham), the Boards of Lindfield and Cuckfield, the Coverts of Slaugham, Christopher Swale and Peter Courthope here in Hurst among others. From 1732 a qualification for inclusion in the Commission of the Peace was ownership of landed property within the county to the value of at least £100. In this chapter we are concerned only with their management of law and order, trying offenders, but at the Quarter Sessions held for us almost invariably at Lewes, they oversaw the operation of the Poor Law, dealt with vagrancy, regulated fairs and markets, wages and prices (particularly of grain during periods of shortage, in order to reduce the risk of bread riots apart from actually helping the needy), weights and measures, supervised highway maintenance, licensed Nonconformist meeting-houses, alehouses and playhouses, badgers (dealers in grain, dairy produce and eggs), drovers and pedlars, and levied rates.

xxvii. Nightwatchman.

Books of Orders from central government instigated many of their activities in the early seventeenth century, such as the 1624 setting of watches

in the highwayes Townes & villages to secure all passengers, . . .
from the violence of theeves and lewde and loose persons . . .

from morneing to eavininge for the Staying and apprehending of
all suspected p'sons of fellonyes and other misdemeanours of
other rogues and vagabonds, and such as deserve punishment . . .
whereof some may be convayed to the Justice of Peace . . .

Petty Sessions were held in the Justice's parlour or study to administer
summary justice for minor offences; there is evidence that in Sussex in the
eighteenth century once-accepted customs like gleaning and estover were
being treated as criminal. At the other end of the scale capital and other
serious offences such as homicide, infanticide, rape, robbery and arson, were
referred to the Assize Court.[9]

xxviii. punishment of vagrants and beggars.

Bringing a charge against a miscreant required the initiative of an individual;
the parish constable, appointed in earlier times by the manorial court and
later by the vestry from among the more solid parishioners, only became
involved when it was necessary to physically apprehend the accused. One of
the corollaries of a rota system was a degree of unwillingness to be too
zealous in the execution of constabulary duty – a year or two later a
neighbour could be constable and might be minded for a bit of revenge.
John Russell did not attend the view of frankpledge held at Buttinghill in
September 1613, officially because of sickness, but one cannot help

wondering if there was any connection between his non-attendance and the fact the Rector, Christopher Swale, was ignoring orders

> to divert his gutter newly made into the King's highway in the town of Hurst where it now runs to the injury of the neighbours . . .

At the same court a year later:

> The parishioners of Hurst are to repair and amend 'a gutter bridge' in the King's highway between Stocker's field and Isaak's field by the Feast of St. John the Baptist next under penalty of 5s. Thomas Whatman arm[iger - esquire] and [Christopher] Swale have diverted their gutters and sinks into the King's highway in the village of Hurst to the great injury of their neighbours and each of them is to stop up his aforesaid gutters and sinks newly made by the Feast of St. James next under penalty for each delinquent of 5s. [10]

The parish constable had to keep accounts:

> March ye 28th 1730: account of the money as Joseph Muzzall disbursed when he was Headborough from St Michael 1728 unto St Michael 1729 – paid to Mr Medley at the court leet for my common fine: five shillings; and paid to Fran: Keed for Beere & Tobacco when Th. Allen was taken and kept in custody five shillings & ten pence –   £   s   d
>   10 10/ severall other small payments I charge nothing for which I paid. [11]

William Sayers, the constable of Buttinghill Hundred, was reprimanded by the Court in 1786 'for not delivering his presentment to the Grand Jury', but a glance beyond Hurstpierpoint shows that many, even most, of the hundred constables in the county were equally dilatory. Another consequence of unpaid officers being selected from their community was that the attitudes of that community were reflected in any charge. For example, goods stolen would be undervalued in order to convert the charge into one of petty larceny. If a very conscientious officer could report to Quarter Sessions that his parish was peaceful and law-abiding, this state of affairs was symbolised by the presentation of a pair of white gloves to the court. The very fact of a case being brought to court implied some degree of hostile local opinion. [12] As late as 1820 a letter from the vestry clerk, William Ellis, reported that the headborough, Penfold, 'put Bartlett's son in the stocks without sufficient cause', and was summoned to appear at Quarter Sessions.[13] Neither recorded indictments nor newspaper reports necessarily reflect the actual level of disorder, as the Justices themselves tried to avoid attracting unwanted attention from central; certainly court activity was somewhat fitful, often a reaction to a perceived threat.[14]

xxix. A double pillory.

All the foregoing might suggest a fragile and unstable society, but this was not the case. Neither paternalism nor the rule of law would have worked without the active involvement of unpaid, annually appointed amateurs. The success of local law administration can be gauged by the absence of intervention by military or other central government forces. For the most part, people went about their daily lives in a law-abiding environment. Against this background, we now need to see how Hurst behaved. The seventeenth century was one which saw perhaps more that its share of upheaval, so we will take a good look at our parish during those years, with an occasional glance elsewhere and at other times.

PARISH LAWBREAKERS

One simple comparison can be made by looking at the published *Calendars of Assize Records*. From 1601-25 a total of 87 individuals from mid Sussex parishes were committed for trial under the supervision of a judge rather than by local magistrates, their offences ranging from failure to repair bridges and maintain roads, through non-attendance at church and keeping unlicensed alehouses, larceny of household goods and farm stock, assault and affray, forcible ejection from premises, to infanticide and murder. There is a distinct impression that the gentry indulged in recusancy and the more violent offences, while the labourers and traders went in for burglary and unlicensed pubs; some of the crimes were clearly drink-related, so the clamp-down on the latter was justified. But in 1621 a Bill empowering Justices to send drunkards to the house of correction was opposed because it might have resulted in gentlemen being committed and whipped.[15] Also to be noted are several instances of the parish constable, headborough or tithingman being accused of dereliction of duty by allowing prisoners to escape, either deliberately or through inefficiency. Only four from Hurst were indicted during those years, so the parish was not particularly disorderly.[16]

One of the earliest records of wrongdoing involving someone with connections here, is one which probably occurred against a background of protection of gentry rights, in particular the protection of deer within empaled parks. In 1541 Thomas Fiennes, Lord Dacre, was hanged at Tyburn for killing a gamekeeper, and his lands, including the manor of Hurstpierpoint, were forfeit. In July 1575 Thomas Lambert, yeoman, with others, broke into the park of the next Lord Dacre and killed a deer without licence; he was indicted for poaching. On to 1578, and it was the then gamekeeper, Thomas Luxford, who did the killing, in an affray between hunters in Danny Park.[17] Another sixteenth century example comes to us indirectly, through the post mortem inquisition entry for 1st July 1553 (7EdwVI):

> Richard Holden died East Grinstead March last; [he held the] Manor of Pakyns and also lands in Hurstpierpoint which came to him by attainder of a certain John Burtenshaw who had committed murder and felony. . .[18]

At the other end of the spectrum Robert Barnes, a labourer, was indicted for grand larceny on 20 January 1597. Grand larceny meant in his case the stealing of four pairs of shoes (4d), a knife (2d), a pair of gloves (2d) and 2 girdles (4d) from John Brooks.[19]

As has been said earlier, concern about bastardy was largely due to the potential expense to the parish and not a direct matter of law and order. Until 1576 there was no provision for punishment, but by 1610 the mother could be sent to the house of correction for a year, an option which remained available to the authorities until 1834. Public confession with naming of the father and whipping for both parents, were frequent in the early seventeenth century, but became less common after 1630; curiously they were officially reinstated in 1723 and 1744 respectively. Sometimes the views of the community representatives were expressed in pretty direct language. At the Assize held at Horsham on 12 July 1603 the Grand Jury (chosen from the minor gentry and substantial yeomen to decide which cases should proceed to trial) presented

> divers harlots and strumpets, having had bastards, refuse to declare who was the father of them, and also escape without due punishment [including] Gillian Cole of Hurstpierpoint [who] had a bastard some years ago and suffered no punishment other than excommunication.[20]

Punishment was not only severe; it was often very swift. On 2nd February 1612 William Morrell a Hurstpierpoint labourer stole from John Constable 39s [today about £150] in money, a hat-band and a shirt-band valued at 6d and 12d respectively. By the 24th he had been found guilty at East Grinstead Assizes and sentenced to hang.[21]

Incarceration, depending on the severity of the offence, was either in the House of Correction, from 1624 to 1778 in Cliffe High Street, Lewes, and after that date in North Street, or at the County Gaol. This also was originally at Lewes, in the Castle, but by 1541 it was deemed to be inadequate, some facilities being transferred to Horsham, where a purpose-built gaol was opened in 1640, It was here, on 4 August 1735, that a 'pretended dumb man' was committed for murdering a Bognor woman, and gained the unenviable distinction of being the last person in England to be punished by being pressed to death with increasing weights on his naked supine body. Lewes Castle tower was demolished in 1763, but by 1813 there was a 'Borough Prison' in the east wing of the Market Tower which had been erected in 1791.[22]

By contrast, many of the hearings at Quarter Sessions were adjourned again and again while the facts were fully investigated, much to the irritation of the Sussex bench in the middle years of the seventeenth century, when they issued a document requiring notice to be given by disputants.[23] This was particularly noticeable in cases relating to the administration of the Poor Law which had not been resolved at Petty Sessions: Settlement Examinations, Removal Orders, Bastardy Maintenance Orders, and Vagrancy. Even so, they seldom had any sense that matters were out of control, probably because the paupers themselves had no say. Runaway pauper apprentices were easy to deal with, at least in the immediate action: committal to the house of correction for a spell, then return to the master, even if that merely resulted in a later repetition of the offence.[24] It was 'rival' parishes contesting responsibility which caused most of the delays. Typically, in October 1647 Thomas Furlonger was ordered to pay 12d per week for the upkeep of the daughter of Whitpayne Elliott until she reached 14 years or was able to get her own living. Two years later Edward Hollingdale 'being a vagrant shalbe taken whipt & sent to Hurstpierpoint being as he confesseth the place of his birth'. Likewise John Jennings stole grain worth 2s in 1656 and was sent to the house of correction as he was a 'wanderer' – guilty on two counts.

In 1589 it was enacted that no cottage could be built unless it possessed four acres of land, deemed sufficient to support a family. In September 1617:

> Richard Butcher son of Thomas Butcher has newly erected a cottage in Hurst contrary to the form of the Statute.[25]

In July 1657 Thomas Haselgrove and his son, also Thomas, both husbandmen, were indicted for contravening this law, but it may have been their appearance six months earlier for assault and battery on Thomas Coulstock that drew their presence to the attention of the authorities. They were still at it two years later, having built another cottage despite their previous offence. It was clearly a law which was difficult to enforce without recourse to the courts, as Thomas Moore too was at Lewes in April 1659 for the same reason. One of the concerns was the risk of subtenants becoming a charge on the parish.[26]

Certain games had been unlawful since 1478. Whether enforcement had always been rigorous is open to debate, and the early Stuart kings encouraged secular recreation as described in the 'Book of Sports', last re-issued in 1633 and vigorously supported by the Rector of Hurst, Christopher Swale, but the Long Parliament swept away its libertarian attitudes in an outburst of reformist zeal. This persisted officially through the Civil War and Commonwealth, but transgressions were inevitable. William Bryan, barber surgeon, was indicted in January 1659 for 'suffering unlawful games and dice to be used in his house and disturbance of the peace'. Things got out of hand in some way, because he was also accused of assault and battery upon Barbara, the wife of George Norton, gent. Another case of violence by a medical man came before the court over a century later, when Richard Weekes, surgeon, was accused of assaulting William Whiteman in July 1783. Others to resort to physical methods were Thomas Coulstock, cooper, who was accused of assaulting Elizabeth Curtis, widow, in 1737, and Thomas Bartley, labourer, whose assault on Henry Shoulder was described thus: ' . . . did beat wound and ill treat so that his life was despaired of'; it might be thought that this was exceptional, but the same phrase was used in cases from other parishes, so we cannot judge how severely Shoulder was injured – and in any case Bartley was found not guilty.[27]

Disputes over property could lead to harsh words, trespass and assault. William Hippisley, gentleman, George Goring's agent, was accused of 'diverse seditious words & speeches' in April 1649 (see also below, with reference to 'social crime'); in October he pleaded not guilty, but was bound over in the sum of 20s for an assault on Richard Whitpayne, and the same for his assault on William Lashmer. By the following January the boot was on the other foot, with Richard Whitpayne, yeoman, his wife Barbara and Joanna Whitpayne (sister) being ordered to pay 12d each for trespass. Another peep ten years on shows Richard Whitpayne as a struggling pillar of the establishment.   He and John Bushell as churchwardens were reprimanded for the 'disarray' of the churchmarks, by which occupiers were required to repair designated sections of the churchyard fence, but they obviously pleaded to good effect, as the parish was ordered to pay 50s towards the cost. It would appear that the Whitpaynes were not quiet for very long, for in January 1661 four of the family, Robert, Robert junior, John and Thomas, all classed as yeomen, were accused of trespass and taking a harvest (growing crops), but the record does not show the name of the victim.   In April 1682 John Hende trespassed ' 'in the close of John Greentree with his horse and doggs'. Greentree was not satisfied with the law's response; he and Elizabeth Hollybone were indicted the following October 'for a trespass in the close of John Hendy at Clayton with his hoggs and horses treading down and brayking his come and grass &c'.[28]

This sort of tit-for-tat behaviour permeated all classes, as a substitute for the outright violence of earlier times. The gentry, concerned about maintaining order, were not above creating some disorder themselves on occasion. Christopher Swale, who was Rector of Hurst from 1607 to 1645, had a very public row with a fellow Justice, Thomas Whatman, a Chichester lawyer, ostensibly over money alleged to be due to a member of Swale's family, but really about status. The wives had a brawl in church, Whatman claimed that Swale's strictures from the pulpit were aimed at him, Swale that Whatman scoffed at him during services and libelled him, all very unedifying for the other parishioners.[29]

A recurring theme was that of failure to repair the highway, a responsibility first laid on the manor by the Statute of Winchester in 1285, and subsequently on the emerging administrative unit, the parish. Everyone occupying plough or pasture had to provide a cart with two men for four days each year, while others had to put in four (later six) days work, either themselves or by substitution. Supervision was entrusted to Surveyors of Highways, sometimes known as waywardens, and they were answerable to the justices, a system which continued until 1835 and later in some areas. In 1662 Hurst, together with neighbouring Cuckfield, Keymer and Clayton were presented for the state of several roads linking these parishes; from Paynes to Wortleford Bridge, from Hoales Bridge, from Wilcombe Warren, the clappers at Beny Bridge (the last still unrepaired a year later). When the actual individual could be identified, it was he who was brought before the Quarter Sessions. In 1663 John Burtwell did not repair his hedge between East House and Randiddles, Thomas Wickham from Mogrumb Bank to the Sandfields, John Marks, bricklayer, 'a certaine highway for the horse and harness called Latchetts Lane'. Thomas Board Esq of Hothenboys (now Abbey Farm) and Thomas Winchester defaulted on their six days provision of labour. Board was still showing some disregard for his responsibilities in 1675,

> continuing a noysome pitt in the highway in Hurstypoint leading
> from Hurst church towards Chayley whereby the anger it inforces
> to the common nuisance'.

In 1680 a fine of 12d each was imposed on Francis Geere and Anna Mugglewood, together with a requirement to carry out repairs on the road to Cuckfield. Hurstpierpoint people owned or occupied property outside the parish as well. Roger Turner encroached on the highway, in the first instance for about five feet in breadth and two rods (11 yards] in length between Keymer and Ditchling, in the second a much larger area between Keymer and Hurst of more than 16 yards long and 11 yards wide. In 1735 the inhabitants of Hurst were presented for not repairing the clappers at 'Cobs Mill Bridge' nor the road from Dannard (Danworth) Brook into town, and in 1768 for similar neglect near Cobs Croft.[30]

'Real crime' was dealt with at different levels. Summary justice could be meted out by a single Justice in Petty Session, while the major offences went to the Assizes; even some of these went no further than Quarter Sessions, usually in response to a guilty plea. In October 1653 Arthur Luxford of Hurstpierpoint, gent., was indicted for assault on Bernard Newton. In 1660 Thomas Spring, a cooper, admitted stealing two pillow coats (cases) and four napkins worth 12s from Thomas Ruscombe. Witnesses were unpredictable, and Sarah Cox a spinster had to give a surety of £10 to appear when John Hillman cordwainer was accused of stealing two linen curtains from Ann Blackmar – he was fined £20. William Borrer thought he had found a culprit in 1742, one Richard Winter, accusing him of theft, but he was discharged. On 7 July 1798

> William Taylor labourer with force and arms at Hurstpierpoint one hand saw and steele value 4s of William Hill did steal take and carry away against the peace of our said Lord the King his crown and dignity.

He was found guilty the following 17th January of grand larceny and sent to the house of correction for 14 days. Later that year Edward Tabby labourer was found not guilty of the felony of stealing 12lbs straw worth 4d and 3 bushels of barley worth 3s from William Borrer. It was in these situations that possible dereliction of duty by the parish officers could be considered. In 1659 James Holden, tailor, was indicted for 'refusing to assist Thomas Luxford, yeoman, constable in carrying of one Overington Wood to the common gaol house who was committed for felony'. By 1662 Luxford had risen in the social strata, being called 'gentleman', but he was himself indicted for an unspecified felony. In 1679 Thomas Freeman of Hurst was the tithingman for the half hundred of Windham which included Cowfold and Shermanbury; he disobeyed 'a warrant of Thomas Board (he of the 'noysome pitt') and Peter Courthope Esq two Justices &c for the removing of William Button and his family from Hurst to Bolney'. On the other hand, sometimes the officers were too officious, as when Penfold the headborough in 1820 put Bartlett's son in the stocks on Church Green without sufficient cause. The manorial courts exercised jurisdiction over some matters, fining Robert Skelton in October 1615 6s 8d for taking cattle 'by force and arms' when they were being led to the pound, also on Church Green. Clearly all the facilities for restraining both men and animals were in the centre of the village, as it was also the site of the lock-up known as the Black Hole.[31]

RESPONSE TO EXCESSIVE CONTROL

'Social crime' took many forms. Sussex was normally self-sufficient in grain, but the markets were exploited by outsiders to produce shortages in spite of the 1586 'Book of Orders' licensing system, leading to dearth locally. For example, after the bad harvest of 1630 the Council allowed a large quantity to be taken from Sussex to London; in 1637 Ouse farmers were accused of making extra profit by private (non-market) transactions, known as regrating; the next year navy demands had left local markets with very little grain – Steyning had one sack for two market days – and people at Shoreham were about to open the navy granaries, forcing the bench to stop all shipments out of the port. At the end of the 1640s five millers were similarly presented; while in the same period Lewes maltsters agreed to keep some grain in reserve. If the Justices failed to control parochial distribution of corn through the overseers of the poor, or via officially appointed badgers selling at subsidised prices, there was a risk of social disorder in the form of bread riots. These occurred in Sussex on several occasions between 1585 and 1649, but the records do not specifically mention Hurst. In the end it was often these same magistrates, in their guise as gentry and wealthy yeomen, who subsidised the poor rates and so defused the situation.[32]

Alehouses were seen by central government and the local gentry as places where crime and immorality were discussed, if not actually pursued, and they were frequently under censure from the bench which claimed they were for travellers, not for locals. To some extent the increase in their activity resulted from the loosening of supervision as living-in servants became wage-labourers. Bearing in mind the known concern with parish expense, they were seen as places where the poor would waste their money and their energies to the extent that they would become a charge on the poor rate. They were also potential breeding grounds for infection, and used up valuable supplies of grain in times of dearth. For all these reasons, their licensing was strictly controlled under an Act of 1552 to 'prevent hurts and trobles, abuses and disorders', but in spite of this unlicensed houses continued to flourish because the people did not accept the law. In 1610 Robert Harris complained that they were 'nurseries of all riot, excess & idleness . . . sheep-stealers, robbers, quarrellers'; they fostered 'filial disobedience, sexual licence, disruption of family life'; they 'encouraged games which led to drunken debauchery'; they were 'a seething cauldron of sedition & opposition to church & state'. Frequent presentations were made to Quarter Sessions by the more upright members of a community, who by doing so alienated themselves still further from their inferiors; and the same alehouse keepers' names appeared time and again. The Caroline Books of Orders already mentioned continued this concern, requiring the justices to suppress superfluous alehouses and strictly control those that were allowed. In part this was to regulate the movement and consumption of corn in times of shortage, but also to deal with behaviour outside the norms of society. 'A Letter from the Councell' in 1625 ordered:

> . . . the suppressing of sup'flouse Allehouse we must agayne require it of you to take a strict course that in such Inns & Allehouse (as shall be allowed) the strength of Beere & Alle to be ther brewed & sowld shall be so moderate and reforemed as thereby drunkeness may be avoyded & vayne consumption of grayne prevented both which in a pte will be remedied if the nomber of Allehouses & tippling houses be abridged & offenders in that kinde strictly punished. . .[33]

In 1664 the bench considered Hurst to have too many such establishments and ordered that 'the Royall Oak be hereby suppressed and put down as a supernumerary and unnecessary alehouse. . .', Richard Vosam being banned from selling beer or ale and ordered to pull down and take away the sign. The licence would seem to have been restored fairly soon after, for we find Richard Stapley of Hickstead Place going to the Royal Oak in 1686, when John Field lived there, and in 1699, when Francis Allcocke was the innkeeper. In 1735 William Greenaway was indicted 'for keeping a disorderly alehouse and selling liquors on the Sabbath Day in the time of Divine Service', while in 1742 Richard Fillary was similarly accused of 'selling spiritous liquors there with licence'. Greenaway was clearly an individual with unacceptable disregard for the norms, as only a few months before his alehouse offence he had been presented with John Goble 'for keeping hoggs and letting them about the streets doeing damage to their neighbours'. It was not until the nineteenth century that the Royal Oak finally ceased business, its licence being transferred to the New Inn opposite. Generally the magistrates gained some sort of control over the problem, as the number of alehouses was reduced from one for every 87 persons in 1700 to one for 232 in 1830. Friendly Societies which started in the mid-eighteenth century, enabled the parish elite to absorb craftsmen and skilled labourers, who thus improved their status, into a much less unruly atmosphere. In Hurst the Union Benefit Society, founded in 1825, met regularly in the New Inn for food, drink, entertainment and fellowship, all approved by the incumbent and the vestry.[34]

Some indictments are difficult to classify because the records give insufficient detail. For example, John Snashall, the Hurst blacksmith, a forebear of the barber-surgeon we have met already, was one of ten men from different parishes accused of 'riott routt and unlawful assembly' at Cowfold in 1685. Was it after closing time at the local, or was it a social protest against some actual or perceived injustice? This sort of activity alarmed government sufficiently for the Riot Act to be passed in 1715, requiring dispersal within one hour of its public reading. On the other hand, crowds were useful in publicising exemplary punishment, such as the gallows, the pillory and the cart's tail for whipping.

Trade, including the buying and selling of goods, was strictly controlled. From the reign of Edward II it was illegal to buy goods on the way to market for resale at a profit, an action known as forestalling, and a continuing fear of dearth led to further Acts of Parliament such as that in 1552 which imposed severe punishments. It was probably this that John Moore had indulged in when he bought ' six calves att Brighthelmston'. Currying (treating of tanned leather to improved its qualities) brought Thomas Tumis before the Bench 'for using his trade [in Hurst] itt being no Markett Towne or corporation and currying of tenne hydes'.[35]

Keeping dogs, nets and ferrets was clearly done with an intention to poach, but Thomas and William Avery were caught in the act – 'tracing and killing one hare in the snow'. They submitted and were fined 5s at the Quarter Sessions held at Lewes in April 1667. Thomas, this time with William Norton, had shown earlier signs of unwillingness to conform when in 1664 he refused to take the Oath of Allegiance. It is probably no surprise to find that poaching was still active two hundred years later, twenty pheasants being stolen from Little Park.[36]

One type of 'social' crime which was actively pursued in Sussex in the eighteenth and nineteenth centuries was the 'free trading' of the 'gentlemen' smugglers. The right of the crown to raise revenue from duties on goods carried into or out of this country goes back many centuries, and by the 1700s covered candles, glass, gloves, hats, leather, playing cards, clocks, beer, brandy, tea, lace and even dogs. It was easy to imagine that these taxes were not popular, and it seemed to be to everyone's advantage if they could be avoided.   But it was the banning of exports of raw wool which particularly affected Sussex. The 'owling trade', so-called because of the smugglers' habit of blacking their faces, led to large numbers of bales of wool going straight from shearing to cloth-workers on the Continent who paid not only in cash but in luxury goods such as brandy and lace.   In Sussex, smuggling was second only to agriculture in terms of the value of the trade until the 1840 repeal of the protective tariffs on these items. Contraband goods were landed on the coast and moved inland as quickly as possible.   From Hove, then no more than a straggle of houses along Hove Street, the route was through Goldstone Bottom, West Blatchington (the church being used for storage), Saddlescombe, Hurst and Cuckfield.[37] Even apparently 'solid citizens' could become involved, for Thomas Marchant records:

> 1719. Sept. 30th.   Talked to Mrs Beard, for Allan Savage, about her horse that was seized by the officers at Brighton running brandy.[38]

The excise men attempted to control the problem; in Hurst we know of four: Mr Pointin at the Swan (Down House) in 1716, John Atkins in 1825, John Page in 1827, and William Austin in 1841.[39] The last date indicates that the authorities still felt the need for the post to be filled even after the withdrawal of the tariffs.

Battles between the Revenue men and the smugglers were very frequent. Mr Still of Albourne, whose daughter married Richard Davey in St Lawrence Church in 1797, had his horse shot from under him more than once on his adventurous rides across the Downs from Shoreham. In his last escapade he was deserted by his confederates and captured, all his stores confiscated and fined £100, a calamity which seems to have hastened his end.[40] 'Running' was the undoing of two other men, as recorded in a letter from Richard Weekes to his son Hampton in December 1802:

> Mst Webbers Eldest Son at Locks in this Parish Smugler was returning unladen from Patcham met Robt Begnall Junr of Clayton when an affray took place between [them] as a consequence of wh[ich] this Begnal, who was employed by the Hurst Excise Man as his Assistant Shot young Webber with a Pistol. . . He lived a week . . . the jury brought in a Verdict of Wilfull Murder therefore Begnall will be tried at Horsham but am inclined to think he will not be Hanged but possibly Transported.[41]

Some fifty years later a particularly cool and audacious escapade took place. In the middle of August 1855 a celebrated wild beast show was set up near the Custom House in Shoreham. The Customs men were given complimentary tickets and they all went to the show, providing the 'runners' with an opportunity too good to miss. Moored to the quay was a vessel laden with stones, allegedly awaiting a purchaser for the cargo. Concealed beneath were bales of tobacco which were quietly put over the side into a barge during the evening. This went up river to Beeding chalk-pits, where the bales were quickly transferred to four vans (covered wagons), one of which was later traced as far as Horsham, another through Hurst and Cuckfield, where the trail ended. Fourteen tons of tobacco had been 'run' under the officers' noses while they were watching the animals.

In spite of the superficial glamour attached to the activity, it was not universally popular, and gradually people became disenchanted, among them a Portslade farmer and a Hurst trader who brought actions for trespass.

Transportation, mentioned above, was first authorised by the Privy Council in 1615; America, particularly Virginia, was the destination until the War of Independence in 1776; Australia took over in 1787; and the eleven year gap led inevitably to grossly overcrowded prisons, even by the standards of the day. There is no Hurstpierpoint entry in the lists of those sentenced to transportation at Quarter Sessions between 1790 and 1825, when Benjamin Shaw was sentenced for life. Subsequently a further nine, of whom six were agricultural labourers, received terms of from seven years for larceny to life for assault, their ages ranging from 41 down to 15.[42]

More obvious social protest occurred in widely differing circumstances. During the middle years of the seventeenth century opinions became polarised. Christopher Swale was a Royalist and used his best endeavours to keep Hurst on the King's side by scoffing at the Parliamentarians' orders. William Hippisley has already been mentioned for uttering 'seditious words and speeches'. He was at Danny, the Sussex agent of the Earl of Norwich, Royalist and father of Lord George Goring, the King's cavalry commander during the Civil War, so he was unlikely to be dealt with sympathetically by Herbert Morley, a staunch Puritan supporter of Cromwell until the 1650s. However he got off due to influence from Norwich's camp.[43]

After the international conflict of the last decade of the eighteenth century, peace in 1801 was celebrated in every community, but not by every individual:

> Hurst was illuminated on Tuesday Evening every house in town except Dodsons [the Rector] and Robert's therefore Dodson had one pane of glass broken.[44]

Earlier mention has been made of the fact that a significant part of the business of the courts was taken up in dealing with the potential instability caused, at least in the minds of the gentry, by the poor. By the early eighteenth century the necessity for houses of correction had been accepted; apart from their deterrent effect, they provided a source of labour to lie alongside the workhouse, for spinning or weaving or knocking hemp. We have also noted the change in employment patterns from living-in servants to day-labourers. Towards the end of the eighteenth century the pauper crisis intensified, was then masked by the extra food demands of the Napoleonic Wars, only to receive renewed impetus as peace returned.

William Cobbett pointed out in 1825 that farmers paid less in wages than the cost of the food they would previously have provided.[45]

During each of these crisis periods, the mid-1790s, 1816 and 1822, unrest occurred throughout the country from Cornwall to Cumberland. The 1800 Bread Act which required only wholemeal flour to be milled, caused riots in Horsham.   Such riots in the cereal-growing south-east became more organised in the Swing Riots of 1830. Apart from protest meetings and riots with various targets such as food shortages and wages, tithe impositions and workhouse conditions, the special outward manifestations of this series of protests were the wrecking of threshing machines which were progressively reducing the need for labour-intensive methods of harvesting, and the firing of grain ricks and barns. These activities were often preceded by threatening letters written by 'Captain Swing', a pseudonym used by anyone actively engaged in the demonstrations; there is evidence that some degree of political organisation was necessary in order to develop the geographical spread which occurred.   Kent experienced this before Sussex, starting in August, but by October farms in East Sussex were suffering and letters were being distributed in the Lewes area on 13 November. A case of arson occurred at Hickstead on the 22nd, and others at Bolney and Cuckfield on 14 and 19 December, but the nearest examples of threshing machine-wrecking were at Crowborough to the east and Goodwood in the west. Against a background of 46 cases of arson and 49 of machine-breaking in Kent, the mid-Sussex experience was one of comparative calm. Nevertheless 52 men and women from all parts of the county were charged at a special assize session on 20 December 1830, those found guilty being imprisoned or transported for long periods.[46] An entry in the Vestry Book c.1825 indicates that Hurst had perhaps already taken steps to reduce the risk of outsiders causing trouble, albeit not for the specific purposes of machine-wrecking or fire-raising:

> In consequence of the Parish being visited by a great number of
> Vagabonds it is become necessary to hire a Beadle, to walk the
> Parish & arrest all he meets with begging & take them before a
> Magistrate, the said Beadle to have a Blue Coat with red collar &
> cuffs & Hat with a silk band, and it agreed that Michael Harmes
> shall undertake the said office & to have 10/- per week.

Wm. Jenner) Churchwardens
John Marchant)
Wm. Marshall) Overseers
Thos. Uwms)

Inhabitants
J C F Tufnell
N Borrer
H Weekes
R Weekes [47]

The nineteenth century saw a gradual move away from local decisions about law and order to a national accountability system. Parish constables were still being appointed here in Hurst as late as 1852, when two each of bakers, carpenters, cordwainers (shoemakers), grocers, one bricklayer, coachman, yeoman, carrier, auctioneer, market gardener, farmer and butcher were appointed, showing the range of occupations involved. But many other parishes had already appointed paid watches, or had taken powers under the 1839 Rural Constabulary Act. Hurst did not have its own police station until 1871. By the last decade of the century, the administrative activities of the bench had been taken over by the newly-formed councils, leaving JPs to concentrate on dealing with crime as defined by parliament.

The absence of any Hurst involvement in periods of great unrest has been touched on in order to emphasise the generally law-abiding nature of the parish. Together with the very small number of indictments for 'normal' crimes, it indicates a community which largely accepted the social structure and the inequalities it provided. To some extent the 'social' crimes, such as poaching and unlicensed pubs, were probably tolerated in moderation as a kind of safety valve. Whether this was merely an outward veneer or an expression of real acceptance of the 'rich man – poor man' relationship of the hymn remains a matter for speculation. Certainly those who were ratepayers did not expect to be accosted by beggars when they should have received appropriate action by the bench. By way of reinforcement, in the last years of the eighteenth century the nationally run Proclamation Society found echoes locally in their campaigns to control Sunday observance, vagrancy, weights and measures, and moral behaviour generally.[48] But to a large extent the various members of a rural society had learned to live side by side with a minimum of disturbance.

NOTES AND REFERENCES

1. Fletcher A (1975): *A Community in Peace and War, Sussex 1600–1660,* 147.

2. Houlbrooke R A (1984): *The English Family 1450–1700,* 118–9, 167–78; Wrightson K (1982): *English Society 1580–1680,* 90–2, 116; Woodcock G (ed)(1967): *William Cobbett, Rural Rides,* 226–7; Jefferies R (1992): *Hodge and his Masters,* 72–7; Howkins A in Short B (1992): *The English Rural Community, Image and Analysis,* 85–102; Hay D & Rogers N (1997): *Eighteenth Century English Society,* 32; Thompson F (1973): *Lark Rise to Candleford,* 212.

3. See page 81

4. Fletcher A & Stevenson J (eds)(1985): *Order and Disorder in Early Modern England,* 1–10, 23–5, 31; WSRO/ Par 400/13/l.

5. Fletcher & Stevenson, *Order & Disorder,* 15; Thompson E P (1991): *Customs in Common,* 98–121; Hey D (ed)(1996): *Oxford Companion to Local and Family History,* 387;Hay & Rogers, *18th Century Society,* 84–5.

6. Fletcher & Stevenson, *Order & Disorder,* 16, 32; Emsley C (1987): *Crime and Society in England 1750–1900,* 2–3; Sharpe J A (1984): *Crime in EarlyModern England,* 77, 87.

7. England, 77, 87; Turner E (ed)(l 849): The Diary of Richard Stapley, *SAC* **2**, 108; Hay & Rogers, *Society,* 134.

8. Eastwood D (1997): *Government and Community in the English Province 1700–1870,* 8–11, 45.

9. Cam H (1963): *The Hundred and the Hundred Rolls,* 9–10, 91–2, 280–2; Renshaw W C (1916): The Hundred of Buttinghill, *SAC* **58**, 6.

10. Hey, *Companion,* 28, 253, 348, 386; Fletcher & Stevenson, *Order & Disorder,* 16, 20, 37; Eastwood, *Government,* 95; Cunliffe E S (ed) (1896): Booke Concerning the Deputy Leiuetennantshipp, *SAC* **40**, 1–37.

11. Renshaw, Buttinghill, *SAC* **58**, 12.

12. WSRO/Par400/28/5.

13. Godschall W M (1787): *General Plan of Provincial and Parochial Police,* 33–5, quoted in Eastwood, *Government,* 101; Sharpe, *Crime,* 79, 81–2.

14. WSRO/Par400/37/125.

15. Fletcher & Stevenson, *Order & Disorder,* 30–1, 36, 38; ESRO/QI/EW9; Renshaw, Buttinghill, *SAC* **58**, 17–20.

16. Fletcher A (1986): *Reform in the Provinces,* 363.

17. *Calendars of Assize Records, Sussex: Elizabeth I and James 1.*

18. *VCH* **7**, 175–6.

19. Hunnisett R F (1985): *Post-Mortem Inquisitions 1485–1649, SRS* **14**, 125.

20. *Assize Records, Elizabeth 1.*

21. 18 Eliz I c. 3; 7 Jac I c. 4; 6 Geo II c. 31; 17 Geo II c. 5; Quaife G R (1979):

Wanton Wenches and Wayward Wives, 217–8; *Assize Records, Elizabeth 1*.

22. *Assize Records, James 1*.
23. *Assize Records, Elizabeth 1*; Topp J (1991): *Sussex Prisons*, passim; *SAC* **19**, 121–5.
24. Fletcher, *Sussex*, 219.
25. Fletcher, *Reform*, 219.
26. Renshaw, Buttinghill, *SAC* **58**, 7–20.
27. 31 Eliz I c. 7; ESRO/QI/EW2; Sharpe, *Crime*, 84.
28. ESRO/QI/EW3, 9, QO/EW33.
29. Quarter Sessions Order Book 1642-49, *SRS* **54**; ESRO/QO/EW8.
30. Fletcher, *Sussex*, 55–6.
31. 13 Edw I, St II c. 5; Tate W E (1969): *The Parish Chest*, 242–4 ESRO/QI/EW3, 4, 9.
32. ESRO/QI/EW2, QO/EW33; WSRO/Par400/37/125; ESRO/QR/E564/46; Renshaw, Buttinghill, *SAC* **58**, 7–20; Mitten B J (1905): *Guide to Hurstpierpoint and Neighbourhood*, 4.
33. ESRO/QR/EW; Fletcher, *Sussex*, 147–50; Charlesworth A (ed)(1983): *An Atlas of Rural Protest in Britain 1548-1900*.
34. Wrightson, *English Society*, 167–70; ESRO/QI/EW7, 9; Clarke P (1983): *The English Alehouse, a Social History1200-1830*, 45–57, 145–6; Eastwood, *Government*, 40; ESRO/QO/EW7; Cunliffe, Deputy Lieutenantship, *SAC* **40**, 1– 37; Turner, SAC 25, 113, 124; *Sussex Agricultural Express* 31.5.1845, 31.5.1859, 3.6.1862, 9.1.1869, 1.6.1869.
35. *Sussex Agricultural Express* 2. 2. 1869.
36. 5&6EdwVlc. l4.
37. *Sussex Agricultural Express* 2. 2. 1869.
38. Waugh M (1985): *Smuggling in Kent & Sussex 1700–1840*, 11, 122.
39. Turner, Marchant Diary, *SAC* **25**, 185.
40. *Ibid.*, 175; parish registers.
41. Woodward W A (1928): *A Soldier in Wellington's Army, Sussex County Magazine*, February 1928, 48.
42. Ford J M T (1987): *The Weekes Family Letters*, 241.
43. Davey R (ed)(1988): *East Sussex Sentences of Transportation at Quarter Sessions*.
44. ESRO/QI/EW3.
45. Ford, *Weekes Letters*, 52–3.
46. *Political Register*, 20 October 1825.
47. Thompson E P, *Customs*, 192; Hobsbawm E H & Rudé G (1969): *Captain Swing*, passim; Charlesworth A (1979): *Social Protest in a Rural Society,Historical Geography Research Series, No. 1*, 30–1.
48. Cited in Packham R A (1993): *The Early History of Hurstpierpoint*, . 4.
49. Eastwood, *Government*, 109.

10. A ROAD SYSTEM EVOLVES

On Foot or by Horse – Roads, Trackways and Bridges

The whole philosophy of transport, travel, and road construction is now entirely different from times past. Today the advertising media present a picture of an affluent society of 'busy people' who, it is felt, have the right to enter their comfortable car, sheltered from the elements, and with little physical effort visit the local supermarket to purchase food which they had no part in growing, collect their children from school, or travel as fast as the law permits wherever they wish. It is equally projected that the authorities have the duty of providing them with the multi-lane superhighways to do so. However true or not this picture is in actual fact, as a contrast, it was only little more than a century ago that the maximum speed of travel on the roads was that of a galloping horse, and the more usual was 3 or 4 miles an hour on foot. Unless one had a horse, or could travel with the village carrier, nearly everyone had to walk. Following compulsory education in 1871 children might have to walk over 2 miles to school and 2 miles home again, perhaps twice a day if they came home for a mid-day meal. Many adults walked or cycled further than this every day. Most people worked hard physically for long hours for low pay, the majority on the land producing the food they ate. Even when one was wealthy enough to possess a carriage, and very few did, travel was slow, uncomfortable, tiring and exposed to the elements. It was only a further similar period before that, when the turnpike roads became general, almost all roads, including the King's highways, were little better than public bridleways of today, churned up by horse traffic.

There are many references to the appalling state of roads in Sussex. Classic statements were those of Horace Walpole in 1749: 'If you love good roads, be so kind as never to go into Sussex'; and of a Dr J Burton in 1751 who queried: 'Why have the cattle, pigs, women, and other animals longer legs in Sussex than elsewhere? Is it not because of the difficulty of pulling them out of so much mud and through its holding power, that the muscles are extended and the bones grow in length?'.[1]

Apart from the normal Sussex wagon, and particularly in the north of the parish and up into the Weald, heavier wagons were 'negotiating execrable roads'. These immense vehicles were making tracks six feet wide with wooden wheels six inches wide protected by strips of iron called strakes rather than metal hoops. There was some merit in the wider wheels, recognised by a reduction of toll on the Turnpikes,[2] as they tended to spread the load more evenly and leave a broader track, but the strakes did a lot of damage. The iron-masters in the Weald had long been the worst offenders in churning up the roads, and they were forced to carry and lay materials for making them good again.[3]

Wagons and carts carried no lights when it was dark apart from perhaps one or two dim oil lamps; and there were no streetlights until the coming of gas in late Victorian times. As the drivers always led their horses or sat exposed to the elements, identification along narrow lanes in the parish was by the sound of perhaps sixteen bells on the harness of the horses or the rumble and creaking of the wagons. The more affluent, who used a light gig, carried a large gig umbrella, rather like today's golf umbrella, to protect themselves from the elements.

We have seen that there were efforts in Roman times to provide an easy route for man and his animals and primitive carts through the southern part of the parish at least, but once the old Greensand Way became disused and decayed there would have been little through traffic. Movement of people was dictated where possible by the ease of passage, particularly of river crossings, and this was locally from the west, dominated by the castle of Bramber, along the top of the Downs, and over the Ouse at Lewes, again protected by its castle. King Edward I came this way with his Court in 1281 when travelling from Canterbury to Chichester and again in 1305.[4] Before fields were enclosed with banks and hedges restricting their passage, travellers found the easiest way, and in the bad weather of winter the way could be very wide as they tried to avoid the ruts, fallen trees and flooded areas. Before the latter part of the eighteenth and early nineteenth centuries there would be a little traffic through the parish. There could be the traveller from Henfield, Albourne and neighbouring areas going either towards the market town of Lewes or a local fair. There might be someone moving sheep or other livestock from the Downland to a market or a vendor over the downs from the fishing village of Brighthelmstone. The major routes for travellers were still well to the east or west of Hurst or along the Downs from Bramber to Lewes. Goods were carried on packhorses. Wheeled vehicles were few, mostly heavy farm carts and travel by all parties, as we have seen, was by horseback or on foot.

It was felt that the roads and tracks in the parish should be for the local population, and the local Church Vestry, despite legislation, had the strongest reluctance to spend time and money to cater for the passing traveller in the maintenance of roads and bridges.[5] The impetus to the improved state, at least of the main highways, was the spread of the turnpike roads by the middle of the eighteenth century. The development of Brighthelmstone necessitated easier and speedier travel and the London–Brighton Turnpike, via Cuckfield, St. Johns Common, Stonepound, Clayton and Pyecombe was established in 1770,[6] and a parallel route via Henfield by 1782.[7] There was not as yet a road of any importance where the A23 now runs, simply a way from Newtimber to Sayers Common. More important to Hurst was the creation of a Turnpike Road in   1777[8] from Crouch Hill, north of Henfield, to Ditchling. The old Manor House to the north of the church had gone and the new road went on the line of the present line of the High Street. The previous route had gone south of the church along Churchfield and round to West Furlong Lane. The old High Street itself was improved. There were tollhouses to the east of the White Horse and just before New Way Lane.

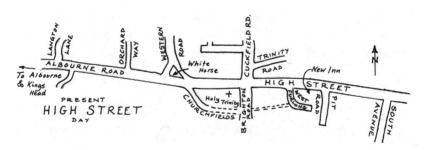

Figure 4. Sketch map of Albourne Road and the present High Street,
showing the earlier line of the west-east route via Churchfields.

It was not until 1808 that there was an Act of Parliament to shorten the distance from London to Brighton, for the benefit of the Prince Regent, by joining up Pyecombe to Bolney and Cuckfield via Staplefield,[9] and not until 1818 was the link from Hickstead to Warninglid made,[10] reducing the distance to 52 miles and the journey time to 5¼ hours. Apparently the Royal

ANNO TRICESIMO OCTAVO

GEORGII III. REGIS.

◆◆

Cap. 7.

An Act for continuing for the Term of Twenty-one Years, and from thence to the End of the then next Seffion of Parliament, the Term, and altering and enlarging the Powers of an Act, paffed in the Seventeenth Year of the Reign of His prefent Majefty, for repairing and widening the Road from a Place called *Crouch Hill*, in the Parifh of *Henfield*, to the Turnpike Road leading from *Brighthelmftone* to *Cuckfield*, and from the Eaft Side of the faid Turnpike Road to the Town of *Ditchling*, in the County of *Suffex* ; and alfo for repairing and widening the Road from *Ubley's Farm*, in the Parifh of *Hurftperpoint*, to the Marle Pit oppofite to *Newtimber Broad Lane*, in the faid County.

[5th *April* 1798.]

WHEREAS by an Act, made in the Seventeenth Year of the Reign of His prefent Majefty, intituled, *An Act for repairing and widening the Road from a Place called* Crouch Hill, *in the Parifh of* Henfield, *to the Turnpike Road leading from* Brighthelmftone *to* Cuckfield, *and from the Eaft Side of the faid Turnpike Road to the Town of*

Preamble.
17 *Geo.* III, recited.

[*Loc. & Per.*]   I   Ditchling,

Mail coaches however still travelled by the Cuckfield and Clayton route with a journey time of 8 hours. The village did benefit from its new turnpike and in 1816 an old fifteenth century house was converted into the New Inn[11] (see page 303) to take advantage of the cross country coach which connected with the London to Brighton coaches at the King's Head, Albourne (see Colour Plate 15).[12] The Parish Vestry must in one way have breathed a sigh of relief over the new turnpikes which they did not have to maintain, but as most were farmers they must have cursed the tolls at the gates every time they and their stock went through the village. At least there were two fewer problems to deal with – they had the greatest difficulty in trying to maintain the old highways. Repairs were usually of flints gathered laboriously from Wolstonbury Hill by the paupers.[13] A pensioned-off labourer unable to do a full days work was employed to break up the pile of flints by the wayside and fill in the potholes. Road construction, including the High Street before McAdam, was to a great extent a matter of filling up the holes and trying to compact the surface. In wintertime they became foul and muddy, while in summer they were watered to keep the dust down.

The far better standard of road construction of the turnpikes enabled the increased use of wheeled vehicles and a consequent greater ease of travel during the Georgian and early Victorian period.

The opening of the London to Brighton turnpike roads began the era of fast coaching along them, and more and more coaches made the journey – at one time between 30 and 40. The names of the coaches, and indeed those of the coachmen, became famous – they were the 'Kings of the Road'. However, this revival of road traffic dramatically declined with the coming of the railway from London through to Brighton in 1841 and the collapse of the Turnpike Trusts in the 1870's. The County Councils, set up in 1880, gave some help but it was not until they were responsible for the maintenance of the highways, including the London to Brighton road, that the situation improved, catering for the new cycling clubs[14] until they were driven off by the advent of the motor car and its vast increase in numbers over the twentieth century. Since the new A23 was constructed the old London–Brighton road has in part become the B2118.

32. Tollgate (Lindfield).

Stone Pound Gate
Clears Patcham Gate
St. John's and Ansty Gates

Y

Patcham Gate
Clears Stone Pound Gate,
St. John's and Ansty Gates

126

xxxi. Tollgate tickets.

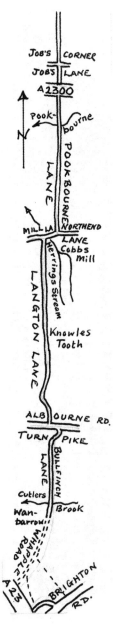

We have seen that two of the important roads in the parish had eventually become turnpikes. Apart from farm tracks most of the others were either leading to Cuckfield or to the 'dirt and mire of St. Johns Common.'[15] What few roads there were ran mostly north and south. Langton Lane, the way to Cuckfield, still a narrow winding lane between hedgerows, was then a continuation of a lane, now Bullfinch Lane which was itself continued southwards by a whapple road towards Newtimber. (There is still a field of Wanbarrow called Wobblegate field). The whapple road was a road, rather like a present bridleway, for horses and foot traffic only and was stopped up in 1798 after the new turnpike road was made.[16] It is possible that the Borrers or a previous owner of Pakyns diverted Bullfinch Lane round their property. Northwards Langton Lane led past Cobbs Mill linking up with an east–west lane where there was a bridge known as Berry Bridge over the Herrings Stream. From there the route was along Pookbourne Lane over Pookbourne Bridge to the parish boundary at Jobs Corner, and northwards again to Stairbridge on a tributary of the Adur and a detached portion of the Parish.

Figure 5.

What is now Western Road, formerly often called White Horse Lane or Chinese Lane, led northwards from the White Horse Inn, around what was then the western boundary of Little Park until it reached Pitts and the Eastfield, where it was later cut across by the new Cuckfield Road. It then swung north and northeast along what is now Danworth Lane, over a bridge at the Danworth Brook (part of the Herrings Stream) past High Hatch farm before crossing Goddards Green and up Bishopstone Lane. Past Wortleford Farm (now gone) it crossed two bridges at Wortleford over the Adur tributary forming the northern parish boundary. Wortleford was in early times of some importance, Christiana de Wertleford being mentioned in a Subsidy Roll of 1327.[17] The estate was always freehold and there was considerable argument in the seventeenth century as to who should maintain the two bridges.[18] The new Cuckfield Road was not constructed until 1835 when an Act of Parliament was passed for a new Turnpike Road from Hurstpierpoint Church to Anstye Cross on the old Brighton Turnpike Road.[19] It had two 'lodges' and the Lamb Inn at its southern end .The lodges are now two shops, one formerly Hilton Electronics, the other now a beauty salon. The turnpike had a gate near Chalkers Lane, but as a source of revenue it cannot have been much of a success for the new railway had come and put an end to such roads. It was still known as the New Road for many years.

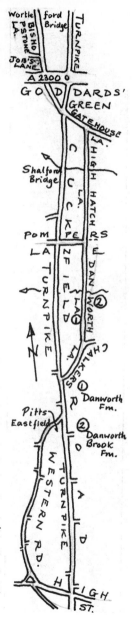

Figure 6.

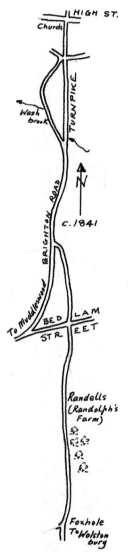

This was in fact only the northern part of a new route as an Act of Parliament had been passed in 1834 for 'making and maintaining a Branch Road from the Town of Hurstpierpoint to Poynings Common'.[20] This, the present Brighton Road, used sections of an old lane which led directly towards Washbrooks, then eastwards along Cutlers Brook, and southwards to Bedlam and past Randolphs Farm and Foxhole over Wolstonbury towards Brighton. The new turnpike led from the church down what is known as the Hollow which indeed may have been lowered at that time, the previously existing slope being too steep for horses (the houses on both sides are up on a bank). The new road then cut across fields in part, swinging west to cross the existing Brighton Turnpike at Muddles-wood, just outside the parish, where there was a turnpike gate.

Figure 7

Plate 33.
The 'Hollow' at the beginning of the Brighton Road

The history of the roads north of the Hassocks Road is a little more complex. Long before St George's Church or Hurstpierpoint College were thought of there were lanes in existence on approximately the same lines. The 1658 map clearly shows Malthouse Lane as 'The way that leads from East Crosse towards St John's Common,' and the only likely position for the Cross would be at the junction of Hassocks Road and New Way Lane. The 1842 Tithe Award map shows a hedge line with a belt of trees on a line northwards from New Way Lane. Perhaps over the years the lane moved to its present position further to the east, and there must have been farm lanes leading to Hurst Wickham. On the site of the College were two small farms, Crisps opposite the College entrance and Cophall or Petwyns on the south of Chalkers Lane. Heading northwards along the lane were Rickmans and Kents divided by the Herrings Stream. They were later combined into one holding. On the same stream to the east was Ruckford Mill, sometimes called Avery's Mill after its owner, and still in use earlier this century. The northern end of Malthouse Lane, where it joined St John's Common, has now disappeared as has the Common itself together with the northern corner of the Parish and Grasmere or Malthouse Farm. The medieval farmhouse is now submerged under a sea of houses as is the rest of this area now lost to the Parish. Gatehouse Lane leading westwards towards Goddards Green still survives although isolated and so does Pangdean Lane, now a bridleway, from Malthouse Lane to Gatehouse Lane. The new A2300 link road cutting across Cuckfield Road, isolates the northern part of the parish, and seals off the opposite end of Gatehouse Lane near Deanhouse.

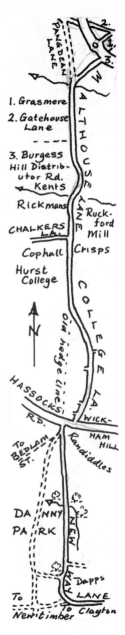

Figure 8

Figure 9

Returning to the Hassocks Road, heading south from the 'East Cross' is New Way Lane. How new is new? It probably dates from the seventeenth century. In 1674, as we saw in a earlier chapter, Peter Courthope was taken to court for blocking a public highway.[21] He had purchased Danny in 1652 and it is likely that the public highway ran right past his door on the line of the present driveway. He was forced to buy a strip of land 30ft wide in 1675 and lay out a new road 'from Dapps to the highway leading to Pyecombe.' Could this be our New Way Lane? From Randiddles at the Hassocks Road corner New Way Lane indeed runs to the east of Danny and forms its boundary, and also is very close to the old Roman road which ran from the Ham southwards over Wolstonbury. At the foot of Wolstonbury the lane turns east but at one time its westerly extension, now a bridleway, was the way to Newtimber and beyond westwards to Portus Aderni – possibly Portslade. The Roman road probably later became the eastern parish boundary which runs in a dead straight line past Crossways and up Belmont Lane and on northwards. New research in that area may tell us its exact route. Well to the north of the village was another of the few routes from west to east. From High Cross on the Albourne–Henfield road it ran eastwards on the line of Reeds Lane to Sayers Common.(This section was probably later as it cut across the field pattern of 1671/2). From Sayers Common the route followed a somewhat zigzag pattern, probable due to old field systems, along Mill Lane, past Cobbs Mill at Berry Bridge, past the way to Naldretts, and to Northend Farm on the later Cuckfield Road. From there it ran northwards to Shalford Bridge on the Pookbourne and on the line of a present footpath to Goddards Green and on to St John's Common. From Mill Lane another lane ran eastwards with the odd name of Pompers Lane serving Longs Farm (later Pickhams) and across High Hatch Lane to Malthouse Lane. There were other lengths of minor lanes and a network of footpaths and bridleways serving the farming community and very many still survive. There are today around 32 miles of footpaths jealously guarded by ramblers and others.

xxxii. Roadmender.

The old roads did not, of course, remain unaffected by events. By the early nineteenth century new houses were built on the north of the new turnpike opposite the Church as far as the White Horse, and new villas to the east of the High Street towards Hassocks. From the coming of the railway to Hassocks Gate in 1841 the village began to expand rapidly with housing development along existing roads and the new Cuckfield Road.[22]

The first soil drainage system in the village was laid from the corner of New Way Lane through the High Street and up 'White Horse Lane' and Cuckfield Road in 1870 to a Sewage Farm near the present village boundary in Cuckfield Road, and piped water replaced the old wells.

The sewage tanks must have proved inadequate. In 1912 the sewer was extended to a new enlarged site beyond Court Bushes, and it is now at Goddard's Green. Water was supplied to Hurst from the Downs at Clayton, and the new water company was re-constituted in 1890 as the Mid Sussex Water Company.[23]

Six street lights lit by oil were erected in the town in 1812,[24] and in 1861 a gas works was established at the northern end of Western Road enabling the houses and roads to be lit by gas.[25] It was not until the 1950's that Electric Street Lights appeared.[26]

Since the beginning of the last century housing estates have multiplied, not only in Hurst but also at Hurst Wickham and Sayers Common. After the new A23 scythed through the parish, the area to the west to the boundary of the old London Brighton Road became more isolated and was transferred to Albourne. Thus after possibly 2,000 years the shape of the parish boundary has changed and parts of our history lost forever.

NOTES AND REFERENCES

1. Cooper JH (1912): *A History of the Parish of Cuckfield*, 180.
2. *Ibid.*, 185.
3. Old Acts of Parliament, *SAC* **15**, 142.
4. Royal Journeys in Sussex, *SAC* **2**.
5. Vestry minutes
6. 10 Geo III, c.95.
7. 11 Geo III, c.99.
8. 17 Geo III, c.74.
9. 48 Geo III, c.101; ESRO/QDP/E13.
10. ESRO/QDP/E66.
11. Weekes R: Glimpses of the Past, Extracts from a Hurst Resident's Diary, *Mid Sussex Times* (nd, pre 1912); Bates A (1969): *Directory of Stage Coach Services 1836*.
12. Weekes, Diary.
13. WSRO/ Par 400/31/26–31.
14. Harper C G (1922): *The Brighton Road*.
15. A Native, A Minor (1837): *A History of Hurstperpoint*.
16. 38 Geo III, c.7.
17. Subsidy Rolls 1296, 1327 and 1332, *SRS* **10**.
18. The Book of John Rowe 1597–1622, *SRS* **34**, 127, 129.
19. 5&6 Wm IV, c.24; ESRO/QDP/E141.
20. 4 Wm IV, c.10; ESRO QDP/E110, 135.
21. ESRO/DAN2071–81.
22. WSRO/Par400/12/3/1.
23. Burgess Hill & St John's Common Water Co., founded 1870.

24. Weekes, Diary.
25. Hurstpierpoint Gas Co., later part of SE Gas.
26. The village was first supplied with electricity in the 1920s by Hassocks &
    Hurstpierpoint Electricity.

11. FARMING WITH MACHINES

Up horn: Down corn
Down horn: Up corn
– traditional

1840 – 1876

The early years of the 1840s are a good moment to take stock of the farming scene. The first detailed census took place in 1841 and the reforms of the tithe law led to the preparation for each parish of detailed maps showing not only the owner and occupier of each farm but the land use for individual fields. High corn prices at the time ensured that a large area of land was under the plough in the parish. James Caird, writing in the early 1850s reckoned yields in Sussex to be around 22 bushels per acre (0.6 tons/acre) compared with modern yields of up to 3 tons/acre.[1] William Wood who farmed a number of Mid Sussex farms including Newhouse and Washbrooks farms and was also a miller during the later part of the nineteenth and early twentieth century recalls wheat selling for 58s 4d a quarter in the late 1840s.[2] This price of £13.40/ton compares with a wheat price in August 2000 of around £58/tonne without any allowance for inflation. So that for the larger farmer 'with ample capital, farming was a good business through the major part of the nineteenth century, up to about 1876. They lived in the style of country gentlemen, were very hospitable, entertained largely, kept a good table and cellar, and enjoyed what sport there was going – enjoyed life to the full'.[3]

The 1841 Census puts names to these farming families. Different members of the Wickham family farmed at Great Danard, High Field, Goldbridge, Dumbrills and Wanbarrow Farms.   The Pickett family (William and Elizabeth aged 70 and 75) farmed Great Danworth whilst Edward (35) and his family occupied Pickhams and Henry (65) worked Newhouse Farm adjoining. The Census also reveals the size of these farming families often also living with both domestic servants and farm labourers in the same house. East Edgerley, for example, was not only home to William and Lois Hallett and their four children but three male servants, probably farm staff Henry and James Noakes and James Wickens together with Jane Reeves and Eliza Killick. Other households would have relied on family labour such as the several generations of Pratts at Naldritts which was home to no less than eleven from the matriarch Sarah aged 94 to George Pratt aged 25. There was only room for one live-in servant, Sarah Standen, a teenager from a village family, who no doubt had to work hard for her keep!

Farming prosperity brought higher rents for landowners. Caird reports average rents in Sussex at 19/- an acre in 1850 compared with 10/9d in 1770. By comparison wages had gone from 8/6d. to 10/6d. a week and farm cottage rents from 1/2d to 1/11d a week in the same space of time.[4] During this period the principle landowners consolidated their position within the parish. Copyhold and small freehold farms were added to the growing tenanted sector. Tott Farm for instance which had been held by the Evelyn family, was acquired as copyhold by the Lord of the Manor William John Campion. The sitting tenant Mary Ann Jenner continued to farm undisturbed. Families like the Borrers bridled at the powers of the Lord of the Manor and the Danny archive contains protracted correspondence in 1851 between the two families' lawyers over the felling by Borrer's bailiff of some trees on copyhold land held by them but subject to the standing timber (except for repairs) being owned by the Lord of the Manor.[5]

William Wood paints a vivid picture of life on a mid-Sussex farm at the time. Hams and bacon hanging from kitchen jacks, cellars full of home-brewed beer (using local hops and malt) and a busy farmer's wife supervising baking and cooking as well as the farm poultry and calf rearing. Some dairying was practised and local cheese was made although it was Wood's verdict that 'a Sussex cheese was too big to swallow and too hard to bite'.[6] The farmer whilst busy supervising his farm staff found time for shooting, reckoned by Wood to be their chief pastime.[7] Market days were very much social occasions and William Wood tells of the Market Ordinaries which were provided by hotels such as the White Hart, Lewes, where on market day 'there was always a choice of thick or clear soup, a choice of fish, joints of beef, mutton or pork, always game when in season, and at other times chicken, duck, turkey or goose and the price was 2s, nearly every man . . . had a bottle of wine'.[8]

Another event which mixed business and pleasure was the weekly Corn Market at the New Inn on Tuesday evenings at 7 o'clock. It was at one such meeting that it was decided to revive the Hurst Ploughing Match, after it had lapsed for a number of years. William Wood relates the tale of its revival 'some forty years ago' (his book appeared in 1938) a ten shilling wager on who had the best crop of green turnips prompted the decision to start a Ploughing Match and Root Show, although the reported sighting of a Hurstpierpoint Ploughing Match horse brass from the 1880s might contradict this tale. The match continues to flourish on the first Saturday in October with a large entry of commercial, vintage and horse ploughmen. The grain and hay competitions remain but roots are no longer shown, reflecting their decline as animal feedstuff. Incidentally at the last meeting of the old Society held at Danny a team of oxen beat the horse teams by ploughing a given acreage in the shortest time.[9]

For the smaller farmer life was undoubtedly harder. He was dependent on livestock for a greater part of his income and on the heavier land in the north of the parish corn yields were much lower. William Wood reckoned on his last farm on the south side of Hurstpierpoint to harvest 10 or 11 sacks of corn to an acre whilst his neighbour to the north would produce 6 and would need three horses to do the cultivation work that two could do on the lighter land.[10]

For the farm labourer life was very tough. The 'hungry forties' saw high corn prices but no improvement in the labourers' wages. As industrialization grew in the north and Midlands the rural south and west were seen as poor areas. Whilst Caird reckoned Sussex wages in 1850 around 10/6d per week, Wood with access to his family's day books reckoned Mid Sussex wages nearer 8/- a week whilst at the same time corn for a time reached 80/- a quarter (£18.7s a ton). Bread was the staple diet providing around 40% of the calorific intake, with each adult consuming an average of 12 lbs. of bread a week and a typical family could eat 56 lbs. of bread a week. A 4lb. loaf would cost in the region of 10d.[11] Vegetables would supplement the diet, but 30% of the labouring households had no purchased meat as shown by Dr Edward Smith's survey in 1863. William Wood confirms this view: 'only the parson and shopkeeper could afford butchers' meat'.[12] As a consequence much of the livestock reared locally met a depressed trade at markets such as Hurst's held on Church Green and undoubtedly cattle continued to be driven north to Smithfield Market which remained a livestock market until 1855.

Nevertheless most farmers and landowners remained paternalistic to their staff. William John Campion left money to be distributed to his farm workers on his death in 1855.[13] Of the twenty workers on Danny home farm nine received the maximum payment of £10 each for working more than twenty years. Henry Mitten and Henry Richardson (bailiff) had both worked 36 years. It is also interesting that members of the same family predominate with three Jupps and Lewrys and two Ganders, Richardsons, Kings, Millers and Pierces being employed.

Much of the work had remained unchanged for centuries. Cutting corn with sickles and scythes would have been the only course during the early part of the period and the grain would have been flailed out in the traditional manner. Steam began to make an appearance and portable steam engines and later traction engines powered mechanical threshing machines. Certainly by 1873 William Cooper of Henfield was thrashing corn at Danny.[14] The heavy Sussex turn-wrest plough had been heavily criticised by contemporary agricultural commentators as being clumsy and inefficient so the Danny Home Farm invested in 1872 in a 'Patent BB No. 2 Plough with two wheels and steel breast'; with coulters and spare shares and skim points it cost after 5% discount, £6.12s from James and Frederick Howard's Brittania Iron Works, Bedford.[15] This was a horse drawn plough but elsewhere on Downland Farms oxen could still be seen working.

Disease was rife and fatalities high. An outbreak of scarlet fever could kill thirty or forty in the locality and smallpox was still prevalent. Infant mortality and death at childbirth were commonplace particularly amongst the poor. Unsanitary water supplies were a frequent cause of disease. Rabid dogs were still a worry and Maude Robinson at Saddlescombe recalls a young farming neighbour being bitten and subsequently dying of hydrophobia in the 1860s.[16]

Cattle diseases were also prevalent. Despite the gradual increase in milk consumption tuberculosis was endemic. Brucellosis (contagious abortion), Johne's disease, and a host of other complaints were commonplace. Foot and Mouth, the greatest fear of twentieth century farmers was not regarded as being so serious in the mid-nineteenth century. Maude Robinson recalls a team of working oxen being nursed through the disease.[17]

Particularly feared was the Cattle Plague, now known as Rinderpest which caused fever and dysentery and frequently death in the infected cattle. The disease swept through the country during 1866. Cattle sales were suspended and the newspapers were full of meetings and debates about the best course of action. The East Sussex Cattle Plague Association met at Lewes and discussed a ban on stock movements, the destruction of infected beasts, limited compensation payments and disinfection of infected premises. With no statutory powers they could only call upon the Government to act. Advertisements appeared for quack remedies:

> Bakers Preventive Medicine – secures farmers Perfect Immunity from this scourge.[18]

The Plague Returns printed in June 1866 revealed that of the reported cases nationally 248,025 animals had caught the disease of which 79,997 had been killed and 121,160 had died.[19]

Hurst held a special church service on 7th March. As there was no compensation scheme the disease could mean ruin to a small stock farmer so no doubt the special hymn for singing in the time of Cattle Plague was sung with feeling. Less serious ailments could be treated by the vet. The Danny Home Farm had Thomas Brush attend. Extracts from his account read:[20]

1873	
Jan 23rd Bottle Mixture for cow	3s
2 Drinks for cow	4s
April 7th Dose Physic for Horse	2/6
Bottle white oil	2s
Pot ointment	2s
April 8th 4 Balls for Horse	4s
12th Giving Horse Dose Physic	2/6
15th 2 Balls for Horse	2s

and later:

Oct 28th Lotion Bullock belly	2s

and still the horse had not recovered:

Dec 2nd Dose Physic Horse	2/6

The Danny archive [21] also gives details of other local tradesmen dependent on agriculture, including the following millers and feed merchants: J C E Hammond at Clayton Mills; Robert Broad at Ruckford 'Water and steam mills near the College' and William Wood at Hammonds Mill, Burgess Hill. The millers also supplied imported Cotton Cake and Linseed Cake for stock feeding as did Broad and Packham 'Coal and Coke Merchants dealers in Best American Linseed oil cake cotton cake Guano direct from the Peruvian Government Agents, Nitrate of Soda etc. Concentrated Manures, Bone, Cereal, Turnip, Superphosphates and Half-inch Bones'. John Leopard also supplied feedstuffs from Hassocks Gate.   Amongst the eighteen mills that Wood recalled in the Hurst area in the 1870s would have been Charles Packham's at Cobbs Mill.   Another trader not mentioned in the Danny archive would have been the Pesketts who were hay merchants as well as shopkeepers.[22] Other suppliers included Mr Webber whose 100 wattles were delivered via the L.B.S.C.R. Co. from Balcombe at a price of £15, and Sutton & Sons of Reading Seed Merchants. Suttons supplied swede, mangold, Kohl Rabe (sic), Drumhead cabbage and mustard seed to grow for animal feeds.   Professional services included those of Mr Edward Drawbridge of Lindfield Agricultural Valuer, whose firm was later taken over by Bannisters of Haywards Heath.

Other problems have a familiar ring.   In September 1854 a barn at Washbrooks Farm was burnt to the ground.   John Lewis the Campions' solicitor writing to W John Campion noted:

> it is a pity that parents should not be more careful in allowing
> their children to have Lucifer matches to play with.

Whilst it was never proven to be children the insurance company would seem to have met the claim of £233 to rebuild the barn.[23]

Finally before leaving this period it is informative to have a look at an Inventory and Valuation prepared in 1869 of the 'Livestock, Implements of Husbandry, Tackling, Hay at feeding price, Whole Manures, Labor (sic) to mould, Cultivations on Great and Little Danny farms' i.e. the Campions' home farm.[24]

Nine horses on the farm were named Darling, Traveller, Trooper, Dragon, Rodney, Sharper, Colonel, Move and Boxer.

The dairy herd comprised 12 Alderney cows, all named, and a half-bred Alderney bull. The dairy young stock were five two year old Alderney heifers '1 Crop bred heifer; 3 yearling Alderney heifers and a young Alderney Bull'.

Beef stock comprised one fat Shorthorn cow; one fat Devon steer; four three-year-old fattening Devon steers and ten two year old fattening Devon steers.

There was a sheep flock of 98 Southdown wethers; 20 Southdown fattening ewes; 21 Southdown wethers and 31 Southdown wether tegs.

The farm equipment and 'tackling' is listed in full and includes ladders for the ricks, horse harness, horse rakes, wooden and iron rollers, carts of all types; three turn wrist (sic) foot ploughs; seed and manure drills; cake crusher, dock pullers and spuds; American hay rake, seed lips, cribs for cattle feeding, 2 Sussex wheel ploughs.

Plate 32. Haymaking.

There were 12 stacks of hay all no doubt carefully thatched for the winter.

The Cultivations listed were for mangolds, turnips, cabbages, beans and peas, and the farm had grown 18 acres of Wheat, 9 acres of Oats, 4 acres of Barley, 13 acres of Beans and 8 acres of Peas. The labour involved in cultivation at the time is illustrated by the work done to establish one acre of mangelwurzel that autumn: 3 ploughings; 6 small harrowings; once rolled with three horses, 27 cart loads of dung and mould; hand drilling; horse and hand hoeing.

The Poultry: 28 hens and 4 roosters; 7 ducks and a drake; 3 hen turkeys and a cock turkey; 8 young turkeys and 40 chickens.

The animal feedstuffs in store included 10 cwt. of foreign oil cake; 50 bushels of potatoes (presumably chat potatoes for animal feed) and 10 bushels of old peas.

In total the value came to:

Livestock	£971. 0. 0
Tackling & Implements	£241.11.6
Tenant Right and Sundries	£1,051.16.6
Poultry	£7.16.0
	£2,272. 4.0

A large investment, which in the next decade was going to show little return.

1876 – 1918
DANNY
HURSTPIERPOINT

May 4th 1879

Dear Sir,

I have instructed Mr Coddington to return to you 10 per cent on the nett receipts of your Rent at this Audit, for the half-year ending March 25th 1879. I make this allowance because I wish the farmers occupying my land to know that I fully appreciate and sympathise with their difficulties during the last two or three years. I make it in order that I may share with them in their losses, but chiefly as an encouragement for them to work their farms with a good heart for the future. . .

Though things may look black just now, I am not disposed to think that a re-evaluation and re-adjustment of rents will be necessary or advisable . . .
I do not pretend to hold out hopes that prices either of wheat or fat stock, will go back to what they were a few years ago. . .
Where we have grown three quarters of wheat we must grow five, or grow something else; when we have fattened one Bullock we must fat two. . . . .but I look with hope and confidence to the enterprise, patience and perseverance which has never yet deserted the English cultivator of the soil.
I need hardly assure you that what affects my tenants affects me as my interests are bound up with theirs.

I am,
Yours faithfully

W. HENRY CAMPION²⁵

Although the repeal of the Corn Laws in 1846 had been predicted to ruin British agriculture it was the opening of the Prairies and cheap imported grain in the 1870s that brought to an end the 'Golden Age of High Farming'. The 1880s and 1890s were particularly bad.

Farmers short of capital cash, many on the verge of ruin . . . The
land around here more than half laid down (much of it dropped
down) [to grass] . . . Whoever attempts to grow wheat at 30s/qtr
must linger out at last a wretched existence in the union house.[26]

Financial ruin was compounded by drought during 1891-94. Refrigeration
techniques enabled cheap meat to be imported, further undermining farming
fortunes. William Wood recalled that of the farming families locally 'I do
not know of one of the old yeoman stock remaining' and blamed their
misfortune on the fact that they had sold their cattle 'their chief asset' whilst
corn was dear and had nothing to fall back on when their 'stiff heavy land
became unprofitable'.[27]

In 1882 Henry and Samuel Beeching gave notice to quit their tenancy of
Randolphs and Washbrooks Farms. They had been there since the 1860s,
and Henry was in his late 70s, whilst Samuel was ten years younger. They
were the Campions' largest tenants on their Sussex estates and had been
prominent families in the parish having farmed also at Blackhouse in the
northern part of the parish and Berrylands at Sayers Common, as well as
trading as butchers in the village.   As usual an inventory and valuation
was prepared, detailing the compensation due to them on quitting and this
shows a number of changes in husbandry techniques compared with the
Great and Little Danny valuation cited earlier.

Plate 33. Corn Harvest on Randolphs Farm

Cropping seemed similar with wheat, oats, cabbage, 'sweeds' (sic), grazing rye, mangolds, trifolium, rape saved for seed, but the land, in addition to being dunged, had in part superphosphate applied and Crabtree Field had one ton of guano (sea gull droppings shipped from Peru) applied. The cultivation work was just as intensive with three ploughings and numerous harrowings being commonplace. Eleven stacks of hay were left and the new tenant was to have the straw for the cost of threshing and carriage of the outgoing tenants' corn to market within 10 miles of the farm. Also included in the total valuation of £789-6s-9d were several roller blinds in the house and 'three bells as hung'.[28]

Randolphs and Washbrooks Farms were offered by Mr Coddington, the Campions' agent, for let. The advertisements which appeared in April and May 1882 read:

> Sussex – To be LET on the CAMPION ESTATE from MICHAELMAS next those well known and useful Farms of RANDOLPHS and WASHBROOKS about 291 ACRES in extent in Hurstpierpoint parish, adjoining Danny demesne having about 155 ACRES of very productive clay and mixed loam ARABLE LANDS with 136 ACRES of good PASTURE and MEADOW LAND good and suitable offices and cottages and dwelling-house pleasantly and healthily situated on rising ground within 8 miles of Brighton by road and 2 and a half miles from Hassocks Station. Is well suited for combining DAIRY FARMING and Sheep feeding with either Nursery or Market Garden purposes. Apply Mr W.H. Coddington, 11, Montpelier Terrace, Brighton.[29]

With wheat and stock prices on the floor the advertisement draws attention to the farms' suitability for dairying and market gardening. Milk had always been produced in the area as shown by the twelve Alderney cows kept at Danny in 1869. Indeed Caird describes in some detail the dairying on a 450-acre Downland farm north of Brighton in 1850. Forty cows were kept with

> comfortable stalls for the milch cows . . . [which] are house-fed during the winter on carrots, mangold, swedes and grain. They are housed during the night in summer and tethered [!] by the head in the day.[30]

Caird went on to question the wisdom of the unusual practice of tethering cows under a hot summer sun. Nevertheless the cows showed a good profit from the milk sold in Brighton.

Plate 34. Mangolds being loaded on to traditional farm cart.

Although the evidence is difficult to find, the reliance on dairying undoubtedly grew through the period. The Census returns show a small increase in the number of farm workers describing themselves as dairymaids, cowmen or cowboys as a percentage of the total workforce between the 1871, 1881 and 1891 returns.[31] Interestingly the number of dairymaids fell, perhaps because domestic work was better paid. Again using the Census returns, they suggest that in 1881 and/or 1891 there were dairy herds on the following farms: Little Danworth, Latchetts, Stuckles, Langton Farm, Paddock Farm, West Town, Danny, Tott, Russells Farm, Randiddles and Washbrooks, there were probably others.

The Census and other records reveal another trend. Farms which in the 1840s and 1860s had supported an independent farming family, were now amalgamated with others, as it became more difficult to find tenants. To try to maintain viability in the face of deepening recession, Washbrooks Farm, farmed in 1841 by Henry Packham, was put with Randolphs Farm and was farmed by Henry and Samuel Beeching until 1882. Tott which had for years been farmed with Randiddles by the Jenner family until Grace Jenner's death in 1869, was let to Richard Broad who had other business interests including a butchery business and a shop let in the village. The farmhouse was lived in by James Bean the bailiff. By 1875 Broad had taken other land including Hautboys (Abbeys) and Dapps which Mrs Harriett Marchant quit in 1870. At the 1881 census Rhoda and Luke Benfield lived in Tott Farmhouse as dairymaid and bailiff respectively. Whilst there were changes contradicting this, the trend is clear: 38 farmers in 1871; 29 in 1881 and 17 in 1891.[32] In twenty years the numbers had halved. By contrast, the number of farm workers fell by 20% from 225 to 180 in the same period.

With their employers struggling there was little prospect of improvement in the lot of the farm worker. Wages rose in Sussex from around 8s 6d in the 1850s to 12s a week in 1880.[33] This was 1s a week below the national average for farm wages and considerably below the wages paid in industrial areas. Mechanisation both with steam and improved horse drawn equipment such as Mr McCormick's self-binder (which won a gold medal in the Royal Agricultural Society's trials in 1879), reduced the labour need but until the twentieth century hand milking was the only practical option.

Increasing intervention from the new public health and sanitation boards could bring some small improvement in the labourer's lot. For example, W H Campion was required to remedy the foul drains which were leaking into the well at one of the Bedlam Street Cottages occupied by the Pierce family in 1875.[34] It could be difficult for farm workers to move to new work outside farming, as their employer, who would need a vacant cottage for a replacement worker, nearly always controlled the cottage that they occupied. During this period the practice of farm workers being housed in the farmhouse virtually died out.[35]

Another change in the period was the closure of Hurstpierpoint Market. In 1855 W J Campion let his coach house and a piece of land on Church Green on Stock Market days to the market committee, represented by W Marshall and James Wood.[36] The coach house was to be used for settling accounts and the rental would seem to have been 2s per annum in total. Wood, who farmed at Berrylands, and Marshall seem to have represented respectively the interests of butchers and farmers on the market committee. In 1880 Mr Smith of the Ham wrote to the Campions' agent, W H Coddington, giving notice on behalf of the 'late Hurst Cattle market to surrender the Piece of Ground lately occupied by them for the Cattle Market held on Church Green'.[37] This almost certainly would have been a private treaty market, rather than an auction market such as Haywards Heath and Hassocks Gate Markets as well as the more distant markets at Lewes, Steyning (an important horse market) and Horsham. Fairs such as St John's at Fairplace in July at Burgess Hill which survived until 1912,[38] and Lindfield in August, were also important outlets for store stock. Most of the village butchers had their own slaughterhouses, including F Botting, who ran an abattoir at Court Bushes.[39]

The turn of the century saw an influx of West Country farmers with experience in dairying. They were particularly drawn to the area as they could market fresh milk direct to the South Coast and London markets. After twenty-five years of falling prices rents had tumbled and some farms in the county were tenantless. Amongst the first in the village was the Harvey family, from east Cornwall. Staunch Methodists, they quickly established themselves with Ernest Harvey taking Goldbridge (Bridgers Farm) in 1900 and Eleazor, his brother, Randolphs Farm in 1901 from the Hannington and Campion families respectively. Later arrivals include the Jenkin family, W I Jenkin taking Tott and other farms on the Danny Estate around 1912 and 1913. The Jenkins moved their farming equipment and livestock from Cornwall by rail to Hassocks Station. 'Don't get off 'til Hassocks' was the advice that had gone back to Cornwall, that is do not take a farm on the heavy wealden clay north of the parish. Another Cornish family that moved to the area at this time (1898) were the Blakes but they did not move into the parish until 1926 when Ernest Harvey quit Goldbridge (Bridgers) Farm.

Ernest Harvey's Farming Day Books for part of this period have been kept by the family and provide a fascinating insight into farming at the time. Meticulously they record the daily output of milk. This, the most important product, was sold to Frowd and Mockett, and the separate business of C.F Frowd, both receiving the milk by rail at their Brighton dairies. Later in the period some milk was sent to London. Production was geared to ensuring an even supply of milk throughout the year and any impending shortfall avoided by the purchase of freshly calved cows, mainly from Haywards Heath Market but occasionally as far afield as St. Ives, Northampton and Yeovil, with the stock being sent back by rail.

The cows were fed during the winter months on purchased brewers' grains – 'bought grains from Sidney Hole'(10/11/1900)[40] – hay and roots, in particular mangolds. The roots were a labour intensive crop and there are frequent references to payments to casual workers, hoeing and pulling mangolds. The weekly wage bill varied with the seasons but seldom topped 16s a man even during harvest 1900. Beer still remained part of the wage costs:

22nd May 1901 – Shearing sheep. Paid for 1 gallon beer.

Tamplin and Sons (Brewers) appear to have made regular deliveries much to Ernest Harvey's disapproval as a Methodist. He generally blamed the brewery cart for any potholes that appeared in the farm road!

A sheep flock was also kept with replacement stock being purchased from as far away as Dorchester Sheep Fair. Chichester Market was also a source of stock:

12th June 1901
Bt. 50 lambs @ 25/- [each] from Mr Dale, E Marden   [£]
                                                       62-10
29th June 1901
Paid L.B.S.C. Rly 50 sheep [from] Chichester   1-0-6
Hurdles 4/4 Oil Cake 9/6 Sheep trough 7d

Once this stock was unloaded at Hassocks it would have been driven back to Bridgers Farm via the High Street. Fat lambs appear to have been sold generally at Hassocks and Haywards Heath Markets. Frank Botting also purchased lambs, as well as rabbits, for sale in his butcher's shop.

A small poultry flock was kept with regular consignments of eggs going to Frowd and Mockett by rail. Sometimes the daybooks record the sale of eggs to locals and village shops. The occasional visitor was also noted:

Fox paid us a visit tonight and killed 2 hens and 10 chickens, 6 big ones and four smaller.
                    19/7/1907
Pigs were also reared:

£8 – 11 bought of Bannisters pigs
recd. of Bannisters [auctioneers] 10 sheep £23 – 15
                    17/01/1901

Their diet included acorns collected by some of the cottage dwellers in Langton Lane:

Paid Sherlock 2½ bushels acorns 2/-.
                    1/12/1900

The arable cropping included wheat, oats and beans. The grains were sold to Mr Hammond and Mr Packham at nearby Cobbs Mill. Hay was sold to Mr Peskett. The farm income was further supplemented by carrying out farm work for other farmers and landowners. An early reference to spraying appears in May 1907:

> Sprayed 6 acres kilk [charlock] for Mr Scrase
> 1 keg of Sulphate of copper £2.

The list of goods in store for Lady Day 1907 reveals a considerable amount of fertiliser including sulphate of ammonia (£12-2-6/ton); nitrate of soda (£11-2-6 / ton); Kainit (45s/ton); basic slag (55s /ton) and superphosphates at 53s 9d. The nitrogenous fertilisers were very expensive in particular and the list of nitrogen fixing seeds also in store show the importance attached to rotations to maintain fertility: Alsike 9d/lb, trefoil 3d/lb, clover 32s a bushel and white Dutch clover 9d/lb together with Italian ryegrass.

Plate 36. Staff of Geer & Son Ltd.

Coupled with the rise in dairying in the area was an increase in market gardening. The comparatively fertile and easily worked soils of the Greensand, along with railway communications to the nearby south coast and London markets, were the spur. A number of families were associated with the trade in the locality; the Sayers family in Hurst Wickham; and the Geers and Starleys. James Starley is mentioned as farming Ubbleys in

1841.[41] His family, famed for their bicycle connections, went on to become market gardeners and nurserymen at Albourne.

Plate 37. Geer's: inside a glasshouse.

In any event, Daniel Starley, together with William Pescott and David King, were listed as market gardeners in the 1845 edition of Kelly's Directory. The 1871 Census reveals David King still working at Whitpain Cottage with other members of the King family at Lahore Cottage. The Wadeys, farmers and market gardeners at Box House, and Frederick Peskett at Breachland Cottage were also listed. The Geers of Erskine Nursery came to the area around 1847 [42] and by 1881 five members of the family were resident at Erskine Nursery. Edwin Geer, who had been born at Washington in Sussex around 1820, founded the nursery. The orchards, including the pear walk, must have been planted out during his tenure. The nursery was rented from Mr Weekes at this time. Hurst was noted for fruit growing. Box House had as late as 1953[43] eight acres of mature orchards including apples, pears and plum trees underplanted with rhubarb stools, gooseberry, currant bushes and raspberries and Emperor daffodils. There were a further 2¾ acres of vegetable grounds as well as over 6 acres of allotments. Box House was farmed by the Holman family for much of this period. Not all the produce went out of the parish. Harry Bransden had a small greengrocers at the eastern end of the High Street growing some of the produce sold on land at Ribbetts and where No. 8 South Avenue now stands.

The outbreak of the Great War caused immediate disruption on the farms. Horace Broad who farmed at the Ham was appointed to requisition horses for the army. Cart-horses were required to haul military supplies in France and were literally taken out of the shafts of the carts and binders harvesting corn. Harold Harvey vividly recalled seventy years later the carters in tears at the loss of the horses they cherished. Harold's father recorded in his Day Book:

> Sold Victor to Mr Broad for the Army At £38.0.00
> Boxer   £51.0.00
> Captain   £51.0.00   6th August 1914

Plate 38. Muster of horses for the Great War.

The family's contacts in Cornwall ensured replacement horses were soon on their way, enabling other horses on the farm to be sold to neighbours who had lost theirs. The assumption that the war would soon be over meant that few steps were taken initially to improve agricultural output which after nearly forty years of depression was at a low ebb. Whilst prices improved during the war it was not until 1917 that the submarine blockade brought the threat of starvation home. In haste the government passed the Corn Production Act and gave greater powers to the War Agricultural Committees, set up in 1915. These committees were organised on a local basis and they carried out farm surveys to establish which ground should be ploughed for corn. The Cuckfield Rural District Committee sat under the Chairmanship of William Wood in the later part of the war. With horses and skilled labour and phosphatic fertilisers in short supply, it was not easy to respond to the ploughing orders. In any event without sprays, wireworm and leather jackets took a heavy toll on the newly sown corn.[44]

German prisoners of war were drafted to work on the land. William Wood recalled a hard working group of Bavarian prisoners being billeted on his farm. As in the Second World War women volunteers took the place of men on many farms, including William Wood's. There two girls took over his Jersey herd of twenty-two cows and 'never before or since was the work in my cow stall better done than it was by these two London girls'. The committees set up tractor depots across the county and Titan tractors were allocated from farm to farm as needed.[45] Although slow and lumbering, they, coupled with Simplex Mogul and Bates tractors which were also making an appearance, helped lift wheat production across the county from 44201 acres in 1914 to 66,823 acres in 1919.[46]

By the end of the war farming had fully recovered and farmers thought they could look forward to a period of prosperity. Stock had doubled in price, horses worth £50 at the outbreak of war now commanded £100 and upwards. The Corn Production Act gave a guarantee of minimum prices for wheat and oats. On a personal note though few families had escaped tragedy and William Wood was no exception, he lost his only surviving son in Mesopotamia in 1916.

1918-1939

> But now that Farmer's Glory's dim
> And agriculture holds no pleasures
> I'd give a lot
> If I had farmed when times like these were not.'
>   A G Street from 'A Farmer's Glory'[47]

1918 saw one of the largest single sales of land in Hurstpierpoint for very many years when Lord Monk Bretton, Baron Hurstpierpoint and Coneyboro, put his lands in the parish onto the market, bringing to an end the Dodson family's long association with the village.

1900 marked the high water mark for the landed estates with probably about 90% of the farmland nationally owned by landlords. Hurstpierpoint was no exception. Much of the north of the parish was in the hands of Lord Monk Bretton; Little Park, Bridgers and Great Danworth Farms were owned by the Hanningtons; and the Borrers had Box House, West Town, Coombe, Clayton Wickham and Highfield Farms shared amongst the family. The largest landowner of all, the Campions of Danny, dominated the south of the parish and beyond.

For nearly forty years rents had fallen, indeed some farms had been let rent free for a time, in particular large Downland farms.[48] Even during the war years legislation had limited rent increases. Estates which had been left entail, that is in trust for yet unborn generations of the family, could now be sold after a series of changes in the law during the last part of the nineteenth century, so 'breaking the tail'. Tithes which had always been a tax on farm produce, had been commuted to a money sum in 1836, based on the average price of wheat over the previous seven years. The liability for the tithe rent charge was switched in 1891 from a hard-pressed tenantry to their landlords. The 1894 Finance Act brought land into the scope of Death Duties for the first time. Lloyd-George's 'People's Budget' of 1909 introduced super-tax and Land Value duties so precipitating the constitutional crisis between the Houses of Lords and Commons, culminating in the ascendancy of the Commons enshrined in the Parliament Act 1911. With all these changes and pressures many of the landed estates began to be dispersed, and by 1946 only 56% of farms in East Sussex were rented.[49]

Lord Monk Bretton's Hurst estate went to auction on 23rd July, 1918. Included in the sale of 1156 acres were Danworth Brook Farm 57 acres, let for £60 per annum to Mr C Bellingham (a family associated with the farm for many years) together with house and buildings and cowhouse for 14; Kents Farm 91 acres, occupied by Austin J Baker; Northend Farm 93 acres, farmed by Richard Crane; Dumbrells Farm 141 acres, held by the Executors of H G Coomber; Wortleford Farm 62 acres, let to Mr Myram; Malthouse

Farm 66 acres, farmed by George Pratt who also farmed a further 33 acres at Gatehouse Farm. Deanhouse Farm[50] was also offered for sale, this let to Arthur Clark who paid £95 per annum for its 161 acres. Interestingly in a reference to the village's feudal past, the particulars made clear that the Crown as owner of Pangdean Farm had the 'right of first cut and carry away of grass' from 1 acre 1 rood and 33 perches of brookland at Deanhouse Farm. These historic manorial rights, including manorial rights over Copyhold property, were swept away a few years later by the fundamental reforms introduced by the Law of Property Act 1925.

In the previous century an estate such as Lord Monk Bretton's would have been competed for amongst neighbouring landowners, but times had changed and the estate became fragmented amongst numerous owners. The Borrers had already begun to reduce their estates with the sale of Highfields Farm and Clayton Wickham Farm to A E Peters, a south coast solicitor, over a period of time between 1911 and 1914.[51]

In fact 1918 had been a good time to sell. War had driven land prices up and the future looked bright. With the lessons of the submarine blockade fresh in their minds, Lloyd-George's post-war coalition promised to maintain some support for agricultural production. Although the Corn Production Act was repealed, it was replaced by the Agriculture Act 1920. The Act contained the basis of a complicated formula for price support, but before this section could be enacted, the grain price collapsed, and to avoid a £20 million bill for support the measures were quietly dropped. Wheat which had sold at 72s 10d per quarter in 1918, had risen to 80s 10d in 1920. By 1923 the price had almost halved to 42s 2d.

A series of wet summers during the '20s and recurring outbreaks of Foot and Mouth disease added to the gloom. Nationally many farmers were bankrupted. Particularly vulnerable were those who had just bought their farm from their former landlord with borrowed money. This dramatic change in farming fortunes hit farm workers as well. At the same time as the Corn Production Act had given a minimum price for wheat and oats, it also created Agricultural Wages Boards for each county to fix minimum wages. With the repeal of the Act and the collapse in prices, wages fell from about 47s/week by 10s within a year and a further 10s in the following year. Although the 1924 Labour government reintroduced the Wages Boards, the economic circumstances meant there was little room for improvement in pay until the Second World War.[52] Locally, however, wages had reached around 60s/week by the late 1930s.

Milk production remained the dominant feature of agriculture locally. Whilst fodder supplies had been short during the last years of the war, cheaper grain after 1923 led to a rapid increase in milk supplies. The introduction of glass lined railway tankers also meant that for the first time West Country milk could be sent fresh to London in volume. This inevitably led to a further fall in milk prices. In an attempt to remove surplus milk from the fresh market, a number of cheese making centres were established across the county, including one at Hurstpierpoint in a former brewery, presumably Couchman's in Cuckfield Road.[53] Whether the product was any better than the Sussex cheeses that William Wood complained of earlier is not known. The introduction of the Milk Marketing Board in 1933 finally brought an end to these cheese making centres.

William Ira Jenkin took a prominent role locally in milk production. Together with dairy herds at both Tott Farm and Newhouse Farm he started his own dairy and traded at 'The Creamery' 121 High Street and in Brighton. Another leading dairy farmer was Sidney Hole. An exceptional man who built a very substantial farming, horticultural and dairying business over his lifetime with farms from Barcombe and Saltdean to Albourne, as well as the Hole and Davigdor Dairies in Brighton. He was nicknamed the 'midnight milkman' reflecting the long hours he worked building up the business. He also turned his mind to wider issues being credited locally with designing a submarine escape hatch, and inventing an electric milk-float, as well as writing on agricultural and economic issues.[54]

The price of all farm commodities continued to fall through the late '20s and early '30s. Milk averaged 1s 1d per gallon (less than 1new penny/pint) between 1927 and 1929.[55] Wheat dropped as low as 20s 9d per qtr (£4.67 ton) in 1934.[56] It had never been as cheap in living memory. The government began to take some action: a 'National Mark' was established as a guarantee of quality to be placed on home-grown produce which reached prescribed standards. In 1932 the Wheat Act was passed to give some support to producers, tariffs were raised to protect horticultural produce and under the Agricultural Marketing Act 1933, the Milk Marketing Board was established, thus stabilising the price of milk. As war came closer, further steps were taken to bolster food production including grants towards the cost of liming and applications of basic slag to grassland (slag is a by-product of the steel industry and is used as a phosphatic fertiliser) and a ploughing up grant of £2/acre.

On 9th May 1935 Harold Harvey returned from honeymoon and took over the running of Newhouse Farm. On the same day he started his Farm Day Book,[57] which he kept until just a few days before his death in 1992. In many ways the workload described in these early entries hardly differs from his father's descriptions of farm work before the Great War.

The dairy herd is still centre stage numbering about forty head, mangolds are grown in copious quantities to feed them through the winter although sugar beet pulp bought from Jenner & Higgs of Haywards Heath now makes an appearance. Horses still do some work but a tractor (probably an International) does much of the heavier tasks such as mowing, cultivating and ploughing: '[ground] very stiff, tractor is doing remarkably well' (20/12/1935).

Sixteen months later a Cleveland Caterpillar tractor is bought from Bexhill for £50. Horses still had a role, [Harold's] 'father sent up a four year old cart mare from Cornwall' (1st June, 1937). But it is obvious that Harold Harvey's interest lay with the new machinery becoming available, 'swath turned [hay] with new Bamford swath turner turns 2 six feet swaths cost £23 10s less 10% makes an excellent job'. Despite this mechanisation, farming remained a labour intensive industry: 'Setting out mangolds in Pomper Field 6 men and myself (Everest, Bert, Jim, Funnel, Adsett & Blackwell)'.

Thomas Peskett of Western Road and the High Street continued to buy considerable quantities of hay as his family had from Harold's father before. Baker Bros., butchers in Southdown Terrace, regularly bought cattle and lambs. The lambs were acquired in August for further fattening from Lyminge sheep sale. Whilst in 1936 it had cost £4 to send 110 back by rail; in 1939 Appleby's were transporting 75 lambs by lorry for 65s and they would have delivered them direct to the farm. Cows were still bought and sold at Haywards Heath Market 'Bought cow at Haywards Heath £25- 10. Sold 2 cows 13 cwt [@] £16; 11 cwt [@] £11' (30/8/1935).

In addition to 'Red Standard' mangolds, kale was grown for cattle feed; Victor and Square Head Master wheat was sown; and Eclipse and Majestic potatoes were grown.

Fertilisers were used in increasing quantities and nitrogen fertilisers had dropped in price since his father's day, sulphate of ammonia £7-1-10d; superphosphates, however, were dearer at £3-5-0d. Basic slag and lime were used, '15 tons lime delivered 28s 6d less 50% Govt. rebate' (27/9/1937).

Advances in crop growing were also being matched with those in livestock husbandry. Whilst Foot and Mouth was still a feared scourge (Haywards Heath Market was shut for over two months because of it, before re-opening on 25th January 1938), other diseases were being tackled by improved veterinary products and techniques: 'Injected heifers against abortion with live vaccine' (15/2/1939); in the same year the cows were drenched with Vitamin E. Tuberculin testing was introduced in 1937 in an effort to rid the national herd of tuberculosis and prevent the passing of infection to the human populace.

Whilst the Government's attempts at support came too late to save many from ruin and still left many badly under capitalised, it is clear that farming production and prosperity were beginning to be restored as the Nation faced war again.

1939 TO THE PRESENT

Shipping space must be saved

Notes on Agricultural Policy for those directing the food production campaign.
Ministry of Agriculture, Spring 1942.

Mary Shelton was fourteen when she started work for Holes Farms in 1940.[58] George Hole, Sidney's son, was in the process of expanding the market gardening enterprise in response to wartime demands. Mrs Shelton recalls that when she started only about a dozen people were employed to run fifteen or so acres of horticultural crops. By 1945 the staff had grown to over 100 and around 150 acres were in cultivation, spanning the easily worked Greensand from Breechlands to Bishop's Place Farm in Albourne. All manner of vegetables, including roots and brassicas, were grown, but the largest area was devoted to potatoes. Seed which had previously been imported, was in short supply, and the Holes turned to producing onion and leek seed in particular. This was dried at a converted barn in Albourne, with any surplus being taken by lorry to Kent for drying in a hop-dryer.

Mary lodged with the Funnells, Fred one of the Holes' carters. The working day started at 5.30 a.m. seeing to the horses. On the market garden work began at seven o'clock, with a 'lunch' break at 9.30 and dinner at midday. The day ended at 5.00 p.m. normally, but at busy times could go on until dusk. After supper the horses, mainly cross-bred Shires, would be bedded down for the night.

By 1943 Mary Shelton had enrolled in the Women's Land Army. The market garden staff was divided into gangs of ten, each of which was given a colour and each gang member a number. Each individual had their own set of tools marked with their colour and number – woe betide anyone who put away a dirty hoe! Whilst Wellington boots were issued, the lack of waterproof clothing was one of the worst aspects of working in all weathers. Nevertheless the Land Army girls were expected to turn out for Church Parade and the occasional march-past in Brighton for events such as 'Salute the Red Army', when they brought up the rear alongside the Boy Scouts. Fanny Hole, George's sister, was the Land Army District Representative, responsible for assisting with welfare and billeting problems. A particular memory was the Christmas party attended by all the staff. The Allen family, who farmed at Blackstone, provided the music, bringing along their collection of Victor Sylvester records.

In the early days of the war British troops were drafted into the fields at harvest. Particular care was taken by the Holes' foreman to ensure that the land girls and the soldiers were kept at opposite ends of the farm. Wednesday early closing meant that Brighton shop-workers could spend an afternoon working on the land. School children were another important source of labour. Donald Blake recalls sharing Sayers Common School with evacuee children, who had their lessons in the afternoons while the local children took their turn in the fields. As the official history records, 'it would have been impossible to plant and lift over one million acres of potatoes if children had not been permitted and willing to assist in the busy periods before 1944 when prisoner-of-war labour became relatively plentiful'.[59]

The lessons of the Great War had been learnt. The County Agricultural Committees were put immediately on a war footing and 'War Ag' became an essential part of Britain's war effort. Before the war 16 million tons of human food and 7 million tons of animal feeding stuffs were imported. In 1942 over 7.7 million ton of allied merchant shipping was sunk, mainly by U-boat action,[60] and 'Dig for Victory' was a grim reality. In addition to 'ploughing up' and drainage grants, the War Ag Committees at both county and district level had draconian powers to direct farmers and landowners. National priority was given to wheat, vegetable, potato, sugar beet, and particularly milk production. The government decreed that the arable acreage be increased 'to the limit of our resources by ploughing all available grassland'.[61] Thus much of the chalk Downland in neighbouring parishes not being used by the military disappeared under the plough.[62] Smaller areas were also brought into cultivation: George Hole cropped the bottom of the sandpit below Breechlands, while Mrs Warton let Five Oaks nurseries to Harold Harvey 'for the duration of the war and three years after'.[63] Dairying remained, however, the priority for much of the parish.

As production increased, fertilisers and animal feeding stuffs became more difficult to obtain. Phosphatic fertiliser in particular was very short after the fall of France. Mrs Shelton recalls George Hole buying dung from neighbouring dairy farms, all of which was hauled out of the cattle yards by the Land Army girls. Sewage was also used; in cold weather frozen lumps of it had to be broken up before being spread. Soot was used by the Holes, Mary remembers the girls being paid 6d a day bonus to stand on the back of the manure drill to poke the soot through with a stick to prevent the drill becoming blocked. Swill was fed to pigs on most farms: 'Tottenham Pudding' was brought down from London by rail, its quality as a feed depending on whether it came from the East End or the West End.

Mechanisation gathered pace. The new found prosperity and War Ag encouragement meant that further investment in farm machinery was possible: 'fetched Fordson tractor from John Woolgar £72 – 10d' wrote Harold Harvey in December 1940, the first of several tractor purchases. John Woolgar ran Stephen Woolgar & Sons, the agricultural engineers at the eastern end of the High Street, until it was taken over after the war by Harper & Eede of Lewes. New techniques were also developing. A shortage of cattle feed had led to a fall in milk production nationally. Harold Harvey's day book details how the land at Five Oaks was sown with oats and tares for silage; the practice of making silage of grass and other green crops finally ousted hay as the principal source of home grown winter stock rations. Machine milking began to be introduced on local farms: 'Put milking machines on cows first time most of them take to it well' (22/4/1940).

In addition to the long hours of farm work, both farmers and workers were expected to join the Home Guard or become Air Raid Wardens:

On A.R.P. duty all night at Sayers Common post 15th January 1941.

Two nights earlier:

. . . bomb dropped in field by Berrylands, just missed houses and buildings, [crater] 35 feet deep.

Another bomb fell on a field of onions near the King's Head, and George Hole rallied his staff to prevent the theft of onions which were in short supply, by villagers viewing the damage. Hurst smelt of burnt onions for a week.

In 1943 the Hender family quit Little Park Farm. B B Hender had been a respected tenant of the Hanningtons for many years, renting Danworth and Latchetts farms as well.[64] The sale of equipment and stock conducted by Bannisters of Haywards Heath was memorable for two reasons: the high prices as noted by Harold Harvey; and the road block across what is now Trinity Road, the police checking that vehicles leaving the sale had the appropriate permits for wartime travel. The auctioneer announced that an alternative exit was available across the fields, and most left by that route to avoid awkward questions.[65] Charles Matthews was the incoming tenant, moving from West End Farm, Burgess Hill, although originally from Staffordshire. There were no dairy cows at Little Park until a herd of pedigree Ayrshires was bought by Mr Matthews in Dumfries and sent down by train to Hassocks.[66] A separate herd was milked at Danworth. Very little of the farm was under the plough. Nora Talbot helped with the Shire horses, taking vegetables to the greengrocer's in the High Street. Her father George was the carter, and also thatched the ricks, working there for over fifty years and being awarded the Royal Agricultural Society's long service medal. In the same year the Waters family took over Highfield farm initially as tenants of the A E Peters Trust,[67] dairying again being the mainstay of the business. The previous tenant had bred dogs in the farmhouse attics, and the property was in a poor state; in common with other farms there was no electricity until the late 1950s.

Victory brought no lessening of the pressure to increase production, as food shortages were if anything more acute after the war. Europe faced starvation, and this country was bankrupt, so the new Labour government followed the wartime consensus that a repetition of the farming collapse that followed the Great War must be avoided. The Agriculture Act 1947 set out a framework of deficiency (top-up) payments to be made if prices fell below a certain level, ensuring cheap food while maintaining farm incomes. The next year the Agricultural Holdings Act gave lifetime security of tenure to farm tenants.

Government investment in research and the work of the National Agricultural Advisory Service, coupled with enormous investment in equipment and buildings led to substantial improvements in output. Wheat yields have grown from 19cwts/acre in 1945 to 60cwts today; potatoes from 7 to 15 tons and more; milk yields which fell during the war from 542 gallons per cow per annum to 484 by 1945, now stand at an average of 1,300 gallons, with some individual cows reaching 2,200 gallons (10,000 litres).[68] Joining the EEC in 1973 led to a changed method of support, with intervention buying of produce, until production outstripped demand, leading to the 'lakes and mountains' of surpluses in the 1980s, although Britain has remained a net importer of food. Reform of the Common Agricultural Policy and a strong pound has led to the collapse in incomes of the late 1990s.

At a local level these changes have had a profound effect. The doubling of milk yields in the post-war years has meant that fewer cows are now kept. Farming economics have dictated that, whilst 30 cows constituted a viable herd, 150 are now needed to maintain a similar standard of living. As a consequence the dairy cow has disappeared from the parish: first the small herds; then those on farms able to grow arable crops; finally the handful left were dispersed when milk quotas capping production were introduced in 1984. Amongst the last to leave were those of the Humphreys family who moved from Little Danworth to a Somerset farm.

Parallel with the farming revolution, the pattern of land-ownership has changed too. The dispersal of the Borrer estate began before World War I, the final portion of Pakyns Manor Estate being sold in the early 1950s. James Hannington became a farmer in his own right at Little Park, Danworth and Bridgers. Danworth was developed with all the latest equipment as a dairy farm, the tower silos being a landmark for many years. With the sale of Little Park land for housing the remainder of the estate was disposed of, much of it to Prince Littler, a theatre impresario, who had substantial farming interests in Mid Sussex. After his death in the early 1970s his land was sold and Danworth Farm was purchased by Nigel Ventham, famed locally for his herd of red Sussex cattle which were finally dispersed in 1998. Alone the Danny estate continued in the traditional manner. After a brief period of farming Little Danny themselves during the early 1960s, the farm was re-let by the Campions, as were other holdings as they became vacant. Finally, however, the estate was offered for sale in the early 80s; after failing to sell at auction it was bought by a property developer.

After the war market gardening slumped. Field-scale vegetable growing in the eastern counties and cheap imported salads undermined the local markets. Supermarkets want vast quantities of identical produce which small local businesses cannot supply.

The Holes switched from vegetable to flower seed production, and the business at its peak required up to 142 men and 72 women full-time, and as many as 200 casuals.[69] The flowers grown included delphiniums, sweet peas, asters, lobelias, violas, larkspur, alyssum and cornflowers. Peter Nelson recalls that the perfume from the flowers was so over-powering that the windows of Wanbarrow Farmhouse had to be kept shut. Vegetable seed was grown under contract and a bumper harvest in 1952 meant that enough leek seed was grown in Hurst to supply the whole of the USA and Britain for seven years. Once the Far Eastern growers with far cheaper labour costs had recovered from the turmoil of war this market too was undercut.

After George Hole's illness his farm manager, Peter Nelson, took on the tenancy of Wanbarrow, he and his sons running a 'Pick Your Own' enterprise using the Holes' old packing station at Breechlands. This was finally closed after the re-routing of the A23. After wartime fruit and vegetable growing Geers nursery, under the direction of Albert Geer, changed to strawberries and flower production. Lupins and Sweet Williams being a particular feature of the fields surrounding the nursery, with Cyclamens grown in the glasshouses. The firm continued to have a stall in Brighton Market until the 1960s. While Geers still trades, other nurseries such as Manor and Court Bushes have disappeared under houses. The watercress beds in Langton Lane have also long ceased to trade.

Plate 39. Seed harvesting at Washbrooks: leeks.

Plate 40. Seed harvesting at Washbrooks: Allysum.

It is perhaps too soon to discuss objectively the change wrought by the break-up of the old landed estates. Certainly there are fewer farmers and farm-workers than ever before. Almost all the local farmers have long since diversified their businesses, and, like Richard Broad and Samuel Beeching in the 1870s and 80s, rely on some non-agricultural income, be it from horses, holiday or office lets, or a children's visitor centre. Full time traditionally employed farm-workers have almost entirely disappeared from the parish. Family labour, contractors and mechanisation have finally completed the change begun by the introduction of threshing machines in the hungry years of the 1840s. Although the dairy cow has gone, sheep and reduced numbers of beef cattle remain.

As food production has declined in importance and profitability, so leisure and the funds to support it have grown. Horses have multiplied and 'horsey culture' is evident in many parts of the parish. The trend which was discernible throughout the twentieth century has accelerated in recent years. Farms have become increasingly fragmented, and cottages and farmhouses sold away from the land they served for centuries. Historically the village was largely self-sufficient in most foods, with meat, eggs, fruit and vegetables all grown locally. Now most villagers look to the superstore for their sustenance, perhaps an appropriate moment to reflect and recall the:

> Makers of land, one of the nameless line
> That fenced, and tilled and overcame the waste,
> And cut the necessary gaps
> And shaped the fields, slow-paced
> Into their permanent design
> Each field with local name, not marked on maps,
> How come by, how begotten,
> Long since forgotten.

V Sackville-West: The Yeoman from 'The Land' (1926)

Plates 41 & 42.
Combining at Coombe Farm before the new A23 was constructed;
haying at Tott Farm 1981.

NOTES AND REFERENCES

1. Caird J (reprint 1967): *English Agriculture in 1850–51*, 474.
2. Wood W (1938): *A Sussex Farmer*, 193.
3. *Ibid.*, 36.
4. Caird, *Agriculture*, 474.
5. ESRO/DAN1771.
6. Wood, *Farmer*, 28.
7. *Ibid.*, Chapter IV.
8. *Ibid.*, 76, 77.
9. *Ibid.*, 92 and 196-197
10. *Ibid.*, 179.
11. Zuckerman L (1998): *The Potato*, 103 (quoting contemporary research by Dr Edward Smith).
12. Wood, *Farmer*, 55.
13. ESRO/DAN1829–30.
14. ESRO/DAN1775.
15. *Ibid.*
16. Robinson M (1938): *A South Down Farm in the Sixties*, 56.
17. *Ibid.*, 57.
18. *Sussex Agricultural Express* 19 June 1866.
19. *Ibid.*
20. ESRO/DAN1775.
21. *Ibid.*
22. *Kelly's Directory* 1874.
23. ESRO/ DAN 1771.
24. ESRO/DAN 1775.
25. *Ibid.*
26. *Sussex Agricultural Express* 2 November 1889 (quoted by Brandon & Short 'Southeast from AD1000).
27. Wood, *Farmer,* 18.
28. ESRO/ DAN 1881.
29. ESRO/ DAN 1850.
30. Caird, *Agriculture,* 129.
31. Bower A (unpublished): Analysis of Hurstpierpoint Census Returns.
32. *Ibid.*
33. Brandon & Short, *South East,* 333 *cf.* Wood, *Farmer.*
34. ESRO/ DAN 1773.
35. Wood*Farmer,* 124.
36. ESRO/ DAN 1775.
37. *Ibid.*
38. Matthews H (1989): *Burgess Hill,* 155.

39. Land Tax Records 1946-47 WSRO/ ADD MS 20,089.
40. Ernest Harvey Farm Day Books 1900–1915.
41. 1841 Tithe Redemption Particulars.
42. Conversation with S Revell of Geer & Son Ltd.
43. WSRO/ SP 2148-2165.
44. Jesse R H B: *Agricultural Survey of Sussex*, Royal Agricultural Society of England *County Agricultural Surveys, No 2,* Chapter XVI.
45. Brandon & Short, *South East,* 329.
46. Jesse, *Survey,* 103.
47. Street A G (1983): *Farmer's Glory,* 10 (parody of poem in *Punch* August 1904.
48. e.g. Home Farm Stanmer let rent free for two years in 1907 by the Earl of Chichester, quoted in Brandon P (1998): *The South Downs,*158.
49. *National Farm Survey of England and Wales* HMSO 1946, quoted in Jesse, *Survey.*
50. WSRO/SP616/SP615.
51. Sale particulars of Clayton Wickham Farm 1973 T Bannister & Co.
52. Much of the preceding information has been taken from Orwin C S (1949): *A History of English Farming.*
53. Jesse, *Survey,* 48.
54. Hole S (1929): *Agriculture and Industry.* The booklet was 'An Appeal for the   Reconciliation of Industrial and Agricultural Economics' by a blend of Agricultural subsidy and Imperial Preference.
55. Ministry of Agriculture's index of prices 1927-1929, quoted in Watson & More (1945): *Agriculture, The Science and Practice of British Farming,* 872.
56. Stratton J M (1969): *Agricultural AD 220–1968,* 147. This price was lower than that reached during the long depression before the First World War.
57. All date entries from Harold Harvey's Farm Day Books.
58. Conversation with Mary Shelton 15 August 2000.
59. Murray K A H (1955): *Agriculture* (part of Civil History series HMSO).
60. Liddell Hart B (1973): *History of the Second World War,* 403.
61. *Notes on Agricultural Policy for those directing the food production campaign,* Ministry of Agriculture Spring 1942.
62. Brandon, *South Downs,* 181. By Spring 1942 the East Sussex Committee had reclaimed 8,000 acres of former turf-covered Downland for wheat with the aid of Fordson tractors and land girls, and yields were extremely high. It was estimated that this land and further Downland scheduled for reclamation in the Eastern Downs, would produce annually enough wheat bread for 240,000 persons, 2,400 gallons of milk

together with fresh vegetables for the coastal towns and sugar ration for 125,000 people.

63. Letter to East Sussex War Agricultural Committee 29 January 1941 (Harvey family papers).
64. WSRO/ADD MS 26,300.
65. Conversation with Relf Waters.
66. Conversation with Margaret Higgs.
67. Relf Waters.
68. HMSO *Survey of Agriculture* 1999.
69. Conversation with Peter Nelson 25 November 1998.

12. SHOPS — A STORY OF RISE AND FALL

The High Street in Hurst is of considerable antiquity, with a mixture of substantial houses, inns and smaller cottages. The population up to the seventeenth to eighteenth century was largely self-sufficient in the necessary food, clothing and fuel with very few premises actually built as shops. These were probably only used by the gentry and well-to-do farmers, whilst the poorer people lived by growing their own vegetables, by barter, by dealing with itinerant hawkers or shopping in the weekly market where items were considerably cheaper.

The earliest references to shopping that are available are in the Marchant Diary. Thomas (1676-1728) was a farmer and freshwater fish (carp and tench) trader who lived at Little Park and was aged 38 when the excerpts from the Diary begin. There are many references to shopping in Lewes and Horsham and one reference to a transaction in Shoreham:

1714 Oct 8	Paid 4s at Lewes for ¼ lb. Tea; 5d for a quire [24 sheets] of paper; and 6d for 2 mousetraps Received a hundred weight of Malaga raisins from Tourle of Lewes at 32s and six lbs of hops of Dick Wood at 2s lb.
Dec 13	Recd 5½ yds of narrow cloath at 6s per yd of Mr Thos Friend of Lewes, and 33 buttons with mohair, and canvass and silk.
Dec 15	May went to Horsham with 5½ yds of cloath to R. Hurst's to make me a great coat, and my old coat for a pattern.
Nov 21	At Shoreham Bought two Cheshire cheeses at 3d per lb.[1]

xxxii. Itinerant Scotchman.

There were many hawkers or pedlars who travelled a regular route in the countryside carrying drapery and hardware from market to fair. These were known as Scotchmen and there are two references to such in the Diary:

1719 June 10	Paid for 6yds of edging at 21d per yard 10s 6d.; for 3 ½ yds of muslin, for a cap and ruffles and to graft an apron, 5s 9d; in all 15s 9d to John Gracie, a Scotchman, for M Balcombe.
1720 Feb 9	pd 3s 8d to a Scotchman for a handkerchief for M Balcombe.[2]

As was usual in country towns, Hurst had a weekly market which was held on Tuesdays on the Church Green and on the Lamb Platt, where London Terrace now stands. Prices were low because distribution costs were low. Later as the number of shops in the High Street began to increase, the market was moved to the New Inn, selling only corn; livestock was later sold beside Hassocks Station, on the Market Ground between the station and the Hassocks Hotel.

There are many references in this chapter to the map of Hurstpierpoint prepared by James Fisher, Land Surveyor and Accountant, in 1841. In the Book of Reference accompanying it, properties listed here are referred to by (F) in the text.

By the middle of the eighteenth century shops were beginning to be established in the High Street, though in the early days it was a case of working in the front room of the cottage or house with probable outworking also.

By the beginning of the nineteenth century, there were two different drivers who ran a carrier's wagon to and from London and Brighton via Stone Pound. George Knowles' wagon brought on different occasions:

Carpet, Cacao, an elephants thigh, pieces of furniture, box of bones, gig and harness, a letter, a wine cask, lace etc, a muff, a close stool, a butter stand, and a carpet sized 14 ft by 11ft'.[3]

These are all referred to in the Weekes Family Letters written to and from members of the family when Richard Weekes' eldest son Hampton was a medical student at St. Thomas's Hospital in 1801/1802.

THE TAILOR

There certainly was a tailor's shop in the High Street at the beginning of the nineteenth century since there are three references to 'Keating the tailor ' as follows:

1802 Ap 6   From Mary Weekes – to Hampton- Let us know wether we shall bespeak you a coat of Keating and what colour etc.

Ap 8   To M A Weekes –Tell Dick I have just been writing to Keating (for I promised I would) for an other good black Coat and I have taken ye liberty of writing for a couple of pair of nankin breeches for ye summer as none I had, and I have strictly enjoined him to make them, and coat large every were and told him that was ye only fault I had to find of him.

Ap 17   To Dick Weekes – Dear Dick I this morning also received my Coat and small clothes from Keating wh. fit me well.[4]

xxxiv. Tailor's scissors.

All through the nineteenth century there were at least three tailors in the High Street, one shop owned by Charles Stevens (father and son) being listed in The Post Office Directory and Kelly's Directory [5] from 1855 to 1918. Tailors made mostly gentlemen's clothes in heavy cloth, all by hand up to the late 1840s when the Singer Sewing Machine was invented. Women's clothing was made at home either by the housewife or by a worker who travelled around the countryside. The materials were supplied by a 'grocer and draper' or by the travelling pedlar. By the 1870s dressmakers had set up in business in the village. One lady, Miss J Knight, who lived at Eardenstowe, 116 High Street, was listed as being in business from 1874 to 1918. By 1903 there were three dressmakers in the village and one milliner. From 1874 Clement Peskett had a tailor's shop at 55 High Street, then it passed to his son, Norman Flavius Peskett. He was succeeded by F Oxenham who had been a traveller in suitings. When he died, his widow and son Billy carried on the business until 1970. Though tailors are listed right up to the latter half of the twentieth century most of their business was in ready-made goods with the exception of one, Leslie Twiner, who had premises at 38 High Street from 1951 until March 1967. He worked in the traditional fashion sitting on the bench cross-legged as all tailors did in the past.

THE BOOT AND SHOEMAKER

Up to the middle of the nineteenth century, boot and shoe making was a skilled handicraft trade. There was no left and right fitting and the product was hand cut and stitched. The tradesman was supplied with leather from leather dressers or curriers, the lining materials and sewing silks from drapers or warehousemen. A development was the availability of pre-cut soles and tops from leather cutters, working up to the mass production industry in the second half of the nineteenth century, when a series of inventions in sewing and riveting machines enabled the machine manufacture of boots and shoes. This naturally led to the disappearance of the hand-making of shoes and outworking. Up to World War One, the upper classes generally wore bespoke boots or shoes, the latter on the whole out of fashion until just prior to the War. There were also no nationally agreed sizes. As the nineteenth and twentieth centuries progressed, the number of multiple shops which stocked a variety of factory-made shoes increased.

This led to the local trade becoming one of selling ready-made shoes with hand working in repairs only.

All through the nineteenth century and early twentieth century there were at least five boot and shoemakers in the village.

In the Weekes letters, there are references to one 'William Randell' who lived at Black Lion Cottage (86F) High Street, and was followed in business by John Randell until at least 1845, according to the Post Office Directory:

1801 Oct 23	Hampton To Richard – As to buck boots I will tell you a something of Attree – has just had a 2d pair so you may suppose they are worth but little, each cost £2-6-6 what think you of that for a pair of brown paper boots for they are litterally nothing else, they are not like Randles wh. I would prefer a great deal. If you were to desire him to make me a pair stiff in the leg and pretty high up, long in ye foot seams on each side of the leg instead of behind, but if you desire I should get a pair here, I will.
1801 Nov 1	Hampton to Richard – Now for Buck Boots, crimping at the instep is quite out of fashion neither do they have any tongues at the instep quite plain, and stiff legd tell Randles to make them round toed and rather longer in the foot than my last Shoes were for they were too short, I would wish them not to be doubled about in packing.
1801 Nov 18	Richard to Hampton – Randles has declind making your buck boots says he don't know how therefore wish you to get a strong pair in London tell them they must be stout and the soal good.[6]

In Pigot and Co's Directory of Sussex[7] there were six shoemakers in the village at this time. William Walker was established as a shoemaker in 1838 in the High Street on the corner of Pit Road in a cottage called Pierce's, (68F) (later called Card's Cottage) according to James Fisher – Book of Reference.[8] The business had become J Walker and Son by 1887 and by

1937 the business had moved to 133 High Street. Another shoemaker, Walter Newman, had a business at 9 Hampton Cottages (now 159 High Street) from before 1894 until after 1937.

George Stevens started in business as a shoemaker at 19 High Street (25F) from 1830 until at least 1924 by which time the firm had become G Stevens and Son. John Bassett Hallett had a shoemaker's shop at Upper Trumpkins (96F) from1839 until 1867, he then moved to Church Terrace until 1894.

Opposite to W Randell and Son on the twitten to Ribbetts, John Gorringe had a shoemaker's shop at North Cottages (89F) (later called Ribbetts Cottages) from 1841 until in 1903 he was said to be in business at 1 Camden Place, opposite the Church.

In 1937 P Woodford and Son trading at 104 High Street advertised a repair service and well-known brands of shoes, his son Percy taking over and trading until the 1990s as the last footwear retailer in the village.

THE BUTCHER

The fact that all through the nineteenth century there were at least three to five butchers in the High Street suggests that the consumption of meat was quite high. It was a skilled trade since to make a living the butcher had to buy expertly (probably locally), kill and cut to serve all sections of the community. At least two progressed to become farmers, presumably to produce their own beasts.

From A History of Hurstperpoint by a Native a Minor,[9] there is a reference to a butcher's shop on the north side of the east end of the High Street made by the author (probably Grace Weekes) of A Slight Sketch of a Picture of Hurst:

> The last house in the place eastwards is a very old established butcher's shop kept by the family who now occupies it, I should think these 50 years with its palisades and 2 or 3 old fashioned cut elms before it [10]

This family was that of James Marshall who by 1841 was stated to live at Lower Trumpkins (107F), and also had a small shop occupied until 1845 by Jonathan Marshall in the High Street (49F), east of the crossroads with the now Cuckfield Road,.

Henry Beeching was another butcher in the village who lived at Nortons (76F) in 1841 which property belonged to a farmer, Edmund Davey. He was Rector's Churchwarden for 40 years and died in March 1888. In 1855 Henry is listed in Kelly's Directory as being in business with Samuel Beeching and by 1867 Henry and Sam are listed as farmers at Washbrooks Farm and Randolphs Farm. By 1887 Henry is no longer listed as a butcher but had moved to Black Lion House in the centre of the village; Sam was given no address. He was still listed as a farmer in 1894, now living at Western Villas. He died in 1907.

A similar progression is listed for Richard Broad who is first mentioned in Kelly in 1855. By 1874 Richard is listed as butcher and farmer thereafter Harry Broad is listed as a butcher in the High Street in 1894 and 1903. Finally by 1913 he had retired to Lissington, Hassocks Road. Horace Broad, possibly a brother, was a dairy farmer at West Town in 1894 and 1903.

Frank Botting started a butcher's shop in 1900 at Townfield Terrace (now 130 High Street) which he called Clock Stores. He took over Harry Broad's shop (now 113 High Street) in 1908, and was succeeded in 1935 by Walter Thair, who named the property Aberdeen House. When Walter Thair retired from the butchery business, he was succeeded by Frank Boone, then A K Smith and in the late 1990s by Barry Shell.

Allen Botting had a butcher's shop and slaughter house in Southdown Terrace (now 50 High Street) from 1882. This was on the site of Walter Fitch's general store that had been destroyed in the great fire of January 1882 and had since been re-designed and rebuilt. He was succeeded by Alfred James Baker, who trained his two sons William Alfred and Cecil Victor in the business, trading as Baker and Son from 1916 and Baker Brothers from 1928. After the retirement of Alfred and Cecil the business was carried on as Baker Bros. by A J Richardson until he retired in the 1960s.

Another butcher's shop was located in Cuckfield Road near the crossroads and in 1909 it belonged to Percy Challen, who also farmed at Langton Farm, until 1914. Charles Jennings ran the shop in the 1920s and was succeeded by H J Box. E C Cuss carried on the business for a considerable time. He was in turn followed by John Cuss and later Clive Miller.

THE GROCER

Up to about the middle of the nineteenth century the grocer was a skilled craftsman, having learnt his trade as an apprentice for some years. He served the well-to-do customer with sugar, spices, tea, coffee and cocoa which had all been supplied to him in large amounts by a specialist wholesaler. He then packed as required in smaller quantities. Aubrey Rees quoted in The Grocery Trade:

> The grocer had been up to 1846 at any rate . . . minister of luxuries to the rich [11]

xxxiii. Victorian shop scales.   xxxiv. Tea-packing box and mallet.

He would supply the less well-off labourer with bulk flour, salt, oatmeal etc. which formed the basis of his monotonous diet. The poorer people supplemented this at the open market, where local farmers offered eggs, bacon, cheese and butter at very much lower prices than the grocer. The large amount of hand mixing, grinding, and packing necessitated several assistants and apprentices and it was understood that they lived in on the premises.

Not only were large windows for display of goods unknown, since plate glass was not available until later in the century, but the display of goods was definitely frowned upon until after the middle of the nineteenth century. Also the practice of haggling or higgling was very common especially in the drapery and haberdashery trade and so goods were not openly price marked.

No less a person than Lord Macaulay refers to the practice in the Edinburgh Review April 1830:

> A butcher of the higher class disdains to ticket his meat. A mercer
> of the higher class would be ashamed to hang up papers in his
> window inviting the passer by to look. We expect some reserve,
> some pride in our hatter and our bootmaker.[12]

As the century progressed, the railways, steamships and refrigeration developed, causing a great increase in the movement of foodstuffs and general lowering of prices. All this resulted in large-scale manufacture of new food products and also of many established items which previously had been produced by the skilled grocer.

New types of food were coming on to the market, one – margarine – was a British product, patented in 1867. There was a very big increase in the display of pre-packed goods, many of which were governed by Resale Price Maintenance.[13] In the inter war years and towards the end of the twentieth century the increase in the number of large scale retailers faced the small specialist grocer with intense competition leading to the closure of many, as in Hurst, where now only a branch of a multiple shop retailer exists.

In 1841 Fisher lists six grocers in the High Street and nearby: Henry Parker at Prospect Cottages (37F), Jesse Gosling, Commerce House (51F), Charles Ellis, Holdens (60F), H W Rowland, Uttica House (The Old Royal Oak) (83F), Thos Wells, Blackford House (85F) and W Hollamby, Lower Trumpkins (102F).

The premises at Holdens (where the Nationwide Building Society now stands) belonging to Charles Ellis, were taken over by Darius and Thomas Davey who developed the grocery business into wine and spirits and new food products, and also many items which previously had been sold by individual retailers such as drapers, upholsterers and general merchants.

Between 1874 and the early 1880s, Darius having died in 1881, Thomas let the premises to Walter Fitch who lived in the west end of the three storey, three block shop with his wife, child and 10 servants and assistants. On Friday, January 27 1882, the entire premises were totally destroyed by fire, though fortunately without loss of life. Between 20 and 30 members of the Brighton Volunteer Fire Brigade and 15 from the Hove Brigade assisted in fighting the fire which was not totally extinguished until Monday January 30. Mr Masters of The Stores kindly placed his premises and stock at his neighbour's disposal though one report stated that Mr Fitch would carry on business temporarily in the Music Room in Manor Road (which became The Somers Clark Institute). He died in 1891 aged 45, and Mrs Fitch lived on at Nortonbury, 100 High Street.

George Masters first appears in The Post Office Directory in 1880 as a grocer and draper and by 1887 he had expanded into upholstery, undertaking, wine and spirits with a Head Office in Lindfield. By 1899 the firm had become the well known Masters and Tulley occupying 93 to 99 High Street (built where Uttica House (83F) once stood) and with a workshop on the south side of the street. By 1956 the business had been taken over by Walkers Stores of Brighton and now has become chiefly a multiple grocer with newspapers (when the last newsagent in the village closed in 1999) owned by Alldays.

Fletcher Peskett is first mentioned in 1887 and he followed George Peskett in business as a grocer, corn and seed merchant at 17 High Street. He was joined by his son Thomas in 1922, until the late 1960s.

The multiple firm, the International Tea Company, had a branch at 87 High Street from 1911 until some time in the 1950s, this being where Threshers Wine Merchants is now in business.

Thomas Wickham is listed as a grocer and draper from 1874 at Church Terrace; here in 1884 his nephew George Prince was apprenticed. Thomas Wickham died in July 1901 and George managed the business for his widow until 1903 when he took it over in his own name as Wickham's Stores (now 36 High Street). This developed with a ladies' department opening next door and a men's department at No. 61 on the other side of the High Street, after Bannister's watch and clock business closed in 1920. In the 1930s Mr Prince opened a branch of his men's department in Keymer Road, Hassocks, with Charles Vigar as manager. This shop still exists today as Princes (Hurst) Ltd, Outfitters, and is owned by the daughter of the late Walter Thair. After Mr Prince's death in 1941, W Thair bought the business and Dick Stenning, who was at one time Chairman of the Parish Council and of the St. Lawrence School Governors, managed the outfitters' side of the business. The grocery continued with L T Usher in charge, until in 1967 The Brighton Cooperative Society took over and added a butchery department. The shop closed in 1981 and today the premises are occupied by a clock shop and an antiques shop.

At the other end of the village, the large building that had been the National School, was sold to Henry Sendall, grocer. He had been in business elsewhere in the village from 1867 and he remained there until between 1874 and 1878. John Curtis followed from 1883 until 1913 when E Robins and Son (wine and spirit merchants) took over until some time after 1924. They were followed by a long established firm of grocers from Brighton, Gravely and Son, who were in business from the early 1930s (run by W J Hobbs and P C Norman), until the mid 1960s since when it became The Players' Theatre.

George Jupp had a large shop on the corner of South Avenue and the High Street from 1887 until just before the beginning of World War One named Southdown General Stores. A picture postcard of Jupp's stores is overwritten:

> Good English Cheddar Cheese at 6½d. /Lb. Good Cheese at the right price—NO King like Edward – NO Cheddar Cheese like Jupps at the price.[14]

The premises are now car showrooms.

Plate 43. East end of the High Street, with George Anscombe sitting outside Jupps.

THE DAIRY

Up to the beginning of the nineteenth century the supply of milk was solely in the hands of the local farmers, who supplied their customers direct. Demand increased tenfold from the 1900s because milk was promoted as a very health-giving product. Consumers were not aware that milk was spreading tuberculosis – 40% of herds being infected in the 30s – because there was no pasteurisation. It was estimated that 40,000 people died yearly from bovine tuberculosis in the years just before the Second World War, then tuberculin testing of cattle began and a health drive was started. This led to better methods of handling, and glass bottling with sealed caps. By 1947, 71% of milk sold was pasteurised. Milk was increasingly sold on retail rounds and the small-scale dairyman expanded his range of goods to carry groceries, bread and yoghurts. Now the largest sale of milk is from multiple shop retailers and supermarkets, pre-packed in cardboard or plastic. There are still at least two firms who have rounds in the village: Unigate, and J B Johnson of Burgess Hill.

Plate 44. William Parsons on his dairy round from Latchetts Farm.

In 1845, J Spratley was listed as a milkman. He grazed his cows in a meadow, Peasecroft, north of the White Horse Inn. D Spratley was listed in 1867 as a dairyman. There are then no listings until 1911 when Jas Clarke is mentioned, as he is in 1913. J R Heafield had a dairy in 6 Cards Place from 1918 until at least 1938 and A J Bignall and Son advertised as Oakmere Dairy at 153 High Street from 1930 until the late nineties. William Ira Jenkin had two farms in 1924, Tott Farm and New House, and by 1937 he had The Creamery, 121 High Street and Randolphs Farm with Horace Jenkin. The Creamery closed in the 1950s/60s.

THE BAKER

In the years up to the early twentieth century most bakers were independent, preparing, baking and selling on their own premises. Home bread making was still common, though often the housewife would take items to the bakehouse for cooking. Mechanical aids to the manufacture of bread came into use in the early twentieth century followed by machine wrapping in the twenties and slicing in the thirties. The independent master baker was greatly aided by the invention of small-scale machinery and he was able to keep up production of specialist breads. He was helped by an increase in the production of flour confectionery of all sorts. Extensive delivery rounds by cart enabled the baker to continue, but now even these have ceased locally, leaving the multiple shop retailer or supermarket to take over most of the bakery trade proper.

Since 1839, there had usually been at least three bakers in the High Street. John Tilley was in business at Ribbetts (88F) until 1874, Thomas Walker at High Street (50F) until 1867, J N Morley had The Hygienic Steam Bakery at Trumpkins from 1887 until sometime after 1913 and F Heathorn and his family were in business at 35 High Street from 1894 until 1938. C Williams had a bakery in Western Road and ran the shop at 115 High Street from before World War Two until the late 1980s.

Plate 45.
Bread ovens in the premises now occupied by Rideaway Cycles in the High Street.

THE IRONMONGER/HARDWARE MERCHANT

The housewife up to the early nineteenth century probably had only a few all-purpose cooking pots and a minimum of knives, forks and spoons in her kitchen which had been made by the local blacksmith as required. Then as the century progressed, factories began to make a widening range of ferrous and non-ferrous metal goods, and ironmongers opened shops to sell them. They also began to sell labour saving devices, oils and pigments to prepare paints, and hand tools. In the first half of the twentieth century, ready-packaged paints became available together with wallpapers, hobby tools and china and glass, to give the shops, now called hardware merchants, the extensive range of goods that is now stocked. In 1890 Arthur Reuben Russell owned the ironmonger's shop in the High Street and the forge in Pit Road. The shop was completely rebuilt, with the adjacent house, in 1895 by the local builder, Alfred Godley. Will Gorringe was in business as an ironmonger from 1861 until after 1894 but only in 1894 is he listed as a smith. By 1918 R Gatland had a shop at 59 High Street on the corner with Cuckfield Road as a hardware dealer and remained there until some time after 1938. At 123 High Street, F A Curd sold china and kitchen goods, decorating materials and useful gifts and also advertised as a plumber, from 1923 until the 1950s. In 1937, at 105 High Street, George Allen took over A R Russell's business to be followed by S Barron in 1958. He was succeeded by Dot Baker and her son Peter. After they closed down, David Robinson re-opened the shop in September 1991, sadly closing in April 2000.

THE WATCH AND CLOCKMAKER

The craft of the watchmaker and clockmaker is of great antiquity and very highly specialised. Obviously his skill was only in demand by the fairly well-to-do section of the community, thus there have only been one or two watch and clockmakers in the village at a time in the last two centuries. A beautiful longcase clock (dated 1705 to 1715) with only one hand is owned by former residents of the village (see Colour Plate 16). It is inscribed:

Thos. Jacket. Hurstperpt

Could this be the Thomas Jacket referred to by Thomas Marchant?

> 1719 Sept. 16   Thos Jacket mended my partridge net this
> morning [15]

Both John Nye and William Atwood were in business in 1839 and 1841, the latter opposite the Church in Church Cottages (40F). T Humphries was in business from 1887 until shortly after 1891 and Charles Bannister had his shop at what became Prince's Men's Department (61 High Street) from 1887 until 1920.

P W Gladman had his shop next to Grapevine Cottage, 143 High Street, from 1911 to World War Two, after starting in a small premises further east along the High Street. He was followed by G Funnell and Son until 1958, and then succeeded by Gordon Boakes who advertised as The Mid Sussex Jeweller, selling also clocks and watches, from 54 High Street. After him came John and Dorothy Callagan, who have recently retired.

THE CONFECTIONERY TRADE

The confectionery and chocolate trade was continuously expanding in the second half of the nineteenth century and the first half of the twentieth century. Up to the beginning of the fourth quarter of the nineteenth century sugar confectionery was mainly sold because eating chocolate was comparatively rare, but by the beginning of the next century one third of the trade was in this form. There was a fairly rapid increase in branded and pre-packed chocolate goods and because of the ease of handling and high gross margins, small scale retailers were favoured and are to this day. The numbers of general retailers selling newspapers, fancy goods and stationery as well as confectionery, have much increased over the small scale confectioner.

From 1871 tobacconists had to be licensed and until the middle of the twentieth century theirs was an expanding trade. In rural districts such as Hurst, tobacco has been sold by non-specialists such as newsagents, grocers or confectioners.

There were three confectioners in Hurst in 1899: William Cockbill at 2 Southdown Terrace, G Marchant and G Withyman, who combined selling tobacco with retailing pork. In 1903 E Chatfield had taken over as tobacconist at Southdown Terrace to be followed by A W Ashby until 1940. Miss Irene Ashby carried on her father's business until the 1970s, when she closed her shop, selling all her sweets at half price. This is now 56 High Street. F Holden had a shop at 119 High Street from 1911 selling tobacco, until sometime before 1924 when the firm became Holden and Rapley thereafter adding newspapers to their stock. (Miss Christobel Rapley was part of the firm until shortly after 1938). This continued to be a newsagent's shop under the name of Foulger, then Cresswell followed by Woods until 1999 when it closed.

FRUIT AND VEGETABLES

The handling of fruit and vegetables had remained firmly in the hands of the small scale retailer from the nineteenth century up to the development of the large supermarket in the latter quarter of the twentieth century. At first, produce was grown locally in neighbourhood market gardens, then with the development of the railway and the motor lorry, speedy movement of goods was possible from much further afield. Now goods are moved rapidly across the world by sea or air.

The first greengrocer is listed in 1874 as John Dorkings at 165 High Street (Hampton Cottages). Mrs Dorkings ran the business until sometime between 1903 and 1911 when H Bransden took over. He is listed as a nurseryman in South Avenue, where he grew his produce, though he had a shop at 165 High Street in 1938. Mrs J Hayes had a greengrocery shop at 7 Church Terrace, High Street from some time before 1899 until 1924 – she served customers from her front door with goods for sale being displayed in the front courtyard of her house. Mrs I P Voyce had a fruiterer's and florist's business next to Curd's at Trumpkins from the 1930s until the 1950s. Her son Billy used a donkey and cart for local deliveries and sales. Hurst has been very fortunate in having two greengrocers in the High Street up to the present day.

THE CHEMIST AND DRUGGIST

Up to the foundation of the Pharmaceutical Society of Great Britain in 1841, there was only a professional body licensing apothecaries to dispense drugs. In that year chemists and druggists were united into one body, though they were not yet examined. In 1845 there was a dispensing chemist and patent medicine vendor, Thomas Wyborn, listed in the village in Pigot and Co's

Directory.[16] He was followed by William Mitten who must have made the name of Hurstpierpoint well known in the botanical world. His father, William Mitten was the butler at Danny House and on his retirement, Townfield House was built for him in the early 1840s by the Danny Estate where he lived for about 40 years. His son William was born on 30 November 1819 and was educated at Lewes and served his apprenticeship in pharmacy there. After posts in Brighton and South London, he opened a shop in the High Street where the old Barclays Bank building now stands. He was registered as a Chemist and Druggist on 31 December 1868, without examination because he had been in business before 1 August 1868. He was very interested in botany, early in his life becoming acquainted with William Borrer, the botanist, of Henfield. He made mosses his particular field of study and through his work on the Hepaticae of New Zealand and of South America he was elected an Associate of the Linnean Society in 1847 (there being only 25 members).

He was in business in Hurst for 56 years, working from 7 am until 10pm, and lived at Treeps. William had many strings to his bow, since he also sold newspapers, books, stationery, was an agent for two insurance companies and for the well known dyers 'Pullars of Perth'. When he died aged 86 years in 1906, he left his wife aged 93 and four daughters. In his obituary[17] he was said to have been a man of serene temper, with a strong vein of humour. Many unobtrusive acts of kindness were done by him, about which few knew. He was the area authority on local history and archaeology. Flora Mitten, his third daughter, studied for the Chemist and Druggist Examination at the South London School of Pharmacy (where she took the medal for Botany and the first certificate in Senior Chemistry, continuing as a visiting examiner), passed the Major Examination and was registered as 'Pharmaceutical Chemist' on 19 December 1883 Certificate No. 1966. She continued to practise after her father died, and remained on the Register until 1934. After her father died, the business was registered in the name of A Spencer Whitby, who moved to Treeps in the early 1920s. When the election of the first Parish Council took place in December 1894, Flora topped the poll on a show of hands, when thirteen members were elected. Colonel Campion, as Lord of the Manor, asked that a written poll be taken. In the following parish poll, Flora came third of the thirteen.

Flora was only one of 8 female Pharmaceutical Chemists on the Pharmaceutical Society's register in 1892 and she reported in the 'Chemist and Druggist Magazine on July 3 1892:

> When I was young and inexperienced I used to meet with rebuffs and discouragement but it never occurred to me to take them seriously to heart or to allow them to daunt me. Our community have been so accustomed to see me here for so many years that they now take my presence as a matter of course and do not object at all. People come to me as freely as they do to my father, and are apparently as satisfied; women come as well, and in many cases have remarked that it was more comfortable to come to me. [18]

xxxv. William Mitten.   xxxvi. Flora Mitten.

By 1911, the Misses Mitten had moved to Culver Croft, where they remained until the early 1930s. Flora died in June 1941 aged 90.

After Mrs Fitch died, Nortonbury (100 High Street) became a pharmacy owned by Walter O' Neale. This was then taken over in 1940 by David Morris assisted by his daughter, Brenda, until 1960. D Grindrod was the last pharmacist occupier of 100 High Street until 1972 when he retired. There was also a pharmacy next door at 1 Cards Place registered as H S Martin (though this gentleman actually had a pharmacy at East Grinstead from 1903 until he died in 1921). This was run by P W Blacklock from 1907, J R Thornton from 1910, J J Hughes from 1912 until 1914 when George E

Heaton became owner until 1920 when he died. A Spencer Whitby moved to these premises and ran the business until the well- known firm of Savory and Moore took over in the 1930s. The shop moved to 86 High Street in the 1990s and was taken over by Lloyds, who run the business today. There was yet another pharmacy in the High Street at No. 59, owned by E A Cox from 1960 until 1976.

THE SADDLER

Since all local transport was horse drawn and horses were ridden by the local gentry until the coming of the motorcar, there must always have been a considerable amount of work for a saddler and harness maker. It is surprising then that in 1841 there were only four such in the High Street: Thomas White, Dunstalls (23F), Richard Talmey, Anglesea Cottage (26F), Henry French, Prospect Cottages (36F) and Jane Brown, Trumpkins (99F). The latter continued in business until sometime after 1845. Henry Brown carried on in the middle 1850s until George Brown took over in the early 1870s until 1912.

Henry French was succeeded by John E Smith in the mid 1880s. He moved to the recently rebuilt premises, 1 Southdown Terrace (formerly Walter Fitch's general stores) now 58 High Street – the Nationwide Building Society. He was in business here until at least 1938.

THE HAIRDRESSER

In the early 1700s wigs were worn by the gentry. This involved shaving the head regularly. There are several references in the Marchant Diary to a local man, John Parsons, who did this for Thomas over the years:

> 1716 Oct 13   Pd J Parsons for shaving head & face –
> received a black wig of him for which I am to
> give him 100 good house faggots.[19]

Thomas's son Willy began to wear a wig when he was 16:

> 1717 Jan 1   Pd J Parsons 2s 6d for new mounting an old
> wig for Willy and for cutting off his hair.[20]

The first mention of a hairdresser in the High Street was in 1874 [21] when it recorded that Mrs M A Bailey was in business and also sold stationery. Her son William Witham Bailey was in charge at Trumpkins from 1881 until 1909, when his son of the same name transferred the business to 120 High Street. This is now Daniel's Restaurant. Here his sister ran a small stationery and toy shop, through which customers had to pass to reach the hairdressing salon. After W W Bailey committed suicide in March 1930, his former customers were compelled to go to S H Jago, at 8 Church Terrace. He had been in competition since 1909 and also did ladies' hairdressing by appointment in a curtained-off area near the window looking out onto the Brighton road. His assistant was Albert Mabbitt, very well known in the village. George Baker was a ladies' and gentlemen's hairdresser at 122 High Street from 1935 to 1963 latterly concentrating on the former.

THE POST OFFICE

By 1839, a Post Office was established at Amwell Place, (116F) William Randell combining the job of postmaster with that of carrier and fly proprietor. He ran regular services to Brighton on four days a week and to Lewes once a week by wagon. It is recorded in Pigot's Directory:

> Letters from London and all parts arrive (by foot post from Brighton) every morning at a quarter past ten, and are despatched every afternoon at four.[22]

When he died in 1844, Sarah Randell took over as postmistress (listed in The Post Office Directory from 1845 to 1867) when:

> Letters arrive from London at ½ past 2 pm; delivered 7 summer and ½ past 7 winter; despatched ½ past 11 pm [23]

This occupation would not have been a sinecure with so much night work. It is recorded that a post office savings bank was started in 1861 and there is a congratulatory telegram dated 16. 12. 1961 celebrating 100 years of its existence.

The scope of business widened considerably and by 1867 this included post office orders, savings bank, and government annuities and insurance. For a short while there was a post office between W Mitten's chemist shop and Black Lion House on the north side of the High Street. Then it was moved to its present location at Number 80. When Sarah died in 1873, first Edward Channing, then Francis Burnett ran the Post Office. By 1874 a telegraph office was in operation to and from which messages were sent by Morse code, being open from 8 am until 9 pm and on Sunday from 7. 30 until 10 am. By 1894, Mrs Clara Emma Carter was the postmistress who had a very busy day, since as listed in Kelly:

> Letters arrive from London &c via Hassocks R S O and deliveries commence at 7 & 11. 15am & 6. 15pm: Sundays at 7. 30 am; Dispatched at 8. 50 &10. 30 am & 1, 2. 30, 7. 20 & 9 pm. Sundays at 9pm.[24]

J Booker took over from Mrs Carter in November 1924, being followed in 1947 by A N Hodson, in 1949 by F E Robinson, by F R Allen in 1966 and in 1969 by R Turner.

There was a sub post office in Hurst Wickham and shop run by Mr and Miss Poundsbery for many years up to the end of the twentieth century.

THE TELEPHONE

The National Telephone Company Limited had a public call box on the first floor of Nortonbury House in 1904, though William Mitten already had a telephone (No 6), one of only 6 lines in the village, in 1896. These were all on a switchboard which had an operator to connect the caller to the number required, by inserting the plug into the jack and clearing the lines when both telephones were back on their rests. By 1906 there were 65 numbers on the Hurst exchange, some of which were in Hassocks and Albourne and several were party lines. All subscribers' lines were transferred to a new exchange in 1937 at 41 Cuckfield Road, this building now belonging to Graham Foster, antique dealer and restorer. The present digital exchange adjacent to Weald Close, was converted from the previous cross bar exchange and was opened by the Chairman of the Parish Council, on 26 July 1989 at 6 am.

THE STATIONER AND BOOKSELLER

Pigot and Co's Directory [25] records that in 1839 W Powell was in business as a bookseller and stationer in 1841(F65) which he had until 1845. By 1855 William Mitten had opened his pharmacy and like many chemists and druggists, also had close connections with the book trade, both retailing and publishing books, postcards and stationery. One of his daughters, Bessie J Mitten, wrote a guide to Hurstpierpoint which was published by W and F Mitten at the beginning of the twentieth century. [26]

A H Homewood had opened a stationer's shop at 3 Southdown Terrace by 1894 and also ran a branch of Mudie's Library. [27] By 1903 he had been followed by Miss Fanny Philpott, until at least 1918. She also continued to run Mudie's Library, to which the annual subscription was 10/6d. Miss Philpott was followed by Mrs S Berdsey until the late 1930s selling also stationery and fancy goods. From 1899 until at least 1924 first Miss M M Carter then Miss P Carter were listed as stationers in Kelly [28] in the High Street, possibly connected with the post office where Mrs E M Carter was postmistress.

SAYERS COMMON

Sayers Common, now named as part of Hurstpierpoint Parish, was first mentioned as a hamlet in the Post Office Directory of 1861 [29] and by 1881 was a separate ecclesiastical parish. The Duke of York Inn was established by then and there had been a shop kept by William Hole since 1845. There was also a butcher named Thomas Walder. By 1874 Mrs Fanny Hole had taken over the shop which she ran until 1894. From 1899 until 1924 John Hole was the owner of the shop combining this with being the local pig-killer. A sub post office had been opened by 1911 on these premises for a population of 445, letters arriving from Hassocks at 7. 50 am and 12. 20 pm and being dispatched at 11. 15 am and 6. 35 pm. Hurst was the nearest money order and telegraph office. By 1937 the shop and sub post office was run by Henry P Clayden and a cycle dealer's shop was operating, run by Albert Garrett, he no doubt doing good business since the road to Brighton passed his door. In the early 1940s Albert and his wife were still in business, she now having a separate haberdashery next door. In the early 1940s the sub post office was run by Mr and Mrs Moore, selling also stationery, soft drinks, sweets and newspapers. This was closed by the early 1950s. In the early 1920s there was also a tobacconist, Miss J Peacock, and a grocer S J Fairlie, but neither of these appears to have been in business for a long period.

Before the Second World War there was a proliferation of shops in Hurstpierpoint up to a maximum of sixty, including two banks, and it was possible to buy all one needed at any time, in spite of the fact that transport was freely available and that cars were within the reach of many. In the last years of the twentieth century, numbers decreased rapidly, with an increase in premises such as antique shops and offices and now most people shop for the majority of their needs outside the village.

NOTES AND REFERENCES

Much background information has been obtained from:

Jefferys J E (1954): *Retail trading in Britain, 1850–1950.*
Alexander D (1970): *Retailing in England during the Industrial Revolution.*

The considerable help of the Museum of the Royal Pharmaceutical Society is acknowledged with thanks.

1. Turner E (ed) (1873): The Marchant Diary, *SAC* **25**, 167, 170, 190.
2. *Ibid.*, 184, 186.
3. Ford J M T (1987): *The Weekes Family Letters*, 102, 103, 108, 134, 155, 212, 228, 240.
4. *Ibid.*, 152, 153, 158.
5. *Post Office Directories, Sussex 1855–1880; Kelly's Directories 1887–1918.*

6. Ford, *Weekes*, 55, 61, 77.
7. *Pigot's Directory 1839*.
8. WSRO/ADD MS 17685 AD908: Book of Reference to accompany Plan of the village of Hurstpierpoint 1841 by Fisher J.
9. 'A Native, A Minor' (1837): *A History of Hurstperpoint*, 66; WSRO/ Par 400/9/3/1.
10. 'A Native of this Village' (probably Grace Weekes)(1826): *A Slight Sketch of a Picture of Hurst*, 66.
11. Rees J A (1910): *The Grocery Trade* Vol 11, 198.
12. Lord Macaulay: Mr Montgomery's Poems, *The Edinburgh Review* April 1830.
13. Resale Price Maintenance: for many years individual manufacturers had been permitted to enforce RPM for their own products; the Resale Prices Act 1964 prohibited all methods of enforcing minimum prices unless goods had been registered. 'Recommended retail prices' have now replaced RPM.
14. David Robinson's collection.
15. Turner, Marchant, *SAC* **25**, 185.
16. *Pigot 1839*.
17. *The Chemist and Druggist* 28 July 1906.
18. *Ibid.*, 3 July 1982.
19. Turner, Marchant, *SAC* **25**, 176.
20. *Ibid.*, 178.
21. *P. O. Directory 1874*.
22. *Pigot 1839*.
23. *P. O. Directories 1845–67*.
24. *Kelly's 1894*.
25. *Pigot 1839*.
26. Mitten B J: *Guide to Hurstpierpoint and neighbourhood*.
27. Charles Mudie in 1842 began to lend mostly new books, of every genre except law, to middle and upper classes, from his shop in Bloomsbury. The subscription was 1 guinea a year for one volume or 2 guineas for four. By 1858 he had 100,000 volumes in stock and was shipping to all corners of the Empire. Eventually local shops held books, which could be taken out for a subscription. The setting up of the public library system brought about the end of Mudie's Library.
28. *Kelly's 1899–1924*.
29. *P. O. Directory 1861*.

13. EDUCATION IN THE 18th AND 19th CENTURIES

Cuckfield had its 'free Gramer Scole' endowed in the early sixteenth century, by Edward Flower's will of 1521 and by the bequest of William Spicer, Rector of Balcombe, in 1529,[1] but we have no records of any schools in Hurst for almost another two hundred years. This does not mean that no teaching was available before then, but it probably indicates that it was restricted to a privileged few, the sons (mainly) of the gentry, who either had private tutors or went to endowed schools of the calibre of Winchester or Eton, Tonbridge or Shrewsbury. The children of the 'middling sort' might hope for some tuition from the priest, curate, parish clerk or the private enterprise of a 'petty' school. Later, at about ten years of age, they might be sent to board in the homes of others, and then be lucky enough to be taught alongside the young of the family at a nearby school, one of the many being founded around the country in the late sixteenth and early seventeenth centuries. The main emphasis would be on 'good manners' and obedience, and it was felt that this would be best achieved away from home.[2] Another approach would be to arrange apprenticeships in specific skills such as husbandry. As with many people nowadays, the whole emphasis of the middling sort was on advancement and improvement. Whatever the method, none of these possibilities would have been available to the lower classes of society, except perhaps by chance at the hands of the curate or parish clerk or by means of pauper 'putting-out' or apprenticeships (and these were often merely a device for reducing the burden on the Poor Rate payers). Indeed, the very idea of educating 'the masses' was viewed with some disquiet by a writer in the Gentleman's Magazine as late as 1797, a disquiet thinly disguised by the phrase 'ignorance is a balm'. A few years earlier Hannah More was faced with outright opposition when she opened a school for poor children, local farmers expressing the view that the poor should be ignorant, as they were intended to be servants and slaves.

CHARITY SCHOOLS

From 1604 a clergyman with a university degree could receive a bishop's licence to teach, but this did not mean that unlicensed men were barred from teaching, and many schools were staffed by unqualified persons for many years to come. After the upheavals of the Civil War the church and the gentry were concerned that nonconformity would continue to disrupt society. A series of

Acts of Parliament, named the Clarendon Code after Charles II's chancellor, sought to control this perceived threat. Among other restrictions, dissidents were debarred from teaching, although a number of nonconformist schools did carry on quietly. The 1689 Toleration Act reversed this trend and unlicensed teaching, although strictly illegal, went unchallenged for the most part. Many villages still had no schools, and in 1698 the Society for the Propagation of Christian Knowledge (SPCK) encouraged countrywide charity schools, with local gentry, farmers and tradesmen contributing the necessary funds. By 1704 the SPCK had published guidelines for the appointment of a master, covering his church observances, his temperament, his handwriting and arithmetical ability, and his discipline; lastly he had to be approved by the incumbent and licensed by the bishop. To many the eighteenth century was not only the age of reason; it was also the age of benevolence, and much of this attitude had its expression in the provision of charity schools, with Anglican clergy playing a leading part. There were fewer than 500 such schools at the end of the seventeenth century, thousands in the next 100 years, but still some country towns without any school of any kind, a situation which was entirely acceptable to many parents, as schooling not only involved positive expenditure, it meant loss of children's earnings.[3] Other methods of funding were endowment or sponsorship by one person, but local subscription and management by the 'middling class' was used in Hurst.

John Hart, a Staffordshire man, came to Hurst in 1714, immediately after taking his degree at Clare College, Cambridge.[4] In May he subscribed to the oaths and declarations required since the time of Henry VIII before he was allowed to receive an episcopal licence to become our first recorded schoolmaster.[5] By 1714 this subscription included a long list: acknowledging the sovereign as supreme governor of the Church of England, the Book of Common Prayer and the Thirty Nine Articles of Religion, conformity to the liturgy, oaths of allegiance, supremacy and abjuration (denying the Jacobite claim to the throne), and rejecting transubstantiation. Thomas Marchant records the further proceedings in his diary:

> 1714. October 3rd   (Sunday) . . . Mr Hart received the
> Sacrament to qualify himself for a
> certificate from the Sessions . . .
> October 8th.   Went to the Sessions at Lewes. . .
> Mr Hart was sworn, and had a Certificate.
> Mr Norden, Mr Whitpaine, John Lindfield,

> Mr Hart and I came home together, and
> drank four pints of wine at John Smith's . . .

Presumably, his appointment was also approved by the Rector, John Dodson, but he is not mentioned by Marchant. From the original diary, as yet unpublished, it is clear that a building existed in that year, for on Saturday 18 December 1714 'Grey carried. . . . a load of flints to make a way to the school . . . .' Apparently a new building was erected, or major alterations were carried out, during August 1717, for there are almost daily entries recording the activities of various workmen.[6] Where the school was situated and when it actually opened are unclear, but it was maintained by subscriptions from local people. Five years later Hart was 'head-hunted', as recorded in the Marchant diary:

1719. March 2nd.	I was at Stephen Bine's with Mr Dodson, Mr Scutt, Mr Whitpaine, and Mr Hart. Mr Hart, who had been sent for to teach chool at Deptford, concluded to stay with us to teach our school, and Mr Whitpaine promised to contribute £7 per annum, Mr Scutt £7, and myself £3, and to be answerable for £1 for my mother if she should object to continue it.

In the same year Marchant 'pd Abram Muzzel 7s 6d for the schooling of Will. Balcombe'.[7] Such voluntary contributions were the only funds these schools received. Marchant did not leave all his own family's teaching to Hart and Muzzell, for we find:

1718. May 14th.	Mr Lun, the dancing master [who also taught at Lewes], began teach at Kester's.
1722. Janry. 16th.	Mr Pointin, of Henfield, began teaching my son William [age 21] arithmetic. He is to come three times a week, and to have 2s 6d for teaching.
April 14th.	Agreed with Mr Pointin to teach Bett [daughter] at an addition of 2s 6d per week; also M. Balcombe on the same terms. Pd 6d for a book for them.[8]

There may be some indication that Pointin was particularly successful, for the Stapley (Hickstead) account book has an entry for 8 October 1730:

> Anthony Stapley went to Board and Schole to Bridghelmstone to board att Thomas Browne for four shillings and six pence a week and he doth go to schole to John Grovers [Quaker] to read and write and cast accounts,

but what would appear to be a final bill was paid on 8 April 1731, and on 10 May Anthony 'went to Tho Pointer *(sic)* by the week to write & read & cast account'. Perhaps Pointin's skill derived from his other occupations as excise man and mapmaker.[9] In some parishes actual payment was by results: 2s 6d for each child who could name the letters of the alphabet, 5s for reading and knowing the catechism, 15s for writing and casting accounts; children did not progress to writing and arithmetic until they were able to read.[10] There is no evidence that this sort of encouragement occurred in Hurst.

Salaries for rural teachers, about £20 a year, often proved to be unattractive by comparison with those offered in towns,[11] but Hart continued to be paid for his work at the charity school for the next twelve years, so he was satisfied presumably. As we have seen already, the Marchant diary ceased in 1728, but the Danny records show subscriptions by Henry Campion of £6 per annum in 1727 and 1728, and also extra payments of £14 pa for boarding one pupil, Jack Shore.[12] Hart had become master of Steyning grammar school by 1733, but probably left Hurst in 1731, as from that time payments were made to Abraham Muzzell at least until 1751, when the school was endowed, an indenture showing Henry Campion paying £5 annual rent for a school in 'a messuage or tenement, erected on a piece of ground in the east corner of a field called Hazle Croft',[13] to teach 20 children to read. (Presumably there were other subscribers as well). Muzzell was nominated as master by Campion, any successors to be chosen by the rector, churchwardens and overseers. In 1769 Richard Pilbeam was a schoolmaster here, living at Hardings (now Card's Place), for we read that he was paid £3 15s for schooling.[14] The 1819 Report of the Commissioners on the Education of the Poor[15] showed that the school was still flourishing; together with other establishments, education was being provided for upwards of 100 children. The background to this continued success is the lack of evidence of neglect or cruelty, but one has to remember that inspections were infrequent, and contemporary standards differed from modern expectations.

There was political controversy surrounding the charity schools too, with vehement articles, public demonstrations and court cases. High Anglicans endeavoured to eliminate nonconformist support for the schools, while Low Churchmen feared Jacobite leanings being inculcated into the children. The Close Vestries Bill of 1716 sought to transfer control to an elected management team instead of a self-appointed group, but these same people controlled the vestries, so trustees and managers largely remained the same.[16] None of this seems to have penetrated as far as our parish, neither was there apparently any local attempt to establish nonconformist schools as occurred elsewhere.

SUNDAY SCHOOLS

In spite of continuing concerns about over-educating those whose job in adult life would be menial, yet another attempt was made to improve the low level of rural literacy. This was about 20 percent in the mid-eighteenth century, as measured by ability to sign a document, although more could read. The establishment of Sunday schools sought to address this. By 1818 twice as many children were receiving basic teaching in reading in Sunday schools as in all other establishments put together. The main objective was, of course, religious, but parents and employers were also in favour for mercenary reasons, as the children's attendance did not prevent them from contributing to the weekday labour force. The eagerness of the children themselves was apparent in the large attendances maintained throughout Sunday. By 1785 the need to coordinate the teaching resulted in the formation of the non-denominational Sunday School Society. Opponents of the weekday schools also perceived that the improvement in education of the poorer children gave them what was considered an unfair advantage over the less well-taught sons of the traders.[17] As we shall see later, the problem of child labour remained acute in rural parishes for many years.

NATIONAL SCHOOLS

National efforts to establish elementary schools got under way in the first years of the nineteenth century. Joseph Lancaster, a Quaker, began teaching poor children and soon had a free school of 1,000 boys. He published the results of his endeavours and by 1808 had started the British and Foreign Schools Society. This nonconformist initiative somewhat alarmed the Church of England, and its leaders were relieved to discover that Andrew Bell, recently returned to England from Madras, had been experimenting with new teaching methods at the same time as Lancaster. By 1811 he had been appointed superintendent of the National Society for the Education of the Poor in the Principles of the Established Church, with authority to develop his ideas of mutual teaching by the pupils themselves, the monitorial system.[18] The members of the National Society proceeded apace with their efforts, and by the 1850s well over one million children were attending their schools, and only about 150,000 those of the British Society.[19]

Such schools were set up in the larger parishes to begin with, but by 1820 William Campion was leasing for one year, to Robert Upperton of Brighton, 'all that piece or parcel of Land with the (disused) Chapel (now intended to be converted into a National School House). . . late of the Revd George Bennett Clk'. The payment for the lease was five shillings, with a peppercorn to be paid at the end of the period. This property was on the site of the present Free Evangelical Church and the Players' Theatre.[20] The premises were released to a group of ten local gentlemen, the document being duly enrolled in Chancery, and continued as our village school until a new site was found on part of Little Park Farm, where it still stands and flourishes. The High Street building was sold at auction at the New Inn in 1869 to Henry Sendall, grocer, with a covenant preventing its use as a place of public worship which seems somewhat curious in view of its previous occupation, perhaps an indication of the concern of the establishment over the perceived influence of nonconformity.[21]

In similar fashion, in April 1843 Dr Avery Roberts and his wife conveyed to the rector, churchwardens and overseers of Hurstpierpoint 'part of Berry Lands near Sayers Common' to be used as a site for a school for poor persons, and residence of master and mistress, in union with the National Society, and subject to inspectors under Order in Council dated 10 August 1840, and to inspection of Chichester Diocesan Board of Education, under the management and control of the rector and curate of the parish'. The school, 'of brick, flint and slate, with a stove', had been built ahead of the conveyance with £300 from Avery Roberts, as it was insured for this amount with Norwich Union three months earlier. In addition to the initial gift for Sayers Common, Avery

Roberts made a bequest in his will, proved in 1862, of £200 'to the Treasurer for the time being of the Parochial National School at Hurstpierpoint'.[22]

Pigot & Co's Directory of 1839 shows that Ronald and Harriet Paterson were in charge of the National Schools. Kelly's Directory, published at intervals from 1845 onwards, mentions the National Schools, both in Hurst and at Sayers Common, and points out the support by subscriptions.

According to a report of 1855, the school in the High Street had 70 boys and 60 girls on its books, with average attendances of 60 and 50 respectively. The stipend of the headmaster was £50 pa and that of the girls' teacher £37. 16s. £35 was contributed by subscriptions from local worthies and a penny a week given by parents for each child. Other income from legacies etc totalled £53, but expenditure was £110, so there was little available for any extras. The school had last been inspected the year before, and it was noted that there was one other school in the parish, for dissenters. At the same time the Sayers Common school had 60 children, the teacher's salary was £30, and other income £11; the last previous inspection was in 1851.[23]

By 1860, the reports were becoming longer and more detailed. We find that the 60 boys (out of 77) and 59 girls (out of 78) present at the examination on 5th June were divided into three classes each. They were examined, usually by the visiting parish clergy, on the catechism, the prayer-book, the old and new testaments; in reading from monosyllables to books of greater difficulty; in writing on slates and in copy-books from dictation or in compositions; in the simpler and higher rules of mathematics; and in geography and grammar. The degree of proficiency found was A or B in a scale ranging from A to E. Particular comments were: 'The [boys] school is in a satisfactory condition . . the third class of young children appear to have more than usual pains bestowed upon them . . . [the girls school] very satisfactory, reading and arithmetic good, writing on slates better than in copy-books which is partly to be attributed to insufficiency of deskroom [later supplied] . . . needlework has due attention paid to it and some of the older children are taught to cut out'. These remarks were made by the Reverend Charles Heathcote Campion, younger brother of William John, one of the original lessees, in his capacity as Diocesan Inspector. He also noted that there was no library or evening school. At Sayers Common there was a library, they were 'doing very well, the upper children receiving advanced instruction in arithmetic and some progress has been made in geography. All the principle subjects are well taught'. In spite of this, intelligence was only rated 'C'.[24]

The 155 boys and girls on the school books at this date represented less than 39% of the total number of children in the parish aged between five and fourteen, as shown by the census returns of the following year.[25] More than ten years later, compulsion brought the school figures nearer to those of the whole child population. Even in the 1860s the need for more desks and a larger room continued to concern the authorities, successive inspectors' reports referring to the problem, but by 1864 plans were afoot to remedy this. On 18 June the School Committee met to choose the best site: Church Green (where the War Memorial now stands), part of Church Field, or the existing site; a letter was sent to Mr Dodson, asking him to sell or give Church Green, but by 8 July no reply had been received. In November 1866 it was reported that the Rector had given a site for new buildings which it was hoped would be commenced the following spring. But no further progress was actually possible until Charles Smith Hannington agreed in 1868 to provide a plot 120 x 177 ft. part of Little Park Farm, abutting on what was then called the turnpike from Hurstpierpoint to Cuckfield 'in trust for a School for the education of children and adults or children only of the labouring, manufacturing and other poorer classes' the management to be vested in a committee of the minister, curate, churchwardens and six other named persons, all of whom to be 20s contributors and communicants of the Church of England, vacancies to be filled by an electorate of communicants contributing 10s or more annually. On Friday 14th August that year the corner-stone of the New Schools was laid by the Bishop of Chichester after a Harvest Festival service at 12 o'clock in Holy Trinity which included the singing of five Psalms and three hymns, the Litany '&c', a procession from the church to the site of all the clergy, the churchwardens and sidesmen, the builder, architect and solicitor, and the donor of the ground, to be followed by the choir and children of the schools, and then the rest of the congregation. The ceremony continued with readings and prayers, and was lengthy enough for the last lines of the Order of Service to indicate: 'Then (if time permit) the 100 Psalm O. V. (Hymn 136) will be sung. And the Bishop will pronounce the Benediction'. All was not over even then, as parishioners were reminded that 'Evening Prayers will be at the Parish Church at Eight o'clock'.[26]

From 1862 any incidents of note had to be recorded for inspection by Her Majesty's Inspector. In Hurst the first logbook entries start in 1863, while still in the High Street.[27] They were kept by Thomas Rooke and Sarah Gumbrill. By contrast with the ceremonial laying of the corner stone of the new school, the actual removal to Cuckfield Road is recorded in remarkably brief fashion:

> 1869 Mar 19 Last day in old school; packing and removal taking place. 22 Assembled in New School.

In common with schools in all other rural areas, they show in repeated entries how school attendance fluctuated wildly, depending on the weather, sickness, the harvest and other out-of-school activities. Random samples, a mixture from both boys' and girls' departments (they were considered to be separate schools, as indeed was the infants' section) from that first year of records, soon give a flavour of the problems confronting the teachers:

xxxvii. 'The written excuse' (Cruikshank cartoon 1834).

1863 Feb 12   children kept at home to fetch soup from Danny

Mar 3   several boys gone to work bean planting

6   lowest attendance this week owing to boys having to stay at home while parents went to Church to apply for meat & beer to be given away on Prince's Wedding Day March 10

Mar 10   General holiday for Prince of Wales Wedding

11   boys all look exceptionally tired from yesterday's exertions on the hill & in the field

12   wet afternoon, v short attendance

20   v short attendance, wet morning

24   weather v fine, several boys away at work

Apr 30   attendance this afternoon not good . . . children [getting] flowers for garlands

May 1   not assembled Garland Day

15   wet, short att

18   many want leave to attend a club which is held nearby; several away to work

19-20   wet, numbers low [41 boys on 19th, 47 on 20th]

28   Hurstpierpoint Club Day, many asked for leave, no attendance pm

Jun 16   only assembled am, attendance not good – a Volunteer Review at Danny pm

19   am very wet many absent

23   many absent on account of haymaking

Jul 6   haymaking still keeps school very thin; several away, St John's Cattle Fair

17   progress of school seems very slow, owing to irregular attendance from various causes, eg sickness, outdoor employment of mothers, and 'looking after little ones'

27   several away, Foresters Fete at Chinese Gardens

31   boys beginning to stay away for harvest . . .

And things did not improve in subsequent years:

1864 Jan 11   attendance not as good as before Christmas, some children never attempt to come the 1st week or two

20-22   V wet, attendance low

Feb 19   day piercingly cold, snowing at intervals,
          only 4 children present
Oct 20   several boys away acorn picking [for pig
          food or as a remedy for diarrhoea]²⁸
     21   low attendance, same reason
Dec 8   short att 46 am & 62 pm, Hurst Fat Stock
          Show
Dec 9   Fox Hounds meet at New Inn . . .
1872 Jul 19   haying & fruiting
     26   Harvesting
1874 Sep 7   Danny Vegetable Show, att low

And so on and on. It would seem that bad weather reduced attendance, while good weather allowed some outside activity to achieve the same effect. There was a widespread belief, even among some HMIs, that the country child could not be educated, an attitude which gave little encouragement to the teachers. The Agricultural Children Act of 1873 attempted to impose minimum school attendances between eight and twelve years of age, but enforcement was not successful until three years later, when full-time schooling from five to ten became compulsory, with registers being required from 1880. Even so, the influence of the agricultural year was sufficient to allow flexibility in ending the summer term, not adhering rigidly to the end of July. For example in 1866, the Hurst term ended on 23 July, whereas in 1875 a late harvest enabled the school to stay open one further week until 6 August, the master knowing that attendance on return in September would be low while some casual farm work still remained to be done. And sometimes the effect of farming activity was even more immediate:

1871 Dec 8   stock show, holiday given as road blocked by cattle
1875 Dec 16   holiday because of stock show held near school

(presumably this was on Lamb Platt, where London Terrace now is on the other side of Cuckfield Road)

Accidents and serious illness were, of course, recorded then as now:

1863 Feb 24   Johnothon (sic) Furlonger away from school on
               account of accident in which his leg was broken
Mar 18   E Rhoudes away, broken leg
May 27   W Henty readmitted after small pox

1868 Jul 22	J Tulley would be absent some time, leg broken
Nov 5	A Dunstan wished to return, but sent home till next week, only just recovered from scarlet fever
10	James Morley away, another infectious disease rife, sister is attacked with it
1869 Apr 14	pane of glass fell from window on to Henley, making deep gash on face
1871 Jun 29	some away, mumps
Jul 6	more away, mumps
1872 Jun 7	measles, 9 away
21	measles, 40 away, attendance 57
Jul 5	measles still bad
1874 Mar 27	measles still prevalent
Apr 17	attendance below average due to measles
1876 Mar 24	measles spreading
Apr 24	measles still prevalent . . .
1878 Mar 7	several away, scarletina, mumps
15	A Miles sent home, scarletina under same roof
18	scarletina increasing
27	Ernest Dunstone 5th Standard died after an absence of five weeks

Sometimes both causes of low attendance were recorded:

1871 Jul 14	week's attendance thin because of mumps and fruit gathering.

At first glance it would seem that there was an excessive concern about attendance shown in the log books, but it should be remembered that grants to the school, and ultimately the teachers' salaries, depended on the average numbers recorded in the registers, not just on those on the lists at the beginning of each term. This control became even more stringent in 1862 under the Revised Code devised by the Vice-President of the Education Department, Robert Lowe; grants were calculated on attendance under a certified teacher, together with a three R's examination by HMI. [29] Continuing absence of significant numbers of children, particularly on examination days, meant straitened circumstances for the school and its staff. But there were other matters recorded.

The National Society laid great emphasis on the religious basis of all the teaching, to the extent that biblical arithmetic textbooks posed questions such as: 'There were twelve apostles, twelve patriarchs and four evangelists; multiply the patriarchs and the apostles together and divide by the evangelists' or 'Jacob had four wives: Leah had four sons, Rachel, Billah and Zillah two each; how many sons had Jacob?[30] This sounds far-fetched to us today, but it required the 1870 Education Act to change this approach; the receipt of a government grant precluded this doctrinaire method. But it was natural in a Church of England school that regular contact with the church should take place. The parish curates were frequent visitors, Canon Borrer and his family less so. They tested the children on the Catechism and other church matters; quantities of needlework, chiefly mending, were sent from the Rectory. On 3rd November 1864 Canon Borrer presented some books as the commencement of the school library, so one of the criticisms of the previous year's inspection was being addressed. The library opened the following week, with a set of rules requiring the payment of 1d per month in advance, a fine of a halfpenny for late return of books, and repairs of damage to be paid for by the child responsible. A further parcel of books came from the Rectory in April 1865; there now being 60 volumes available for borrowing. That these contacts were not just routine is shown by the entry for 26 June 1868:

> Rev F Parnell's last visit, all v sorry he is going to leave Hurst.

Sometimes it would appear that such attentions were not universally welcomed:

> 1875 May 19   Miss Borrer did not visit on account of
> complaint [unspecified] of Mrs Burt.

This did not sour relationships for long, because we find that on 28 May 1878 the school was dismissed at 11 am to be present at the wedding of Miss Blanche Borrer, 'buns distributed after the service'.

There were regular attendances at Holy Trinity Church by the various classes, while the whole school was involved on special occasions, some happy, some sad:

> 1863 May 14   Ascension Day, 1st & 2nd Divisions at church
> Sep 4   Service at church specially for thanksgiving
> for late harvest. Tea for children at 5 o'clock at
> New Inn
> Oct 15   Wedding of Rev J B Orme, curate

1866 Mar 7   Special church service held for the 'Cattle Plague'
   Sep 7   Harvest Home, church am, holiday pm
1869 Feb 4   dismissed at 11, Miss St John's wedding
1872 Feb 22   Ash Wednesday, took all boys to Church am
1887 Oct 14   George Pierce died in Children's Hospital
     19   funeral, boys & teachers joined mourners as
            they passed school gate, sang hymn 337 at
            church, 289 at grave.

The monitorial system initiated by Andrew Bell was adopted here as elsewhere. By the time of the extant log-books they had been joined by another grade of assistant, that of pupil-teacher, created in 1846. So we find:

1863 May 11   Arthur Eve Pupil Teacher away, ill-health
     15   Arthur Eve still away, class taken by George
            Humphrey [monitor]
     18   A Eve PT returned
   Jul 2   A Eve away, ill-health

But, even in good health, he did not stay very long:

1864   Mar 1   Written testimonial to Arthur Eve, leaving [for
            Montacute] as school not able to pay salary.

On 21 March two boys were appointed as monitors to replace him. By June 1865 a new system of monitorship had been introduced, whereby boys of the 1st section of the 1st class did the job for three or four days, and were then replaced; they were marked on keeping the class in order, the marks being totalled for a prize to be awarded before Harvest Holidays. In 1871 it would appear that there were three pupil-teachers, under five-year apprenticeship indentures, £10 per annum being an average male wage, while some of the girls received less than £5. The master or mistress had to promise to give the pupil 'daily opportunities . . . of observing and practising the art of teaching', and to devote at least one and a half hours 'before or after the usual hours of school keeping' to personal instruction (in a mixed school, properly chaperoned). Her Majesty's Inspector had to approve the arrangements. The pupil-teacher was required to be able to read with fluency, write in a neat hand, know simple arithmetic, the parts of speech, and elementary geography, and be able to teach a junior class.[31] Thus it is that we find these three being entered for examinations. On 13 May 1871, Talmy obtained 132 marks, Anscombe 124 and Dunstone 112, and on 28 September they went to Brighton for an external test. How they performed we are not told, but for two of them it became irrelevant:

> 1872 Feb 9   Dunstone & Talmy found in possession of
> books &c, admitted taking them, both publicly
> expelled . . .

Anscombe survived, to be joined by H Holman and F Humphreys; their accumulated marks by January 1873 were 1264, 1445 and 1192 respectively; by Mar 29 they were 2390, 2510 and 2275. In spite of this, Her Majesty's Inspector was not impressed – on 5 December he wrote 'Pupil Teachers must improve'. Anscombe did, for in 1874 he was clearly serious about pursuing a career in teaching, and a medical certificate dated 21 October states 'I hereby certify that Alfred Anscombe is in good health, & that he has no failing to incapacitate him for a teacher. H Martin Holman MD'. The path to success was still not clear, for less than three months later he contracted rheumatic fever, not returning to school for nine weeks. He failed his arithmetic and Euclid exams in November, but HMI took note of the illness and said that his result would not prevent him from following his chosen profession.

In 1839 a number of Diocesan Training Colleges were set up around the country, one being King Alfred's at Winchester. The regime was frugal; lessons on secular subjects took place against a background of daily religious observances, starting at 6.15 am. The aim was that 'the master [should go] forth into the world, humble, industrious and instructed'.³² On 3 July 1876 Anscombe went there to try for a Queen's Scholarship, only about a quarter of all candidates being successful. Not all of those who did pass the examination were able financially to take up the Training College place offered, and the probability is that Anscombe was one such. The alternative since 1852 had been the grade of assistant teacher; on 13 November 1876 HMI reported that he was now qualified and on the 24th he left Hurst, having been appointed assistant master at Southwick. In 1884 W White, a paid monitor, also entered for the Winchester scholarship, but the result is not recorded – we must fear the worst, but it is evidence of a standard being aimed at. 1879 saw the arrival of Mr R E Williams as assistant master and his sitting his first examination in London; he finally received his certificate in November 1881 and left for pastures new on October 1883.

The monitors and pupil-teachers enabled the management committee to keep the expenses to a minimum.   However, any success the school achieved depended on the qualified staff, and Hurst experienced fluctuating fortunes in this regard.   In July 1866 Thomas Peters replaced Thomas Rooke for less than three years, but he was in charge when the move from the High Street took place, with pretty laconic entries in the log-book:

> 1869 Mar 19   last day in old building, packing books pm
> 22   first day in new school, 87 boys attended

The 1871 census shows Sarah Gumbrill and Sarah Redford as living on the premises, the first occupants of the rooms in the centre of the building; Harriet Turner was at Sayers Common School.   George Rawlinson, newly arrived, was a lodger in the High Street house of James Wadey, builder, and his wife; ten years later we find him at Rectory Cottage with his wife, four daughters and a son.

Plate 46. Boys' entrance to School, showing track to Little Park Farm (now Trinity Road).

It would seem that problems with discipline bothered each of the early teachers in turn. Sarah Gumbrill made the following entry:

> 1863 Aug 25   child in lowest class severely punished before all the school, first for inattention (habitual) to junior teacher, second for disobedience and sauciness to myself (caution to all given)

And in the infants log-book:

> 1870 Jun 28   all boys kept in til 5 o'clock for being noisy
> Jul 26   punished Thomas Parsons for stealing a child's dinner; gave lesson to whole school on 8th commandment

Sometimes the seriousness of the offence warranted external judgement:

> 1868 Dec 7   Mrs Sayers complains that Lewry ill-used her girl going home
> 14   Revs Molyneux, Rose & Methuen enquired into disgraceful conduct of Lewry, found guilty and punished before whole school.

Although Thomas Peters supervised the transfer to the new premises on 22 March 1869, by 31 March Jonas Rawson was the new master. He increased both punishment and detention, but the HMI report the following year indicated that the new regime had not succeeded in maintaining discipline. So he was succeeded in turn by George Rawlinson, who started his duties on 9 January 1871, aged 21, to the accompaniment of burst pipes, with an enforced week's holiday. The pipes were still leaking over a week later, despite workmen in the school all day, the whole crisis supervised by the Revs Barton, Brown & Borrer – not a propitious start for Mr Rawlinson. Emily Brown had become mistress of the girls' school in 1872, with Sarah Redford in charge of the infants. By 1894 the staff had increased throughout: James Harbour and Arthur Stenning were assistant masters, Sarah West had replaced Emily Brown and also had two assistants, and the infants needed two teachers. At Sayers Common Mrs Fanny Field was joined by Alice King.

George Rawlinson's 'reign' was a long one, with very favourable inspection reports throughout. In his second month he instituted a school garden, divided into ten plots, each to be looked after by two boys in partnership. He required pupil-teachers to arrive at 7 am for their own lessons, the implication being that previously they had learned as they went along. At the end of his first year HMI reported that 'Mr Rawlinson appears to be painstaking and industrious, under his management the school promises to do well'. In early 1872 he distributed Rules for the School, so that both staff and children should know clearly what was expected of them. His approach was one of encouragement throughout, and this bore dividends; the Diocesan Inspector's report of 29 February speaks for itself:

> Every boy passed, school very hopeful, great care in RI, influence must be good, whole school has most careful supervision, singing tone excellent, utmost reverence, discipline remarkably good, hymn sung very correctly if rather too loud considering its character.

Rawlinson's compassionate attitude is shown in the following:

1874 Mar 20   Henley sometimes late in consequence of his having to clean shoes, if not in before the registers are marked in the morning his mark is left blank until after morning school when if he comes in before 10 m he is credited with a 'present', if after 10 'absent'.

This did not mean that he never punished. It was he who expelled the pupil-teachers, he who made the following entry:

1874 Nov 13   Jess Walder broke Girls' School playground door handle off, seen by 2 boys & 3 girls, sent home to say it must be paid for by parents, received impertinent refusal from Mrs Walder, as he is still owing 8d for tearing a reading book and 3d for breaking a slate, & this not being the first time, resolved . . . to enforce payment & therefore sent him home until full payment is made.

Results in various external examinations and competitions showed his continuing influence:

> 1878 Feb 1 H Holman, F Humphreys & W Walker gained
> prizes in essay competition
> 8 H Holman 1st in 1st Class £2 prize in Diocesan
> Inspection, F Humphreys 2nd Class, W Holman
> 3rd Class

H Holman and F Humphreys passed their pupil-teacher exams in December, Humphreys to become a qualified assistant master. W Holman's partial success was not sustained. On 10 February he announced his intention to leave at the end of the quarter & have his indentures cancelled, but never got that far – he was expelled for immorality on 21 February!

But the general trend was upwards. Rawlinson took ten boys to Brighton to receive RSPCA essay prizes in March 1879, and another group for more prizes in a separate competition in July. The following year's inspection was 'most satisfactory, Mr Rawlinson very able, it is a pleasure to come into contact with his work. . .', and even more boys (18) received RSPCA prizes. It became 'a privilege to examine such earnest and intelligent boys', and 22 out 23 gained prizes. All this success produced an extra holiday granted by the Rector. And on 16 May 1890 the Diocesan report said 'Mr Rawlinson's department maintains its almost unrivalled position in rural schools'.

It was not just the external authorities who thought well of him. In 1969 the centenary of the opening of the Cuckfield Road building was commemorated by asking elderly ex-pupils for their memories. One said 'I was at Hurst School 73 years ago [1896]. . . I have many fond memories of Mr Rawlinson. . . [who] was liked by all the boys and I have no memory of punishment. . .'[33]

This pensioner remembered a professional footballer coaching the boys, thus starting an interest which lasted all his life. There is evidence in the log-books that sports were very much part of Mr Rawlinson's approach, although some games activities were recorded earlier:

> 1864 Jul 21 Mr Campion gave leave for cricket in Sand
> Field Danny, bats & stumps to be obtained at
> Jupps

1865 Aug 18	boys to cricket at Sandfield; match v Ditchling in contemplation
1887 Jul 27	cricket: boys 52, YMFS 49
1888 Nov 17	played Milton Grammar Scool at football 2-3
Dec 8	played Burgess Hill at football
1889 May 6	commenced cricket
Sep 25	began football in Mr Combridge's field
1890 Feb 24	match v Milton Grammar postponed (influenza)
Nov 3	football v Milton Grammar 5-2
1891 Feb 16	football: choir 5 rest 0
May 11	cricket Town v Country, former victorious
Jun 5	match with Hamilton Lodge won by 10 wickets
Jul 3	match with H Lodge, HL won by 14.

Plate 47. Stoolball in Danny Park.

These log-books show how thoroughly the schools were a part of the parish. We have already noted the influence of the farming year on attendance, but annual events staged by various local organisations were reflected in both attendance and actual school involvement. In addition to the Hurstpierpoint Club, there were the Foresters Fete and other treats at the Chinese Gardens, treats at Danny, the Fryers (sic) Oak Club, the meets of the Southdown Foxhounds, the Hassocks Gate Club, the Albourne Club, the Danny Vegetable Show, the White Horse Club, the Oddfellows Anniversaries – life seems to have been one long round of parties.

It is evident that the school prospered, for by 1886 the need for extending the premises became apparent. Some 40 landowners agreed to a voluntary rate of 1s in the pound to help to finance the new buildings; they raised nearly £9,500 by this method. Fifteen other owners refused, while some seemed to have found excuses for not contributing: Charles Sergison of Cuckfield Park, who owned land in Hurstpierpoint, wrote to the Rector to inform him that he could only offer £1 (instead of the £11 10s 6d due from the rate) as he had received very little by way of rents and had had expensive repairs carried out, as well as having to use £170 'of my own money' for a new slaughterhouse. An application was made to the National Society for a grant, but the Society laid down very strict requirements for the building, and it was not until 1891 that the work was carried out.[34]

It has to be remembered that this was all the schooling the vast majority of children received. We have already noted the many occasions when those on the school books were absent in order to supplement the labour force. At fourteen they were available for full-time work.

PRIVATE SCHOOLS

Throughout, private enterprise entered the scene alongside charity. The Sussex Weekly Advertiser for 11 July 1796 contained an advertisement for a Grammar School run by the Reverend E Edwards with an able and respectable assistant to teach boys classics, writing and 'Mathematical Learning'. We have yet to find any clues as to the site of this school, but accommodation was limited to eight boarders paying 18 guineas a year, while day pupils were accepted at one guinea each quarter. Six months later the much shorter insertion in the newspaper referred specifically to 'Hurst Grammar School', and only gave the start date of the new term.[35] Although similar advertisements for other schools in the area appeared at intervals over the succeeding few years, no further mention was made of the Hurst Grammar School.

We find evidence of another private boarding school from an unexpected source, the accounts of the radical political activities of the poet Percy Bysshe Shelley, from his letters and from various biographies.[36] Elizabeth Hitchener (1782–1822), the daughter of a one-time smuggler turned inn-keeper at Friar's Oak in Clayton parish, went to the Lewes school of the Misses Adams and became imbued with the forthright and unconventional attitudes of the younger Adams sister, Hannah.[37] Elizabeth's emerging radical ideas were based on those of writers such as Thomas Paine, himself in Lewes a few years earlier, and fostered by William Godwin and his associates in London during the period in which she was developing her skills as a teacher. By 1811 she was running her own school in Hurstpierpoint, in a house later owned by Dr Henry Holman, and now known as 'Abberton'.[38] One of her pupils was the daughter of a Captain Pilfold who lived at Cuckfield and was an uncle of Shelley. As a result of this she met the poet, some ten years her junior, and 'struck up an extraordinary intellectual friendship, with hours of long and candid arguments on the subjects of religion and philosophy',[39] progressing into frequent, lengthy and often gushing letters between June 1811 and June 1812. Things took a more sinister turn when a package of Shelley's political tracts, addressed to Miss Hitchener at Hurstpierpoint for distribution in Sussex, was opened by the authorities (when he had failed to pay sufficient postage), and she was watched thereafter on the instructions of the Earl of Chichester, joint Postmaster-General. She was so much in sympathy with Shelley's aims, that she agreed to join him and his wife and sister to found a radical commune in Wales, closing her school in order to do so; Shelley even suggested that she should bring some of her pupils with her. In the event, the Shelleys were forced to leave Wales, and Miss Hitchener joined them at Lynmouth in Devon, and the radical propaganda was continued from there.[40]   But Shelley soon found the association with the schoolteacher less attractive, and she was asked to leave the group and return to Hurst, where 'she found that she was the subject of much laughter and scandal, and generally regarded as Shelley's cast-off mistress'.[41] She went abroad and married an Austrian officer, returning later to run a successful school in north London. In 1822, the year of her death, she published a long poem 'The Weald of Sussex'.

However little these events concerned the inhabitants of Hurst until the final humiliation, they implicitly show that some children in those politically turbulent times were being taught more than the three Rs, as it is inconceivable that Elizabeth Hitchener would not have passed on her deeply held views to the next generation.

Moving on, Pigot's 1839 Directory records three private establishments, run by Ann and Elizabeth Barker, who took premises previously occupied by the Black Lion (both day and boarding); Mrs Hewish (day); and Mrs Patterson (boarding). Kelly's from 1855 records the arrival and development of St John's College, of which more later; but makes no reference to any other teaching establishments. This repeated omission reminds us that these directories were commercial undertakings: with brief introductory details about the locality, even the best are far from comprehensive.

For example the 1871 census includes Belle Vue School (now Lamb House), Cuckfield Road, run by Mary Ward with three other teachers, two servants and 21 girl pupils; Antonio Martineau 'Professor of Language' (where is not stated); at Gothic Cottage (now House) Fanny and Elizabeth Rowland and Catherine Beard taught four girl boarders aged 9-12 (possibly there were other day pupils); and at Hamilton Lodge in the central section of the High Street Louisa Wise and three assistants ran a boarding school for fifteen boys. By 1881 Belle Vue had added three more to the teaching staff and four more pupils; Hamilton Lodge had increased to 26 boys.

The 1881 census just missed Aubrey Beardsley, the well-known black-and-white artist of the last years of the century, who, at the age of seven, was sent to Hamilton Lodge from his home in Brighton because of a weakness in the lungs. During his time in Hurst, 1879-81, he wrote home frequently. The first letter, to his mother Ellen dated 1 October 1879, seems to describe a fairly relaxed regime: 'I do not do very many lessons, I go lots of time into the playground'; there were outings to the circus and frequent ones to the Chinese Gardens, fireworks on 5th November, Valentines and other enjoyments. His stay obviously improved his health, for on 27 February 1880: 'Miss Barnett. . . will take care of the prescription, but I am quite well, and don't want any medicine yet'. In the same letter: 'I am getting on better with my music now. At first Miss Barnett was quite bald with teaching me. . .' But no mention was made of any other subjects![42]

PUBLIC SCHOOL

The history of Hurstpierpoint College has been recorded elsewhere,[43] but we should look at the relationship between the school and the parish during our period.

Nathaniel Woodard went to Shoreham in 1846, where he found no organised education beyond that of the church primary school. Within a year his first school had started, and on 1 August 1848 Lancing College was founded, with Hurst following exactly one year later, although at that time it was known as St John's Middle Grammar School and housed at Star Lane, Shoreham, under its headmaster, Edward Lowe. With fees of 18 guineas a year, expenditure was kept to the minimum and life was frugal, but numbers increased and Woodard looked for a new site. This he found at the Mansion House in Hurst High Street, moving there on 25 January 1850.[44]   Four days later 34 boys were at Holy Trinity among a large welcoming congregation of clergy, gentry, ladies and local traders, who then had lunch at the New Inn.

Lowe attended many parish functions and had good relations with the local farmers and traders. A number of their sons become scholars. William Campion entertained visitors on Lowe's behalf; gave permission for cricket matches in the park at Danny; allowed access for the annual Ascension Day climb of Wolstonbury; and awarded prizes, as the family had already done at the National School. The emphasis on High Church observances produced opposition, but Woodard and Lowe weathered this, and the school expanded, using other properties in the neighbourhood. The larger numbers increased the risk of cross-infection, and scarlet fever occurred in both 1851 (with two deaths) and 1852. The Bishop of Chichester understandably showed more than a clerical concern, as he had a son at the Mansion House, and wrote a stiff letter to the Vestry in 1862 about the lack of effective sanitation in the village; the vestry replied, unwilling to accept any interference; but a new cess pool was built.[45]

A free place scholarship was offered to the village, and this continued through the years. George Rawlinson's log-book entry for 14 March 1892 indicates that John Stevens had been elected by the Vestry for this award.[46]

The new buildings, on 12 1/2 acres of Copthall Farm bought from Nathaniel Borrer for £800, were opened on 21 June 1853 with great ceremony. Once fully functioning, the neighbours were regularly reminded of the religious basis of the school, with hymn singing at twice-daily services and processions with banners and robed choristers. It was this aspect which made the Woodard foundations different from earlier public schools.[47] St John's College has meant that Hurstpierpoint has become known throughout the country and beyond.

NOTES AND REFERENCES

1. Wright M (1991): *A Chronicle of Cuckfield*, 21–2.
2. Houlbrooke R A (1984): *The English Family 1450–1700*, 146–151.
3. Jones M G (1938): *The Charity School Movement*, 3, 5, 16, 19, 33.
4. Caffyn J (1998): Sussex Schools in the 18th Century, *SRS* **81**, 304.
5. WSRO/Ep. II/1/1.
6. Unpublished Marchant Diary
7. Turner E (ed)(1873): The Marchant Diary, *SAC* **25**, 167, 184–5; unpublished diary.
8. *Ibid.*, 191.
9. ESRO/HIC472, 5, 8, 9; Turner, Marchant, *SAC* **25**, 175; Turner E (Ed)(1866): The Stapley Diary, *SAC* **18**, 157
10. Jones, *Charity Schools,* 67, 79–80.
11. *Ibid.*, 100.
12. ESRO/DAN2198.
13. 'A Native, A Minor' (1837): *A History of Hurstperpoint*, 43.
14. Cited in Caffyn, Sussex Schools, *SRS* **81**, 152.
15. Jones, *Charity Schools*, 112–3.
16. *Ibid.*, 86, 150, 152.
17. *Ibid.*, 153.
18. *Concise Dictionary of National Biography* (1992), Vol 2, 1711–12; Vol 1, 197–8.
19. *Report of Royal Commission, Parliamentary Papers* 1861, XXI, Part 1, 592.
20. WSRO/ Par 400/25/12, 15: the full list of lessees is: William Borrer of West Town House, Rev John Kenward Shaw Brooke of Eltham, co. Kent, William John Campion, jun., of Danny, William Borrer, jun., of Henfield, Hampton Weekes, M.D., Edward Turner, Nathaniel Borrer, Richard Weekes, jun., surgeon, Henry Holman, surgeon, all of Hurstpierpoint and Thomas Turner, jun., of Oldland in Keymer, gent.
21. WSRO/ Par 400/25/15.
22. WSRO/ Par 400/ 25/13, 14; Par 400/24/95.

23. WSRO/EpII/40/1.
24. WSRO/EpII/40/5.
25. 1861 census records 556 children aged 5–14, year total varying from 66 to 41.
26. WSRO/ Par 400/25/22.
27. WSRO/ E 400/12/1; some books still held at St Lawrence School.
28. Horn P (1974): *The Victorian Country Child*, 200.
29. Horn P (1978): *Education in Rural England*, 125.
30. *Ibid.*, 118.
31. *Ibid.*, 62–75.
32. Sir James Shuttleworth, Secretary of the Privy Council Committee on Education, cited in Horn, Education, 91.
33. WSRO/ ADD MS 42164.
34. WSRO/ Par 400/25/17.
35. *Sussex Weekly Advertiser* 11 July 1796, 16 January 1797.
36. Cameron K N (1951): *The Young Shelley*; Jones F L (1964): *The Letters of Percy Bysshe Shelley*; Holmes R (1974): *Shelley, the Pursuit*.
37. Caffyn, Sussex Schools, *SRS* 81, 415.
38. 'A Native, A Minor', *Hurstperpoint*, 3n.
39. Holmes, *Shelley*, 71.
40. *Ibid.*, 85, 131, 136–7, 140–5.
41. *Ibid.*, 175.
42. Maas H, Duncan J L & Good W G (eds)(1970): *The Letters of Aubrey Beardsley*, 5–13.
43. King P (1997): *Hurstpierpoint College 1849–1995*.
44. *Ibid.*, 7–8.
45. *Ibid.*, 8–12; Vestry Book 1862–1984, 15–17.
46. Log-book held at St Lawrence School.
47. King, *College*, 16, 48.

14. ONE FOR THE ROAD

Ale has been drunk in England since long before the Romans came, and the tavern or hostelry, especially in the Middle Ages, has always been a place where all classes and types of people could meet and exchange news. The amount of ale consumed was enormous, as it was drunk by all ages at all times, taking the place of water which was often tainted and unfit for drinking.

In the thirteenth and fourteenth centuries celebrations of saints' days at the local church often took the form of a feast called a leet-ale, scot-ale or church-ale, at which the food and ale was given by local people and any profits from the sale went to the church. The clergy were regularly forbidden from taking part, but probably to little avail, as these celebrations usually took place in the churchyard. At weddings there was usually a bride-ale, where the bride dispensed ale to the guests in exchange for gifts. At burials, not only was much ale drunk at the wake, but there was free ale given to the poor, so that the peasants and craftsmen had many opportunities of drinking without having to buy from the alehouse.[1]

Tea and coffee did not come into Europe until the seventeenth century, and they were so expensive that they were only drunk by wealthier families. In fact tea was so costly that it was kept in a locked tea-caddy so that servants were not able to use any, only the re-used tea-leaves which came from their mistress's table.

Brewing was universal, every village supplying its own needs. A government survey in 1577 listed well over 17,000 drinking houses (inns, taverns and alehouses) in 30 counties in England.[2] Small beer, a weaker liquid made from the second run of the wort, was usually drunk by children, and brewed in the home. The 1711 probate inventory of William Webb, a thatcher in Hurstpierpoint, lists a brew-house containing a brew-vat and mash-tubs, and also a buttery with 2 barrels and 14 glass bottles.[3]

From early times much ale was sold in 'ale-houses', where it was made in the kitchen and sold and drunk in the front room. In Hurstpierpoint there are two buildings in the High Street where rooms have been added at the front for this purpose. Care was taken to prevent the use of impure water, and there were regulations for the control of the trade. It is clear that they were hard to enforce, it being more profitable to pay the fine for breaking them than to abide by the law. At Shoreham in the thirteenth century the brewers paid 2 ½ marks (probably more than £800 in today's money) to escape appearing at the manorial court. Ale was supposed to be sold in measures on which the capacity had been stamped by an official, but this was often ignored, perhaps because the customer brought his own jug. The ale-conner tested the strength by arriving unannounced, buying some ale and pouring a little on a bench on which he would sit in leather trousers for half an hour; if the ale stuck to the trousers it had too much sugar in it. In London in 1364 Alice Causton filled the bottom of a quart measure with pitch and sprinkled it with rosemary, herbs sometimes being used to flavour the ale – she had to 'play bo-pepe throwe a pillery' (with her head through a pillory). Brewing was mostly in the hands of women called ale-wives, the husbands working elsewhere. Running an ale-house was thought to be a respectable job for a woman.[4]

In spite of this, female visits in the sixteenth and seventeenth centuries were regulated by social convention. Women might go to the alehouse with their husbands, particularly when they were on a journey or if there was a family or neighbourhood celebration. Groups of married women could go together, typically to celebrate christenings or churchings. Unmarried women might visit the alehouse with a boyfriend if they were courting. These were the principal occasions when a woman could enter a victualling house without risk to her reputation. Her presence there in other circumstances was likely to provoke loud comment from neighbours; an unattached woman who went to the alehouse on her own was usually regarded as promiscuous and might well be turned away by the landlord, accosted or assaulted.[5]

The malt used in the brewing was to be 'clene, swete and drye and wele made'. Andrew Borde writing in his *Dyetary of Health* in the first half of the sixteenth century says:

> Ale is to be made of malt and water, and the which do put any other thynge to ale than is rehersed except yeast . . . Ale for an Englysshe man is a natural drynke. Ale must have these propertyes, it must be fresshe and clere, it must not be ropy or smoky . . . Ale should not be dronke under v [five] days old. Newe ale is unholesome for all men, and sowre ale . . . is good for no man.

Beer came into the country from Flanders but for more than a century was not drunk by Englishmen. Borde disapproved of it:

> Bere is made of malte, of hoppes and water, it is a natural drink
> for a Dutche man.

Cider also was widely drunk in the Middle Ages. In 1341 seventy-four parishes in West Sussex gave tithes of cider as part endowment to the church. Borde also defined this drink:

> Cider is made of the juce of peeres or the juce of apples . . . but
> the best cider is made of clene peeres, the which be dulcet.[6]

Hops which were used instead of the spices, were grown locally, in a garden north of the High Street between Ribbetts and St Georges. There was a malthouse at Tott Farm in 1703 together with the messuage, barn and 22 acres held by Mrs Eveling. Richard Haynes was a maltster in 1768; Thomas Smith's 1841 premises were on the north side of Hassocks Road between Tott Farm and Randiddles, while Jack Spratley had his own malt-kiln near the White Horse; William Stevens lived in Malthouse Cottage in the late nineteenth century, Philip Smith in Townfield Cottages. George Saltman was employing six men and a boy in 1881. The survival of 'Brewhouse' and 'Malthouse' as names for houses and roads shows how much this industry has become part of our history.[7]

Over the years there have been many inns, beer-houses and later, public-houses, in Hurstpierpoint.

> From Crowboro' Top to Ditchling Down
> From Hurstpierpoint to Arundel town,
> The girls are plump and the ale is brown,
> Which nobody can deny.
> Hillaire Belloc: 'In Praise of Sussex' in The Four Men.

Inns catered for the horse and carriage trade and were usually large fashionable establishments, with stables and rooms for travellers to stay overnight, and even a blacksmith's for any repairs which might be needed. In 1686, the year after the Monmouth rebellion, a national survey was made of guest-beds and stabling at inns and ale-houses, so that, in case of a further uprising, the militia could be housed and so protect the safety of both King and kingdom. In a list including Ditchling and Henfield, Hurstpierpoint had eight guest-beds and stabling for eighteen horses in several inns. Any unfortunate travellers staying in those beds would have had to make way for the militia.[8]

Taverns sold wine to the more prosperous, but without the extensive accommodation of the inns.

Beer-houses, or formerly ale-houses, were for the traveller on foot or the poorer local drinker, and were normally smaller premises, serving ale or beer (and later spirits) and providing rather basic food and accommodation. Entertainments took the form of games of dice, cards, backgammon, tick-tack or marbles, to name but a few. There were often alleys for bowling or skittles. Sometimes communal games or entertainments would spill outside into the yard, street or nearby green. These could be football, morris dancing, bear-baiting or cockfights. There were mummers at New Year, and fiddling and dancing at Candlemas, May Day and many other festivals.[9] They were much frowned upon by the authorities as being a source of drunkenness and, especially any in isolated places, as being haunts for thieves or even highwaymen.

> We . . . having great Reason to suspect that Gaming, Drunkenness and Disorder have been too frequently committed and suffered in your Houses to the great Annoyance of the principal Inhabitants . . . that you Houses have been kept open on the Lord's Day and that Riots Quarrels and fighting has of late been committed . . . [10]

Charles Booth, who pioneered social survey methods, wrote in 1889:

> Public houses play a larger part in the lives of the people than clubs or friendly societies, churches or missions, or perhaps than all put together.[11]

The earliest record we have found in Hurstpierpoint relates to 1582 when Thomas Luxford of Clayton, Gent

> holdeth a ten'th called Pipelears now used as an Inn and the sign of the Hatchett in the north side of Hurst Street.

He was evidently not a satisfactory tenant, and was taken to court as

> The barn fallen down with a plot of ground on the backsyde
> where sometime was an Orchard but the good tenents have cut
> them down.

Plate 48. White Horse, early years of the 20th century.

A 'pub crawl' through the village from west to east starts at the White
Horse, part of the present building displaying the date 1591. In 1817
Thomas Wadey, the landlord or victualler, applied to the parish for a
reduction of his rental

> . . . as 2 cottages were to be built on part of the land and losing
> the use of the stables.

On 13 June 1817 the Overseers, Richard Davies and John Hugget, agreed to
a reduction of forty shillings per year to £10. 12s to be paid on Lady Day (25
March) and Old Michaelmas Day (29 September). George Cripps was
employed to build the two cottages, valued at £230.[12]

There was also a White Horse at Albourne, just south of the junction to Hurst, until April 1823, when Mr Tamplin applied to the parish to remove the licence to 'the House erecting at Sayers Common' [the Duke of York], to which they gave their consent.[13]

Moving along the High Street, the premises now occupied by the vet was earlier one of the buildings with an added front room, a small beer-house called the Oak; the name was revealed during re-decoration and carefully re-painted. Incidentally, it was while digging the foundations for the extension in the early 1800s that part of what was thought to be the old Hurstpierpoint manor house was found. Just a few doors away was the Red Lion (now a private house) with a similar front extension; in 1852 the landlord was John Peskett. These two establishments were only licensed to sell beer, and operated from the beginning of the nineteenth century until the late 1950s.

In Cuckfield Road the Sussex Arms Hotel was on the corner of Manor Road next to Hurst Brewery (now offices and Maxim Lamps), run by George Saltmarsh from 1862 to 1884, and bought in 1887 by John Edwin Couchman, who was described as 'brewer & maltster, wholesale & retail spirit merchant & mineral water manufacturer' (see Colour Plate 17). Violet Morley recalls that she

> . . . had to pass it every day to go to school, and we used to look through the windows. One machine used to fascinate us. We could never understand how it worked. Bottles with a little glass ball inside would be filled with lemonade which brought the ball to the top, placed in the machine which sealed the contents, I suppose by suction. The man operating this machine wore a wire mask to protect him from any that got smashed. These glass balls were called 'couches' after the brewery owner. We liked to get hold of them for marbles.

Marbles were played throughout Sussex. Gordon Tulley, writing in June 1967, remembered

> On a Good Friday I have seen as many as 100 boys playing marbles on the Green, this was the end of the marble season and ended at noon on that day.

He also remembered Hurst Brewery when he was a boy, seeing Mr George Chart, who lived nearby in Manor Cottages, wearing a perforated mask.

> The beer was made from the spring water beneath the brewery, and the malt was laid out on the concrete floors, turned by maltster Mr Curd, who wore a red stockinet cap with a tassel!

The barrels were mended on the premises and all the beer and mineral waters were delivered by horse-drawn drays.[14]

Plate 49. Hurst Brewery cart.

Mr Couchman lived in Dene House (now the Rectory), running the brewery until 1913 when it was taken over by the Brighton firm Smithers & Sons. His non-business activities included the village school and local charities, helping to found a trust fund to provide cottages for working people at reasonable rents, as well as becoming an authority on archaeology and local history, as mentioned in an earlier chapter. The brewery became a cheese factory in the 1920s, to be followed in the next decades by Slazengers, the tennis racquet makers. The Sussex Arms which had been the 'brewery tap', continued to trade until about 1970, the sign still showing faintly on the wall.

At the top of Cuckfield Road on the east side was another beer-house, the Lamb, believed to have been built in the early nineteenth century by Richard Weekes as a coaching inn, hoping for trade from passengers using the new turnpike (New Road as it was called) from Cuckfield to Brighton. Unfortunately the favoured route went via Friar's Oak, Stonepound and Clayton Hill, hence the descent to a beer-house. James Beckworth was landlord in 1895 and also proprietor of the fly, the horse-drawn cab ferrying people around the village and to Hassocks Gate station. His successor, George Stoner, was responsible for watering the dusty High Street from a water-cart, and for 'scavenging' (acting as dustman).

A short distance along the High Street was the Swan (now Down House), where Thomas Marchant went on several occasions:

> 1716. Feby. 28th.   Spent 2s with Mr Pointing, the exciseman, at the Swan in the evening.
>
> 1717. March 5th.   I met Mr Whitpaine at the church to consult about mending a bell. Went from thence to the Swan. Stay'd late, and drank too much. There was Mr. Chantler of Cittinly, and a butcher that came with him, and Stephen Bine.
>
> 1720. Janry. 20th.   At the Swan with Mr Courthope, Mr. Dodson, Mr. Beard, Mr. Scutt, Mr. Burry, Thos. Norton, of the North-end, and Mr. Whitpaine, when we executed the assignment for the Letchford Charity money, and Mr. Whitpaine paid the money, £100, to Mr. Courthope. Spent 5s. on the parish account.[15]

The Royall Oake (opposite the New Inn) in 1663 was part of Stylers and occupied by William Briant, the rent of 4d per year being unchanged for about 150 years:

> ... a messuage, garden and orchard in Hurst Towne.[16]

In December 1686 the landlord was John Fields. Richard Stapley of Hickstead Place:

paid to Mr John Whitpaine for writing a copy of an exemplification of my father's will, the sum of 20s, at John ffields house, called the Royal Oake, in Hurst Town.

By 1699 the inn holder was Francis Allcocke, who obviously acted as a collection point for goods, as Richard Stapley records:

I delivered my new perriwigge in a pasteboard box, to be sent to Wallis, ye perriwigge maker, to be changed for a larger wigge in ye head and cawl . . . I delivered it to ffrancis Allcocke at ye Royal Oake in Hurst parish aforesaid, and he promised to take care of it as abovesaid. I recd. Another wigge of ffrancis Allcock ffebruary 15th.[17]

On 15 March 1715 a court was held, attended by Thomas Marchant

. . . in obedience to the notice on Sunday given by Jos. Muzzell. He called it a Court Baron. There I found Mr. John Norton, and John Stone, who, with myself, were all the tenants present: and no business appearing, Mr. Warden [steward of the lord of the manor] did not keep a court.

Four years later the steward was Mr Osbourne, who kept a Court Baron at the Royal Oak on 10 October.[18]

The licence was eventually revoked due to disorderly behaviour and transferred across the road to the New Inn (see Colour Plate 9):

This day was decided the grand contest for licensing another public house in Hurst, but which, by the desire of the gents was terminated in favour of a second house opposite the Royal Oak.[19]

As has been shown in the chapter on roads, the New Inn played an important part following the development of the turnpikes. It was taken over by Thomas Smith in 1839, and he remained landlord for 20 years, owning as well a bowling alley in Randiddles and a malthouse on the Hassocks Road. He and his wife Jane had a son Philip, who became a miller. He died in 1883 aged 78. The inn was larger than it is now, with stable and probably a brew-house to the east. Kelly's Directories record it as a hotel in 1867, a posting house and commercial inn in 1874, and note in the 1894 edition that the corn market was held there on Tuesdays.

Plate 50. The New Inn 1836 (note stabling).

On the north side of the High Street the Black Lion was situated by Ribbetts, with Black Lion Cottages next door, where Randell the cobbler plied his trade. By 1841 the beer-house had closed and the Misses Barker were running a ladies seminary in the building.[20]

The last public house was the Queen's Head (now The Poacher), part of Lower Trumpkins, Upper and Lower Trumpkins together extending from Ribbetts to opposite South Avenue. William Peskett was landlord in 1867; by the 1891 census Henry Mewett had taken over as innkeeper, with Elizabeth Anne and Rose Mewett as barmaids.

The Chinese Gardens were pleasure gardens in Chinese Lane (Western Road) opened in 1843 by Adam Adams, the landlord of the White Horse, with 5 ½ acres of parkland, woodland walks, lily ponds and a large lake for fishing and boating; summer houses in secluded spots, a goodly-sized ballroom, a large public bar and tea-rooms. However it took another year before it was really established, and there was a 'Grand Re-Opening' on 27

May 1844. For amusements there were lawn billiards, bowls, a shooting gallery, darts, a coconut shy, and a brass band. The gardens were very popular, with visitors from all the surrounding villages and towns. These included outings by various organisations, for example:

> On Monday last, the members of the Philanthropic Society paid their fifth annual visit to the gardens, the members numbering about 700, arrived by train at Hassocks Gate Station about one o'clock, and proceeded in procession to the gardens, attended by the Railway Band which played through the town. The day being very fine the members and their friends amused themselves most pleasantly with the many games the gardens afford. Weir's celebrated quadrille band was in attendance, and contributed much to the amusement of the day; the admission to the gardens was upwards of 1, 000. Mr. Adams, with his usual liberality, gave up the gardens for the day to the Society, for the benefit of the above institution. Perhaps we shall not be much out of order stating that, during the season, the benefits received by various charitable institutions amounted to upwards of fifty pounds. This day's pleasure ended with a good display of fireworks, and the eruption of Mount Vesuvius etc.[21]

Plate 51. The Chinese Gardens.

In the 1930s much of the land was sold for the building of houses, with an additional condition in the deeds that they should not be used for the trades of 'a Licensed Victualler, tavern keeper or Vendor of Malt or Spirituous Liquor . . .' and later a codicil was added that 'no roundabouts, fairs, swings or other like matters' should be permitted which might cause annoyance to Mr C Hannington (the owner of the land) or his heirs. It eventually became just a public house with a large function room for hire. Towards the end of the 1960s the name was changed to The Pierpoint. In the 1990s it was closed, the buildings pulled down, and more houses built on the site.

Outside the village, at Goddard's Green crossroads, in 1847 stood the Magpie, becoming the Jolly Sportsman in 1859 when Henry Payne was landlord, followed by his widow Charlotte. It is now known as the Sportsman.[22] Thomas Hole was landlord of the Duke of York at Sayers Common in 1855 as well as being a blacksmith; twelve years later he was still the blacksmith, but the landlord was Joseph Whitaker. The King's Head, just outside the parish in Albourne, was 'a public house erected at Ublies' in 1817. It was a coaching inn in the nineteenth century, with cottages to the south turned into stables.[23] In 1937 a new King's Head was built with a bright copper dome which had to be camouflaged during the Second World War, but it ceased to be an inn when the new A23 was built and took away the passing trade.

There also appear to have been rather a lot of 'retailers of beer' during the second half of the nineteenth century, most only trading for a few years. Kelly's Directories between 1841 and 1894 list at least fifteen.

Although most of the beer drunk nowadays has been brewed by the big commercial concerns, there are still a few privately owned or common brewers surviving. The nearest to Hurst are Harveys of Lewes and King & Barnes of Horsham.[24]

NOTES AND REFERENCES

1. Clark P (1983): *The English Alehouse, a Social History 1300–1830*, 25.
2. *Ibid.*, 2.
3. ESRO/W/FN265.
4. King F A (1947): *Beer has a History*, 20–21; Salzman L F (1923): *English Industries of the Middle Ages*, 287–9.
5. Clark, *Alehouse*, 131.
6. Salzman, *Industries*, 285–301.
7. WSRO/ Par 400/37/98; WSRO ADD MS 17683A: Fisher Map 1841; censuses 1841-91; *Kelly's Directory 1894*.
8. WSRO/ Par 400/37/120; PRO WO/30/48/7788, quoted by Pennington J: Inns and Alehouses in 1686, in Leslie K & Short B (eds)(1999): *An Historical Atlas of Sussex*, 68.
9. Clark, *Alehouse*, 5, 154.
10. ESRO/DAN1126, ff 192r–226r; ESRO/DAN1118.
11. Clark, *Alehouse*, 1.
12. WSRO/ Par 400/37/115, 116.
13. WSRO/ Par 400/12/1/11.
14. *Kelly's Directory* 1895; Morley V (nd, 1990s): Memories of Hurstpierpoint, 6; Tulley G: Old Hurstpierpoint, *Meeting Point* June/July 1967.
15. Turner E (ed)(1873): The Marchant Diary, *SAC* **25**, 175, 180, 186.
16. ESRO/DAN1118.
17. Turner E (ed)(1849): The Diary of Richard Stapley, *SAC* **2**, 113, 124.
18. Turner, Marchant, *SAC* **25**, 172, 185.
19. *Mid Sussex Times* (nd, pre-1912): Glimpses of the Past, Extracts from a Hurst Resident's Diary.
20. WSRO/ Fisher Map.
21. *Sussex Agricultural Express* 3 September 1853.
22. *Kelly's Directory* 1867.
23. *Mid Sussex Times*: Hurst Resident's Diary; Packham R A (1997): *Hurstpierpoint in old picture postcards*, Vol 2, 16.
24. Holtham P: Malting and Brewing, in Leslie & Short, *Atlas*, 113.

15. HURST IN THE TWENTIETH CENTURY

It is probable that life in Hurstpierpoint developed slowly until the coming of the turnpike roads; the inhabitant of 1500 would have recognised the Hurst of 1750. But new and better-maintained roads, followed by the railway and the internal combustion engine, expanded the horizons enormously. If we then add radio and television, air travel, the computer and the Internet, we can easily imagine how someone from the 1830s would feel utterly bewildered now. Change seems to come upon us almost weekly, and at what to many is an alarming rate. To record all of these changes in detail would require, not just another chapter, or another book, but a whole library of books. But, of course, such books exist already, and it would be tedious to repeat their contents. Much of the story of the land and its use has been brought right up to the present time, appropriately, as this is central to our story. What we can now try to do is to take some of the other themes of this book a little further on in time and examine a few of the more dramatic changes, enlivening them with appropriate oral memories from some of the residents of Hurst who have lived through them. This inevitably will be something of a 'rag-bag' of disjointed records, but it may help to emphasise that our recent memories build on what has gone before, and that history is being added to all the time as we go about our daily lives.

THE ESTATES

A stag hunt ended one day in the Laundry Field, where the animal had to be shot because it could not escape from the small enclosure. George Anscombe was among a number of boys who acted as beaters for a shoot at Danny, being paid eight shillings and a rabbit. Lunch of bread and cheese and a jug of beer was too much for one lad, who was found beating round a single tree, shouting loudly.[1]

At the start of the twentieth century the farmers from Cornwall who came to mid Sussex did so in response to the concerns of the local landowners that the hunting-shooting-fishing types were tending to neglect the farms. Mr J E Couchman, mentioned in earlier chapters dealing with local archaeology and the brewery, travelled to the south-west to encourage them to move.[2]

In the late 1940s there were a few major landowners and tenants: the Holes, the Hanningtons, the Orlebars at Pakyns, and the Danny estate. Even then the last-named was very much smaller than in earlier times: the Gorings could walk on their own land from Eastbourne to Wiston. Now it has been totally fragmented, with no fewer than 17 landowners in New Way Lane alone.[3]

Some of the estate cottages, such as Randiddles, still had outside 'privies' and pumps for water.[4] These cottages were tied to the farm workers' employment, so that loss of job meant loss of home. Even as recently as 1963, when a man who had worked on one farm for 50 years died, his daughters were given notice to vacate the premises forthwith, although in this particular instance the cottage was never again occupied by an agricultural worker.[5]

THE FARMS AND FARMING

London Terrace at the top of Cuckfield Road was built at the turn of the nineteenth century on ground which had been called Lamb Platt. It was here that cattle and sheep fairs were held until the early years of the twentieth century.

King Brothers had a dairy at Latchetts, and came round with a big churn on a milk float, for the women to fill their jugs in the street. Clayton Wickham farm delivered milk twice a day; sometimes even skimmed milk had enough cream on top to turn into butter.[6]

The Cornishmen mentioned above saw the benefits of farming near to the railway as they were able to milk their cows and sell the milk in Brighton and London the same day, rather than having to make it into cheese, cream and butter which meant working until 2 o'clock in the morning. Most of the corn was milled locally by Mr Packham at Cobb's Mill, already mentioned in the chapter on e Craftsmen and their Trades, but the very top-quality wheat might be sold in London to firms like Hovis or Rank. Incidentally the mill recharged the accumulators for the wireless batteries as well. Any market-garden produce not sold on a local direct delivery round was fed to the animals. Farm-made ice-cream was sold locally as well as bottled milk.[7]

Domestic service at the big houses had a number of benefits. During the First World War food was very short, but at Little Park there were always eggs, chickens and rabbits, and a huge tub of cattle treacle, some of which went on the breakfast porridge. Every year a pig was killed and cut into joints, the hams being salted or smoked over a gentle fire of oak sawdust, with homemade sausages as well. Milking was done by hand. As the herd was large it would be evening before the milk had cooled and been put into churns to be taken to Hassocks station.[8]

Jack Spratley was born in 1923 at No.1 Western Cottages (since demolished) opposite the White Horse. It was his grandfather who had the dairy farm on land now occupied by Pickett White's garage, as recorded in the chapter on the shops.[9]

Women were employed on the farms as well as men, particular in wartime. Nora Talbot recalls working long hours helping with hay-making and stacking, looking after and feeding the horses, collecting root crops and cabbages from the fields and taking them in a cart to the greengrocers in the High Street, mucking out the sheds and taking the dung to the fields for spreading. When other girls were called up into the Land Army, she was not allowed to join, and so did not get a uniform.[10]

Mixed farming prospered after the Second World War. Ford tractors arrived under 'Lease-Lend' from the USA; a boy of 12 with 200 day-old chicks reared to lay could make £100. In the mid 1950s Plumpton Agricultural College gave tuition in harnessing horses as well as in tractor hydraulics. Rent was about £3 per acre; now up to £100. Three or four bullocks could be driven 'on the hoof' from the farm along the High Street to be slaughtered and hung within 2 miles of their pasture. Sheep were driven from Ditchling to Henfield, taking two days with an over-night stop at Stroods.[11]

Ploughing matches are still events which are contested annually, and are watched by many. Olive Beckett recalls the farmer at Randiddles, who 'used to spend half the night polishing the horse brasses'.[12]

THE CHURCHES AND CHAPELS

In 1902 the east window of Holy Trinity Church, depicting the Ascension, was removed, to be replaced by a second one depicting the Crucifixion, dedicated in memory of a member of the Campion family who died in the South African War. Miss Harriet Gurney, who provided St Christopher's Home for the village, discovered the discarded glass and arranged for it to be shipped to a church in Ontario, Canada, where it is now installed.(see Colour Plate 18).[13]

Every Sunday Tommy Newman, the boot maker, wore top hat and tailcoat to sing in St George's choir.[14] The children used to find out in advance who was preaching at the Parish church and St George, in order to avoid what they thought would be a dreary sermon.[15]

Olive Beckett recalls Sunday School being run by Mr Prince, who 'made the Parish Room look like a church with pictures hanging round the walls, and kneelers'. The children from the whole diocese collected money for St Cuthman's, Brighton which had been bombed. Later Olive herself became Superintendent at a time when there were about 60 children. She took them on one outing to Eastbourne which was memorable in an undesirable way. Although no swimmer, she tried to save one of the girls who had dropped into deeper water; they both ended up in hospital for one night, and Olive received a Commendation from the Royal Humane Society.[16]

Before the Second World War, the College had little or no contact with the village; the staff did not go to church, worshipping instead at the Chapel. After the war, some attempts were made to change this: the new Rector, Theo Franklin, involved a number of lay people in various activities, the wife of one of the masters returning from holiday to find she was running the Mothers' Union.[17]

When Canon Franklin arrived Holy Trinity was so filthy, probably because the verger who was paid to clean it had a wooden leg, that picking up something from the floor inevitably meant picking up cobwebs as well. The Church was shut for a week, the pews were all washed with vinegar, the hot water coming from the house opposite. It was agreed that such a state of affairs could not be allowed to recur, and the Martha & Mary Guild was formed, Olive Beckett becoming the founder secretary, the Marthas volunteering to clean the church on a regular basis, and the Marys contributing money for the purchase of cleaning materials and equipment. Theo Franklin was also a prime mover in getting the village school named after St Lawrence, and in restarting St Lawrence Fair.

TRADES AND CRAFTS

Tommy Newman, the boot maker, sat in the window at Hampton Cottages working and singing hymns all the time. Harold Poundsbery in Hurst Wickham used to repair the boots for the College boys. Russell the blacksmith would mend George Anscombe's broken iron hoop for a penny. He regularly got drunk on Saturdays and sacked all the men, only having to go round on Mondays to their homes to ask them to come back.[18]

George Anscombe left school in 1917, aged 14, and worked in the paint shop and blacksmith's at Woolgars, the wheelwrights [Harper & Eedes], first learning to shoe the donkey which brought the laundry cart from Danny to Chichester House (training school for domestics). The odd remains of paint were mixed together, always coming out green, and used for the farm wagons. Metal tyres for these were put on a load of lit faggots, made red-hot, fitted to the wheels with sledge-hammers, and sprayed with water to shrink them on.

Mr Simms was a photographer living in a cottage opposite Randiddles. He had a studio with old-fashioned curtain drapes and a stool for the sitter. His sisters mounted and tinted the pictures. There were lots of pictures of children around the village sitting on the same stool.[19]

OTHER OCCUPATIONS

George was a member of one of six families of Anscombes: his father was a Prudential agent, as were two uncles; one was a gardener, one the manager of the gas company towards the bottom of Western Road; Uncle Joe was the Registrar of Births and Deaths; and Uncle Henry was the undertaker, so one recorded your arrival, the other saw you out. When George was young he was given a trial as a telegraph boy, bringing telegrams from Hassocks station to Hurst Post Office. Riding his bike back, he hitched on to Brown's coal lorry, reached to the High Street in record time, and got the job.[20]

The Post Office employed another teenager, in what was probably an even more responsible position, that of Sub-postmistress, at Hurst Wickham, in the front room of a small terrace house. Phyllis Poundsbery undertook this, selling cigarettes, soft drinks and other goods, for over 57 years, doing at least a 12-hour day, until a succession of three burglaries eventually made her 'call it a day' in 1989.[21]

On leaving school, Jack Spratley worked at Manor Nurseries, then at Erskine, so his call-up was deferred as he was on agricultural work. Tom Lewry was a master bricklayer; he built the cesspit at Washbrooks, but later went on the dustcart. Patrick O'Flaherty, known as Dummy because he could not speak, lived in an old shack down College Lane, and went around muck-spreading, mangel-pulling and so on, but bought the 'Irish Independent' newspaper, writing his order on a scrap of paper for Ray Packham.[22]

THE HIGH STREET

George Anscombe, born in 1903, was bitten on the forehead by a dog as he was going to school; he had to go to Miss Mitten's, the chemists [later Barclays Bank], sit on the floor and have it cauterised. He remembers being sat on a soap-box to have his hair cut by Bill Bailey for tuppence; Bill's sister had a small toy shop selling marbles, fishing hooks, slates and slate-pencils, and canes. Next door Miss Packer ran a haberdashery shop until she married Thomas Peskett, the grocer. George became an errand boy for Jupp's Stores [on the corner of South Avenue](see picture on page 303), and remembers the shop being dressed to the ceiling with honey pots, Mr Jupp saying that was how it should be done, only to have the lot crash to the ground when a steam-roller went past. One winter the son of the saddler George Brown threw a snowball at the bald head of Mr Gillam the fishmonger, with dramatic results: he was 'driven mad' and one of Walker's cabs had to take him to Hellingly Hospital. Later George worked at Masters & Tulleys [Alldays, etc] on the provision counter, making pats of butter, slicing bacon, and dressing the window. The shop assistants had to buy their own aprons and jackets and use their own bikes. They had regular customers for Collins' meat pies; there were dummy pies filled with sawdust on top of a glass case, and one day a customer in a hurry grabbed one and left her money on the counter, only to be discovered when her husband cut into the anticipated Saturday supper treat.

He was promoted to taking orders out in the country, at cottages as well as the farms and larger houses, cycling about thirty miles each day. When Walkers took over, George asked for a van; when it did not come at the promised time, he left and went to Graveleys [Players' Theatre] where a van was available immediately. His order round remained the same, as all the customers went with him. But Masters & Tulleys gave in eventually, as Ted Crane was driving for them later.

Bakers the butchers provided meat for George to take on his rounds. Charlie Jennings, the butcher at the crossroads, was also a bookmaker; George's bets were more successful than his father-in-law's, in spite of not studying form. Also at the crossroads was Gatland the ironmonger, who went round the country selling paraffin, oil, candles, and cleaning materials for the kitchen, including blacking for the grate and whitening for the hearth. Bannister the watchmaker next door had a red squirrel in a wire netting run in the backyard.[23]

Jack Spratley's mother was one of the women who worked at St George's Laundry, ankle-deep in water, scrubbing over old tubs for about ten bob [50p] a week in the 1920s and 30s. Opposite the church were Edgar Voyce the greengrocer, Mansbridge's shoe shop, Kate Garner's café, and Fred King the tailor, who lived in the two cottages, 41 and 45 High Street, with a central gateway to the public baths. Fred Heathorn sold Jack and his friends lemonade and cakes, rock-hard little scones with about half a dozen currants, strips of sponge for trifles and fairy cakes with a dollop of whiting and a cherry on top. When asked for two pennyworth of stale cakes, he would say 'H'm, I don't know whether I can help you there boys, because I don't bake any stale cakes, but I'll give you some of yesterday's,' and fill an old paper bag with these 'plumb-heavies'.[24]

Nobody thought of shopping outside the village; there was no need. Apart from the many shops, there were traders who came in to sell their goods.

Fishermen came from Brighton, another boiled whelks and winkles, a coloured man from Ditchling sold tea, and Mr Faccenda sold ice-cream called 'Hoky Poky' from a pony-cart with a pretty awning over it.[25]

A few families have influenced the development of the buildings in the High Street to a great extent. Among these were the Weekes, whom we have met earlier. Apart from Matts, where Richard had his home and medical practice, they owned at various times: Down House, Norton House, Hampton Lodge and Howard Lodge and the Mansion House. Joan Black's mother was a Weekes, born in yet another property built by the family, Dean House [the present Rectory in Cuckfield Road]. Her great grandfather came to the Mansion House in the eighteenth century, and it remained in the family until it was sold during World War II. When Joan's father retired from his medical career he returned to Hurst, to Norton House, with his wife and Joan and an aunt of hers.

HEALTH

In the first years of the century medical treatment in rural areas still used many traditional remedies. George Anscombe knew a gipsy clothes-peg seller named Martha who told an inhabitant of Ribbetts cottages to bind a young cabbage leaf tightly on his knee; the next morning the water on the joint had reduced and the leaf had disintegrated. She also recommended a fresh cow pat for the butcher who had cut his hand open with a meat hook, again effecting an apparently miraculous cure.

The local doctors also relied on simpler methods than those available today. George Anscombe's stomach-ache was easily diagnosed by Dr Beach the day after some apple scrumping: 'You picked the wrong apples – they were cookers'.[26]

By the 1930s the management of the health of the community had progressed to the acquisition of a car for the three District Nurses as the result of a public subscription instigated by Mr Harding, the Rector. A group of doctors, including Ralph Green, Edsel Pembery and Peggy Denman, established practice premises at Eastern House in Hassocks Road.

EDUCATION

In 1905 Miss Whittaker was head of the Infants school. In winter she brought milk to school to warm on top of a coke stove to give the children a drink in little 'dolly' cups. Some children had to walk from as far as Hurst Wickham and Ruckford Mill, a long way for four-year-olds. Older children came from Sayers Common, Albourne and Newtimber. There was an outcry when the entry age was raised to five, as the mothers wanted to go out to work. So that more children could join in the Maypole dancing, the teachers fastened tapes round two or three trees in the playground. On Empire Day the children dressed up to represent members of the colonies, saluted the flag and bowed to Britannia, seated on a throne, dressed in white with a brass helmet borrowed from a fireman father. In about 1909 the school went to the crossroads one day to see King Edward VII pass by in an open car – one little girl was disappointed that he did not wear his crown. Violet Morley won top prize, and some others, in a weekly national essay competition run by one of the Sunday newspapers.[27]

George Anscombe went to the Church of England School in 1908 when he was five, the then headmistress, Miss Whitaker, living at 'Eastfield', Cuckfield Road. The children used slates and pencils, and George soon found an aptitude for painting, always getting top marks. It was a skill which he developed again when he retired, and one of his paintings occupies a proud place in the present building.[28]

A scholarship to the grammar school would cover fees and rail fares, but nothing else, and Violet Morley was one who could not take advantage of her success for lack of money.[29]

In the 1920s Jack Spratley was taught in the Infants' classes successively by Miss Lacey, Miss Dunstone and Miss Ratcliffe the headmistress; then moving to the Senior Boys, whose headmaster was Harry Scofield (father of Paul, the actor). 11+ exams meant a few went to grammar school; the rest stayed and had old Harry ('Come out sir, and fetch my stick.'), who caned the boys; they used to rub orange peel on their hands to take the sting out. Games were played wherever there was space, for example the park at Danny for cricket.

Some of the private schools mentioned in an earlier chapter survived into the twentieth century. Olive Beckett went to Belle Vue at the top of Cuckfield Road, where Miss Heren and Mademoiselle Maury were the joint headmistresses, enforcing very strict discipline. This included not speaking to the children who went to the Church of England village school; as this was almost next door, with next-door neighbours going to and from school together, the girls took no notice. The lessons covered most subjects, and were very good, learning geography, French, grammar, tables and so on by heart. French sentences on the blackboard were absorbed while sewing and darning. The few boarders had to sit on chairs with a bar across the back to keep their backs straight. There were no school dinners for the day girls, so it was school and back twice a day.[30]

Other small schools were run in various houses around the village. One such was lower down Cuckfield Road, run by Miss Evans; a number of ironstone ink bottles were dug up in the garden as evidence of writing activity.

Before the Second World War, staff at the College had lived in a somewhat monastic environment. There only about 12 masters, practically none married. Those returning from war service felt it was no place for a family with young children. However, attitudes were changing, the College itself was expanding, and gradually masters were to be found living in various properties around the village.[31]

COMMUNICATIONS AND UTILITIES

Mr Cherriman used winter (closed in) and summer horse-buses, the last knife-board bus being specially painted to go in the Lord Mayor's Show in London. George Anscombe saw 'Tringy' the bus conductor fall off the platform into a puddle, having to blow his whistle to get the bus to stop. The tail-board proved to be dangerous in Ernie Cragg's carrier business too, one of his men falling into the road. Taxis were horse-cabs hired out by Mr Walker at the shoe shop. His horses also pulled the fire-engine, so when both were out on hire, the fire-engine had to be man-handled from its station to a fire at Washbrooks Farm. George's uncle built the fire station in 1905 [at the entrance to Holly Mews in the High Street]. When the fire bell was rung, both the Queen's Head (the Poacher) and the New Inn were ready to load beer for the men on to the appliance, depending on which way it went.

Plate 52.
Horse-bus at the White Horse with the Cherrimans, father and son, on the right.

Plate 53.   George Stoner filling water-cart before sprinkling the High Street.

Mr Stoner from the Lamb Inn used to fill up the water-cart from Mr Holman's memorial fountain, removed when the area was redesigned for the War Memorial, before watering the street to keep the High Street dust down in summer.[32] The roads were repaired by tipping on tar with grit and sand and then rolling it with a huge steam roller, the foreman having written authority to replenish the water supply from any householder. Although there was less traffic, there was more noise due to the iron wheels. When someone at the Mansion House was ill, straw was laid on the road to deaden the sounds of the carts.[33]

Plate 54. Another view of the fountain, with the Danny coach in the foreground.

The Mansion House is remembered by others. Ted Crane's father came to work there in 1909 as chauffeur/engineer to Arthur Black, Joan's father, who had bought 'a lovely Wolseley car with a very unusual bulb horn blown by the exhaust with a brass pedal on the floor through two organ pipes, very melodious'. Bringing Bishop Bell from Chichester one day he said 'Let the Bishop hear the Gabriel'; when Ted's father pushed the pedal he said 'I don't know Arthur, it doesn't sound all that angelic to me'. When the car was sold, Joan's brother Carey had the horn transferred to his sports car. Later the Mansion House had a Rolls Royce, still driven by Ted's father, who also serviced cars belonging to several other owners in the village. He also taught Joan Black to ride a motorbike. In the early days petrol was sent in 5 gallon tins by passenger train to be picked up at stations on long journeys. Steam cars were more reliable; when you put them away at night, you knew they would start in the morning.

Plate 55. Steamroller and gang on Cuckfield Road.

In time, Cherriman's horse-buses were replaced by motorised vehicles. Ted Crane was taught to drive by the Army during World War II, and when he returned to Hurst he joined Southdown, driving buses for the next 35 years, the last ten between Hurst and Hassocks.[34]

Plate 56. Laurence Cherriman in front of the first motor-bus in West Furlong Lane.

LEISURE

George Anscombe recalls Maypole dancing in the village playground, and going on farmer William Wood's wagons to the swings, boat-swings and helter-skelter at the Orchard Tea Gardens at Hassocks, followed by a Charlie Chaplin film at the Hassocks Hotel. Later, a travelling cinema would visit Hurst with such film serials as 'The Perils of Pauline'. After school at Miss Hannington's Scallywag Club the children made jigsaw puzzles, watch-stands and picture frames; they rang hand bells, playing Christmas Carols at places such as the Sunshine Home (Little Torch). There were circuses and fairs on the Laundry Field at the eastern end of the High Street, and the Chinese Gardens with its boating lake and swings. Later George joined the village band, playing flute and piccolo, while his brother played the clarinet. On Carnival Day the children collected a lantern on a pole at the New Inn to join the procession, getting a bottle of ginger beer and a Heathorn's bun when the lantern was returned. The boys hired bicycles from Chandler's for sixpence to cycle to Brighton for the football or to go swimming at Brill's

Baths in Pool Valley, never needing to padlock the bikes. In the Recreation Ground they put a stone in each corner of a handkerchief and threw it in the air, hoping to catch a bat. Another time, they threaded a cord through all the door knockers at Hampton Cottages, tying it to the end one; when No.1 answered the door it lifted the next knocker and so on, to Tommy Newman at No.9, and they all came out on the pavement talking to one another and looking for the culprits – all innocent fun, no mugging or vandalism.[35]

The village cricket club played matches at Danny on Wednesdays as well as Saturdays, with Simon Campion, one or two gentlemen farmers, Harry Scofield the school headmaster, Morley Tidey a round-arm bowler, and Fred King acting as umpire.

Jack Spratley's mother was first married to an Italian chef who drowned during World War I; his half-brother repaired old gramophones and sold boxes of needles at their house at the bottom of Cuckfield Road, but only after he had put his apron on and opened his little shop. Jack and his pals would take Fred Heathorn's 'plumb-heavy' scones to Church Field and soak them in his lemonade to make them soft enough to eat while they played with a couple of cocoa tins and a piece of string to listen to what was being said the other side of a 'castle' of hay.[36]

Around 1900 the Hurstpierpoint Bonfire Boys had their headquarters at the White Horse. Gordon Tulley recorded his memories of their celebrations.

> They held a procession of burning torches, pulling a burning barrel of tar through the streets on a three-wheeled trolley. Young men and women in fancy dress, carrying torches, marched in the procession with bands playing and fireworks being let off *en route*. The local Fire Brigade followed in readiness with the horse-drawn fire engine complete with hand-pumps. The shops were boarded up and gratings covered to prevent damage. Some of the fireworks were home-made and the most frightening of all we called the Lewes Rouser, that scared the life out of the ladies. When the procession arrived back at the White Horse, my father, who had ridden in front of the procession on horse-back, got off the horse and mounted a scaffold in front of the bonfire and read the Riot Act before the fire was lit. The Bonfire Boys would then throw their torches to set light to the bonfire. There was a grand display of fireworks set off by Mr George Withyman in the plat in

front of the Inn. At the rear, where stables used to be, a huge bonfire was lit at ten o'clock and the glow could be seen for miles around.   As the fire blazed away there was a supper of hot sausage rolls and baked potatoes in their skins awaiting them in the big room in the Inn. The next morning the High Street was littered with burnt-out fireworks, and the roadmen were kept busy clearing away the mess.   A new law of about 1917 stopped fireworks being set off in the highways, and the Society was disbanded.[37]

WARTIME

A Methodist Sunday School treat at Bexhill had to be cancelled at the last minute – the date was 4th August 1914. Instead the schoolgirls would darn socks for the convalescent soldiers at the Sunshine Home (Little Torch) and go to the drill hall to roll bandages. Entertainment included a play produced by the schoolteachers and performed around the district, in which Violet Morley was Robin Hood.[38]

The village War Memorial[39] stands by the crossroads on land owned by the Campion family, and was unveiled on St George's Day, Sunday 23 April 1922 by Colonel Campion. It records the names of 77 men 'who died for their country in the Great War 1914–1919' on the plinths of a large Celtic cross. The one in the Campion Chapel of Holy Trinity Church, in Derbyshire alabaster, lists 78 names,[40] the difference due to an addition to the later memorial, unveiled some four years later by the Colonel's widow, Mrs Gertrude Campion.[41] In a letter to the Rector in 1919 [42] she explained that the crucifix above had been brought to a Brighton curiosity shop by a soldier from the battlefields of France, and she hoped that it would eventually form part of the memorial. To both memorials the names of 17 men and one woman were added after the Second World War.

In the Second World War the College OTC and all the masters were in the Local Defence Volunteers (later the Home Guard). There were three defence points: Lock's Manor, College Lane, and near the fire station. There were regular anti-aircraft units in the parish, moving from place to place for security reasons.[43] Joan Black became an Air Raid Warden, and the post was in their house, with the siren on the roof. The shops kept going, selling what they could, with plenty of vegetables available.

To help the war effort, scrap was collected, rose-hips and acorns were gathered, the grass verges cut for hay, and many people kept pigs. Sayers Common schoolchildren helped the land-girls with George Hole's harvest. Farm-hands were so few that a boy of five to eight years of age was safely strapped to the binder immediately after school to relieve the man who had to hand-milk the herd.[44]

Canadian troops, Commandos, Land Army girls, school and business evacuees were all accommodated in the village which was designated a 'reception area'.[45]

Girls from Raine's Foundation Grammar School in East London arrived in September 1939 with their teachers, most of the Raine's boys going first to Brighton and then to west Surrey. Initially the girls had lessons at the Chinese Gardens Hotel (later the Pierpoint), but subsequently Holmcroft (South Lodge) in South Avenue was rented and used as classrooms. Belmont House was a hostel for some of the girls, and school lunches were also served there. Boys from Keeton's Road L.C.C. Secondary School in Bermondsey also came to Hurst, having lessons in various buildings around the village. Hurstpierpoint College, apart from providing science lessons for the Raine's girls, took in 90 boys from two houses of Westminster School, 42 accommodated at the College, the rest billeted in the village, other Westminster boys going to Lancing. Margaret Haugh, the headmistress of Raine's, wrote:

> When the war is over, and we return to our own place, we shall be able to say in all truth that we were never made to feel as strangers in a strange land, and we shall look back on evacuation with ever-pleasant recollections of our sojourn in this Downland village in 'Sussex by the Sea'.

Villagers billeting the children were paid 10s 6d for one evacuee and 8s 6d for each extra child, to cover full board and lodging. In 1941 a 2lb loaf of bread cost 4d, a pint of milk about the same, while butter and cheese were 1s 7d and 1s 1d per pound respectively.

Land Army girls, some local, some evacuees, replaced men on several local farms and nurseries. While Hurst men were being called up to serve elsewhere, soldiers from the French Canadian Regiment de la Chaudiere and the Seaforth Highlanders Regiment of Canada were billeted here, at Danny, Belmont School and in Hurst Wickham. They would go into Hurst Wickham Post Office when officially on guard duty at Wickham Place, carrying fixed bayonets, to buy cigarettes or whatever else they wanted.[46] British Commandos carried out some of their training on the Danny estate, and the village received from their C.O. 'thanks to the people of Hurstpierpoint who uncomplainingly billeted the men under my command'.

The cellars of the brewery and the adjacent Sussex Arms were used as an air raid shelter for the children from the school and the Somers Clark Institute in Manor Road, while the empty premises above, together with other nearby rooms, were used by Slazengers. When their London factory was bombed the Hurstpierpoint buildings were used to make rifle butts and snow shoes for the Russian front as well as for reconditioning tennis balls.

Only one casualty of direct enemy action occurred. In February 1943 a bomb exploded near the house in Cuckfield Road of the Reverend B T Lamb, the Evangelical Free Church minister, killing his four-year old daughter Heather.

Through all this the Hurst WVS helped to organise the billeting of over 1,000 adults and children. There was, of course, an element of compulsion involved, and some official contribution towards the cost was made, but the words of the headmistress of Raine's School and of the Commando officer confirm that, when the need was recognised, Hurst was indeed 'kind and charitable'.

Plate 57. Ribbett's Cottages with criss-crossed sticky paper on the windows to reduce the risk of flying glass during air raids.

NOTES AND REFERENCES

Much of the source material used in this chapter comes from tape-recorded conversations with several long-term residents of the parish. Space makes it impossible to include all of their reminiscences, but we are very grateful to each and every one of them for their help. Specific research was also carried out by Janet Johnson and Miriam Patrick, and this is acknowledged in the references below.

1. Conversation with George Anscombe 5 November 1997.
2. Packham R: personal communication.
3. Conversation with Peter Nelson 25 November 1998.
4. Conversations with Olive Beckett 4 February & 25 March 1998.
5. Conversation with Nora Talbot 5 June 2000.
6. Anscombe; Conversation with Phyllis Poundsbery 5 July 2000.
7. Blake.
8. Typescript memories of Violet Morley (nd).
9. Conversation with Jack Spratley 22 September 1999.
10. Talbot.
11. Blake.
12. Beckett.
13. Norris J (1973): *Notes on Holy Trinity Church*, 19.
14. Anscombe.
15. Beckett.
16. *Ibid.*
17. Conversation with George Lambert 26 January 1999.
18. *Ibid.*; Poundsbery.
19. Beckett.
20. *Ibid.*
21. Poundsbery.
22. Ray Packham with Spratley.
23. *Ibid.*; conversation with Ted Crane 22 April 1998.
24. Spratley.
25. Morley.
26. Conversation with Joan Black 15 July 1997.
27. Anscombe.
28. Morley.
29. *Ibid.*
30. *Ibid.*
31. Beckett.
32. Lambert 5 February 1999.
33. Anscombe; conversation with Margaret Georgeson 24 July 2000.
34. Morley.

35. Crane; Anscombe.
36. *Ibid.*; Morley.
37. Tulley G (1967): Old Hurstpierpoint – Gordon Tulley Remembers, *Parish Magazine* November 1967.
38. Packham with Spratley.
39. Morley.
40. Research on the War Memorials carried by Miriam Patrick.
41. The additional name is that of Cornelius, son of Joseph King, bricklayer from Ribbetts and his wife Sarah.
42. 19 September 1926.
43. Parish Magazine 1919.
44. Blake.
45. Research on the evacuees carried out by Janet Johnson.
46. Poundsberry

GLOSSARY

advowson	Right of presentation to a church benefice.
agist	To pay for pasture, normally on a headage basis.
andirons	Pair of bars with hooks for supporting roasting spit.
appropriator	Ecclesiastical body, other than parish priest, with rights to tithes.
badger	1. Licensed dealer in grain.
	2. Pauper required to wear badge.
bailiff	Agent of lord of manor.
beadle	Parish messenger, crier, assistant to constable.
bede roll	List of church benefactors.
Borough English	Custom of inheritance by youngest son.
box iron	Flat iron with space for hot coals.
bride ale	Church function to help newly married to set up home.
broadcloth	Cloth two yards in width.
buckram	Linen stiffened with gum.
bush	Sign outside alehouse to indicate that wine is for sale.
bushel.	See separate lists of weights, measures and coinage.
buttery	1. Ale store.
	2. Cool room for provisions; tableware.
calico	Unprinted cotton.
cambric	Fine linen or cotton imitation.
card	Implement for combing wool or flax before spinning.
cartulary	Charters of an estate.
chaldron	See separate list of weights and measures.
chamber	Upper room.
chattels	Moveable goods including animals.
chevage	Annual payment to lord of manor by serfs.
church ales	Forerunner of parish garden party.
churchyard rails	Fence maintained by owners of particular property.
clapper	Raised platform or stones for passage through floodwater in road.
close	Enclosed piece of land.
close studding	Narrow panels between studs (vertical timbers).
close-stool	Commode.
coffer	Chest for money, valuables.
copyhold(er).	Customary tenancy of the lord of the manor, converted to freehold 1925.
Cordwainer	Shoemaker.
corrody	Board provided by monasteries to benefactors.

court leet	Held in manor or hundred, with jurisdiction over petty offences and civil matters.
crape	Wool for shrouds.
cresset	Iron lamp, sometimes suspended on a pole.
croft	Enclosed ground near house for arable or pasture use.
curtilage	Court or yard attached to house.
custumal	Written collection of manor customs.
damask	Patterned wool, linen or cotton.
demesne	Land kept for use of lord of manor.
denshiring	Paring turf or stubble, leaving it to dry, burning and spreading ashes to improve soil.
deodand	Article causing violent death, offered to God in expiation.
dowlais	Coarse calico.
drage/ dredge	Mixed cereals.
ell	See separate lists of weights, measures and coinage.
enfeoffment	Land in trusteeship.
engross	To buy corn wholesale to hoard and retail against rising prices.
engrossing	Acquisition of land in one ownership.
entail	Restriction of land inheritance, including right of disposal.
escheat	Legal reversion of land to the King or lord of the manor on tenant's death without heirs.
essoin	Excuse for absence from manor court.
farm	To let land, tithes, rents for fixed period.
farthing	See separate lists of weights, measures and coinage.
felloe	Segment of rim of wheel.
feoffment	Granting of a fee for conveyance of land.
field	Large area of arable land divided for crop rotation.
fifteenth	Tax for special purpose of one-fifteenth of income.
flitch	Side of animal, salted and cured.
flock	Wool refuse used for stuffing.
forestall	Buy food privately before market or fair.
frankpledge	The pledge of a tithing for the good behaviour of all over 14 years of age.
free bench	Widow's one-third of husband's income.
furlong	Coarse woollen cloth.
fustian	Sub-division of arable field; see separate lists of weights, measures and coinage.
gallon	See separate lists of weights, measures and coinage.
garner	Small corn-barn.

garth	Yard or garden attached to house.
gate, gait	Right of pasture for one animal.
gavelkind	Equal inheritance.
gill	See separate lists of weights, measures and coinage.
gridiron	Grid placed near fire for roasting.
grist	Corn to be ground at one time; inferior corn.
gutterlog(ge)	Drain made from hollowed out log.
hayward	Responsible for hedges and controlling open-field cultivation.
headborough	Deputy constable.
heriot	Paid to lord of manor on death of tenant, best beast.
hide	60-100 acres land.
Holland cloth	Fine linen.
homage	Loyalty to lord of manor; assembled tenants.
hovel	Outhouse for corn, farm implements; low-roofed, open-fronted cattle shed.
huckerback	Rough surfaced linen, eg towelling.
husbandman	Tenant farmer.
hutch	Large wooden storage box.
imprimis	Firstly.
impropriator	Layman with right to tithes.
indenture	Contract between two parties, each keeping half of document cut along indented line.
iron box	Box-iron with source of heat in cavity.
joined	Made by a joiner, eg stool, bed.
journeyman	Waged artisan who has completed apprenticeship.
kail pot	Cooking pot for broth.
keeler	Large tub for brewing.
kerchief	Cloth to cover head.
kersey	Coarse, ribbed, woollen cloth.
kettle	Deep cooking vessel.
kneading trough	For kneading dough or butter.
knobstick wedding	One imposed on pregnant woman by churchwardens.
L.B. & S.C.R.	London, Brighton and South Coast Railway.
Lady Day	25 March quarter day.
laine	Open field.
lammas land	Common land for part of the year.
latchetts	Shoe fastenings.
latten	Metal alloy resembling brass.
lead	Water container.
lease	Wheat free of impurities.
lees	Winter-feed for cattle.

liberty	Group of manors where the lord, not the sheriff, has jurisdiction.
linseywoollsey	Mixed fabric: wool/linen, wool/flax, inferior wool.
linchet	Turf between arable strips; terracing.
maslin	1. Mixed corn; 2. Brass-like metal; 3. Kettle made from (2).
merchet	Payment to lord when beast sold, daughter married or son sent to school.
mercy	Amercement, fine.
messuage	Dwelling and outbuildings, garden.
Michaelmas	29 September quarter day.
month's mind	Memorial service a month after burial.
mortmain	Non-transferable bequest.
mow	A rick or heap.
nail	See separate lists of weights and measures.
nuncupative	Verbal (will).
outfangthief	Right of lord to pursue a thief beyond his own manor.
owler	Smuggler (especially of 'exported' goods).
oxgang	Half-yardland.
panakin	Very small pan.
pancheon	Large cask.
pannage	Payment for pasturing pigs.
peck	See separate lists of weights, measures and coinage.
peculiar	Ecclesiastical area exempt from bishop's control.
peel	1. Square fortified tower; 2. Paddle for placing dough in baker's oven.
perch	See separate lists of weights, measures and coinage.
pie powder court	For summary justice at markets and fairs.
pintado	Coloured chintz cotton.
pipe rolls	Sheriff's audit records.
ploughland	Area cultivable by eight-ox plough, four yardlands, eight oxgangs; 80-200 acres.
pluralism	Holding of more than one benefice.
posnet	Cooking pot.
possett	Hot milk with ale or wine, sugar and spices.
post-mill	Windmill on post to allow rotation to face wind direction.
powdering tub	For salting or pickling meat.
presentment	Statement on oath at church or civil court.
pricket	Candlestick.

quarter	1. Division of large parish; 2. Eight bushels (see separate lists of weights, measures and coinage).
quartern	Quarter-peck (see separate lists of weights, measures and coinage).
quern	Hand mill.
quit claim	Release of legal rights.
regrate	Buying corn for resale.
relict	Widow(er).
rood	1. Quarter acre; 2. Eight yards; 3. Cross of Christ (especially over chancel entrance).
rotulet	Small roll of parchment.
scutage	Payment to lord *in lieu* of military service.
seisin	Right to possession.
selions	Parallel strips of arable in open field.
serge	Twilled worsted or worsted/wool.
skim(m)er	Brass ladle for removing scum from cooking.
smock mill	Windmill fixed to ground (*cf.* post mill).
solar	Private upstairs room (for ladies).
spud	Small spade for cutting weed roots.
stallage (stolledge)	1. Fee for fair stall; 2. Support for barrels.
stint	1. Limit on number animals on common; 2. End of selion (*q.v.*).
tallage	Arbitrary tax or levy.
tally	Stick notched as record of money transaction, then split in two, each party retaining half in order to resolve any subsequent disagreement.
teg	Sheep in its second year.
tenant right	Occupier's entitlement to compensation on quitting a farm for cultivation; hay, straw, etc. left for incoming tenant.
tenement	Holding of house and land.
tenter	Wooden frame to stretch cloth to dry without shrinking.
terrier	Inventory of land (especially church) possessions.
Tester	Canopy over a (four-poster) bed.
thrum	1. Unwoven warp-threads; 2. Coarse or waste yarn; 3. Tool for retaining malt in brewing tub.
tithe	Percentage of produce to maintain parish priest.
tithing	Group of householders, originally ten, within Hundred.

tithingman	Petty constable.
toft	Site of house in village, especially one with rights of common.
tow	Hemp fibre refuse.
treen	Wooden bowls and platters.
trencher	Flat platter for meat.
tup	Ram.
turbary	Common right of cutting turf or other fuel.
twitten	Narrow path between walls or hedges leading from one street to another.
tyre	Flax.
vallence	Curtain round bed.
vestry, closed	Incumbent, churchwardens and substantial land-occupiers acting as the precursor of the parish council.
vestry, open	Meeting of parish governing body, which all could attend to deal with local matters.
vill	Norman French name for township.
villein	Land-holding serf.
virgate	Quarter of a hide (*q.v.*), 15-60 acres.
wain	Large cart.
watch and ward	Patrolling town by night and day respectively.
waywarden	Responsible for highway maintenance.
wether	Castrated male sheep.
wista	Yardland, virgate (*q.v.*).
witnesses	Godparents.
yardland	20-50 acres, virgate, wista (*q.v.*)
yeoman	Owner-occupier; small farmer.

WEIGHTS AND MEASURES

Weights

16 drams	=	1 ounce		
16 ounces	=	1 pound	=	454 grams
2lbs 4oz (approx)	=	1 kilogram		
8lbs (beef)	=	1 nail		
14 pounds	=	1 stone		
28 pounds	=	1 quarter		
4 quarters	=	1 hundredweight (112 pounds)		
20 hundredweights	=	1 ton (2240 pounds)		

Volumes
Liquids

4 gills	=	1 pint	=	0.57 litre (approx)
2 pints	=	1 quart		
4 quarts	=	1 gallon		

Dry goods

4 pecks	=	1 bushel
8 bushels	=	1 quarter
5 quarters	=	1 load
36 bushels	=	1 chaldron

Wool

7 pounds	=	1 clove
4 cloves	=	1 todd
6 ½ todds	=	1 wey (182 pounds)
2 weys	=	1 sack
240 pounds	=	1 pack

Hay

1 truss	=	36 pounds
1 load	=	38 trusses

Corn (average)

1 bushel wheat	=	60 pounds
1 bushel barley	=	47 pounds
1 bushel oats	=	40 pounds

Linear Measure

12 inches	=	1 foot
3 feet	=	1 yard
39.37 inches	=	1 metre
5 ½ yards	=	1 rod, pole or perch
1100 yards (approx)	=	1 kilometre
4 poles	=	1 chain (22 yards)
10 chains	=	1 furlong
8 furlongs	=	1 mile (1760 yards)
3 miles	=	1 league

3 barleycorns	=	1 inch
3 inches	=	1 palm
4 inches	=	1 hand

9 inches	=	1 span
18 inches	=	1 cubit
45 inches	=	1 ell

Square Measure

40 square poles	=	1 rood	
4 roods	=	1 acre (4840 sq.yds)	= 0.4 hectare (approx)
640 acres	=	1 square mile	

Cloth

2 1/4 inches	=	1 nail
4 nails	=	1 quarter (9 inches)
4 quarters	=	1 yard
5 quarters	=	1 ell

COINAGE

Farthing (1/4d)	=	one quarter of a penny		
Halfpenny (1/2d) =	half a penny			
Penny (1d)				
Shilling (1/-)	=	12 pence (12d)	=	5p
Florin (2/-)	=	2 shillings (2s)	=	10p
Halfcrown (2/6d)	=	2 shillings 6 pence		
Ten shillings (10/-)	=	120 pence	=	50p
One pound (£1.0.0)	=	240 pence	=	£1
One guinea	=	£1 pound 1shilling		
One mark	=	13 shillings 4 pence (13s.4d)		

INDEX

Personal names are often spelt differently. Therefore it has been decided to list all similar names together

Abberton, 134
Acts of Parliament
    Conventicle, 191
    Gilbert's 1782, 164
    Poor Law Amendment, 138
    Settlement, 139, 155
    Toleration, 199
air raid shelter, 373
Alehouses, 232, 355
Allen
    George, 306
Alwin
    William, 82
Anscombe
    George, 303, 330, 331, 356, 360,
        361, 363, 364, 365, 369, 374,
        375
Apprenticeships, 143
Ashby
    Irene, 307
Ashfold
    John, 212
Atwood
    William, 306
Avery
    Nathaniel, 63, 64, 80, 119, 251
    Thomas, 194, 235
    William, 235
Bailey
    Mrs M A, 312
    William W, 312
Baker
    A J, 298
    Dot & Peter, 306
    George, 312
Ball
    John, 176

Bannister
    Charles, 307
Barker
    Ann & Elizabeth, 339
Barnes
    Robert, 226
Barron
    S, 306
Barry
    Charles, 45
Beach
    Henry, 210
Beache
    Ralph, 30
Beadle, 238
Beard, 37, 62, 116, 185, 195, 196,
    235, 350
    Daniel, 63
    Nicholas, 194
Bearstakes, 132
Beckett
    Olive, 358, 359, 365, 374
Bedlam Street, 178
Beeching
    Henry, 298
    Samuel, 287, 298
Belle Vue, 339, 365
bells, 20, 39, 41, 48, 93, 101, 117,
    243, 266, 369
Bennet
    George, 210
Bennett
    Geeorge, 322
Berdsey
    Mrs S, 314
Bevan
    Richard, 135

Bieldside, 119
Bignall
  A J & Son, 304
Bishop's Place, 281
Blossams Well, 110
Boakes
  Gordon, 307
Board
  Thomas, 232
Booker
  J, 313
Borrer
  Canon, 329
  Carey Hampton, 44, 45, 48, 50,
    64, 135, 204, 208
  Nathaniel, 44, 50, 79, 101, 103,
    111, 135, 136, 148, 209, 239,
    257, 341
  William, 50, 51, 52, 63, 120, 127,
    231, 309
Borrer Chapel, 51
Botting
  Allen, 298
  Frank, 298
Bourton
  John, 84
Bower, Bishop, 40, 105
Brand's Dial, 47
Bransden
  H, 308
Breachland, 4, 273
Breechlands, 281
brewery, 278
British and Foreign Schools Society,
  322
Broad
  Harry, 298
  Hortace, 274
  Richard, 268, 287, 298
Brown, 96, 129
  George, 361
  Henry & George, 311

Jane, 311
Buckwell
  Edmund, 127
  Susan, 37, 86
Bullfinch Cottages, 111
Bullfinch Lane, 248
Burnett
  Francis, 313
Burrell
  Timothy, 124
Burt, 117, 130, 178
Burtenshaw
  William, 110
Butcher
  Richard, 221
Buttinghill Hundred, 60
Byne
  Stephen, 127
Callagan
  J & D, 307
Campion
  Charles, 323
  Henry, 133, 177, 320
  William, 44, 46, 47, 51, 57, 62,
    63, 68, 102, 177, 180, 210,
    257, 259, 261, 268, 309, 320,
    322, 335, 340, 359, 370, 371
Card's Place, 128
Carter
  Miss M M, 314
  Miss P, 314
  Mrs C E, 313
  Mrs E M, 314
Cattle Plague, 260, 330
Chalkers Lane, 249, 251
Chandler, 91
  George, 91
Channing
  Edward, 313
Chatfield, 124
  E, 307
  Richard, 141

cheese making, 278
Cherriman
    Laurence, 369
    William, 97, 365
Chichester House, 88, 119, 360
Chinese Gardens, 103, 326, 336,
    339, 352, 369, 372
Chinese Lane, 249
Church House, 42, 118
Clarke
    Jas, 304
Clayden
    Henry P, 315
Cobbe
    Thomas, 18, 30
Cockbill
    William, 307
Colby
    William, 111
common, 15, 16, 27, 38, 39, 62, 66,
    87, 219, 224, 230, 231, 354, 380,
    381
Compton
    Bishop, 36, 213
constable, 21, 88, 197, 220, 221,
    223, 224, 226, 231, 376, 378, 381
Cooper Samson, 177
Corke
    Charity, 37
Couchman
    J E, 6
    Mr, 349
Coulstock
    Thomas, 228, 229
Court Bushes, 16, 63, 253, 269, 286
Courthope
    Barbara, 133
    Peter, 40, 57, 61, 133, 199, 222,
        232, 252, 350
Courtness
    George, 91
    William, 38, 39, 126, 134, 148

Cowdrays, 115
Cowdry
    Cordelia, 115
    Richard, 115
    Thomas, 115
Cox
    E A, 311
Crane
    Ted, 362
Croskey
    Stephen, 143, 155
Crosskey
    Stephen, 82
Crouch House, 110, 111
Croweher
    Thomas, 29
Culver Croft, 310
Curd
    F A, 306
Curtis
    John, 302
Cuss
    E C, 299
    John, 299
Cutler's Brook, 90
Cutlers Brook, 4, 250
Dacre
    Thomas, 16, 44, 226
Danny, 6, 9, 15, 16, 23, 53, 56, 58,
    59, 61, 62, 68, 76, 94, 97, 111,
    118, 119, 122, 192, 193, 194,
    226, 237, 252, 257, 258, 259,
    260, 261, 265, 266, 267, 269,
    276, 285, 309, 320, 326, 327,
    335, 337, 340, 356, 357, 360,
    364, 370, 373
    Estate, 8
    Park, 4
Danworth Brook, 249
Davey
    D & T, 301
    Richard, 52, 90, 152, 204, 236

Denman
    Dr Peggy, 363
Dodson
    Christopher, 39
    Jeremiah, 39, 40, 41, 42, 43, 44,
        47, 62, 64, 94, 118, 126, 145,
        173, 177, 276, 319, 350
    John, 39, 43, 64
Domesday, 4, 12, 13, 23, 25, 26, 53,
    79, 221
Dorkings
    John, 308
Down House, 119, 235
drainage, 175, 215, 253, 282
Dunstall
    John, 118
    Thomas, 87, 118
Dunstalls, 87, 118, 311
Dunstone, Miss, 364
Eardenstowe, 295
Eastern House, 363
Edgerley
    East (Big), 62
    West, 62
Ellis
    Charles, 300
    William, 224
Emigration, 165
Erskine Nursery, 273
Evangelical Church, 213
Fairlie
    S J, 315
Farm
    Danworth Brook. See . See . See
        . See . See . See . See . See .
        See . See . See . See
Farms
    Clayton Wickham, 277
    Coldharbour, 6
    Danworth, 209, 285
    Deanhouse, 277
    Gatehpouse, 277

Highfields, 277
Kents, 131
Malthouse, 277
New House, 132
Newhouse, 256, 278, 279
North End, 252
Randolphs, 8, 9, 11, 61, 130, 131,
    250, 265, 266, 268, 269, 298,
    304
Tott, 63, 64, 74, 81, 90, 94, 115,
    117, 130, 131, 134, 149, 221,
    230, 249, 250, 251, 253, 257,
    276, 277, 278, 345
Wanbarrow, 114
Washbrooks, 8, 10, 14, 15, 57,
    62, 71, 72, 250, 261, 265, 266,
    268, 298, 365
Wortleford, 59, 64, 230, 249, 276
fire engine, 188
fire station, 365
firemarks, 123
Fitch
    Walter, 298, 301
Fowle
    Henry, 129
Fox
    George, 171, 194, 200
Franklin
    Theo, 359
French
    Henry, 311
Friendly Societies, 234
Funnell
    G & Son, 307
Furlong House, 135
Gander
    Ann, 146
Garrett
    Albert, 315
Gatland, 362
    R, 306
Geer

Albert, 286
Edwin, 273
Gladman
  P W, 307
Goring
  George, 24, 34, 56, 57, 133, 192,
    229, 237
Gorringe
  John, 297
Gosling
  Jesse, 300
Grape Vine Cottage, 129
Grasmere, 17, 64, 132, 251
Gravely and Son, 302
Graves
  American War of Independence,
    48
  Victoria Cross, 48
Green
  Dr Ralph, 363
Greenaway
  William, 154, 234
Greensand, 3
  Way, 6
Grindrod
  D, 310
Grover
  John, 197, 198, 199, 320
Gurney
  Harriet, 167, 359
Hallett
  John B, 297
Ham Farm, 8
Hamilton Lodge, 339
Hamper
  John, 129
  Thomas, 129
Hampton Cottages, 297
Hampton Lodge, 135
Hampton Lodge Mission, 213
Hannington
  Charles, 49, 51, 135, 208, 324,

    354
  James, 26, 35, 37, 39, 41, 49, 50,
    54, 84, 94, 115, 151, 152, 172,
    178, 184, 189, 268, 285
  Samuel, 142
Hardings, 127, 128, 320
Harman
  Richard, 210
Hart
  John, 90, 257, 290, 318, 319, 320
Harvey
  Harold, 206, 269, 270, 274, 279,
    282, 283
Haselgrove
  Thomas, 228
Hastings
  James de, 26
Hautboys, 27
  Peter of, 268
Hayes
  Mrs J, 308
Hazelgrove
  Richard, 85
Hazlegrove
  John, 165
Heafield
  J R, 304
Heathorn
  F, 305
  Fred, 362, 370
Herbal remedies, 114, 182, 186
Herrings Stream, 4, 248, 249, 251
Herriott
  Richard, 127
Hider
  Henry, 176, 203, 204, 206
High Hatch Lane, 253
Hind
  Edward, 197
  John, 197
Hippisley
  William, 229, 237

Hitchener
  Elizabeth, 338, 339
Holden
  F, 307
Holder
  James, 88
Hole
  Amos, 96
  Edward, 96
  Fanny, 281
  George, 280, 282, 283, 286, 372
  John, 314
  Sidney, 107, 114, 232, 270, 278,
    282, 314
  Thomas, 96
  William, 314
Hollamby
  W, 300
Hollingham
  Edward, 118
Holman
  Constantine, 188
  Henry, 134, 188, 273, 331, 338,
    367
Home Cottage, 117, 118
Homewood
  A H, 314
Howard Lodge, 135
Humphries
  T, 307
Hundred of Buttinghill, 221
HundredButtinghill, 93
Huntingdon
  Selina, Countess of, 210
Hurst Brewery, 6, 348, 349
Hurst Grammar School, 337
Hurstpierpoint College, 9, 63, 175,
  251, 340, 372
inventories
  Marchant, Thomas, 86
  William Webb, 75

Jago
  S H, 312
Jenkin
  Horace, 304
  W I, 304
Jenner
  Edward, 40, 144, 177, 182, 268
Jennings
  Charles, 299
Jobs Corner, 248
Jordan
  William, 32, 120
Jupp
  George, 302
Juxon
  William, 122
Killingbeck
  Ann, 197
  Humphrey, 194, 197, 199
Knight
  Jesse, 129
Knowles Tooth, 64, 80, 90, 130
Knowls Tooth, 63, 176
Lacey, Miss, 364
Lamb Inn, 249
Lamb Platt, 75, 293, 327, 357
Lambert
  Thomas, 226
Land Army, 372, 373
Langton Lane, 12, 79, 80, 90, 109,
  110, 111, 248, 271, 286
Latchetts, 63, 230, 267, 283, 357
Leppard
  John, 82
Letchford
  Leonard, 35, 39, 41, 42, 80, 142,
    193, 194, 195, 196, 197, 198,
    200, 350
Lewes Priory, 6, 15, 19, 23, 24, 27,
  29, 56, 94, 102, 104, 157, 159,
  180, 195, 227, 292, 318, 319, 354

Lindfield
  William, 64
Little Park, 16, 17, 42, 49, 51, 57,
  61, 62, 76, 97, 122, 123, 124,
  125, 126, 135, 141, 173, 208,
  209, 235, 249, 276, 283, 285,
  292, 322, 324, 358
Loyalist Associations, 218
Luxford
  Arthur, 231
  George, 115
  Mary, 196
  Richard, 115
  Thomas, 131, 141, 195, 200, 226,
    231, 346
Luxfords
  Thomas, 32, 58
Mabbitt
  Albert, 312
Malthouse Lane, 15, 80, 131, 251,
  253
Manor cottages, 167
Manor road chapel, 206
Manors
  Leigh, 63
  Tottington, 63
Mansion House, 62, 120, 121, 122,
  135, 175, 195, 340, 363, 367
Marchant
  Elizabeth, 187
  G, 307
  John, 177
  Mary, 199
  Peter, 115
  Thomas, 37, 39, 40, 41, 47, 52,
    54, 61, 62, 64, 71, 72, 84, 85,
    86, 94, 100, 101, 104, 105,
    106, 115, 117, 119, 123, 124,
    126, 127, 130, 136, 137, 141,
    142, 153, 156, 159, 173, 174,
    176, 177, 180, 182, 185, 186,
    188, 198, 200, 235, 268, 292,

    306, 311, 318, 319, 320, 350,
    351
  William, 123
market gardening, 266, 272, 280,
  285
Marshall
  James, 298
  Jonathan, 298
  Richard, 33, 101, 106
Martha & Mary Guild, 359
Masters
  George, 301
Masters and Tulley, 301
mathematical tiles, 115, 119, 122
Matthew
  James, 195
milk yields, 284
Miller
  Cl, 299
millers
  Avery, Nathaniel, 80
  Ede, Antony, 80
Millers
  Bishop, George, 80
  Broad, Robert, 78, 80
  Cooley, George, 78
  Harraden, Edward, 80
  Harris, Stephen, 78
  Henty, Philip, 78
  Mitchel, James, 80
  Oliver, John, 80
  Packham, Benjamin, 81
  Whiting, John, 78
mills
  water, 4
  wind, 78
Mills
  Bolney, 4
  Cobbs, 4, 64, 78, 79, 261
  Hammonds, 4
  Herrings, 4
  Hookers, 4

Leigh, 4
Leigh/Lye, 81
Ruckford, 4, 63, 80
Mitchell, 96, 129
John, 96
Mitten
Flora, 309
William, 309, 313
Mogrumb Bank, 230
monitorial system, 330
Monk Bretton, Lord, 64, 276
Moore
Mr & Mrs, 315
Thomas, 127, 129
Morfee
Peter, 134, 158, 161, 188
Morley
Herbert, 237
N, 305
Morrell
William, 227
Morris
David & Brenda, 310
Mr Faccenda, 363
Mr Prince, 359
Mr Simms, 360
Muzzall
Abel, 111
Abraham, 111, 126, 127, 147
Henry, 52
Joseph, 224
Muzzell
Abraham, 40, 85, 86, 319, 320,
351
Naldritts, 257
Napoleon, 68, 103
Nelson
Peter, 285
New Inn, 91, 100, 103, 121, 132,
208, 234, 257, 293, 322, 327,
329, 340, 350, 351, 365, 369
New Way Lane, 6, 15, 19, 68, 132,

149, 244, 251, 252, 253, 357
Newman
Tommy, 359, 370
Walter, 297
Norfolk House, 135
North End Mission, 213
Norton, 18, 32, 58, 298
George, 229
Richard, 29, 86
Thomas, 43, 159, 350
William, 235
Norton House, 135
Nortonbury, 301, 310, 313
Nye
John, 306
Thomas, 160
O' Neale
Walter, 310
Oaklands Park, 134
Osbourn
Francis, 96
Oxenham
F, 295
Packham
Charles, 54, 80, 81, 82, 106, 271,
357, 374, 375
Henry, 268
Pakyns, 15, 16, 44, 59, 76, 79, 103,
109, 111, 119, 120, 226, 248,
285, 357
William, 110
parish constable, 223
Parker
Henry, 300
Peacock
Miss J, 315
Pembery
Dr Edsel, 363
Peskett, 261, 271
Clement, 295
George, 301
Norman, 295

Thomas, 279, 301, 361
William, 79, 82
Pest House, 154, 178
Philpott
Fanny, 314
Pickhams, 253
Pierce
William, 212
Pierpoint
Simon de, 12, 16, 24, 26
Pigwidgeon, 110
Plundered Ministers, 193
Pointin
John, 47, 117, 235, 319, 320
Policeman's Lane, 115
Pond Lye, 81, 84
Poor Law Amendment Act, 139,
164
Poor Rate
1629, 141
Poundsbery
Harold, 360
Miss, 313
Phyllis, 361, 374
Powell
W, 314
Prince, Mr, 302
Providence Chapel, 208
public houses
Black Lion, 352
Duke of York, 354
Jolly Sportsman, 354
King's Head, 354
Lamb, 350
Magpie, 354
Queen's Head, 352
Red Lion, 348
Royal Oak, 350
Sussex Arms, 348
Swan, 350
public Houses
The Oak, 348

Public houses
White Horse, 347
Randall
William, 212
Randell
John, 296
Sarah, 312
William, 296, 312
Randiddles, 358
Randolphs, 4
Randulfslonde, 27
Ratcliffe, Miss, 364
Rawlinson
George, 166, 332, 333, 334, 335,
340
Resale Price Maintenance, 300
Richardson
A J, 298
Rigge
Ambrose, 191, 195, 196, 197,
198, 200
River
Adur, 4
Roberts
Avery, 63, 64, 68, 142, 322, 323
Robins
E, 302
Robinson
David, 306
Rooke
Thomas, 89
Rowland
H W, 300
Royal Oak, 233
Russell
A R, 306
Sandfield House, 149
Sandfields, 230
Savege
Richard, 29
Sayers
William, 120, 224

Sayers Common, 3, 14, 15, 46, 48, 49, 63, 68, 96, 97, 132, 142, 212, 213, 244, 252, 254, 265, 281, 283, 314, 322, 323, 332, 333, 348, 354, 364, 372
Scofield, Harry, 364
seed production, 285
Sendall
  Henry, 302, 322
Sewage, 175, 253, 282
Shaw
  Minhard, 39
  Robert, 44
  Sir John, 4, 37, 39, 44, 237
Shaw-Brooke
  J Kenward, 44
singing gallery, 37
slaughterhouses, 269
Small Pox Hospital, 178
Smith, 130
  Charles, 119
  Henry ('Dog'), 41, 42, 141, 142, 318
  John E, 311
  Robert, 127
smuggling, 203, 220, 235
Snashall
  John, 185, 197, 199, 234
Soale
  Philip, 120
Speenhamland, 163
Spotted Cow, 110
Spratley, 129
  D, 304
  J, 304
  Jack, 148, 345, 358, 361, 362, 364, 370, 374, 375
St Christopher's Home, 167
St George's Church, 50, 55, 209
St George's Laundry, 362
St George's Church, 251
St John's College, 46, 49

St John's Common, 66, 87, 149, 251, 253
Stenning
  Dick, 302
Stonepound, 6, 10, 25, 93, 178, 244, 350
Stoner
  George, 350
street lights, 254
Streete
  Humphrey, 35
Swale
  Christopher, 32, 33, 34, 36, 47, 56, 80, 135, 192, 193, 195, 222, 224, 229, 230, 237
Swayne
  Anne, 122
Swing Riots, 69, 238
Talbot
  Nora, 6, 8, 283, 358, 374
Talmey
  Richard, 311
  Ted Crane, 367, 368, 374
Thair
  Walter, 298
The Creamery, 304
The Oak, 348
Tilley
  John, 305
Tithe Act of 1836, 43
Tithe Commutation Act, 70
tollhouses, 244
Townfield House, 309
Transportation, 237
Treeps, 117, 309
Trumpkins, 96, 127, 128, 129, 210, 211, 297, 298, 300, 305, 308, 311, 312, 352
turnpike, 61, 93, 145, 220, 242–244, 246, 248, 249, 250, 253, 324, 350, 356
Twiner

Leslie, 295
Unwins
  Henry, 79, 82
  Thomas, 82
Urry
  John, 28
Vallance
  James, 212
Voyce
  Edgar, 362
  Mrs I P, 308
Wadey
  Thomas, 347
wages, 69, 103, 163, 164, 222, 238,
  257, 258, 268, 277
  1813, 69
Wakear
  John, 210
Walker
  Thomas, 305
  William, 296
Walkers Stores, 301
War Agricultural Committees, 275,
  282
War Memorial, 371
Wealden house, 109, 121, 132
Wealden House, 110
Webb
  William, 127
Weekes
  Grace, 102
  Hampton, 87
  Richard, 42, 54, 62, 64, 72, 94,
    101, 105, 106, 107, 120, 121,
    135, 136, 154, 174, 175, 176,
    177, 180, 182, 186, 187, 188,
    208, 229, 236, 239, 273, 294,
    296, 350, 363
weekly market, 292, 293
Weeks
  Richard jnr, 40, 151
Wells

Thos, 300
West End Cottage, 119
Westbourne, 34
Western Road, 249
Whatman
  Thomas, 36, 224, 230
Wheat yields, 284
Whitaker, Miss, 364
White
  Thomas, 311
White Horse, 370
Whitpain Cottage, 273
Whitpaine, 30, 32, 37, 41, 59, 119,
  159, 185, 199, 318, 319, 350
  John, 37
  Richard, 32
  Robert, 130
  Thomas, 37, 141
Whitpayne
  Barbara, 229
  Joanna, 229
  John, 229
  Richard, 229
  Robert, 229
  Thomas, 229
Wickham
  Thomas, 302
Wickham Farmhouse, 130
Wickham Hill, 8
Wickham House, 82, 121, 122
Wilford
  Thomas, 33
Willett
  Alfred, 74
Williams
  C, 305
Withyman
  G, 307
Wolstonbury, 3, 5, 9, 20, 23, 57,
  102, 246, 250, 252, 340
Women's Land Army, 281
Wood

Richard, 37, 48, 49, 52, 54, 55,
    62, 112, 148, 151
William, 82, 134, 175, 257, 258,
    261, 265, 268, 275, 278, 369
William,, 88, 119, 134, 143, 149,

    175, 189, 190, 231, 256
Wortleford, 230, 249
Wyborn
    Thomas, 308